King of the Night

Oil painting of General Juan José Flores by Antonio Salas in Biblioteca Juan José Flores, at the Universidad Católica del Ecuador (Quito). Photograph by Mark J. Van Aken

King of the Night

Juan José Flores and Ecuador, 1824–1864

MARK J. VAN AKEN

UNIVERSITY OF CALIFORNIA PRESS
Berkeley   Los Angeles   London

University of California Press
Berkeley and Los Angeles, California

University of California Press, Ltd.
London, England

Copyright © 1989 by The Regents of the University of California

Library of Congress Cataloging-in-Publication Data

Van Aken, Mark J.
 King of the night : Juan José Flores and Ecuador, 1824–1864 / Mark
J. Van Aken.
 p. cm.
 Bibliography: p.
 Includes index.
 ISBN 0–520–06277–9 (alk. paper)
 1. Flores, Juan José, 1800–1864—Views on monarchy. 2. Ecuador—
Politics and government—1830–1895. 3. Ecuador—Politics and
government—1809–1830. 4 Monarchy—Ecuador—History—19th century.
5. Ecuador—Relations—Foreign countries. I. Title.
F3736.F5V36 1989
986.6'05—dc19   88-20606
                                                                        CIP

Printed in the United States of America

1 2 3 4 5 6 7 8 9

For
Dolores, Philip, Yoonhee,
Leslie, and Kelly

Contents

Acknowledgments

I am most indebted to my wife Dolores for all the assistance she has rendered through the years, taking notes in archives and at microfilm readers, helping to decipher Spanish diplomatic dispatches, and offering suggestions in preparing the manuscript.

I am also very grateful to Jaime Rodríguez O. for providing copies of Rocafuerte's letters before they were published in book form, to Robert N. Burr for trusting me with his notes on Chilean diplomatic correspondence, to Barbara Good for helping me to obtain microfilm copies of French diplomatic correspondence, to David Bushnell for reading the first chapter and for his comments, to J. León Helguera for help with documentation on Colombia, and to Douglas Gower for his editorial assistance. I must also express gratitude to Juan Freile-Granizo and Nadia Flores de Núñez for their assistance at the Archivo Nacional de Historia in Quito, and to Sergio Fernández Larraín in Santiago, Chile, for permitting me to read much of his manuscript copy of Senén de Buenaga's account of General Flores' activities in Spain, which provided an insider's view of the failure of the monarchical expedition of 1846.

The Social Science Research Council provided me with a grant-in-aid; the Organization of American States gave me a research grant for work in Ecuador; and Duke University provided a Research Grant in International Studies. Two Small Research Grants from California State University, Hayward, paid the expense of some of the typing of the manuscript.

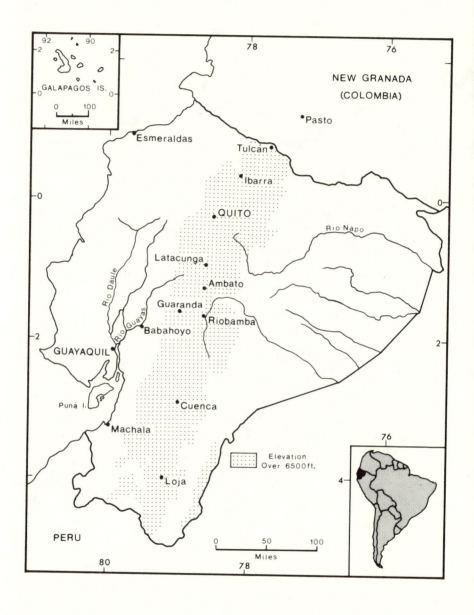

GALAPAGOS IS.

0   100
Miles

92   90

NEW GRANADA
(COLOMBIA)

•Pasto

•Esmeraldas

Tulcan•

•Ibarra

QUITO•

Rio Napo

Latacunga•

•Ambato

Guaranda•

•Riobamba

Rio Daule

Rio Guayas

Babahoyo•

GUAYAQUIL•

Puná I.

•Cuenca

Machala•

Elevation
Over 6500ft.

•Loja

PERU

0   50   100
Miles

76

4

78   76

80

78

INTRODUCTION

The subject of monarchism in nineteenth-century Latin America has attracted little scholarly interest. Most studies of the new Spanish American nations in the early years of independence have focused on the problems of leadership, constitution-making, church–state relations, federalism versus centralism, militarism, economic development, and fiscal turmoil. Discussion of all these subjects is important and has shed light on Latin America's difficult transition from colonialism to nationhood. But to neglect or ignore the strong attachment to monarchical forms and beliefs in the region is to leave a very important factor out of the political equation.

Perhaps our familiarity with the relative ease with which the United States made its transition from British monarchical rule to republican form has led many Latin-Americanists in this country to underestimate the significance of monarchism in nineteenth-century Latin America. To be sure, the United States passed through some difficult times as a fledgling nation, especially during the confederation period, but these early difficulties served only to provoke a move toward stronger central government under a new constitution, rather than a movement to restore monarchy.

It is true, of course, that there were a few mutterings in the United States during the War of Independence and after about the superiority of monarchy, but royalism never numbered many serious advocates. Some of Thomas Jefferson's letters and some of his remarks in *The Anas* have given the impression that monarchism was a menacing force in the 1780s and 1790s. However, Jefferson greatly exaggerated the influence of royalist thought and distorted the views of his political opponents.

1

Gordon S. Wood and others have demonstrated that Americans were "republicans by nature" and that monarchism was not supported by more than a handful of public figures.

Latin American historians are well aware that the political experience of Latin American nations following Independence differed quite markedly from that of the United States. The new countries were plagued with a host of difficulties far more serious than the set of problems faced by the United States. Two nations, Brazil and Mexico, chose monarchy from the outset of independence as the best means of governing societies steeped in authoritarian royalism as a result of three centuries of colonial rule. In nineteenth-century Brazil the effective governance of two emperors of the Portuguese royal family provided the nation with a high degree of stability and unity until nearly the end of the century. Mexico's first essay in monarchism was much less fortunate than that of Brazil. The inept Agustín de Iturbide (Agustín I) managed to hang on to his crown for less than a year before he was ousted by a military uprising.

The dismal record of monarchs in Mexico, first Iturbide and later Maximilian, has probably contributed to the widespread belief that monarchism was not worthy of serious scholarly attention. Most studies of royalism in Mexico have centered on dramatic episodes and personalities, especially the doomed reign of Maximilian and Charlotte in the mid-1860s. Much less attention has been given to the unpopular and fumbling Iturbide. The monarchical project of General Mariano Paredes in the mid-1840s is little known and might have been ignored completely without the work of the Spanish historian Jaime Delgado. The only general study of Mexican monarchism is a little-known doctoral dissertation by Frank J. Sanders, "Proposals for Monarchy in Mexico, 1823–1860."

Although monarchism in the Argentine region was less important than in Mexico, it has received a surprising amount of scholarly examination. The various royalist efforts of Mariano Moreno, Bernardino Rivadavia, and others have been studied extensively by a number of historians, notably Ricardo Piccirilli, José Miguel Yrarrázaval Larraín, Bartolomé Mitre, William Spence Robertson, and Julián María Rubio. Whether advocates of monarchy continued to have importance in Argentina between 1834 and 1860 is not clear, but in 1861 Juan Bautista Alberdi became a convert to monarchism and began work on *La monarquía como mejor forma de gobierno en Sud-América*. It was surprising that Alberdi, who provided much of the intellectual inspiration of Argentina's liberal Constitution of 1853, should argue the case for restoration of monarchy. But Alberdi was responding to a political crisis in Argentina and to a wave of republican pessimism then sweeping through much of Spanish America at a time when monarchist projects were developing in both Mexico and Ecuador. The fact that such a prominent Argentine intellectual as Alberdi shifted ground from republicanism to monarchism in the 1860s indicated that the attraction of kingship was not limited to a few reactionary eccentrics in Mexico.

Almost all Latin American monarchists felt that it was necessary to conceal not only their political views but especially any plans for establishing thrones in the New World. No doubt they sensed that their views clashed with popular opinion and that a forthright declaration of restorationist plans would provoke a vigorous reaction of republicans. Royalist beliefs were kept private and were acted upon only with the greatest circumspection. An example of this is to be seen in the case of General José de San Martín, who supported monarchist proposals both in Argentina and Peru during the struggle for independence. He even sent agents to Europe in quest of a prince for a projected throne in Lima, but San Martín maintained a cloak of secrecy over his views and his plans. The secret got out, but few admirers of the great Argentine hero of Independence were prepared to accept the evidence that their hero was a monarchist. A prize-winning biography of the great general by Ricardo Rojas insisted that San Martín was not guilty of the sin of monarchism.

There was nothing shameful about monarchism in early nineteenth-century Latin America. Three centuries of colonial rule under the Iberian crowns had shaped society and governmental institutions along authoritarian and aristocratic lines that differed markedly from Anglo-Saxon society of North America. The natural-rights school of political philosophy and representative government played only a minor role in Hispanic experience and thought. Richard Morse's brilliant essay in *The Founding of New Societies,* edited by Louis Hartz, underlines the incongruities of Anglo-Saxon and Hispanic institutions and historical experience. Morse points out that the collapse of the patrimonial state as a result of independence "required the intervention of a strong *personalist* leadership," that is, dictatorship. "The energies of such leadership," he goes on, "had to flow toward investing the state with suprapersonal *legitimacy.*" This essential condition of legitimacy might be supplied by governmental emphasis on cultural traditions, nationalism, and constitutionalism. But personalist leadership had many serious weaknesses, according to Morse, among them "untransferable legitimacy" and a tendency to govern by impulse and intimidation.

Given such serious problems, it was natural for reflective and responsible leaders like Simón Bolívar and his associates to worry about political instability and the difficulties inherent in erecting new republics ostensibly based on the will of the people. Salvador de Madariaga, in a fascinating but hypercritical biography of Bolívar, has described in great detail the consideration given by Bolívar and some of his advisers to monocratic and monarchical solutions of the political problems of Spanish South America. On the basis of a considerable body of evidence Madariaga concluded that Bolívar favored the establishment of monarchy and encouraged his confidants to pursue discussions with European diplomats aimed at creating a Spanish American throne, but the Liberator ultimately chose monocratic rule rather than monarchy because he feared that the imposition of royalist government might misfire and destroy his reputation.

Madariaga's biography stirred up strong opposition among the hero-worshippers of Bolívar, partly because of the Spanish writer's negative attitude toward the Liberator, but mainly because of his portrayal of Bolívar as a monarchist. The Venezuelan historian Caracciolo Parra-Pérez quickly answered Madariaga's assertions with a lengthy and meticulous study, *La monarquía en Gran Colombia,* which defends Bolívar from every imputation of monarchism. The Venezuelan's erudite attack on Madariaga's work, though painstaking and impressive, made Bolívar look somewhat like the proverbial piano player in a bawdyhouse who claims to know nothing of the activities in the rooms upstairs. Nevertheless, Parra-Pérez's study seems to have carried the day, and most Bolivarian scholars believe that the Liberator never favored monarchism.

Whether Bolívar longed for a crown or not is less important than the fact, clearly made by Madariaga, that the Liberator and many of his closest advisers gave serious consideration to both monarchy and monocracy (dictatorship, lifetime presidency) as alternatives for controlling the anarchical political forces in Spanish America. In fact, Madariaga's chief contribution to our understanding of post-Independence developments is the linkage he pointed out between monocracy and monarchy, which explains why disillusionment with the results of republican government led directly to thoughts of restoring kingship. The option of monocracy was merely a temporary solution that restrained by means of intimidation and repression. But dictatorship failed to solve the underlying problems, as Morse has shown, of legitimacy and orderly succession. From this perspective monocracy was inadequate.

The historical record of Spanish America reveals that dictators have made interesting efforts to solve the dilemma of orderly succession by attempting to install a homegrown dynasty. In Paraguay Carlos Antonio López managed to arrange for his inept son, Francisco Solano López, to succeed him, but any hope of a López dynasty went up in the smoke of the Paraguayan War in the late 1860s. Another example of attempts to bridge the gap between monocracy and monarchy was provided by the conservative General Rafael Carrera of Guatemala. In 1854 Carrera proclaimed himself "Perpetual President" and declared that he was to be succeeded first by his wife and then by his son when the latter came of age. Some of the mystique of monarchy was furnished by Guatemalan Indians who called Carrera "The Son of God," and by a curate who sermonized that the Perpetual President was a "representative of God."

The "perpetual presidency" of Carrera illustrates the close relationship between monocracy and monarchy. Both governmental concepts appealed to the authoritarian political philosophy and the historical experience of Hispanic peoples. Both concepts promised to restore order and to maintain the customary social hierarchy. But monocracy, without the mystique of royalty and divine ordination, could not resolve the twin problems of legitimacy and succession. Carrera's attempt to win clerical support for the divine authority of the "perpetual presidency" and to provide for his son's succession proved no more successful in the long run than the efforts of Iturbide in Mexico. Carrera's failure proved the great difficulty of converting a dictatorship into a monarchy without the mystique of royalty.

Monarchy appeared to offer several advantages over dictatorial rule. It would solve the problem of legitimacy and it would be in harmony with tradition and the hierarchical social system. General acceptance of a prestigious European prince, monarchists believed, would eliminate the need to govern by intimidation. Under monarchical rule greater freedom and a moderate opposition could be permitted without fear that the government's opponents would overthrow the regime.

If we exclude the unlikely possibility of selecting a lineal descendant of the rulers of one of the Indian empires of the New World, it was necessary for the Spanish American monarchists to find a European prince to carry out the task of restoration. The need for European royalty was a mixed blessing for monarchists. On the one hand, European monarchical governments, with the exception of Spain, were not eager to supply a prince and involve themselves in the internal political affairs of Spanish American nations. On the other hand, European leaders were often flattered by requests for assistance, especially when they were asked to provide protection from the aggressive designs of the United States. Several of the monarchical plans involved proposals for European protectorates, in part because the national crises that prompted the monarchist plans involved a foreign threat to the nation seeking a European prince. Additionally, Spanish American royalists believed that the offer of a protectorate was tempting bait for European nations eager to extend their influence throughout the world.

Great Britain, the greatest maritime power of the century and the most attractive prospective sponsor of monarchy, declined all overtures of Spanish American royalists. British leaders decided that the risks in a monarchy–protectorate arrangement were greater than the prospective benefits. A deep involvement by England in the affairs of a Spanish American nation could jeopardize British trade relations with the entire region and might provoke retaliatory action by the United States. France was almost as wary of royalist schemes as Britain, though Napoleon III succumbed to a Mexican proposal in the 1860s, with fatal consequences. Spain was a poor choice to sponsor monarchy, largely because of military weakness and a tarnished reputation as the former mother country. Nevertheless, monarchists tendered proposals to Spain, and Spanish authorities were all too willing to accept the offers. In the mid-1840s leaders of both Mexico and Ecuador enlisted the assistance of Spain to establish thrones in their countries. Both projects, one of them the centerpiece of this book, aborted badly.

The greatest obstacle to the successful restoration of monarchy was the problem of managing the transition from republic to kingship. Most monarchists evidently believed that their political ideas were not popular and that their plans had to be carried out in secrecy. Juan García del Río's *Meditaciones* is one of the few published works that openly advocated monarchy. The secrecy in which royalist projects were shrouded not only made difficult the implementation of restorationist plans but also obscured most of the historical record of monarchism in nineteenth-century Spanish America. As a consequence much of the history of monarchism has been consigned to the realm of rumor and hearsay, beyond the interest of most historians.

The full story of monarchist activities in the post-Independence era of Spanish America will probably never be known. The advocates of kingship did not leave a paper trail of all their thoughts and schemes. But occasionally the subterranean stream of monarchism surfaced and left a trail. Such was the case in 1861 when García Moreno's letters to a French diplomat were published in Peru to embarrass the Ecuadorian president for having proposed a French-backed monarchy in Quito. But this was a unique instance, and revelations of restoration projects have been rare.

Diplomatic correspondence provides the best single source of information on monarchist activities in Spanish America for the simple reason that invitations to establish thrones and protectorates had to be addressed to diplomatic agents of European governments. The files of diplomatic correspondence in England, France, and Spain contain a great amount of information about monarchist proposals, especially for Mexico and Ecuador, but for other countries as well. The British dispatches contain the best reporting, but the correspondence of other major powers is valuable. The quality of reporting by United States diplomats varies greatly and seldom provides vital data, because North Americans were never approached directly about monarchical plans. All of the diplomatic materials must be used with caution, of course, because even the most able and experienced agents had their biases and limitations.

Though the reporting of the Spanish agents in Ecuador was not of high caliber, the Spanish correspondence has provided the most important information for this study, because it shows conclusively that General Flores proposed a monarchical project not only for Ecuador but also for Peru and Bolivia, and that Spain agreed to the proposal. Though Spanish dispatches do not provide all of the answers to questions about the nature of the Ecuadorian restoration scheme, they do prove conclusively that General Flores was at the center of a major plot to restore monarchy in South America.

The best reporting came from the pen of Walter Cope, British consul at Guayaquil and later chargé d'affaires in Quito, from 1828 until his death in late 1859 or 1860. Cope gathered a wealth of information from presidents, ministers, merchants, and others and passed it on to the Foreign Office in lengthy dispatches. From his reports one even gets a notion now and then of the state of "public opinion," especially when he reports on rumors and attitudes toward government policies.

For general background on Ecuador during the period of Flores' monarchical intrigues there are the usual historical sources: government documents, official and independent newspapers, pamphlets, broadsides, and private correspondence. These sources cast much light on the economic, social, and political development of Ecuador during its first three decades of evolution. The background information shows how difficult it was to govern Ecuador, which in turn helps to explain why Flores, and later García Moreno, sought to restore monarchy.

But all of the nondiplomatic sources put together do not reveal for certain that General Flores sought to impose royal government on Ecuador. Even the private papers of the general provide no information of crucial importance, though interesting supplemental material is to be found there. The lack of concrete and specific information on restorationist activities in the Ecuadorian sources explains why Luís Robalino Dávila, Ecuador's leading historian for this period, was unable to determine for certain if Flores was actually engaged in monarchical projects.

By combining the diplomatic sources with all other historical materials it is possible to trace a fairly complete story of the activities of Ecuador's first president. The record shows that General Flores became convinced that Ecuador was ungovernable under representative institutions and that only a monocracy under his own control or a foreign protectorate under a European prince could rescue Ecuador from chaos. Though Flores fell from power before his scheme could be implemented, he never gave up his belief that monarchism was better suited to Spanish America than was republicanism. Flores' efforts to regain power contributed to a major foreign and domestic crisis in Ecuador in 1859 which spurred another leader, García Moreno, to attempt yet another restorationist project. The failure of García Moreno's initiative put an end to any serious monarchist thought in Ecuador, just as Maximilian's regime ended monarchism in Mexico.

Parenthetically it should be remarked that this study of General Flores is essentially a political biography and should not be taken as a general history of Ecuador from 1830 to 1864. Information on social and economic conditions in early nineteenth-century Ecuador is included, but the emphasis is on political history, especially on the quality of leadership displayed by Flores and on the effects of this leadership on the development of the nation. One might think that native Ecuadorians would have devoted exhaustive research to the life of their first president, but they have not, largely because Flores was not admired. Nor was he hated. The result has been neglect by the historians. No one has been motivated to dig far enough into the historical documents to discover the true nature of Flores' leadership and the political views that shaped his leadership.

With the benefit of hindsight it is clear that monarchy had little or no chance of success in the new nations of Spanish America. There were too many obstacles to a successful restoration movement. But monarchism was more important than is generally recognized, especially in the more conservative countries with intractable political and social problems like Ecuador and Mexico. Nevertheless, monarchism could, and did, crop up in other nations as varied as Costa Rica, Guatemala, Peru, and Argentina. It appealed mostly to leaders who distrusted representative institutions and liberal reforms that disturbed the traditional Hispanic order. Monarchists were not always the most reactionary of conservatives, for many advocates of restoration argued that by recapturing legitimacy a crowned head of state would allow greater freedom than would a dictator. But their dream of greater liberty was probably illusory, because it failed to take into account the determined opposition, and likely civil war, that would be stirred up by the imposition of a foreign prince backed by foreign troops. Monarchy probably could not have recaptured the elusive quality of legitimacy (certainly Maximilian did not), because restoration seemed to deny the entire Independence movement and the emerging sentiment of nationalism.

Despite its futility the subject of monarchism merits careful historical examination. Though restoration had little or no chance of success in Spanish America, important leaders secretly believed in the doctrine and sometimes acted on that belief. Though advocates of monarchy believed that royal rule would save their nations from disorder, it was ironic that those who engaged in monarchist schemes, like General Flores of Ecuador, succeeded only in creating more disorder. The irreconcilable differences in political beliefs which separated republicans and monarchists in the post-Independence period were part of a flawed political process that continues even today to disturb and confound efforts at orderly republican rule in Latin America.

1

BOLÍVAR'S MAN IN QUITO, 1824–1830

Between 1810 and 1825 the great empire of Spain in America passed through a destructive civil war that resulted in the independence of all of Spain's territories in the New World save for Cuba and Puerto Rico. Independence would have come sooner or later, but it was hastened by Napoleon's armed invasion of the Iberian Peninsula in 1807–1808 and his disruption of monarchical rule by taking King Ferdinand VII captive. French occupation of the peninsula and Napoleon's heavy-handed attempts to win control of Spain's overseas territories quickly provided New World leaders with an opportunity to move for independence.

Spanish Americans were not spoiling to throw off the yoke of empire, though many were discontent with aspects of imperial rule. Most black slaves, Indian peasants, and members of the classes of mixed races led a miserable existence, but the dark-skinned classes lacked effective leaders to initiate a successful movement to sever ties with the mother country. Only the upper-class Creoles, those Americans reputedly of Spanish descent, had sufficient education, prestige, and ability to move against imperial rule. The native-born Americans of Hispanic lineage and culture resented the hauteur of their peninsular masters, disliked the economic system that drained profits from the New World, and hankered for high government offices that were usually denied them. But their complaints were not so grievous as to stir many Creole leaders to armed insurrection. Not until French troops occupied the greater part of Spain and held the king captive did the hesitant Spanish Americans take the first steps toward independence. When the Creoles finally moved against imperial rule, by forming governing juntas in

the major cities, they did so by proclaiming their loyalty to the
captive Spanish king.

There was an element of artful pragmatism, perhaps hypocrisy, in pledging allegiance to an absent and powerless monarch, but it was politic to pay obeisance to sovereign authority.
Public declarations of fealty to the king provided a convenient
formula for uniting conservatives and radicals behind the patriot juntas. In addition, support of Ferdinand VII gave a color
of legitimacy to the novel juntas and made it difficult for Spanish authorities to cope with these suspicious governing bodies.
And finally, raising the banner of Ferdinand VII appealed
strongly to the majority of Spanish Americans of all classes who
continued to accept the tradition of monarchical rule.

In the course of some three centuries Spain had managed to
inculcate a deep respect in her colonies for royal authority.
Spanish monarchs and their agents had created a formidable
administrative structure in America, a complex and stratified
social system supportive of kingly rule, a highly regimented
commercial order, and a system of law and justice crafted specifically for the New World. Through a hierarchy of viceroys,
audiencias (administrative courts with jurisdiction over subdivisions of viceroyalties), captains-general, provincial governors,
and a host of other officials the Crown of Castille imposed its
centralized authority over the transatlantic territories. Though
scattered riots and tumults disturbed the peace now and then
through the centuries, most of the time the king's subjects
showed a high degree of loyalty and obedience to the sovereign
and his agents.

Late in the eighteenth century new forces penetrated the
Hispanic world and began to undermine the bulwark of Spanish monarchism. Writers of the Enlightenment like Montesquieu, Voltaire, and Rousseau spread ideas of liberty and reform among educated Creoles. The War of Independence in
North America provided a vivid example of colonies casting off
imperial ties and establishing effective republican government,
while the French Revolution and the Terror aroused lively debate about the virtues and the faults of republics.

Arguments over monarchism and republicanism were largely
abstract and theoretical among Spanish Americans, who were

allowed almost no participation in government except for membership in the lowly municipal councils. Spanish policy deliberately excluded Spanish Americans from most high offices. Though a few exceptional Creoles managed to break the barrier and gain high appointments, in the late decades of imperial rule most of these Creoles were systematically eliminated from the upper echelons of government. The Spanish monopoly on high office doubtless provided many Creoles with a strong argument for both independence and republicanism. During the wars of Independence the question of monarchism versus republicanism would remain a lively issue in the minds of patriot leaders.

By 1825 the patriot legions of Simón Bolívar (the "Liberator") and San Martín (the "Protector") had completed the emancipation of Spanish South America. The administrative structure of the empire lay in ruins and most imperial officials were driven from the continent or obliged to make peace with the conquering patriots. The work of demolition by the patriot armies, though bloody and costly, proved to be easier than the laborious task of creating a new political order. The destruction of the time-honored institutions of monarchy required the formation of new governments that could earn general acceptance and maintain order. Responsibility for the establishment of new governments fell to those Creoles who had made the revolution. Wealthy landowners, merchants, lawyers, and other respectable Creoles, who dominated town councils and patriot congresses, tended to favor representative institutions. Some of these influential citizens preferred constitutional monarchy, but most advocated republicanism. The diverse written constitutions that they prepared for their regimes drew heavily from North American and European models.[1]

In the turbulent aftermath of the wars of Independence, however, it was not the civilian Creoles who controlled the destinies of most of the emergent nations, but rather the Creole military leaders. For better or worse, the generals in command of the victorious troops became the charismatic leaders of the liberated people of Spanish America in the early stages of nationhood. The military campaigns spawned all kinds of officers, some cultured and high-minded, and others vulgar, vain, and pompous. Bolívar, San Martín, and Antonio José de Sucre unquestionably represented the very best type of revolutionary general, but there were others, like Agustín Gamarra and Andrés de Santa Cruz, for example, whose virtues were less conspicuous. The withdrawal of San Martín from public life in 1822 and the deaths of Sucre and Bolívar in 1830 left the field open to the ambitions of lesser figures. If none of the second-echelon generals, save possibly Francisco de Paula Santander, equaled the virtues of the great Bolívar, few of them were as brutish and unscrupulous as the worst of the military clan.

One of the relatively obscure generals who sprang into prominence during the wars was Juan José Flores. A Venezuelan by birth and protégé of Bolívar, he traveled southward down the Andes with the patriot troops and in 1824 arrived in his land of opportunity, the District of the South, soon to be called Ecuador. Six years later Flores was named president of the new nation. With the cooperation of leading public figures of the region he founded the new government and dominated its affairs for the next decade and a half.

General Flores was a complex person who made vastly differing impressions on those who met him. A young French military officer who met the future president in 1828 was impressed by his handsome appearance and his gracious manners. He described Flores as a "man of the world, made for the habits of an elegant life." But four years later Dr. Adrian Terry of Connecticut saw a very different sort of person in Flores, a man who, Terry said, received guests in a threadbare coat, wearing "soiled linen," and with three days' growth of beard. The Yankee physician noted that Flores was small in stature and his appearance seemed to corroborate the rumor that he had "a tinge of Negro blood."[2]

Flores' contemporaries in Ecuador, some of them political adversaries, have pictured the first president as a person of varied traits and talents, a mixture of good and evil. Pedro Moncayo, a staunch foe of the young Venezuelan, has depicted Flores as a man with the personality of a "prankish boy" who forever involved himself in "gossip and mischievous lies." Moncayo once claimed that Flores had the duplicity of Catherine de Medici and the arrogance and ferocity of Caesar Borgia.[3] A more dispassionate contemporary and a noted historian, Pedro Fermín Ceballos, praised Flores for his winning manners, so extraordinary, he said, that "few people could resist" him. Ceballos pointed out that Flores' social charm was not an unmixed blessing, for the general carried affability to such an extreme that he frequently promised the impossible. One of Flores' saving traits of character, as seen by Ceballos, was his ability to confess his errors and to show repentance.[4]

General Flores may have acquired his conversational charm and congenial manners from his association with Simón Bolívar during the wars of independence and afterwards. Bolívar was noted for his lively salon manners and his ability to captivate listeners with brilliant conversation. Flores, an apt student of the Liberator's style, put these techniques to good use not only in Ecuador but later in the salons of Spain where he charmed Queen Mother María Cristina and, as shall be seen, won her support of an ill-starred scheme to establish a throne in Quito.

General Flores' urbanity, so often used to win friends, was also employed to disparage and discredit persons he disliked. His sardonic wit and ridicule were well known, and Ceballos tells us that Flores carried off his attacks "with grace," but he sometimes turned his opponents into unforgiving enemies.[5]

Flores' wit and good manners gave the superficial impression of a man born to wealth and privilege. But the effect was misleading, for Flores had risen to the highest post in Ecuador from very humble and obscure origins in Venezuela. One of the few facts about his birth generally agreed to is that it occurred in the little seacoast town of Puerto Cabello. Even the date of Flores' birth is not known with certainty, though the inscription on his tomb in the cathedral of Quito asserts that "The Founder of the Republic of Ecuador, Its First President and General-in-Chief of its Armies was born . . . on June 19, 1800." Perhaps, but no baptismal record has yet been found, and Flores gave contradictory information about his age from time to time. He may have been born in 1795; then again it may have been in 1802. The year 1800 can be taken as a likely compromise.[6]

The mother of the future president has been variously described as Creole, Indian, mestiza, and a mixture of Indian, Negro, and white. Flores claimed that his father was a Spanish merchant, but detractors of the "Founder of the Republic" say that the elusive father was either Indian or mestizo. Political adversaries have taken spiteful pleasure in emphasizing the rumored dusky racial origins of Ecuador's first president.[7] Oil portraits of Flores in Quito do not confirm the racial allegations. Large paintings show a proud man in full dress uniform, slender and short but well proportioned, with a handsome countenance that radiates quick intelligence and a commanding presence. A trim mustache accents an olive complexion. The general's features are small and well defined, hinting at Spanish and probably Indian antecedents, but not African. If Flores in fact had negroid characteristics, his portrait painters chose to obscure them.[8]

As a child in Venezuela young Juan José apparently enjoyed little if any contact with his father and received scant formal education under the care of his impoverished mother. The latter placed him in a military school or hospital at about age fifteen.[9] He could have received no more than the most rudimentary instruction before he was caught up in the wars of Independence. By the time his military career had elevated him to prominence in Ecuador in the late 1820s he had begun to feel anxiety over his defective education and he wished to improve his mind. In letters to Bolívar the young Flores sought to impress his correspondent by dropping names of authors he was familiar with—Rousseau, Montesquieu, Holbach, Vattel.[10] In 1826 he asked for and received a shipment of books from General Santander, then vice-president of Gran Colombia.[11] It is doubtful that the young general sought learning out of a hunger for knowledge for its own sake but rather from a desire to add luster to his conversation with the distinguished members of Quito society and to embellish his correspondence with metaphors and learned allusions to impress the citizens of Gran Colombia. Even after he had become president of Ecuador Flores continued his efforts to improve his intellect by engaging prominent men such as the poet José Joaquín Olmedo as tutors.[12]

If General Flores had commenced his studies at a younger age, he might have been more successful in acquiring the culture he aspired to. Unfortunately for him, and for Ecuador, by the time he occupied the presidential chair he had already reached the age of thirty. It was too late for him then, for his personality and character had been molded by his life and experiences in Bolívar's legions. He had become a professional soldier and a man of action who lacked the sedentary habits that might have permitted him to enter the aristocratic world of cultivated minds. He was content with the superficial rather than the profound and often settled for form without substance. The shallowness of his learning was apparent to members of the cultured elite of Ecuador who snickered behind his back. When the professors at the University of Quito bestowed an honorary doctorate on Flores in 1842 he immediately became the target of ridicule by his adversaries who referred to him sarcastically as "Dr. Flores."[13]

Acquisition of intellectual sophistication might have made Flores a more interesting chief executive, but not necessarily a better one. Vicente Rocafuerte, who followed Flores in the presidency, was a very learned aristocrat, but he was a rather ineffective executive who angered men in congress by his hauteur. The cultured Rocafuerte left office an embittered man with relatively few accomplishments to his credit.[14]

It is likely that Flores could have offered Ecuador firmer and sounder leadership if he had gained a better grasp of history and politics at an earlier age. Unfortunately it was not until later in his life, in the 1860s when he was no longer president, that he acquired a deeper knowledge of history, philosophy, and government. By that time, of course, it was too late, both for Flores and for Ecuador.[15]

The military campaigns of Bolívar's patriot armies were more important in the education of this young man than all the tutors of Quito. In 1815, when Flores was yet an adolescent, he was swept into the fighting between Spanish loyalists and Venezuelan patriots. Apparently he began his career as a private in the loyalist forces of General Pablo Morillo, but he switched sides after being captured by the patriots. In a series of actions he distinguished himself for valor, skill, and intelligence and was promoted to the rank of colonel shortly after the famous battle of Carabobo in 1821. For a young man of about twenty-one years this was rapid promotion.[16]

After helping to protect General Bolívar from a nearly disas-

trous defeat in the battle of Bomboná, Flores was sent by the
Liberator to the southern province of Pasto to help subdue the
troublesome and tenacious loyalists of this region. The assignment in Pasto was fateful, for it excluded Flores from the campaign to liberate Peru and it placed him relatively near to Quito,
future capital of the Republic of Ecuador. His elimination from
the Peruvian wars could not have pleased the young Venezuelan officer, but military command in Pasto was important, for
north–south communications between Bogotá and Quito depended upon patriot control of this region. Moreover, the difficult guerrilla warfare of Pasto would put Flores' abilities to a
severe test.

Although Flores has been criticized for his harsh treatment
of the Pasto loyalists, it must be stated in his defense that he
merely continued the severe and sometimes ruthless policies
against loyalists adopted earlier by Bolívar. In spite of shortages
of funds, supplies, guns, and seasoned troops, Flores managed
to bring the Pasto region under secure patriot control for the
first time. By July 1824 Pasto was so peaceful that Flores began
to think of marrying and settling down to live "eternally as
governor of this province"—unless the Liberator should find a
better post for him farther south.[17]

It soon became apparent that Pasto was much too "peaceful,"
to the point of boredom, and that the city of Quito offered
more excitement and opportunity for an ambitious young officer. So eager was Flores to shake off the dust of Pasto that he
did not wait for Bolívar to transfer him to the desired post. In
late 1824 or early 1825 the young officer, on his own account,
simply turned up in Quito where he undertook to impress people with his abilities and accomplishments. Full of strut and
swagger, he went on a spree with his fellow officers, entertaining the townspeople with equestrian sports, one of which consisted of lancing the portraits of the Spanish presidents of the
defunct audiencia.[18]

Flores apparently took pleasure in shocking the conservative
upper classes of Quito, for he joined with a group of Freemason
friends to publish an irreverent newspaper called *El Noticiosito*.
The saucy and antiaristocratic tone of the paper provoked the
"old Christians" of the quiet and conservative city to respond

with the publication of *El Pensador quiteño,* in which they attacked Flores and so angered him that he shut down the paper and scattered the printer's type in the streets.[19]

At about this time Flores tried his hand at managing an election for Gran Colombia and did rather well at it. In October 1825 he reported to Santander that, thanks to his own leadership, the electors of Quito had voted unanimously for the reelection of Bolívar and Santander as president and vice-president of Colombia.[20]

Apparently Flores had moved from Pasto to Quito while Bolívar was occupied with Peruvian affairs. Though the Liberator had intended to place another officer in charge of Quito, he later acquiesced in Flores' bid for command by promoting him to the rank of general (1826) and by appointing him intendant (governor) of the "Department of Ecuador," the territory around Quito.[21] The appointment as intendant placed the young general in command of the most prestigious of the three departments comprising the "South" of Colombia, sometimes called the "District of the South," which in a few years would emerge as the nation of Ecuador.[22] A little over a year later Flores managed to obtain an additional appointment as interim intendant and commandant-general of the Department of Guayas, thus effectively establishing his preeminence in southern Colombia. Early in 1828 Flores' military primacy in Ecuador was made clear when Bolívar elevated him to the position of commanding general of the Army of the South.[23]

Before the year 1825 Juan José Flores had not figured prominently among the officers of the Bolivarian forces. He had not taken part in the decisive battle of Pichincha, which liberated the Audiencia of Quito, nor was he present later at the climactic battles of Junín and Ayacucho in the struggle to free Peru. Flores was overshadowed by a galaxy of stellar figures, such as Antonio José de Sucre, Rafael Urdaneta, and Manuel Valdez.[24] It was only after his arrival in Quito and his promotion to the rank of general that Flores emerged as one of the trusted lieutenants of Bolívar.

From 1825 to 1830, while Bolívar was occupied with the pacification of Peru and the governmental problems of Gran Colombia, General Flores exercised supreme military and civil authority in Quito. Though his position of command gave him considerable power, it was not altogether advantageous, for Flores was actually in charge of an unpopular army of occupation. It was his difficult task to play the role of protector of people who were unconvinced of a need for "foreign" protection. Both Flores and his Colombian troops were regarded by many Ecuadorians with a mixture of suspicion, resentment, and hostility. Flores' success in overcoming enormous obstacles during these turbulent years attested to his exceptional skills as a leader. When unpaid troops from his rag-tag army mutinied and mistreated the local population he disciplined the wrongdoers. If he did not succeed in maintaining the strictest discipline, he was hardly to be blamed, for Bolívar and Sucre had similar difficulties with their troops.[25] Few armies of occupation, if any, have been loved and appreciated, and the Colombian army in Ecuador was no exception.

Flores' situation in the south was made more troublesome by the existence of strong royalist, pro-Spanish sentiments among some of the people of the former audiencia. Loyalty to Spain did not disappear with the defeat of the viceregal forces at Pichincha. Nor were Ecuadorians reassured by the heavy-handed exactions of money and property carried out by the Liberator and his chieftains as they prepared to invade Peru in 1822–1823. General Sucre admitted that the vexatious behavior of his soldiers and the imposition of high taxes made Ecuadorians think they lived in a "conquered country." Bolívar, probably exaggerating somewhat, told Vice-President Santander that the economy of the Quito region was "ruined in four days" of warfare. For the Bolivarian forces the south was little more than a region to be exploited for the support of continuing military campaigns against the royalist army in Peru. In his efforts to complete the liberation of Peru, Bolívar and his subordinates sought to take every available recruit and to extract the last peso from this distressed land. Harsh measures provoked resentment against the northern "liberators" and raised doubts in the minds of Ecuadorian patriots about the blessings of independence.[26]

Many of the leading citizens of the south were bitter about the sufferings and sacrifices that accompanied the wars of liberation and their aftermath. The municipal government of

Quito grumbled that its citizens were taxed beyond their means, that their lives and property were jeopardized by the excesses committed by rebellious, unpaid troops, and that their poverty was made worse by government policies that ruined the factories and textile mills of the highlands.[27] The citizens of Guayaquil complained that the port city had been prostrated by recruitments and "violent exactions" which forced the abandonment of agriculture and the desertion of shops. According to people in Guayaquil, agents of the Colombian government had reduced the Department of Guayas "to the condition of the ancient Roman provinces."[28] Flores' travels about the southern district led him to confirm the view that there was discontent with taxes and exactions, but he believed that the inhabitants' protests of inability to pay were exaggerated.[29] Whatever the truth of the matter, when Flores attempted to obtain an emergency contribution from the Department of Ecuador he was unable to collect the money. Because of strong resistance to taxation he refrained from exacting forced contributions except in grave emergencies.[30]

General Flores' desire to marry and settle down, first expressed in Pasto, was carried out in Quito. Early in 1825 he married Mercedes Jijón y Vivanco, a member of the local nobility, even though her branch of the prestigious Jijón family possessed little wealth. The importance of this marriage alliance in the career of the young Venezuelan can scarcely be exaggerated, for it established a firm social bond with the native aristocracy of the highlands. By means of this matrimonial contract Flores managed to identify himself with Quito (or *quiteña*) society and to diminish his unfavorable image as a foreign military adventurer. Though many prominent people would continue to look askance at him as a parvenu and an outsider, Flores had taken an effective step toward joining the local elite. As his children were born in rapid succession, he was able to establish those all-important spiritual and political ties of *compadrazgo* (godfathership or ritual kinship) which are the sinews in the Latin-American social body.[31]

Though Flores' private life from 1825 forward was marked by a newfound social acceptance, his responsibilities in public life left him little time to enjoy the tranquil pleasures of his familial status. In the late 1820s the southern departments became embroiled in a tumultuous power struggle between Peru and the government of Gran Colombia. Ambitious generals of Peru (Agustín Gamarra, José de La Mar, and Andrés de Santa Cruz among them) resented Bolívar's grand design for personal leadership over a great federation of Gran Colombia, Peru, and Bolivia. Responding to regional and personal interests the "Marshals of Ayacucho," as the Peruvian generals were sometimes called, set out first to weaken and then to demolish the fragile Bolivarian political structure. They made life so miserable for Marshal Sucre, Bolívar's presidential designee in Bolivia, that in 1828 Sucre quit his high office in disgust and returned to his family in Quito. Simultaneously the Peruvian leaders decided to undermine the Liberator's control over the southern departments of Gran Colombia.[32] This latter decision put Flores' military leadership in the south to a severe test.

In the power struggle between Lima and Bogotá Flores maintained unswerving allegiance to Bolívar and Gran Colombia. When the renegade Third Division of the patriot army in Peru invaded the departments of Azuay and Guayas in April 1827, Flores, acting without significant support from Bogotá and in the face of covert opposition from Vice-President Santander, managed to expel the invaders.[33] Victory brought only a respite, however, for the Peruvian government soon began preparations for a new attack. Flores alerted Bolívar to the danger, urged a preemptive strike against Peru, and then was forced to wait for several months before receiving orders from the Liberator to recruit and train an army. With almost no help from Colombia, Flores built an army of 5000 by means of large-scale impressments and forced loans from the wealthy inhabitants. Once the army was assembled Bolívar placed the trusted Marshal Sucre in command of the southern defenses. Flores not only accepted this demotion in good form but played a major role in the fighting when the Peruvians invaded. At the decisive battle of Tarqui (28 February 1829) Flores received credit for inflicting a stinging defeat on the invaders.[34]

The battle of Tarqui marked a high point in the military career of Flores and helped the young general to recover his reputation and popularity in the south, a reputation that had suffered from the heavy exactions he imposed on the people in order to raise an army. For his valor in battle he received from Marshal Sucre the special Medal of Tarqui and a promotion to the rank of division general. Sucre, who earlier had quarreled with Flores over a taxation question, singled out the young officer as the hero of the battle and called him "the Prince of Tarqui." Bolívar sent "ten million thanks" to Flores for his "immense services to the fatherland and to the glory of Colombia."[35]

Before the victory of Tarqui Bolívar's opinion of Flores had fluctuated widely. At times the Liberator viewed this young officer with marked favor and granted him preferment. But at other times he criticized Flores as "ambitious" and "conceited" and removed him from military command, as in the case of the Peruvian invasion of 1828. On balance, Flores' loyalty and skill-ful management earned the approval of Bolívar. After the bat-tle of Tarqui the Liberator toasted Flores as an "angel" and "a young hero."[36] In conversation with a French officer Bolívar declared that Flores was "one of the generals of the Republic in whom I have genuine confidence." Bolívar meant what he said, for a few months later he promoted Flores to the position of prefect-general of the south, the highest administrative post in Ecuador, directly under the authority of the Liberator.[37]

Flores' admiration of the Liberator was immense, even exces-sive. It is true, as Flores' critics have pointed out, that the youth-ful apprentice worshiped Bolívar to the point of servility. In all fairness it should be noted that the Liberator was idolized by many people, but Flores certainly carried it to an extreme. In his letters to Bolívar Flores declared that Bolívar was "the idol of my heart," the "GREAT MAN OF THIS CENTURY," and "the divine anchor of our salvation."[38] Bolívar had only to hint of some personal need or desire and Flores would fly into ac-tion to fill the need. On one occasion the Liberator asked his young lieutenant to carry a message to a lady friend in Quito. Flores, playing the role of a sycophant, rejoiced at the opportu-nity and promised a "brilliant result in the affair," no matter how risky the errand might be.[39]

Whether by accident or by conscious imitation, Flores shared many personality traits with the Liberator. Both men made a point of displaying republican simplicity when the occasion demanded it, but both were inclined toward aristocratic values. Both eagerly sought knowledge in books and were fond of exhibiting their familiarity with the ideas of great men. Although Bolívar easily surpassed Flores in learning, neither of the two was a profound thinker. Each was a man of action. Bolívar's love of dominating discussions by wit and eloquence was fully shared by Flores. Both were fond of social gatherings, and not infrequently they behaved in an unrestrained manner. Prodigality, womanizing, love of glory, and hunger for adulation were characteristics of both men.[40]

If Flores was guilty of sycophancy, he was also stoutly loyal to the Liberator. In June 1826, shortly after receiving a draft copy of Bolívar's rather odd and impractical Constitution of Bolivia, which provided for a lifetime presidency and an aristocratic three-house legislature, Flores announced his complete approval of the document—without bothering to read it. Later, after studying the new charter of government, Flores published an article entitled "Presidente vitalicio" in the leading newspaper of Guayaquil in which he praised the Bolivian constitution, declared that the welfare of Colombia depended on the will of the Liberator, and hinted approvingly that the proposed form of government was a step in the direction of monarchy. Though he did not state clearly that Bolívar ought to be the monarch of the new regime, Flores may have had this idea in mind when he declared that "every man of modest enlightenment would look to [Bolívar] for the stability of a good government."[41]

In supporting the Bolivian constitution General Flores acknowledged that in earlier years, when he knew less about politics than about war, he had favored representative government. But recent experience in the south, he said, had changed his views. There was truth in this confession, for apparently a wave of reaction against liberal republics passed through Quito in the mid-1820s, and this probably influenced Flores' thinking. In Bogotá, Vice-President Santander received reports of strong monarchist sentiments among the upper classes of the south, and it was said that the "authorities" of the region supported constitutional monarchy.[42]

Flores' support of the Bolivian constitution and his cautious suggestion of monarchy appear to have been in agreement with Bolívar's thinking at the time. It was well known in the mid- and late-1820s that France and other members of the Holy Alliance entertained notions of implanting monarchy in Spanish America, and it was generally assumed that Great Britain preferred constitutional monarchies to republics in the New World. Bolívar, disheartened by the emergence of vicious political rivalries and near anarchy in Spanish America, began to explore the possibility of monocratic solutions for the problem of governmental instability. Though he carefully avoided open commitment to either monarchy or dictatorship, from 1825 until the year of his death Bolívar was involved directly or indirectly in a variety of speculative conversations, contingency plans, and semiclandestine projects aimed at establishing either monarchy or a lifetime presidency in Colombia.

The historical record shows clearly that the Liberator discussed the feasibility of monarchy in America with foreign diplomats, Spanish American statesmen, and trusted military officers. In his oral discussions and in his correspondence he usually presented his own position in somewhat ambiguous terms, but he did not discourage others from looking into the possibility of adopting monarchy. At times he publicly rejected royalist proposals, but these denials were not clear-cut and definitive. As Salvador de Madariaga put it, "Bolívar was both attracted and repelled by the Crown."[43]

Bolívar's private views on monarchy remain a matter of scholarly controversy that cannot be settled here, but more germane to the point at hand is the fact that a group of trusted generals, all closely associated with Bolívar, and often referred to as the "faithful friends," spearheaded a monarchist movement. Leader of this inner circle by virtue of his dynamism and devotion was General Rafael Urdaneta, companion-in-arms of the Liberator from the early days of the wars of independence and later president-dictator of New Granada. Other members of the select group were Generals José María Carreño, Tomás Cipriano Mosquera, Mariano Montilla, Pedro Briceño Méndez, and Juan José Flores. Latecomers to the "faithful friends" activities were Generals Sucre and Daniel F. O'Leary, two of Bolívar's most intimate associates who endorsed a plan in 1829 for a French-backed throne. In addition to the generals there were many civilians who supported royalist proposals, among them the cultured Colombian Juan García del Río who espoused monarchism in 1821 while serving as minister of foreign affairs under General José de San Martín in Peru.[44]

The correspondence of the "faithful friends" reveals that they wanted a strong, monocratic government. If monarchy could not be established, then they would accept dictatorship under Bolívar. There was a general recognition among the members of this inner circle that republican institutions had a strong hold on the minds of most people and that any move to implant monarchy would meet with vigorous opposition in some quarters. For this reason they were sometimes attracted to the concept of the Bolivian constitution of 1826, which was a compromise between monarchy and republic. Dictatorship, in the absence of a king, also appealed to them, because it seemed to promise stability and an ordered society in turbulent times. Both dictatorship and monarchy, as Madariaga has pointed out, were monocratic in nature. Either form of government would allow for the kind of authority that the Liberator and his "faithful friends" deemed necessary to create "solid institutions" and to restrain the "demagogues" and "factions" that, in Bolívar's opinion, were causing anarchy in Spanish America.

From 1826 to 1830 Juan José Flores championed the Bolivarian monocratic schemes in southern Colombia. His support of the Bolivian constitution is a case in point. In response to a request from Bolívar, Flores persuaded the leading citizens of Quito and Cuenca to adopt proclamations calling for the reform of Colombia's constitution and for a dictatorship under the Liberator.[45] During the years 1827 and 1828 Flores' letters to Bolívar were filled with declarations of his devotion to the principles of dictatorial rule and a lifetime executive. He stated repeatedly his vigorous opposition to elective institutions and reported that he had succeeded in turning "public opinion against elective governments." In one of his interesting letters of this period Flores noted the instability of political institutions throughout Spanish America and concluded:

America presents a vast picture of revolution, and Your Excellency is the genius called upon to rule the destiny of the people. . . . This is the era of Alexander and Napoleon. . . . All is for Bolívar.[46]

When the Convention of Ocaña was convoked in 1828 to reform the Constitution of Cúcuta, Flores worked with his associates throughout the southern district to elect delegates who favored Bolívar's viewpoints. His efforts were so successful that all but two of the southern deputies were committed to support the Liberator in his bid for dictatorial powers.[47] Fearing that the advocates of monocratic government would not prevail at the convention, however, Flores urged Bolívar simply to declare a dictatorship. To assure the triumph of an autocratic regime Flores offered to proclaim the dictatorship of Bolívar in the south, to gather an army, and, together with General Urdaneta, to march on New Granada.[48] This offer was not mere bravado, for Flores coordinated secret plans with Urdaneta "to inundate the Departments of the Center [New Granada]" with troops if they were needed and sent a petition signed by almost all of the army officers of the south demanding that supreme power be granted by the convention to the Liberator in order to save Gran Colombia, as Flores put it, "from the infernal anarchy which is sweeping it to inevitable destruction."[49]

The public documents from the municipalities and the Army of the South relating to the Convention of Ocaña did not speak of monarchy, but rather of "energetic government," "supreme authority," and "unitary government capable of maintaining public order." Flores, however, in his private letters to the Liberator revealed that he expected that a Bolivarian dictatorship would be the first step toward the establishment of a monarchy. "The newspapers of Brazil," he said to Bolívar, "speak divinely of Your Excellency and they assert that Colombia will not be free and independent unless a constitutional monarchy is created." Flores had the Brazilian articles reprinted in newspapers of District of the South to give greater publicity to the monarchical idea.[50]

Together with other "faithful friends," Flores worked diligently to promote the royalist cause. His knowledge of the clandestine activities of Urdaneta was inadvertently revealed in a letter to Bolívar when Flores reported the publication of an article in a newspaper of Cuenca which advocated the creation of a great "Empire of the Andes" under the scepter of the Liberator. Though the article was written by Fray Vicente Solano, a polemical cleric, Flores mistakenly attributed its authorship to General Urdaneta "who is," he said, "a madman for monarchy." Flores confided to Bolívar that the article had good points and bad, but "is useful to us because it says that the sword and the tiara ought to unite against the demagogues."[51] He was later disappointed to receive a letter from Bolívar expressing disapproval of Solano's proposal. Curiously, though, Bolívar took pains to have the article reprinted with an editorial indicating his disapproval of the project—thus giving additional publicity to the idea that he ostensibly opposed.[52]

Bolívar's proclamation of a dictatorship in June 1828 pleased General Flores and the other exponents of monocratic rule, feeding their hopes of creating a throne in the near future. The roots of monarchism had penetrated deeply into the soil of southern Colombia during the period of Spanish colonial rule. The bishop of Quito was known for his strong royalist views and there were reports of many army officers and conservative citizens in the south who aspired to become dukes and marquises under a monarchy disguised as a "perpetual presidency."[53] Buttressed by public opinion and encouraged by the knowledge that he worked in collaboration with the most trusted associates of the Liberator, Flores continued to support dictatorship while fostering the cause of monarchy.[54]

Late in 1828 and early in the following year, shortly after an unsuccessful attempt on Bolívar's life, there was a new burst of monarchist activity in Gran Colombia which once again involved Flores and other "faithful friends." The plot was far-flung, stretching out to Venezuela, Ecuador, and Peru, but it was centered in Bolívar's most-trusted ministers of state who negotiated secretly with a French diplomat to obtain French participation in the royalist enterprise. The project came to naught in 1829 when Bolívar finally backed away from it, apparently out of fear for his "glory" if the scheme failed.

Details of this episode, which go beyond the scope of this

study, have been amply described in the controversial writings of Salvador de Madariaga and Caracciolo Parra-Pérez.[55] The role of the vacillating and ambivalent Bolívar in the monarchical machinations will long be a matter of scholarly dispute, but the role of General Flores is clear. Though fully engaged in the military task of expelling Peruvian forces from Guayaquil, Flores lent his personal support to the royalist project. In letters to Bolívar he urged the adoption of a government of force and denounced opponents like Páez of Venezuela for having "blasphemed" against the "monarchical form of government which rules the enlightened world."[56] Flores also wrote a report that favored "more decisive steps toward France," and, sensing that the Liberator might not give his approval, he urged the dictator "not to turn back on the project for monarchy." As if to whet Bolívar's appetite for power, Flores wrote that he had joined with others in a "large project" embracing all of Gran Colombia, Peru, and Bolivia under monarchy. "I will manage things with skill and wisdom," he vowed, "to win an advantage without compromising Your Excellency."[57]

The royalist "project of General Flores," as Bolívar called it one time, was not carried to fruition. For many months the Liberator responded to the urgings of Flores and others with ambiguous remarks that neither endorsed nor rejected monarchy, while behind the scenes Bolívar and his closest associates worked feverishly to prepare a new monocratic constitution. Ultimately, faced with declining health and with dangerous opposition from Santander, Páez, and others, Bolívar decided in late 1829 to disown the entire project. In January 1830, disillusioned and weak from a disease that would take his life in less than a year, the Liberator tendered his last resignation from the presidency and withdrew to semiprivate life on a country estate.[58]

News of the collapse of the royalist project came as a shattering blow to General Flores. At first, to judge by his correspondence, he seemed not to believe that Bolívar really intended to retire from public office or that the Congress in Bogotá was giving serious consideration to a federalist plan calling for the creation of regional legislatures. He gave his word to Bolívar that he would maintain "the tranquility of the South," but he warned that a federal legislature would bring "license, disorder, and revolution, all in the name of law. . . . May God deliver us and give me the strength to ward off the storm," he declared to Bolívar.[59]

Bolívar's final resignation from the presidency put an end to the project of reconstituting Gran Colombia under a monocratic form of government. In attempting to promote the ill-fated plan Flores had figured importantly, though briefly, among the select friends of Bolívar who sought to erect a European-backed throne in the New World. Flores had not been a prime mover in the affair, but he had cooperated enthusiastically. Though the effort failed, Flores gained political experience through his participation. Through his correspondence and personal communication with Bolívar, Sucre, O'Leary, and others during this period he learned something of the complexities of politics and of the subtleties of European diplomacy. He developed a distrust of "the rabble," of representative government, and especially of federalist institutions modeled on North American government. His antipathy toward representative regimes was not so strong that he would refuse to serve under an elective government (as events would soon demonstrate), but his personal and public commitment to monarchy in the last years of Bolívar's rule made it clear that his allegiance to a republic would be conditional. There was always the possibility, given Flores' one-time adoption of royalist views, that he might revert to the opinions of the Liberator's "faithful friends."

Monarchy in 1830, however, was unthinkable without Bolívar. The Liberator's withdrawal from public life not only demolished the hopes of the monarchists but hastened the political disintegration of Gran Colombia. This great nation, largely the creation of Bolívar, could not survive without the prestigious leadership of its founder.

On 13 January 1830, General José Antonio Páez, caudillo of Venezuela and a staunch opponent of monarchy, declared the independence of the eastern region under his control. The authorities of Bogotá were powerless to coerce the Venezuelans into obedience, even though they knew that Venezuela's defection would promote still more regional separatism.[60] Inevitably the rebellion of Páez brought on more uprisings, first in the province of Casanare and then in Pasto, just north of Quito. Unrest spread like an epidemic into Ecuador.

In several letters to the Liberator, Flores promised to do everything possible to maintain the loyalty of the southern departments. As he hastened from Guayaquil to Quito he learned that citizens were restless and apprehensive over the unsettling news from Venezuela and the north. But he also noted, with much satisfaction, that the troops and the people received him with great respect and friendliness. Once in Quito Flores took stock of the situation. His first reaction was to conclude that the "revolutionary torrent" in the north could not be stopped, but on March 27, perhaps in a last-ditch effort to stop the rush toward separatism, he wrote to Bolívar inviting him to come to Quito where he might rule and "save his glory." Three weeks later the news of a pronunciamiento (declaration of an uprising) in the Cauca region (just north of present-day Ecuador) produced great excitement in the south, and Flores reported that "everywhere opinions in favor of separation are heard." Pasto was in such a restless state that he planned to go there and reestablish order.[61]

On May 6 Flores wrote to Bolívar saying that the situation in the south was critical and that he had received many invitations to imitate the example of Venezuela and Cauca. Then, somewhat ominously, he reported:

> I have answered to everyone that I am with the people and that I will allow them complete liberty when Your Excellency has resigned from command, because I have duties and commitments to fulfill in order not to be ungrateful or a traitor. I am astonished to see the spirit of revolution which has spread through the entire Republic, and above all, the men who promote it. If I am to speak to Your Excellency with my heart I must say frankly that I have lost hope that public confidence can be restored.[62]

As evidence of his continuing loyalty to the Liberator, Flores forwarded petitions from citizens of Quito and Azuay, which he had helped to prepare, begging Bolívar to come to the District of the South. The gesture came too late. When news of the Liberator's definitive resignation from the Gran Colombian government arrived in Quito plans were already prepared for a declaration of independence in case of such an event. On 13 May 1830, the authorities of Quito proclaimed Ecuador to be "a free and independent state," though they also declared that the new state held out the hope of ultimate federation with Colombia. The departments of Azuay (extreme south) and Guayas (coastal lowlands) quickly followed the lead of Quito, and the work was complete. An assembly of prominent citizens named General Flores supreme civil and military commander, but not president, of the new government and instructed him to convoke a constituent congress. Flores accepted the honor, arranged for the elections of deputies to a congress, and assumed executive authority over the new nation.[63]

Most Ecuadorian historians have portrayed Flores as a conspirator and conniver, disloyal to Bolívar, who maneuvered in Machiavellian fashion to break away from Bogotá and take charge of the southern district.[64] Blaming Ecuadorian independence on a wily general is superficially plausible, for Flores was in a position to coordinate a regional political movement if he had chosen to do it. By 1830, with five years of residence in the equatorial region, Flores enjoyed supreme military command and had acquired important family connections through his marriage. He knew the sentiments of most of the leading citizens. Unsubstantiated rumors about Flores' alleged separatist views had circulated for years, but these rumors were based on allegations that Flores was disloyal to Bolívar and would gladly follow the example of Páez—a speculative view that has never been demonstrated and lacks credibility.[65]

The preponderant evidence shows that Flores remained loyal to Bolívar until it was clear to almost everyone that the Liberator lacked the will and the power to put himself once more at the head of a strong government in Bogotá. Flores' invitation in late March to Bolívar to come to Quito and build a new political base in the south was certainly evidence of continuing good faith in very difficult times. Moreover, recently discovered documents reveal that in the last weeks before Ecuador's declaration of independence General Flores was struggling to maintain allegiance to Gran Colombia by ordering subordinates to guard against the subversive activities of a mysterious secret agent from Bogotá who was stirring up separatist sentiment in the south and spreading malicious rumors about Bolívar. Flores also defended the existing Gran Colombian regime by ordering an investigation into a rumored separatist plot by the prefect of the department of Ecuador.[66]

Finally, on the question of Flores' loyalty, it can be said that the military commander in Quito received what amounted to a blank check from Bolívar to deal with political problems in the southern region as he deemed best. In a letter to Flores dated 2 January 1830, more than four months before Ecuador's declaration of independence, Bolívar lamented the impending disintegration of Gran Colombia, warned of "an immense torrent of anarchy which is going to inundate America," and admitted that Flores was going to be placed in a "very embarrassing situation" as a consequence. "I would not know how to advise you," declared the Liberator, "beyond saying that advice in such occasions is useless." He went on, nevertheless, to advise his subordinate to be prudent, to avoid hasty action, and to do "whatever you might believe necessary." Bolívar recognized that Flores probably could not contain the powerful political forces that had been set loose and that the young general in Quito would have to cope with incipient anarchy and regionalism as best he could. Although some of Bolívar's words were typically ambiguous, the letter seemed to say that Flores was on his own.[67]

Ecuadorian independence was not caused by disloyalty or treachery on the part of Flores. Rather, as Roger P. Davis' careful research has demonstrated, it was a product of the growing discontent among the elite classes of Ecuador who disliked the policies of the government of Gran Colombia. A broad range of issues dating back to 1822 irritated the Ecuadorian residents and caused them to think in terms of regional welfare and look for an opportunity to throw off the yoke of Gran Colombia. Economic grievances were the most troubling. The costs of the campaign in Peru, measured in money, manpower, and lives, had rankled for several years. The precarious state of the treasuries of Quito and Cuenca had been made worse by the temporary abolition of Indian tribute, a major source of revenues in the Sierra. Bolívar's imposition in 1827 of a head tax of three pesos on all citizens had provoked angry opposition from all classes and races. Yet another source of friction was the low-tariff or "free trade" policy of Gran Colombia which allowed cheap British textiles to flood the markets that had formerly been served by the highland textile mills known as *obrajes*. Bolívar had given some temporary relief to Ecuadorians by reinstating tribute and raising customs duties somewhat, but he also aroused animosity by imposing a controversial salt monopoly that caused an enormous increase in the price of salt.[68]

Besides economic grievances there were also religious and political complaints. Suppression of minor religious orders in 1826 by the Bogotá government caused the conservative and pious classes to fear further attacks on the Church by Colombian "radicals." There was little hope of redressing grievances because Ecuadorians were inadequately represented in all branches of the Gran Colombian government. Various Creole juntas and *cabildos abiertos* of the south had addressed petitions and protests to Bogotá in 1827 and 1828, without receiving a satisfactory response to any of their complaints. By 1829 Bolívar had received numerous reports of strong federalist and separatist sentiments among the Ecuadorians. Both Flores and Sucre, while working to maintain loyalty to the Liberator and Gran Colombia, warned Bolívar that separatism was gaining ground. In May 1829, General Sucre declared prophetically that "the South is lost." The centrifugal forces of political, religious, and economic discontent in the south were too strong to be controlled by the waning power of Bolívar and Bogotá.[69]

Guayaquil was always prone to go its separate way, but in 1828 and 1829 the civilian leaders of Quito and other southern cities also became increasingly impatient with the Liberator and the leadership of Bogotá. In May 1830 the leading citizens of Quito seized the initiative, convened a *cabildo abierto* (a meeting of the municipal council with most of the prominent citizens) and entertained proposals for autonomy of the south. To avoid countermeasures by Colombia it was necessary to use caution and secrecy. Members of the cabildo paid a hasty visit to General Flores at his hacienda near Quito and invited him to play a leading role in establishing the independence of the south. Flores accepted the invitation without delay.[70]

Historical documents currently available do not reveal Flores' reasons for accepting the cabildo's request, but his chief motives are quite obvious. Bolívar's resignation from power four months earlier had relieved General Flores of his personal obligations to the Liberator as head of Gran Colombia. Bolívar's successor, General Domingo Caicedo, had abolished the post of prefect-general in the south, thus effectively removing Flores from high military and civil command. Flores could not help but resent the Caicedo administration for what amounted to an unceremonious dismissal from office. Finally, it was abundantly clear that independence of the south was now inevitable. Hence it was best for Flores to throw in his lot with the patriots of Quito while the opportunity was at hand.

From the viewpoint of the city fathers Flores' chief asset was his military ability. The patriots of Quito were fearful of opposition to Ecuadorian independence, and they counted on General Flores to provide protection from any prospective military attack. Their fear of Colombian resistance was also revealed in the fact that members of the cabildo carefully refrained from any denunciation of "Colombian tyranny." They praised Bolívar for his "eminent services in the cause of American independence." It was evident that the moderate men of Quito, with Flores as their chief spokesman, sought to give no provocation to the authorities of Bogotá.[71]

Three weeks after Quito's declaration of independence a despicable act of violence occurred—not in Ecuador but in the vicinity of Pasto—which stained the history of both Colombia and Ecuador and permanently clouded the reputation of General Flores. On 4 June 1830, Marshal Antonio José de Sucre was shot from ambush and killed in a remote location called Berruecos, on the road from Popayán to Pasto. The murder, especially heinous because of the sterling character and reputation of the victim, was apparently a political assassination. An impenetrable mystery has surrounded the "Crime of Berruecos," for the identity of the killers and the possible involvement of important figures have been subjects of historical polemics down to current times. Greatest suspicion has fallen upon General José María Obando, a caudillo of the Cauca region associated politically with the anti-Bolivarian federalists, as the man who ordered the killing. A substantial body of evidence has linked Obando with the killing.[72]

Suspicion also fell upon Flores, who, according to his accusers, viewed the grand marshal as a potential rival for the presidency of Ecuador. Though the evidence linking Flores with the crime was circumstantial and suppositional, and has been discounted by Ecuador's leading historian of the twentieth century, the mere fact that he was suspected and accused meant that his critics and adversaries could exploit the matter to Flores' great disadvantage.[73] If he was innocent, which seems likely, then Flores must have felt outrage at the unfair charges later heaped on his head by such political foes as Vicente Rocafuerte and Pedro Moncayo.[74] On the other hand, if Flores was responsible for the deed, then he must have been hounded by a deep sense of guilt during his long years in public life.

As a faithful lieutenant and admirer of Bolívar, General Flores had the difficult task of reporting to the Liberator not only the news of Ecuador's independence but also Sucre's assassination. On the very day of Quito's declaration of autonomy Flores wrote to Bolívar that he had acquiesced in the severance of ties with Bogotá only because Gran Colombia had rejected the Liberator's leadership. He promised to renew the severed bonds if Bolívar returned to power. On 29 June Flores reiterated his desire for reconciliation with New Granada (the central portion of Gran Colombia, with its capital in Bogotá) and reported the murder of Sucre, which he blamed on Obando. "My General," Flores wrote, "I cannot express the mortal grief in which I live as a result of my separation from Your Excellency and the abominable killing of General Sucre."[75]

Bolívar reacted to Flores' report of the murder with sorrow and warned that the death of the "immaculate Sucre" left Flores as a lone target of infamous men in the south. "My dear Flores," wrote Bolívar, "you will be the next victim."[76] As for the political events in Ecuador, Bolívar accepted the "excuses" given by Flores but declared that he could not give approval to the separation of the south, because it was not for him to give. Bolívar assured his fellow general that he had never doubted his "heroic fidelity," and in letters to others he rejected indignantly charges that Flores had conspired in the assassination of Sucre.[77]

Before Bolívar's death Flores received one of the Liberator's last letters, one which has attracted widespread attention. The importance of this communication is twofold. First, the letter acknowledged the independence of Ecuador. And, second, it offered some somber and bitter advice to the Ecuadorian leader. Bolívar summarized "lessons" learned from twenty years of military and political command in the following manner:

> First, for us America is ungovernable; second, he who serves a revolution plows the sea; third, the only thing one can do in America is emigrate; fourth, this land will inevitably fall into the hands of the unbridled masses, to pass later to petty, almost indiscernible tyrants of all colors and races; fifth, devoured by all kinds of crimes and consumed by ferocity as we are, Europeans will not deign to conquer us; sixth, if it were possible for a part of the world to return to primeval chaos, America would do it.

In the same letter Bolívar reminded Flores of the horrible effects of the French Revolution on Haiti and concluded: "You will see that the whole world is going to surrender to a torrent of demagogy. Oh Hapless peoples! Oh hapless governments!"[78]

Bolívar's warnings of impending doom failed to persuade Flores to draw back from his decision to lead the movement for Ecuadorian autonomy. The signs of enthusiastic support that Flores had recently received from municipalities and from military officers seemed proof enough that Ecuador was in little danger of a descent into "primeval chaos." As for the menace of "unbridled masses" and "petty tyrants," able leadership, enlightened policies, and executive firmness could be counted on to ward off the perils of anarchy. Bolívar's brooding pessimism simply failed to overcome the youthful optimism of General Flores as he prepared to embark upon his new career in government and politics.[79] Bolívar's sun was setting; it was the dawn of a new day for General Flores.

2

PROBLEMS OF NATIONHOOD

The land governed by Juan José Flores in 1830 was, and is, one of the most dazzling and picturesque countries in the world. Straddling the equator, for which it was named, Ecuador is dominated geographically by the massive cordillera of the Andes whose highest peaks in this region reach twenty thousand feet. Mountain streams that begin their courses in the cool regions of the sierra traverse the tablelands and plunge westward to the coastal lowlands in their descent to the Pacific Ocean. The tropical coastal plain, roughly equal in area to the highlands, is drained in the north by the Esmeraldas River and in the south by the Guayas and other smaller streams.[1]

The sultry climate of the coastal savannas provided a basis for commercial agriculture, while the cooler climate and rugged terrain of the sierra fostered pastoral and agricultural production based on servile Indian labor and oriented largely toward internal consumption. The geographical contrast between the two major regions of Ecuador was illustrated by the sharp differences between the two major cities of the nation. Guayaquil, with a population of no more than twenty thousand, was a thriving and dynamic port, located on the Guayas River about twenty-five nautical miles from open sea. Though not on a par with major Latin American ports, the harbor sheltered large oceangoing vessels that visited this city in substantial numbers. Besides its mercantile spirit and its plantation agriculture the coast was distinguished by the predominance of people of African descent in its society. The high concentration of blacks in western Ecuador was a consequence of plantation agriculture, which from colonial times was associated with slavery. In the racially stratified coastal society privileged whites, who represented no more than one-sixth of the total population, looked down on the colored classes of blacks, Indians, mestizos, and mulattoes.[2]

The Guayas region was distinguished from the sierra by a vigorous mercantile spirit that was promoted by the dynamic merchant class of the port. Guayaquil provided a market for tropical agriculture oriented toward maritime commerce. Ecuador's chief exports, such as cacao (the chocolate bean), cotton, agave fiber, tobacco, and coffee, enjoyed a brisk demand on the Pacific Coast and in the West Indies.[3]

The isolated and static society of the highlands contrasted sharply with the commercial orientation of the coast. Economic production of the sierra, backward and inefficient, rested largely on pastoral and agricultural activities of large haciendas. Most of the labor was provided by Indians, many of whom toiled under a peonage system called *concertaje*, which made them "as hopelessly slaves as the blacks" of the coast.[4] Although techniques of agriculture were ancient, the highland soil produced large amounts of food products for domestic consumption, while small textile mills (*obrajes*), in diminishing numbers, manufactured coarse fabrics.[5]

The lack of adequate roads not only separated the sierra from the coast but completely cut off the lands east of the cordillera from the rest of the nation. Everywhere provincialism thrived on poor communications. Provincial capitals, like city-states of Renaissance Italy, vied with each other for economic and political advantage. In the highlands, Quito, the national capital and major city, had its rivals in Cuenca and Loja to the south and in Ibarra to the north. But its major rival was always the vital port city of Guayaquil.

Under Gran Colombia the District of the South was divided into three large "departments": Guayas (the coast), Azuay (southern sierra), and El Ecuador (northern sierra), with Guayaquil, Cuenca, and Quito as their respective capitals. Departments were composed of provinces and had boundaries that corresponded roughly to major geographical regions. The metropolitan ambitions of each departmental capital, together with economic interests and social similarities, gave cohesion to each region.

Rivalries and antagonisms most frequently pitted coastal Guayas against the northern-highland Department of El Ecuador, while Azuay in the southern sierra sided with either of the major departments, according to its interests. The basic antagonism lay in the opposing interests and viewpoints of the commercial coast and the agrarian highlands, between the centers of power in the cities of Guayaquil and Quito. But political alignments of the three major regions tended to shift according to the issue of the moment. Quito's pretentions over Azuay were never completely realized, nor could Guayaquil always rely on the support of the northcoast province of Esmeraldas. The transient loyalties and conflicting interests of departments and provinces posed grave problems for those who would build a nation.[6]

The most important source of interregional tension rested in the clashing economies of the two major geographic sections. The interests of commercial agriculture and international trade of Guayaquil were sharply at odds with the traditional agrarian regime and the primitive manufacturing of Quito and the sierra. In 1831 the *Gaceta del Gobierno del Ecuador,* the official newspaper of the nation, spoke for the highland interests when it declared the economy of the sierra was decadent because of the importation of cheap foreign commodities. The paper called for the exclusion of "many foreign goods."[7] Spokesmen of the coast, on the other hand, generally favored low tariffs and few restrictions on foreign trade. Though there were a few individuals in both regions who disagreed with the predominant views in their respective areas, most highlanders favored protectionism, while most coastal people supported free-trade ideas.[8]

Yet another economic issue that divided the nation was the question of government monopolies (*estancos*) on tobacco, salt, liquor (*aguardiente*), and flour. The economic traditionalism of the sierra led highlanders to favor the estancos, while people of the coast tended to favor the replacement of estancos by private enterprise.[9] The entrenched opposition of highlanders to change and their indifference to efficient methods of production contributed to economic stagnation and decay, a condition noted by many observers, especially North American diplomats. "Lifelessness and decay," noted one of these envoys, "are the characteristic features of the country."[10]

Economic backwardness and regionalism were not unique characteristics of Ecuador, but rather were a generalized feature of Latin America in the nineteenth century. Argentina, for example, had severe difficulties, but in this case the chief port was also the national capital, which allowed Buenos Aires to bend the nation to its will. Mexico also offered an example of debilitating regionalism, although the centrifugal forces there were more complex and could not be reduced to the simple polarity of two major cities or regions.[11] Nowhere in the hemisphere was the conflict between coast and interior more acute than in Ecuador.

Guayaquil had two major sources of strength in its contest with Quito. First, it enjoyed an unchallengeable maritime monopoly on which the rest of the nation was dependent for trade and customs receipts. Second, the rainy season conferred virtual autonomy on the city for about four months every year, during which time impassable roads made it very difficult for highland troops to suppress revolts in the port. Rebellious *guayaquileños* understood these advantages very well. They also knew that they could turn for aid to Peru and New Granada, whose leaders were often eager to encourage the separatist inclinations of Guayaquil.

Coping with the unfriendly attitudes of Ecuador's next-door neighbors proved to be one of the most troublesome problems of the new government in Quito. New Granada (called Colombia after 1863) to the north was loath to accept Ecuadorian independence, which if acknowledged posed likely boundary disputes and raised questions of Ecuador's share of the Gran Colombian foreign debt. Peru, to the south, harbored designs on both the Guayas region and the Amazonian territory claimed by Ecuador. Quarrels over borders would lead to costly wars with both of Ecuador's Spanish American neighbors. One of President Flores' first official acts was to send envoys to Bogotá and Caracas to make friendly overtures, but he also made the mistake of indirectly asserting sovereignty over the northern regions of El Carchi and Pasto, claimed by New Granada since independence. Before the end of 1830 New Granada would seek, in retaliation, to topple the Flores regime and to reincorporate Ecuador.[12]

If handling foreign affairs proved dangerous, in the realm of domestic affairs the task of creating a stable, constitutional government was no less difficult. General Flores, acting as interim chief of state, convoked a constituent congress in May 1830, to meet in Riobamba, a highland city situated, significantly, midway between Quito and Guayaquil. In August and September the assembly drafted a constitution, passed thirty-seven laws and decrees, and elected Juan José Flores to the presidency and José Joaquín de Olmedo, the prestigious Guayaquil poet, to the vice-presidency.[13]

In most respects the Constitution of 1830 was an undistinguished document, largely an adaptation of the Constitution of Cúcuta (1820) of Gran Colombia. It provided for a government of three branches, with a unicameral legislature in which the three departments (El Ecuador, Azuay, and Guayas) had equal representation. (The lack of a second legislative chamber deprived the nation of a convenient way of compromising the question of popular versus territorial representation.) Like most Latin American constitutions of this era the new charter created a highly aristocratic government. Substantial property requirements for suffrage excluded well over 90 percent of the adult population from a voice in public affairs, while a three-tier system of indirect elections placed control in the hands of a small oligarchy. Though the Constitution of 1830 listed a few "civil rights and guarantees," it failed to forbid arbitrary arrests and to provide for a meaningful right of petition.[14]

The framers of Ecuador's first constitution attempted to limit the power of the chief executive by specifying a four-year term of office without reelection for eight years, and by denying the president an absolute veto over legislation. The chief executive was forbidden to "infringe the Constitution" and could not be granted "extraordinary powers," nor could he issue decrees on a temporary basis.[15]

Nevertheless, the president enjoyed very broad authority over the budget, the armed forces, and appointments. His patronage powers over departments and provinces gave him virtual control over all political subdivisions of the nation. Additionally, the prestige of the chief of state in Ecuador's authoritarian society caused people to look to the president as the supreme authority and allowed circumvention of the constitutional limitations on executive power. Only a very vigilant and determined legislature could hope to control an ambitious chief executive.

On 23 September 1830, President Flores promulgated the new constitution without benefit of a popular referendum or ratification by the electorate. From that date the new nation on the equator was endowed with a fundamental charter of government. It remained for the president, his advisers, and the members of the next congress to cope with the gargantuan social, economic, and finanical problems of the country.

One of the most difficult problems facing the new regime was the question of the role to be played by the dark-skinned peoples, the "dangerous classes," in the words of a modern Argentine social scientist. Of the 600,000 or so inhabitants of Ecuador in 1830, about 85 percent or more were Indians, mestizos, and blacks. Indians alone comprised 55 or 60 percent of the total, and in some parts of the sierra the proportion of Indians was 70 percent or more.[16]

The native people, who lived in villages apart from Hispanic society and who spoke little or no Spanish, were largely concentrated in the highlands. They were subject to various forms of exploitation, including forced labor and a head tax called "tribute" that took from the Indians about one-quarter of their meager income. Most native peoples lived in dire poverty, and a large number lived as dependent laborers on large estates under conditions that approximated serfdom or slavery. Through three centuries of harsh colonial rule Indians had learned to accept their menial condition and to resist white authorities only if the latter threatened to make matters worse.[17]

Many political leaders, including President Flores, sympathized with the Indians and wished to adopt reforms to improve their condition and to integrate them into Hispanic society. Though granting full and equal citizenship rights was never considered seriously, Ecuadorian leaders actually made attempts, some half-hearted, to carry out humanitarian reforms. The results were meager and disappointing. The issue of ending the unjust Indian tribute hung fire for almost three decades, until its final abolition in 1857.[18] Other reforms included legislation forbidding whipping, outlawing exploitation by the clergy, and prohibiting the buying and selling of peons, but most of the legislation was relatively ineffective because of the deeply ingrained exploitative habits not only of the Creoles but also of mestizos and free blacks who took advantage of the lowly and submissive Indian.[19]

The lack of conspicuous success in efforts to aid the Indian did not necessarily reflect insincerity or hypocrisy on the part of President Flores and his successors. Flores attempted on two occasions, at great political risk, to relieve the natives of the unfair burden. In the second attempt (1844–1845) he triggered a successful rebellion against his regime by mestizos and whites who opposed the humanitarian tax reform.

Much less is known about Afro-Ecuadorians than about Indians. In 1830 there were about 45,000 blacks (7 or 8 percent of the total population), most of whom lived in the tropical coastal plains of Guayas and Manabí. There were about 5200 slaves at this time, only about 11 percent of the black population. In 1843 the British consul reported that most slaves were domestic servants and that those who worked as fieldhands were "quite as well treated" as free blacks.[20] The Flores administration continued the New Granadan policy of gradual emancipation under a law of free birth, but the process was slow. The last slaves were not freed until the mid-1850s.[21]

The long delays in ending Indian tribute and in emancipating slaves were a clear indication of Creole fears of racial strife and of desires to protect their property interests. Members of the white elite were reluctant to grant full citizenship rights to the "dangerous classes," most of whom did not understand the principles of representative government. In an era of mounting democratic pressures, Ecuador was dominated by a powerful oligarchy ("impenetrable aristocracy," in the words of Friedrich Hassaurek) that was imbued with the values and loyalties associated with a monarchical society that had long protected the property and privileges of the upper classes. It was not surprising that this powerful elite should shun democratic ways and should prefer aristocratic, even monarchical, ideas.

Several foreign observers noted the artificial and discrepant nature of republican forms in Ecuador. Dr. Adrian Terry remarked in 1832 that social conditions were "incompatible with a republican form of government."[22] In 1845 an American diplomat reported "a constant burlesque" of republican ways, and a European traveler lamented "this caricature of republican institutions."[23]

The wholly inadequate educational system of Ecuador was an important factor in the malfunctioning republican process. Not only were the lower classes almost universally illiterate, but even the Creoles were largely uneducated. An illiteracy rate of 95 percent of the entire population would be a conservative estimate.[24] The few schools that survived the chaos of the 1820s were grossly deficient in number, size, and quality. As late as 1837 students in a church school were still being taught cosmology according to the Ptolemaic system.[25] The clerical monopoly over education had much to do with the wretched condition of the schools, for most ecclesiastics were poorly trained in seminaries of mediocre quality at best.[26]

The influence of the clergy in education was merely one of several issues between church and state that beset the new nation. Like other Spanish American nations, Ecuador in its Constitution of 1830 asserted the authority of royal patronage (*patronato*) over the Church, that is, the authority of the national government over the Church, especially in clerical nominations. The decision to claim the patronato was not necessarily anticlerical, but the bishop of Quito angrily denounced the decision and refused to take an oath of loyalty to the constitution.[27] Though the Constitution of 1830 forbade the toleration of other cults and guaranteed the Catholic Church's system of laws and courts (the religious *fuero*), there was friction over taxation of the clergy, the future of religious orders, and the toleration of Freemasonry. It was not reassuring to the priesthood to know that President Flores was a Mason, and many clerics feared that he might mount a damaging attack on the Church.[28]

Clerical immorality, dating back to the colonial period, was yet another problem for the new government. Concubinage, profligacy, gambling, and flagrant violations of monastic rules were scandalously common among the Ecuadorian clergy, but Presi-

dent Flores, perhaps because he sensed grave political risks, was
not disposed to attempt to cleanse the Church. In the early 1830s
Quito's chief of police had the temerity to arrest large numbers
of monks for violating a law requiring members of religious
orders to be within monastery walls after six in the evening. But
ecclesiastical authorities secured the release of the monks and
the removal of the obnoxious police chief, after which the
pleasure-loving regulars resumed their nocturnal carousals.[29]
Both Flores and the second president, Vicente Rocafuerte,
wished to curb the clergy, but neither dared initiate a major
reform of the Church. Nevertheless, clerical leaders worked behind the scenes to organize opposition to the government.

If the clergy represented the immoblizing force of tradition,
journalists typified the new forces of change. Newspapers dated
from the Spanish era, but it was not until the Independence
period that the press became a weapon of war and an instrument of politics. Harsh journalistic assaults on government policies and officials often proved shocking in a society of authoritarian traditions and with strong feelings of personal honor.[30]

General Flores was especially sensitive to journalistic criticism
for several reasons. He was vulnerable because he was a "foreigner" from Venezuela, because of gossip about his personal
wealth (so quickly acquired), and because of his alleged complicity in the assassination of Sucre. When newspapers assailed him
as a "foreign adventurer" and as the "assassin of Sucre" they not
only wounded Flores personally (sense of honor) but they undermined his presidential leadership. Flores permitted newspapers to criticize if their words were mild and impersonal, but
the full weight of government power was brought against publishers who, like the ill-fated Colonel Francis Hall, broke the
unwritten rules.[31]

An even greater threat to political stability than the press was
the army. The remnants of Bolívar's famous Ejército Libertador posed enormous difficulties and threatened at times to
overwhelm the young nation. The framers of the Constitution
of 1830, mindful of the dangers of militarism, attempted to
subordinate the army to civilian control by placing the highest
military command in the hands of the president, reserving to

Congress the right to declare war and determine the military budget, and creating a national militia as a counterweight to the army. But they surrendered a great part of the government's authority over the army by granting it a separate legal system under the military *fuero*.[32] The constituent congress also chose a general (Flores) as the first president, thus uniting in one person the highest civil and military authorities in the nation. A dubious precedent was set in selecting a general as president, even though Flores worked diligently to hold the armed forces in check.

Military insubordination was a major problem in the early years of Ecuadorian nationhood. In 1832 Dr. Adrian Terry encountered a battalion of soldiers near Latacunga in the highlands and left the following description of the disorderly troops:

> Soon after sunrise we encountered straggling parties of the hangers-on of a camp; squalid, miserable looking women, some with child, others with knapsack or kettle hanging from their shoulders, here and there a sick soldier . . . , then a donkey half starved and beaten to death, urged along by a troop of hooting ragamuffins, next to two or three mules forcibly seized to transport the baggage and driven by their unwilling owners. . . . Before long these signs of the march of a body of men led us to . . . where the troops had bivouacked . . . ; they were just mustering for the march, and greeted our approach by the most unearthly yells and insulting language which sorely jarred with my companion's ideas of military subordination. Indeed this corps, which is called *el batallón Flores,* from the President, had the reputation of being the most turbulent and undisciplined of any one in the Ecuador. . . .[33]

A few days after Terry's unpleasant brush with the Flores Battalion these same troops rebelled, killed their officers, and began a march toward Guayaquil. Their revolt was blamed on a shortage of rations, lack of pay, and fear that they would be forced to fight in a war against New Granada that had just broken out. (Veterans of the battalion were New Granadans and Venezuelans of African ancestry.) The white inhabitants of Guayaquil, fearing a black insurrection in the port in sympathy with the renegade battalion, hastily readied a volunteer militia, but loyal troops caught and killed the rebels before they could reach Guayaquil.[34]

The tragic revolt of the Flores Battalion illustrated the enormous difficulties posed by an unpaid army composed mostly of foreigners of African ancestry. Even without the racial factor, most Ecuadorian creoles resented this "liberating army" that lived off the land, impressed men into service, and arbitrarily seized food, cattle, and pack animals. They devastated the land like swarms of locusts.

The armed forces presented Ecuador with a dilemma. On the one hand, troops were needed to preserve order and defend the nation. On the other hand, the loyalty of military commanders was precarious, and undisciplined army units caused major disorders, especially when they were not paid. Military revolts disrupted the economy, which wasted national revenues and in turn prevented the government from paying the troops—a vicious circle. The result was an ever-present tendency toward anarchy.

The perennial poverty of the national treasury was undoubtedly the greatest problem faced by Ecuador in its early years. Enormous deficits began to pile up in the 1830s, and, as Linda Rodríguez's *Search for Public Policy* has shown, the consequences were numerous and grave. Unpaid troops rebelled. Unpaid government employees transferred political loyalty to the opposition. Forced loans, debased coinage, worthless paper notes, and desperate fiscal measures turned large numbers of people against the government from time to time. The need for austerity was clear, but the achievement of economy and efficiency in the treasury was an almost insuperable task. To reduce expenditures in the army, for example, would reduce the nation's military strength to defend its borders and might provoke a military rebellion that would cost the treasury dearly.[35]

The drafters of the Constitution of 1830 inadvertently helped to assure fiscal difficulties by failing to establish a separate ministry of the treasury, apparently in the naive belief that a single minister of state could administer all of the complex business of the executive branch, including finance. Enormous deficits began to pile up immediately, and Flores soon found the government on the verge of bankruptcy. The hasty (and unconstitutional) appointment of a minister of the treasury in 1832 failed to resolve the crisis, which was aggravated by an inadequate monetary system, widespread counterfeiting, and a large foreign debt.[36]

Many Ecuadorian leaders hoped that a new spirit of patriotism and "public virtue" (a favorite term of journalists and moralizers of the time) would resolve the problem. But when public virtue failed to materialize, it became evident that only an efficient and ruthless minister of finance could stem the graft, corruption, and fiscal confusion that threatened to destroy the fledgling government.

The formidable problems facing Ecuador in the 1830s were in most ways like those of the majority of Spanish American republics, but some of the hazards faced by the Quito government were exceptional. The conservative influence of the Church, for example, was greater than in most other republics, with the exception of Mexico. Budgetary deficits, too, were less manageable because of the frail economy and the small tax base. Finally, Ecuador's geography not only caused a coast–highland schism but also clamped the nation in the jaws of a vise between Peru and New Granada. The obstacles to effective government in the 1830s and 1840s were truly enormous.

3

FORGING A NATION, 1830–1833

On 22 September 1830, General Juan José Flores took possession of the presidential office, swearing "by God and the Holy
Scriptures to uphold the Constitution." He received warm ap-
plause for a short address he delivered to the members of Congress and assembled guests in which he pledged that "the Constitution would be the only norm of his political conduct." In
accordance with the general's love of display and conviviality,
his inauguration was honored with music and festivities, permitting the young president—he was only thirty years old—to show
off his dress uniform and his many decorations. Henceforth he
was treated as "His Excellency."[1] Though this form of address
had overtones of aristocracy and monarchy, Flores' oath of allegiance to the constitution implied that he had abandoned, at
least for the time being, his earlier preference for monarchy.

In anticipation of his new responsibilities, President Flores
was ready with names of prominent individuals to fill the highest posts in the new government. In a rapid series of announce-
ments he made appointments to the executive branch. Dr. José
Félix Valdivieso, a wealthy and eminent citizen of the southern
highland city of Loja and a close associate of Flores, was named
secretary-minister of the Cabinet. General Vicente González of
New Granada assumed the post of chief of the General Staff.
Lesser posts were promptly filled by respectable citizens of the
highlands area, no thought being given to the appointment of
guayaquileños for the sake of geographical balance in the administration.[2]

The promptness with which the new president assembled his
administration was appropriate, for the nation needed effective
leadership. Flores and his advisers quickly turned their atten-

tion to the major problems of the nation. Working with the constituent congress, which assumed ordinary legislative functions once finished with the constitution, the chief executive approved a large number of laws and decrees dealing with a variety of matters ranging from taxation and education to the maintenance of roads and the provision of a fundamental law code for the armed forces.[3] But the constructive work of domestic legislation was not destined to occupy most of Flores' time, for late in the year 1830 the president's attention was attracted to the embroiling and delicate business of foreign policy.

On 20 December President Flores signed a decree formally approving the incorporation of the northern Department of Cauca into Ecuador. This action touched off an angry dispute with the government of New Granada which had governed the Cauca region for a decade. Soon the territorial dispute would turn into a costly, fratricidal war between the two neighboring nations.

Ecuador's claims to the Department of Cauca had a solid basis in history. Although the boundaries of the former Spanish Audiencia of Quito had not been delineated with complete precision, it was clear that the jurisdiction of the administrative court at Quito extended eastward into the lowlands of the Amazon and Marañón Rivers (subsequently appropriated by Brazil and Peru) and northward to include Pasto, Popayán, and the Pacific Coast port and province of Buenaventura.[4] It was this territory north of the Carchi River, known now as the Department of Cauca, which Flores formally incorporated into Ecuador in the last days of 1830.

The complicated story of the Cauca movement for separation from Colombia and for annexation to Ecuador need not be told in detail. Some of the inhabitants of the Cauca region had shown their discontent with Bogotá rule as early as April 1830 (two weeks before Quito established its own government), when residents of Pasto formally requested annexation of their province to the District of the South. Subsequently, several other cities of the region declared their separation from the strife-torn government of New Granada and requested admission into the new state of Ecuador.[5]

Colombian historians and Ecuadorian opponents of Flores have attributed the Cauca dispute to the secret intrigues and machinations of General Flores. His critics have portrayed Flores as the bête noire in this unfortunate episode. The apparent truth of the matter is that there were abundant examples of machinations and stealth on both sides of the dispute. It is doubtless true that Flores secretly gave encouragement to some of the Cauca petitioners and that he actively and rather openly sought the cooperation of Pasto and Buenaventura. But the politicians and military leaders of Bogotá were not less active, nor were they less inclined to use military force as a means of intimidating the hapless citizens of Cauca. As for the military, civilian, and ecclesiastical leadership of Cauca, no one could outdo them in the slippery business of political intrigue during this period.[6]

Assigning personal blame or credit in the Cauca episode is largely a waste of time. A few significant facts are clear. First, both nations had a logical claim to the region and neither was willing to yield without a test of arms. Second, vigorous opposition in Cauca to the dictatorship of General Rafael Urdaneta in Bogotá and regional sentiment in favor of federalism produced a separatist movement that Flores was quick to exploit. And, third, there were still significant political ties between the Cauca region and Quito which had survived a decade of rule from Bogotá. These bonds of union stemmed from centuries of colonial experience during which time the region looked to Quito for justice and administrative authority. Then, too, there were important economic ties in the form of north–south commerce which provided a foundation for political union. The existence of gold mines in the disputed area undoubtedly constituted an important consideration for Ecuador, which suffered from a serious shortage of money and precious metals.[7]

In his Cauca policy President Flores correctly interpreted the wishes of the nation's leaders, a fact which the members of Congress readily demonstrated by adopting a law approving the presidential decree of incorporation.[8] From the Ecuadorian perspective the assertion of authority over the Department of Cauca was not an "annexation" but rather a reassertion of

Quito's historical authority over territory formerly under the jurisdiction of the colonial audiencia.

Considerations of political and diplomatic strategy almost certainly entered into the thinking of General Flores in his decision to lay claim to the Cauca, although it is not possible to document this view. As a professional military leader Flores favored bold and decisive actions to keep opponents off balance.[9] In December 1830 the Flores administration faced a critical situation with the government in Bogotá, openly hostile toward Quito and strongly opposed to recognizing the independence of the new "state" of Ecuador. Colombian hostility toward Ecuador was so great that President Rafael Urdaneta of New Granada had already set in motion a plan to topple the Flores regime and to reincorporate Ecuador at the very time Flores was preparing to claim Cauca.[10] Since Urdaneta's plot began to unfold before the attempted annexation of Cauca, Flores' move was probably intended as a strategic counterblow to keep New Granada off balance. Such a ploy must have appealed to the military mind of General Flores.

The presumed weakness of the Bogotá government undoubtedly encouraged Flores and Ecuadorian congressmen in the idea of preemptive action. Not only was political opposition in New Granada to the dictatorship of Rafael Urdaneta strong, but secessionist movements in the provinces of Casanare and Panama appeared to weaken the military posture of Bogotá. Therefore, the move to incorporate Cauca seemed perfectly timed. If New Granada should put up unexpected resistance to the Ecuadorian initiative, it seemed likely that General Flores would be more than capable of meeting any military challenge.

But appearances differed from reality, and Flores' Cauca policy proved to be a grave miscalculation of the relative strengths of the two nations. An undetected vulnerability of Ecuador began to come to light even before the formal annexation of Cauca took place. General Luis Urdaneta (cousin and agent of the president of New Granada) turned up in Guayaquil in November 1830 for the purpose of carrying out a secret plan to end Ecuador's bid for independence. Urdaneta soon raised the banner of revolution, allegedly in the name of

Bolívar, to restore Gran Colombia. Invocation of the Liberator's name quickly worked its magic among the Colombian and Venezuelan troops who comprised most of the Ecuadorian army. The revolt spread like a prairie fire, even briefly affecting troops in Quito.[11]

President Flores, who was in Pasto arranging the forthcoming incorporation of Cauca, had to rush southward to deal with the challenge of Urdaneta. Through a strategy of flexible armed resistance and negotiations Flores reached an agreement in February 1831 for Ecuador to rejoin Gran Colombia if Bolívar was actually at the head of the government.[12] The pact with Urdaneta was cleverly contrived by Flores, for he yielded nothing he did not already favor. Possibly Flores knew already of Bolívar's death in the past month of December. At any rate, news of the Liberator's demise, which reached Guayaquil just five days after the pact was signed, quickly demolished the revolt and Urdaneta fled the country.[13]

The Urdaneta affair should have served as a warning to Flores of the unreliability of Ecuador's armed forces. The sudden defection of so many troops was certainly a bad omen, but Flores seemed emboldened by his easy victory over Urdaneta and he pressed ahead with his aggressive plans in the north by sending garrison forces to Pasto and Popayán. Many cities of Cauca, encouraged by the presence of Ecuadorian troops, issued pronunciamientos in favor of annexation. The Ecuadorian government responded by scheduling elections for later in the year.[14]

Congressmen from Cauca, however, never took their seats in Quito. General Flores had underestimated the tenacity and resourcefulness of New Granada and, worse still, he had overestimated his own military power. Insubordination in the Ecuadorian armed forces was so widespread that the troops could not be used effectively against New Granada. The fact that most of the officers and soldiers were Colombians and Venezuelans meant that they were reluctant to fight against their fellow countrymen. Equally important, army units were restless over the government's failure to pay them and provide rations on a regular basis. An Ecuadorian historian has aptly described the soldiers of this period as "hungry, naked, and immoral."[15]

Between April 1831 and August 1832 the Flores administration was jolted by three military mutinies, two of which threatened the stability of the government. General Flores and a handful of loyal men quickly smothered the first uprising, but six months later a major unit of the army, the Vargas Battalion, rebelled, seized the central part of Quito, and demanded food and back pay. At the risk of his own life General Flores helped to quell this uprising, only to have the renowned Flores Battalion mutiny a few months later. Once more authorities put down the revolt bloodily, but the economy and the prestige of the government suffered serious damage.[16]

Enfeebled by military insubordination and fiscal bankruptcy, President Flores sought to escape from defeat by opening a diplomatic offensive. Almost simultaneously he initiated negotiations with New Granada over the Cauca dispute and offered to enter into military alliances with Peru and Bolivia. Unfortunately for Ecuador the two Andean nations to the south were on the brink of war with each other, and neither was disposed to help Ecuador in a war against New Granada. In July 1832 the Flores administration initialed a worthless treaty of alliance with the Lima government which provided for the surrender of disputed borderlands to Peru but secured no military assistance. Negotiations with Bolivia failed to yield an agreement, but they were historically important because they put Flores in touch with the wily General Andrés de Santa Cruz for the first time. A few years later Santa Cruz would come to Ecuador and the two leaders would begin to collaborate on a project to establish monarchy in Peru, Bolivia, and Ecuador—a sort of grandiose version of Flores' proposal for a triple alliance in 1832.[17] But for the time being monarchical dreams lay in the future.

Without international support Ecuador could not continue the struggle against the preponderant strength of New Granada. After several months of difficult bargaining with agents of the Bogotá government Ecuador signed the Treaty of Pasto in December 1832, giving up all claims to the Cauca region, including the province of Pasto. The Carchi River was accepted as the boundary between the two nations. The only concession granted by the victorious government of New Granada was the recognition of Ecuadorian independence.[18]

The Flores administration hailed the Treaty of Pasto as a glorious accomplishment "which reconciles us with the Granadan people."[19] Jubilation in Quito was restrained, however, for nothing could hide the fact that the peace settlement was a humiliation for Ecuador and a severe reverse for General Flores. An opposition newspaper may have overstated the case against Flores in blaming him for "seeking war without need, pursuing it without resources, and ending it without honor."[20] As president and commander of the military forces General Flores had major responsibility for the debacle in the Cauca affair, but it should be remembered that the Congress strongly supported the Cauca policy in the early stages because an aggressive territorial posture appealed to nationalist sentiment. Failure of the policy, of course, brought second thoughts in the matter, and critics fixed the blame on the brash young president.[21]

More important among the adverse effects of the Cauca imbroglio than the loss of presidential prestige was the retardation of national development. Mobilization of the armed forces, accompanied by the usual arbitrary impressments and forced loans, strained the scant human and material resources of the new nation to the limit. The backward and sluggish economy received a serious setback.[22] What is more, the war diverted Ecuadorian leaders from urgent domestic matters at a critical time in the history of the new nation. Military obligations in the north forced President Flores to delegate his executive responsibilities to others on more than one occasion.

In spite of wartime distractions General Flores did find some time to consult with advisers and to tackle important national problems that required attention. In his dealings with the legislature he seemed eager to shed his earlier reputation as a rash advocate of authoritarian government and to appear now in the role of the solemn and responsible statesman, dedicated and faithful to the constitution. His address to Congress in 1831 gave no hint of arrogance toward the proud aristocrats who composed the legislative body and whose cooperation he needed. With rather florid rhetoric President Flores sought the deputies' support of his Cauca policy, drew attention to the "poverty of the Treasury," and urged a reduction in expenditures. In the succeeding months an administrative program of domestic development began to unfold as legislative proposals came forth from the executive branch.[23]

Adversaries of General Flores have portrayed him as a despot and a tyrant, but during his first term in the presidency he neither earned nor deserved such epithets. He was not above attempting to influence the Congress through friends and supporters in that body, and he may have tried to shape the outcome of some provincial elections, as his opponents have charged, but activities of this sort were common in Latin America at this time. If there were elements of authoritarianism and paternalism in Flores' leadership, these characteristics hardly qualified him for the title of "tyrant," unless the same label is to be pinned on almost all Latin American executives of the early national period, including such revered liberals as Bernardo O'Higgins of Chile, Bernardino Rivadavia of Argentina, and Vicente Rocafuerte, archrival of Flores in Ecuador.[24]

It is true, of course, that late in his first presidential term, fearing armed rebellion and angered by caustic criticisms in the press, Flores briefly exercised "extraordinary powers" granted to him by Congress. But this episode, unfortunate though it was in some respects, was brief and uncharacteristic of the rest of Flores' administration. The overall record of his four-year term in office shows that Flores governed by legal and constitutional means.

Even if Flores wanted to dictate to the Congress of 1831, he probably could not have done so, for the legislators were not overawed by the chief executive. One of the first important acts of the deputies was to refuse to seat six officers of the executive and judicial branches of government who had been elected to Congress. The legislators also rebuffed the administration by refusing to accept a report from the chief of the General Staff because it lacked specific information on military expenses.[25]

In a variety of other ways the deputies demonstrated their independence of the executive. Although the Congress approved all military promotions requested by the president, it prohibited the executive from increasing the size of the armed forces without specific legislative authorization. When friends of Flores proposed to confer the title of "General-in-Chief" upon the president and to declare him "Protector and Savior of the

State," the legislators refused. Similarly the Congress rejected a proposal to have the state "adopt" the firstborn son of Flores and to assign him a handsome income of one thousand pesos for his education. In turning down this proposal one of the deputies declared that such adoptions might be suitable in a monarchy, but not in the "perfectly democratic" nation of Ecuador. In yet another rebuff to the president the legislature rejected an executive request to make governors of provinces responsible to the president rather than to the prefects of departments.[26]

Congress, though jealous of its prerogatives, was not openly hostile toward the president. As if to compensate for its denial of the title of "General-in-Chief," it voted to proclaim Flores as the "First Citizen of the State" and to honor him as "Meritorious of the Nation in High Degree" (Benemérito de la Patria en Grado Eminente). Flores, irritated by the earlier snubs, turned down the honors, claiming he had already received the highest praise possible after his victory over the Peruvians at Tarqui.[27]

Friction between the two major branches of government was also evident in some aspects of church–state relations, though in general the deputies shared with the chief executive a moderately anticlerical viewpoint. Both the president and the Congress favored assumption of the patronato by the state (an arrangement stipulated in the constitution), but they differed on questions of detail in exercising patronal rights. Though they clashed over procedures for making nominations to clerical vacancies, the two branches agreed on the need to tap Church funds for the national budget. The congresses of the years 1831 to 1833 adopted a series of measures that increased the government's share of the tithes and assigned ecclesiastical revenues to the support of public schools. A law that denied the traditional clerical immunity to taxation angered the ecclesiastics in Congress, but the moderation of the government in Church matters was evident in the defeat of a blatantly anticlerical proposal in 1833 to exclude priests from Congress.[28] Flores worked harmoniously with the liberal Congress in the elaboration of liberal policies that restricted somewhat the freedom of the Church, appropriated some of its revenues, and divested the clergy of some of their traditional privileges, but these policies did not go to extremes and did not strain relations with the Church to the breaking point.

For the most part Flores and Congress collaborated effectively and were able to promote modest progress in such areas as education and culture. The president created a General Administration of Education, expanded elementary schools in Guayaquil, and created scholarships for poor children.[29] The government upgraded the University of Quito with the creation of two academies, one of mathematics and the other of national history. The administration also made efforts to create and develop a public education system, but progress was slow and disappointing largely because of a shortage of funds.[30] Flores welcomed scientists and professors to Quito, created a national theater, and authorized the publication of Juan de Velasco's *Historia del Reino de Quito,* an important work on the colonial history of Ecuador.[31]

Education and culture did not suddenly begin to thrive in Ecuador as a result of the government's efforts. But a healthy beginning was made. Educational and cultural needs were recognized and measures adopted to commence the slow process of expanding and improving a grossly inadequate educational system. Shortages of funds and defective administration would retard growth, but the direction of development established under Flores would continue until the 1860s when a president with sharply differing views shifted the direction toward clerical domination of instruction.[32]

President Flores showed his concern for the education of Indian children when he issued a decree in January 1833 ordering the creation of primary schools for Indians in all parishes of the nation. The same decree provided funds for fifteen scholarships and established a rudimentary curriculum that included religion, ethics, the three *R*s, and study of the constitution. Following the ill-advised example of the Gran Colombian government of Bolívar and Santander, Flores stipulated that "surplus lands" from the Indians' *resguardos,* or communal lands, were to be auctioned off to help pay for the new schools. The underlying purpose of this policy, which typified most official programs for the Indian during the nineteenth century, was to

integrate the aboriginal people into white society. Fortunately
for the Indian peasants, who preferred separation from Hispanic society, few auctions took place. In May 1833 the government suspended indefinitely the policy of auctioning resguardos, and the auctions were not resumed. Few lands had been
sold because local authorities were slow to carry out national
policy on education for peasant children.[33]

If the Indians' lot did not improve substantially in the early
1830s, it was not because the Congress and the president ignored the problem. Besides its attempts to provide for primary
education, the government adopted a series of measures aimed
at protecting the native people from exploitation by tax collectors, local officials, and priests. One of the chief concerns of the
Flores administration was to restrain the greedy practices of the
clergy who systematically exploited the Indians, in violation of
civil and canon law. The minister of the interior, acting for the
president, ordered prefects of departments and the bishop of
Quito to put a stop to the practice of charging fees for confession, marriage, and other sacraments. In a letter to the primate
of Quito the minister pointed out that the exactions demanded
by priests for wedding ceremonies were so exorbitant that they
prevented most Indians from getting married.[34]

A few months later the government adopted a law of broad
scope intended to protect Indians from abuses by civil authorities and to mitigate some of the evils of the peonage system.
This law ordered tax collectors and other officials to refrain
from seizing the property of natives who were in arrears in
their tribute payments. Imprisonment of wives and children for
similar cause was also prohibited. The law forbade all arbitrary
punishments such as whipping, arrests, and other penalties
deemed "too rigorous or contrary to modesty." Similarly, all
Ecuadorians were barred from requiring "personal services"
from natives "without their consent and without stipulating
wages."[35]

The extent to which Indians may have benefited from the
reform law is difficult to say. Probably their condition improved
but little. This is not to impugn the motives or intentions of the
legislators and the executive. The language of the statute, the
provisions for enforcement, and the content of the congres-

sional debate that accompanied consideration of the new law indicated that the spirit of philanthropy underlay the legislation. Punishments for violating the law were harsh, and all fines levied were earmarked for the support of Indian schools. What is more, the statute required parish priests to read the law to the peasants in their native language every three months, and all Ecuadorians were empowered to bring charges against anyone breaking the law.[36]

One important reason for the failure of the government's program to protect Indians (peasants) was the fact that concertaje, the contract labor system of the haciendas, was left intact. Congressmen were aware that many rural laborers were bound to the land in a kind of servitude sanctioned by law and social custom. They lamented the abuses and cruelties that attended concertaje, but they dared not overthrow the labor system upon which so many landowners depended. The governing class of Ecuador sought to ameliorate the Indian's condition by regulating the terms of labor contracts, specifying the nature of debts recognized by law for labor obligations, and by guaranteeing the Indian's right of movement within the country. But the concertaje system, administered privately on landed estates under consuetudinary law, remained basically unchanged by reform measures.[37]

The taxation of Indians was yet another problem which the first Flores administration addressed without making substantial progress. From early colonial times adult male Indians were required to pay a burdensome tax known as tribute. During the wars of independence tribute was briefly abolished, but Bolívar reinstated it because of the need for revenues. Bolívar also renamed the tax *contribución personal de indígenas*. At the time of Ecuador's separation from Gran Colombia the annual tribute rate was three and one-half pesos.

It was generally agreed by men in government that the contribución personal de indígenas was unjust because it exacted large sums from the social class least able to pay, but the government desperately needed revenues. President Flores managed to persuade the Congress in late 1831 to replace tribute with a graduated income tax known as *contribución ordinaria*. This remarkably progressive tax set rates on the basis of ability to pay and exempted Indians, beggars, minors, and people over fifty years of age. Thus tribute was briefly abolished. Unfortunately, the contribución ordinaria proved uncollectible because the Ministry of Finance and its tax officers were unable to prepare in time a workable system of collection. Faced with a total collapse of the tax system, the Flores administration replaced the new income tax with the old tribute and some new consumption taxes, chiefly on salt and tobacco.[38] Though the attempt to relieve the Indians of capitation failed, the earnest attempt by Flores to institute a progressive income tax tended to refute charges that the president was a political reactionary who cared nothing for the welfare of the poor.

A proposal intended to integrate the Indian into Hispanic society and to benefit the national economy, was yet another aspect of the Flores program of the early 1830s, a program hitherto ignored by historians. In June 1831 the *Gaceta del Gobierno* published an editorial setting forth the administration's position on the need for land reform. The article pointed to the unhealthy concentration of most arable land in the hands of a few individuals and the exclusion of most Indians from ownership. "Our Congress ought to pay serious attention to the means of increasing the number of proprietors," declared the writer of the editorial. The anticipated results of land reform, according to the article, would be greater prosperity in agriculture and an augmentation in the number of landowners whose private interest would lead them to support the government. Citing the example of land policies in the United States, the *Gaceta* urged that small landholdings be assigned to all Indian families without cost to the Indians if possible.[39]

After failing to win support in Congress for land reform, the Flores administration took unilateral action in 1833. Citing a Colombian decree of the year 1821 as his basis of authority, the minister of finance ordered the sale at auction of all public lands in the Department of El Ecuador for the purpose of putting them in private hands. Unfortunately the government's solicitude for Indian welfare had diminished since 1831, for the auction regulations did not specify that the lands should go to Indian families. However, squatters on public domains were to be granted preference in all sales and Indian communal lands were specifically exempted from auction.[40]

Indians probably lost more than they gained from the land reform program of the Flores administration. The original intention of the government appeared to be humanitarian and forward-looking, but the auction system allowed little opportunity for native families, who generally lacked the means to pay for lands even if they were given preference as squatters. Some lands claimed by Indians were auctioned off, but the government proceeded very slowly with the land-sale program, partly because of strong threats of violent resistance by the peasants. As a consequence, not much land appears to have changed hands.[41]

The dismal condition of the national economy, a matter that affected not just Indians but all Ecuadorians, was also a major concern of the Flores administration. When Flores assumed the presidency the economy appeared to be in ruins. Ecuador had no monetary system, no banks to provide credit for large transactions, and no legal code for the guidance and regulation of domestic and international trade. President Flores and the Congress, working together, began the task of building a national economy. Their principal actions may be briefly summarized.

Agriculture, the most important sector of the economy, received a very modest stimulus from a law that reduced the interest rates on Church mortagages and liens (*censos*) to a maximum of 3 percent.[42] Commerce and industry were favored by the founding of a bank in Guayaquil to serve the merchant community and to handle the redemption of government notes. To remedy the chronic shortage of precious metals and to provide a basis for an expanding coinage system Congress and the president approved a law authorizing the creation of a quasi-public mining corporation and the national government ordered provincial officials to send mineral samples to Quito for testing. A variety of other measures called for the repair and construction of bridges and roads, permitted the opening of secondary ports on the Pacific (in the hope of breaking the Guayaquil monopoly and expanding foreign trade), and provided a new commercial code based on a Spanish model.[43]

The adoption of the Spanish commercial code of 1829 to govern merchants and trade pointed up the persistence in Ecuador of Spanish influence and mercantilistic attitudes. In adopting the new commercial code legislators took pains to protect the privileged legal and judicial system of the merchants and guaranteed the continuation of the merchant guild of Guayaquil, the Consulado.[44]

Another significant example of the persistence of mercantilistic institutions in early national Ecuador was provided by official policies regarding the estancos, or government monopolies of tobacco, salt, and aguardientes. The constituent congress of 1830 appeared to favor a regime of economic freedom when it decided to abolish all three estancos.[45] But, mindful of the need to preserve sources of government revenues, the legislators substituted a licensing and tax system in which private producers and traders took the place of the former governmental administrators of monopolies. This half-hearted move toward private enterprise produced few beneficial effects, however, for the licensing system sharply limited the number of entrepreneurs and perpetuated monopolistic practices while the new taxes boosted prices and promoted bootlegging.[46]

The licensing system gave the impression to a foreign observer like Dr. Terry that the estanco system had not been abolished, for he reported in 1832 that government monopolies were stifling economic growth:

> They shut up certain channels of prosperity and wealth from all but a favored few; and forbid that competition which gives healthful life and vigor to trade. These *estancos* are farmed out to individuals, by government, making these individuals the sole importers and sellers of articles. Were they only instituted in relation to luxuries, such as ardent spirits, wine, and tobacco, they would be less reprobated; but, by their operation, the common necessaries of life (as in the case of bread and salt, which are *estanco* articles) are raised to an enormous price.

In 1835 Congress reacted to the difficulties of the licensing system by reestablishing the old estancos.[47]

One of the major deterrents to the development of a flourishing economy was the lack of a sound monetary system. Like many other young nations of this era, Ecuador ran into severe difficulties in its attempts to remedy the shortage of money and to meet the government's financial obligations. The Flores administration first issued one hundred thousand pesos in paper money, but the bills were turned in for redemption so quickly that they failed to circulate as currency. Subsequent emissions met the same fate. Late in 1831 Congress adopted a coinage law that provided for a gold peso nearly equal in metallic content to the United States dollar, and a silver *real* containing 2.9598 grams of silver. The government also established a mint at this time and began to issue metal coins. Unfortunately the silver real was undervalued in its legal relationship to gold, resulting in the exportation of silver coins almost as fast as they could be stamped out. Efforts to halt the outflow of the silver were unsuccessful.[48]

To make matters worse, the counterfeiting of coins commenced on a large scale and quickly undermined public confidence in the monetary system. The making of false coins was apparently facilitated by the fact that Ecuadorian coins were of the same weight and type as those of New Granada, a fact that permitted the circulation of Colombian coins at par in Ecuador. Unfortunately the New Granada mint in Popayán was turning out coins that were readily imitated by the silversmiths of Quito.[49]

Reportedly there were hundreds of counterfeiters in Quito who manufactured great quantities of debased and illegal coins. According to the historian Ceballos, they carried on their work almost publicly. "The sounds of minting the coins were heard clearly by those who governed and were governed," said Ceballos, "and they nevertheless shrugged their shoulders as if convinced of their impotence to cut off the devastating torrent of false coins."[50]

Flores' political adversaries went even further than Ceballos by charging that prominent officials in the executive branch were in collusion with the manufacturers of false coins.[51] The fact that the epidemic of illegal money grew worse in the years 1832 and 1833 gave weight to the belief that the government connived with the counterfeiters. But the truth of the matter is that the president and his ministers made strenuous efforts to halt the illegal practice, which was causing havoc in commerce.

In a series of decrees and circular letters the president and his finance minister warned the makers of false coins of the penalties for their crimes, exhorted police and local officials to pursue the criminals, and authorized forceful entry into shops of suspected counterfeiters. In other measures to alleviate the monetary crisis the administration forbade the export of coins and encouraged the importation of foreign coins.[52]

The flow of cheap coins continued, notwithstanding the best efforts of the government. On the assumption that the counterfeiters could not be stopped and that false coins were better than no coins at all, the authorities tried a short-lived experiment in redemption of illegal issues. But newspaper criticism and the high cost of redemptions caused the Flores administration to abandon the experiment and to renew its attack on the illicit manufacture of debased coins.[53] Many counterfeiters were arrested, tried, and convicted, thus attesting to the administration's determination to enforce the law and punish the criminals. But in October 1832 Congress voted to grant a collective pardon to all convicted counterfeiters on the very dubious grounds that it was wrong to punish *some* of the criminals when so many others had not been apprehended or convicted.[54]

Late in 1833 Congress made amends for its earlier indulgence by adopting some stern measures against counterfeiting. After approving a presidential decree authorizing forcible entries without warrants into houses, the legislative body approved the death penalty for counterfeiters and those found guilty of permitting the use of government dies for stamping false coins. Imprisonment for ten years was the penalty for anyone convicted of distributing the forbidden specie. But even such harsh punishment failed to wipe out the abuse. Certainly it was wrong to blame Flores for the failure, because his successors in the presidency were obliged to continue the war on counterfeiters. As late as 1847, when Flores was in exile, the problem persisted.[55]

Counterfeiting was a vexatious problem, but it was a minor matter in comparison with the momentous dilemma of the unbalanced national budget. During its early years of nationhood Ecuador suffered from large, chronic deficits that undermined the credit of the government and even threatened the state with extinction. José Fernández Salvador, president of the constituent congress of 1830, warned his colleagues that the government lacked funds to pay the troops and civilian employees. If financial resources were not found to meet these obligations, he declared, the country would face discredit, bankruptcy, and upheaval.[56] Fernández Salvador did not overstate the case, for, by the end of the first year of independence, the government had received only six hundred thousand pesos in revenues with which to pay out more than nine hundred thousand pesos in budgetary commitments. As a result of this deficit the treasury fell badly in arrears on the payroll and could make no payments on the foreign debt. Late in 1831 President Flores warned the first Congress of Ecuador that if it failed to adopt the legislation necessary to balance the budget, "the Executive will not be able to assure public tranquility." Seeking to emphasize the gravity of the situation, Flores predicted the "destruction of the state" if Congress did not provide the desperately needed financial resources.[57]

Political opponents of Flores and most Ecuadorian historians have blamed the first president for the enormous deficits of the government in its early years. The vituperative pen of Vicente Rocafuerte contributed much to the general condemnation of Flores for alleged waste, embezzlement, and financial corruption. In his widely read essays published under the title *A la Nación,* Rocafuerte vilified his political opponent for "immorality," "prodigality," and "Asiatic luxury." The president's haciendas, this critic charged, had been purchased with embezzled public funds. Similar accusations that appeared in a liberal, opposition newspaper, *El Quiteño libre,* also made a deep impression on historians.[58]

The notion of Flores as a corrupt architect of financial disaster in Ecuador is in large degree unfair and misleading. Of course, some of the criticism of the president doubtless contained elements of truth. Flores bore much of the responsibility for the unfortunate Cauca war that helped to drain the treasury. It is also true that Flores acquired several valuable landed estates, sixty slaves, gold washings at Playa de Oro, and a beautiful mansion in Quito with funds that are not completely accounted for—but that is not to say that fraud supplied Flores with the money. Much of his property came to him either as booty of war or from the turmoil of the Bolivarian period. For example, in 1826 Flores purchased four haciendas at auction, a perfectly legal transaction, but reasons for the auctions are not explained. In January 1830 he purchased a large sugar plantation near Babahoyo from the prominent Novoa family. Thus, Flores appears to have acquired most of his landed wealth before the independence of Ecuador, a fact that casts serious doubt on Rocafuerte's charges. Like many other generals of the revolution President Flores rose from poverty to great wealth as a result of ambition and opportunism.[59]

Flores apparently lacked strong scruples in private financial dealings, but it does not follow that he was necessarily to blame for fiscal mismanagement in the government. Responsibility for the budget rested primarily with the Congress, not the president—a point ignored by Flores' critics. Looking carefully at the entire record of performance of both executive and legislative branches for the years 1830 to 1835, it appears that the president and his financial ministers deserved less blame for the deficits than the members of Congress who were generally inept and timorous in dealing with budgetary problems. But it would also be unfair to point the accusing finger solely at the legislators, for such a judgment would not take into account a number of other factors such as the inefficiency of the inherited government bureaucracy, the general lack of public spirit, and the impact of fortuitous and disastrous events like the costly Urdaneta revolt.[60]

To put the fiscal problem in perspective, it should be noted that treasury deficits, and even incipient bankruptcy, were by no means peculiar to Ecuador in this period. The struggle by the new Spanish American governments to balance expenditures and revenues was waged from Mexico to Argentina with uncertain outcome. The government of Gran Colombia, most pertinent to the present discussion, perennially bordered on financial collapse. Lurching from crisis to crisis, the administrations of Bolívar and Santander failed to solve the riddle of unbalanced budgets. Leaders of the revolution found it easy to abolish hated Spanish taxes, but not to reduce expenditures and impose new taxes.[61] Colonel Francis Hall, a young British military officer who took part in the Bolivarian wars, blamed Colombia's financial difficulties on "inveterate Spanish habits," confused budgets and accounts, and "the general corruption of all the subordinate magistrates and agents of the government." Colonel Hall might have added, in fairness to Spain and Hispanic nations, that fraud and corruption were also widespread in the government of his native England.[62]

General Flores could not give very effective leadership in fiscal matters because his expertise in the subject was negligible. Flores' first ministerial appointee, José Félix Valdivieso, was a wealthy landowner and an intelligent man, but the management of his private fortune hardly qualified him for handling the complexities of the treasury and the national budget. Besides, as the single minister of state, Valdivieso was overburdened with responsibilities for guiding foreign relations, internal affairs, and all other business of the executive branch. It was not surprising, therefore, that Valdivieso asked Congress to create a new ministry of finance and that the legislators promptly approved the request, even though the constitution allowed only a single ministry.[63]

The new cabinet post was soon filled by the appointment of Juan García del Río, a New Granadan and an itinerant statesman of outstanding, if controversial, credentials. During the wars of independence he had first served New Granada as a diplomatic envoy to England, and later, in Peru, he had served General San Martín as minister of foreign relations and then once again as an envoy to Europe. After San Martín's retirement from public life García del Río came to enjoy the trust of Bolívar as a confidential agent, adviser, and publicist for monarchical ideas. In 1830 and 1831 he figured prominently in New Granada first as minister of foreign relations and later as a member of the Council of State. After a change in government he was sent into exile and he turned up in Ecuador bearing a letter of introduction from President Flores' monarchist friend General Montilla.[64]

Unfortunately for the Flores government, the new finance minister soon became unpopular, especially among liberals and the political opposition. García del Río's foreign birth, like that of Flores, was an offense to the budding spirit of nationalism in

Ecuador. He was an outspoken conservative and his preference for monarchism was widely known, though the extent of his secret efforts under San Martín and Bolívar to establish monarchy in Peru and Gran Colombia was not general knowledge.[65] His royalist leanings and aristocratic hauteur provoked strong reactions among liberal congressmen and young nationalists. But it would be wrong to accept uncritically all of the virulent criticism directed at García del Río, especially the fierce attacks in *El Quiteño libre* and the partisan writings of Rocafuerte. The minister of finance, on the basis of the historical record, worked conscientiously to bring order, rationality, and honesty to the chaotic fiscal system of Ecuador. His major fault was not indifference to corruption, as alleged by his partisan critics, but rather a rigid determination to set things straight. His zeal offended the lax and corrupt officialdom of the treasury, accounts, and revenue departments.[66]

Even before the appointment of García del Río, Flores and Valdivieso made strenuous efforts from 1830 to late 1832 to subdue the budgetary beast that threatened the nation. A few highlights of the administration's actions illustrate the character of the fiscal program under Valdivieso. In September 1831 the minister of state asked Congress for urgent consideration of measures to deal with the emergency, including an extraordinary tax to help meet commitments. The deputies sidestepped the tax proposal and voted instead to reduce government salaries to one-half on a temporary basis.[67] A few weeks later the president, exercising special powers voted by Congress, imposed an "extraordinary contribution" of thirty-six thousand pesos on the three departments of the nation.[68] Valdivieso and Flores then proposed drastic reductions in the government payroll, including the suspension of some departmental courts of justice and accounting offices, a sharp cut in pay for military officers on inactive duty, and a graduated income tax (the *contribución ordinaria* described earlier). The legislators failed to agree on the austerity proposals of the president, though they approved the unworkable income tax which led the administration into still greater difficulties.[69]

Not surprisingly, the financial crisis worsened in 1832 and the administration was forced to impose another special contribution, forty thousand pesos this time. The government's need for quick cash was so urgent during the year that it became necessary to farm out the collection of Indian tribute, the *alcabala* (sales tax), and the tobacco tax.[70] Finally, after the president once more implored the Congress to act, the deputies approved a reduction in the armed forces (while Ecuador was at war with New Granada), but refused a request for prorated reduction in government salaries.[71] Belatedly the legislature assented to the president's request to economize by eliminating some government positions and by cutting the salaries of prefects and governors.[72]

It is evident that the actions of the Flores administration under Valdivieso's leadership do not support the charges of reckless waste that have been leveled at the first president. Far from advocating irresponsible expenditures, General Flores and his minister of state took the initiative in seeking to balance revenues and expenditures. It was the legislators, not the executive, who dragged their feet on fiscal matters.

When García del Río stepped into the post of finance minister in November 1832 the administration's drive for economy and efficiency received a new impulse. The new minister immediately sought and received from Congress limited emergency powers to reorganize the revenue offices, to abolish some positions in the administration of finance, and to "correct" tariff schedules.[73] Armed with augmented authority, García del Río initiated a vigorous campaign to streamline the department of finance and to terminate abuses that deprived the government of badly needed revenues.

In a rapid series of blunt and resolute actions President Flores and his finance minister ordered departmental and provincial administrators to mend their loose ways. Crisp letters to prefects demanded complete accounts of all revenues, expenditures, and obligations for the year 1832. The minister also informed his subordinates that monthly statements of accounts would be required henceforth. Tax collectors were directed to collect all delinquent taxes, to prevent tax evasions, and to require payments in cash. Mindful of the large sums that export and import taxes should have been producing, the minister asked for a detailed statement of accounts from the cus-

tomhouse and instructed its director to require prompt settlement of all accounts in arrears.[74]

Reports that the alcabala was capturing far less in revenues
than expected caused President Flores and his minister to order
reforms in the sales-tax offices, to establish a uniform accounting procedure for all offices, and to impose heavy fines for
evasion of the alcabala. The zeal of the Flores administration
for fiscal reform was further indicated by its reaction to the
refusal of priests and other ecclesiastical personnel to pay their
share of a special war tax. García del Río publicly denounced
this "scandalous disobedience" and threatened to seize and auction off Church property if the tax was not paid in eight days.[75]

Improper practices of the regional treasury offices were costing the government enormous sums of money. The first of
these abuses was the issuance of *libranzas*, or local treasury
drafts against anticipated revenues, a practice begun in the
1820s because of chronic deficits and continued in the 1830s,
though contrary to the law. The second costly abuse was the
payment of usurious interest rates to the government's creditors and contractors such as provisioners of the army.[76]

The losses from these abuses, along with losses from contraband and other forms of tax evasion, probably deprived the
government of more than half of its revenues. The libranzas
were especially pernicious, not only because of the lack of central control over their issuance, but because of the resulting
exploitation of innocent citizens. Government employees who
received the treasury drafts in payment of salary were forced to
sell them at huge discounts when the treasury did not promptly
redeem them, as usually was the case. Speculators then bought
up the discounted libranzas and cashed them in, frequently in
collusion with local treasurers or customs officials, thereby pock-
eting large gains. Not infrequently the government treasurers
redeemed the drafts at discounts and embezzled substantial
sums through dishonest accounting procedures.[77]

The Flores administration mounted a concerted attack on
these abuses. Prefects received instructions to terminate the
use of the illegal libranzas and to cease all interest payments in
excess of 6 percent. Explaining the reasons for the new prohibitions, García del Río declared to the prefect of Guayas that

continuation of high interest rates "would lead inevitably to the destruction of the treasury and the corruption of public morality." The government would not pay interest above the legal ceiling, insisted the finance minister, no matter what the consequences.[78]

Efforts to control interest rates may have been modestly beneficial, but the struggle of the Flores administration to reform the fiscal system cannot be called a success. Large deficits piled up year after year. Speculators, usurers, and embezzlers continued to sap the treasury of large sums. Faced with disappointing results, the president and his finance minister apparently came to the conclusion that the abuses could not be completely eliminated and that it was necessary to tolerate a bad situation. Cries of anguish from the holders of libranzas convinced the administration temporarily that it would be expedient to resume the exemption of the illegal drafts secretly. Ecuador's select creditors bought up the depreciated libranzas from unsuspecting citizens and cashed them in at handsome profits. When news of the secret redemptions leaked out, García del Río and the president were accused of corruption, though they were probably guilty only of bad judgment.[79]

In fairness to the Flores administration it must be recognized that the task of reforming the treasury was so difficult that successive administrations through the 1850s also failed to eliminate deficits and fraud.[80] One of the major obstacles to efficient fiscal management was the nature of the treasury system inherited from the Spanish colonial regime. Spanish financial methods depended upon a complex network of treasury offices whose accounting methods ignored annual balances and at times defied rational analysis.[81] A small army of bureaucrats who staffed the departmental treasuries, the tax collections offices, and the customhouse had become accustomed to irregular and often illegal methods of collections and disbursements which concealed balances and denied remittances to the government in Quito. Peremptory orders from the finance minister to adhere to legal methods and to submit regular accounts had little if any discernible effect on the inert and grasping bureaucrats.[82]

The stubborn resistance of the antiquated fiscal organization, however, was not the sole cause of the failure of the financial reforms of 1833. Dishonesty on a monumental scale was undoubtedly the most important cause of budgetary deficits. Unbridled greed, rooted in human nature and honored in Ecuador by custom, permeated the entire system of revenues and disbursements. The extent of graft and theft will never be known, but it is generally recognized that the malfeasance of tax collectors and treasury officials was horrendous. An example of the magnitude of the problem was offered by the customhouse that in the year 1832 yielded to the national government only four thousand pesos out of collections totaling two hundred thousand pesos.[83] Ninety-eight percent of the collections were used either to defray the expenses of the Department of Guayas or to line the pockets of government employees, usurers, and speculators. The amount of revenues lost to contrabandists has not even been estimated.

The executive branch had almost no power to deal effectively with grafting civil servants, for the constitution forbade the discharge of employees without formal judicial action proving charges of illegal activities. When President Flores attempted to discipline some wayward tax collectors, the Congress reprimanded him for violating the constitution.[84] The arrogance of unscrupulous tax collectors became so flagrant that one of them complained to Congress that the finance minister lacked authority to transfer him from a sales-tax office to a less lucrative position in accounts.[85] The spectacle of a minor functionary accusing the minister of finance before Congress and, in effect, defending his right to graft, was symptomatic of the frustrating absurdities with which the first Flores administration had to contend.

By the middle of 1833 the financial crisis had begun to generate a political crisis. The best efforts of Flores and his advisers to secure the Cauca region, discipline unruly troops, stimulate the economy, improve communications, build a public education system, and improve the lot of Indians were not enough to prevent the growth of a determined political opposition. The inability of the government to solve the problem of budgetary deficits became a focus of discontent. Congressmen, on the whole, had been laggard in discharging their constitutional duties in the area of budget, but critics of the government blamed the flow of red ink on the president and his finance minister, not the Congress.

In republics it is the president who, in the public mind, usually bears the responsibility for shortcomings in governmental leadership. There were shortcomings in the case of president Flores in his first term, of course. He was not above using his position as chief executive to make personal profits, as we shall see. He made mistakes of the sort that might be expected of a youthful general who lacked extensive preparation and experience. He miscalculated badly in the Cauca affair. He made slow progress in promoting institutional development, but his administration failed to produce the revenues needed to pay the troops and the bureaucrats. As a consequence his opponents were emboldened first to challenge his leadership and ultimately to defy the government with armed force. Thus, the first presidential term of Flores, which commenced with rejoicing and optimism, ended in discord and bloody revolt.

4

THE REVOLUTION OF THE
CHIHUAHUAS, 1833–1835

The rise of a political opposition to the Flores administration was predictable, even inevitable. On personal grounds alone, General Flores would have become a target of criticism and opposition even if he had been one of the wisest of statesmen. There were many Ecuadorians who would not forgive him for his foreign origins, and others who despised him for his lack of high social credentials. Still others resented the fact that he was a soldier, one of those military adventurers in the legions of the Liberator who went fortune hunting in South America and seized upon Ecuador as the promised land.

Faultfinding with the president was at first muted and confined to private gatherings, to the conversations of native aristocrats in their salons and of students in the university.[1] But before long opponents of the government began to utter harsh words publicly and to publish their views in opposition newspapers. Like Bolívar and Santander before him, Flores would begin to suffer the barbs of the press.

In 1832 Ecuador witnessed the birth of an opposition press. In July of that year *El Republicano,* a weekly newspaper, appeared in Quito. It proclaimed libertarian principles, denounced despotism, and called for a patriotic struggle against "selfishness and unbridled ambition." The editors apparently believed that President Flores intended to establish a dictatorship and to perpetuate himself in power, for they warned darkly that "no power is permanent." "All ambitious men have fallen and all have bequeathed a sinister and horrible name to posterity," said the paper, "all have flashed like a bolt of lightning and have been buried in ignominious darkness."[2] General

Flores, offended by the outspoken attack on his presidency and apprehensive about the threat of an opposition press, suppressed the fledgling paper. In its last gasp *El Republicano* managed to tell its readers that freedom of the press was essential to the dignity of man and should not be taken for granted. It might have added that press freedom was guaranteed in the constitution.[3]

In early January 1833, President Flores attempted to ease political tensions then building in the nation by issuing a decree of general amnesty that permitted all political exiles to return and declared that no one would be disturbed for his political opinions.[4] This liberal decree apparently gave encouragement to Flores' foes in Guayaquil, for three newspapers unfriendly to the government suddenly burst upon the political scene in that city. Little is known about two of those papers, *El Pichincha* and *El Hombre libre*, but their titles reflected nationalist and liberal viewpoints. The third of the journalistic trio, called *El 9 de Octubre* in honor of Guayaquil's declaration of independence from Spain in 1820, appealed to regional sentiments in Guayas and favored replacing Flores with a guayaquileño in the presidency.[5]

The eruption of a journalistic clamor in Guayaquil caused alarm in the highest circles of the administration. Rocafuerte later reported that Guayaquil was like a "storm cloud charged with revolutionary electricity, ready to discharge against Flores and his dismal regime." The president evidently drew a similar conclusion, for he hurried to the coast to calm the storm. *El Pichincha* and *El Hombre libre* quickly succumbed to presidential pressure and disappeared almost without a trace. *El 9 de Octubre* survived for a time only because its editor and publisher, Dr. Francisco Marcos, agreed to support the Flores administration. The precise terms of the arrangement between the two men remained secret, but they probably included a presidential promise to foster Dr. Marcos' election to the presidency of the forthcoming Congress of 1833. For many years Marcos remained one of the general's most loyal political supporters.[6]

While Flores was occupied with political problems on the coast, new storm clouds were gathering in the sierra. In May 1833 a journalistic thunderbolt struck the highlands when the now famous *El Quiteño libre* published its first issue. This new opposition paper, destined to be the most sensational opposition paper in early Ecuadorian history, was the journalistic organ of a political and intellectual group known as the Sociedad El Quiteño Libre. Most of the members of the association were university students, young professionals, and prestigious aristocrats like Roberto Ascásubi, José Cevallos, and Pedro Moncayo. Don Manuel Matheu, Marqués de Maenza, a patriot of the 1806 independence movement, and General José María Sáenz, brother of the famous Manuela Sáenz, were two of the older generation who joined with the young militants in opposition to Flores.[7]

The prime mover in this society of young nationalists was, ironically, a foreigner, Colonel Francis Hall, one of the many British officers who had flocked to South America to serve in Bolívar's armies.[8] Colonel Hall was well known for both his military and journalistic activities. After taking part in several major military actions in Gran Colombia, including the battle of Pichincha in 1822, he founded a newspaper in Caracas, Venezuela, that sought to spread the views of English liberalism. His criticism of the government of Gran Colombia so angered Vice-President Santander that Hall was ordered to leave Caracas. Eventually the young English gadfly turned up in Ecuador and settled in Quito where he apparently became a university professor and soon gained a reputation for zealous liberalism and staunch opposition to General Flores.[9]

Both Colonel Hall and General Matheu, who soon joined Hall's group, harbored grudges against the man who occupied the presidency of Ecuador. Flores had publicly humiliated the marqués for having called the president a "little mulatto" and for having made other derogatory remarks of a personal nature.[10] Colonel Hall had run afoul of Flores before Ecuador's separation from Gran Colombia when Flores was attempting to promote a Bolivarian monarchy. Though Hall was indebted to Flores for financial assistance rendered earlier, Hall nevertheless turned against his benefactor and openly denounced the monarchical scheme. Flores then expelled Hall from the District of the South.[11] Thus, it is clear that political motives were mixed with personal enmity in the journalistic activities of the Society of El Quiteño Libre.

In the brief span of four months, starting in May 1833 *El Quiteño libre* shook the Flores regime to its foundations. Whether the editors of the paper and the members of the sponsoring society set about to overthrow the government is not clear. The editorials published in its columns claimed that the paper sought only "to defend the laws, rights, and liberties" of Ecuadorians and "to denounce all kinds of arbitrariness, waste, and plundering of the public treasury."[12] But the attacks on Flores and his ministers were not merely direct and frank but often fierce and angry. Their language was frequently extravagant and personally offensive to government officials. If the editors of *El Quiteño libre* did not at first intend to promote a revolution (and probably they did not), certainly their aggressive style and their unremitting accusations of "tyranny," "despotism," "corruption," and "oppression" gave the vivid impression that they sought at least to justify a revolution, if not provoke one.

Week after week *El Quiteño libre* printed news accounts and bold editorials accusing the government of a wide variety of abuses. The chief criticisms of the paper focused on public finance, the defective monetary system, irregularities in elections, abuses of the military, and infringements of the freedom of the press. News accounts and editorials in the paper held Flores and his ministers responsible for the problems of counterfeiting, debasement of the coinage, fostering usury, and the practice of issuing libranzas. In one of its issues the paper revealed that the government, apparently with the president's personal approval, had canceled a substantial tax obligation owed by an in-law of Flores. To prevent acts of favoritism and to assure orderly and equitable practices in the future, *El Quiteño libre* demanded regular monthly publication of treasury accounts—a reasonable suggestion that was honored by some administrations later on.[13]

An indirect way of wounding Flores and damaging his administration was to criticize the armed forces and denounce "militarism." Thus, the editors published articles declaring that the regular army was not only unnecessary and too costly but was "dangerous to liberty." Troops in the urban centers, the paper reported, intimidated voters in elections, and a recent case in Cuenca was cited to imply that General Flores used the army for political purposes. *El Quiteño* urged the creation of a voluntary militia to replace the unpopular standing army.[14]

If the editors were sometimes indirect in their criticisms of the president, at other times they made direct accusations, especially on the subject of financial mismanagement. They reported, for example, an allegedly improper payment of fifteen thousand pesos to the president by a provincial treasury. The implication of the news story was that the general had either stolen or embezzled the money. Flores defended himself by asserting, quite plausibly, that the money was simply a repayment of personal loans he had made to the government during the military emergency with New Granada.[15] More serious, perhaps, were charges that the president had secured an illegal loan of thirty-two hundred pesos and that Indian peons were forced, in violation of the law, to work on one of his haciendas.[16] The first accusation, which was apparently true, indicated that Flores was guilty of using his position to cheat in minor financial matters (a contemptible practice by a person holding the highest office in the nation), while the second charge showed only that his haciendas operated on the same basis as most other large estates of Ecuador.

The most sensational attack made by *El Quiteño libre* on Flores was its report that the president had established a private monopoly on the sale of salt in the highlands. The paper explained in great detail how the monopoly worked, disclosed the names of Flores' cronies (army officers) who acted as his agents, and stated that Flores' hacienda La Chima was used for storing salt supplies. The president's corner on the salt trade not only caused a sharp increase in the retail price of the commodity, declared the paper, but also deprived poor Indian farmers and traders of a traditional source of income. "Is it proper," asked *El Quiteño libre*, "for the Father of the State to make himself an instrument of the misfortune of the weakest part of the population?"[17]

Many of the articles in *El Quiteño libre* appear to have been written not merely to discredit but to infuriate President Flores. For example, a news account of the president's return to Quito from a trip reported sarcastically that a dozen or so schoolboys, rounded up for the occasion, shouted "Viva el Presidente" while "the people maintained the most expressive silence."[18]

Equally provocative was an article condemning Flores for the evil practice of seizing pack animals from poor peasants to transport the baggage and supplies of presidential parties.[19] The charge was doubtless true and it pointed to an abuse that required correction, but the practice harked back to colonial customs and was widely used by the liberating armies of Bolívar, as Colonel Hall and General Matheu knew. Flores was merely continuing the tradition. Yet another example of *El Quiteño libre's* provocative journalism was its condemnation of the Flores administration for alleged complicity in counterfeiting and its criticism of the government's stern measures taken against counterfeiting.[20] This contradictory exploitation of both sides of an issue by the opposition paper must have been exasperating to Flores and his ministers.

As *El Quiteño libre* expanded its circulation and began to attract widespread attention to its anti-Flores offensive, the president responded with a counterattack. At first he had his ministers print replies to *Quiteño's* charges in the pages of the official newspaper, *La Gaceta del Gobierno,* but, seeing that the tongues wagged more than ever, he arranged to have several progovernment newspapers in Quito, Guayaquil, and Cuenca defend his administration and attack the troublesome opposition paper.[21] When his carefully orchestrated offensive failed to muffle the strident voice of criticism, the president attempted to win over the militant editors by flattery and by the offer of a diplomatic post to General Matheu. Unlike Francisco Marcos of Guayaquil, the editors stood fast, however, and Matheu declined the honor.[22]

The journalists of *El Quiteño libre,* saw themselves as white knights crusading against the tyranny of a foreign military adventurer. But Flores viewed the antagonistic editors as his personal enemies and as dangerous men bent upon the overthrow of the government. As president of Ecuador Flores was obligated under the constitution to protect freedom of the press within the limits of "public decency and morality." He also bore the responsibility of maintaining order and respect for the government. Flores persuaded himself that the upstart editors posed a threat to the security of the state.

In June 1833, when Flores was in Guayaquil dealing with

political and administrative problems in that city, he received a
letter from García del Río warning of a plot against the government. The minister of finance did not name the newspaper or
the Society of El Quiteño Libre in his letter, but it was easy for
the president to guess the identity of the alleged conspirators.
The finance minister warned of a possible attempt to assassinate the president, and he urged Flores to return to Quito
immediately "to save your friends, the nation, and yourself."[23]

Flores reacted to the warning by issuing a proclamation declaring the nation to be on the verge of revolution because of
"perfidious and turbulent" disturbers of the peace. He simultaneously ordered that troops be transferred to Quito to augment
the garrison of the capital. Soon afterwards Flores undertook a
quick return march to Quito to take personal command of the
government during the emergency.[24]

García del Río and other presidential advisers who warned of
a conspiracy may have overreacted to the journalistic assault on
the administration. The editors of *El Quiteño libre* firmly denied
the existence of any plot against the government and charged
that troop movements were intended as a weapon to silence the
newspaper.[25] If the editors were truthful in their denials, it
must be said that their persistent defiant accusations did nothing to clear the troubled atmosphere of Quito. President Flores
believed that the Quiteño Libre Society was secretly organizing
a revolt, for in July he wrote to Santander in Colombia that "the
tranquility of Ecuador" was threatened by Hall, Matheu, Sáenz,
and others.[26]

When it became apparent that *El Quiteño libre* would not moderate its criticisms the Flores administration decided to prosecute the troublesome editors for "defamatory libel." The prose-
cution accused the publishers of libeling the president in its
stories on the salt monopoly. Flores and his ministers fully expected to win the case, even though it was to be tried by a jury,
because the existing law on libel held that harsh criticism of
government officials was libelous even if factually true. To the
astonishment of Flores, the jury found the editors not guilty of
the charges.

El Quiteño libre praised the impartiality of the jury and assured the nation that "freedom of the press was perfectly guar-

anteed in Ecuador."[27] The joy of the editors was premature, however, for the president and his ministers were indignant at what seemed to them a miscarriage of justice. It did not take them long to propose to Congress a stern new press law that, when approved by the legislature later in the year, forbade "impious, obscene, and libelous" publications, dropped the jury system in libel cases, and provided a penalty of ten years in exile for anyone convicted under the law.[28]

While the new press law was still pending before Congress the Flores administration faced a deepening political crisis that induced the legislators to approve a temporary grant of extraordinary powers to the president even though the constitution made no provision for such a grant. The crisis, though aggravated by the dissident press, was brought on by many difficulties, especially by the government's failure to solve enormous fiscal problems. As deficits mounted, troops and civil servants went either unpaid or on a small fraction of their regular salaries. Though the president and his finance minister strove to stem the flow of red ink, their efforts (described in the previous chapter) were mocked and disparaged in the pages of *El Quiteño libre*.

The financial difficulties of Ecuador were quickly translated into a grave political predicament when two prestigious public servants left office amid great controversy. The first to depart was José Joaquín de Olmedo, prefect of the Department of Guayas, a poet of great renown, and the first vice-president of Ecuador.[29] Olmedo's resignation was brought on by his toleration of corruption in Guayaquil and his anger at García del Río's stern demands for fiscal reform. When someone passed a copy of Olmedo's letter of resignation to *El Quiteño libre*, people were shocked to read in the pages of an opposition newspaper that the nation's greatest power had been driven from his government post.[30]

The publication of Olmedo's letter soon triggered the dismissal of Flores' chief minister of state, the aristocratic José Félix Valdivieso. The president suspected that Valdivieso was the disloyal member of his administration who had given a copy of Olmedo's letter to the opposition press. Valdivieso protested his innocence, but rumors of a rift between Flores and his chief minister soon spread and papers loyal to the president accused Valdivieso of financial peculations and connivance with members of the Quiteño Libre Society. Valdivieso replied with a public statement in which he rejected all charges including the allegation of disloyalty to the president. He admitted, probably disingenuously, that he had counseled Flores against seeking reelection in violation of the constitution, but he denied the existence of any rift between himself and the president.[31] Valdivieso may have been sincere in his effort to mend relations with Flores, but he made two tactical blunders. First, his mention of a possible reelection of Flores sounded more like an accusation than a conciliatory remark. And second, Valdivieso chose to have his statement published by the same press that printed *El Quiteño libre*.

If a split had not occurred before the appearance of Valdivieso's statement, a yawning chasm opened between the two men afterwards. The president, no doubt angered by the implication that he was seeking an illegal second term, dismissed his minister of state and justified the action with a scathing anonymous public attack on Valdivieso. Flores flatly denied that he had ever discussed the possibility of reelection. He also publicly accused Valdivieso of lying about financial matters and he reminded Ecuadorians that Valdivieso had earlier favored both monarchy and a lifetime presidency.[32]

The clamorous departure of two prominent leaders from public office left the Flores administration in disarray. The president was seriously embarrassed and discredited by the accusation of plotting to arrange for his own unconstitutional reelection. Making matters worse, Flores had demeaned himself and the office of the presidency by publishing an anonymous denunciation of the former minister of state which called him a liar and a monarchist. Meanwhile Flores presided over a floundering government that lacked money to pay and feed the troops.

By early September 1833 serious discontent had spread through the nation and the government had received new reports of plots and revolutionary plans. The pages of *El Quiteño libre* boldly accused the government of tyranny and dictatorship, thus giving the impression that the paper now favored revolution. Behind the scenes, according to Flores and his spokesmen, members of the dissident society were attempting to organize a revolt. Though no specific reports of insurrectionary plans in Guayaquil had been received, it could be assumed that trouble was also brewing in that restless city.[33]

In a secret session of Congress on 14 September the ministers of state reported that a national emergency existed. The administration had proof, they said, that secret meetings of conspirators were taking place, that weapons had been bought and stored, and that attempts had been made to "corrupt the troops." The executive branch lacked authority to deal with the crisis, the ministers testified, and would not be responsible for the consequences if Congress did not take appropriate action. The deputies quickly understood that the administration, without making a direct and specific request, was presenting a case for a grant of *facultades extraordinarias,* special powers that would permit a temporary dictatorship.[34]

A precedent for such a legislative grant existed, for in 1831 Congress, on its own initiative, had conferred extraordinary powers on the president to deal with the revolt of the Vargas Battalion.[35] On that occasion Flores had exercised the augmented authority for a brief time (chiefly to impose a special tax to pay the troops) and had relinquished the attribution six weeks later when the danger had passed.[36]

The situation in 1833 differed from the precedent of 1831 in that the problem was an alleged conspiracy rather than an actual military revolt. Also the initiative came from the executive rather than the legislative branch. In 1833 a vocal minority of deputies strenuously opposed the proposal on the grounds that no clear danger to public order existed, that a grant was unconstitutional while Congress was in session, and that the establishment of a dictatorship would be unfortunate. One deputy, a liberal cleric, declared that facultades extraordinarias had brought ruin to Gran Colombia under Bolívar.[37] But Flores refused to yield to these objections, and thus he precipitated a political crisis.

After heated debate the deputies voted fourteen to seven to approve the presidential request for special powers. No time limit was specified, but the resolution seemed to imply that the grant was to last only six weeks, the period during which Congress was to be in session.[38] Immediately after the vote to confer dictatorial power Flores moved against the newspaper and the members of the Society of El Quiteño Libre. The police arrested all the members of the society they could lay their hands on, including the chief editor, Pedro Moncayo. Those not arrested went into hiding or fled the country. Publication of the newspaper was halted, and it was rumored that the government went to the ridiculous extreme of arresting many of the paper's subscribers.[39]

It soon became apparent that the Flores administration had blundered. The harsh and arbitrary measures used against *El Quiteño libre* provoked an immediate and drastic response by the most determined antiadministration deputies in the Congress. José Miguel Carrión, deputy from Loja, who had strongly opposed the grant of dictatorial powers, sent a message to Congress declaring that the legislators had violated the constitution in permitting the suspension of civil liberties. Carrión announced that he was quitting the legislative body. Angered at what they regarded as "insulting and disrespectful" language used by Carrión, pro-Flores deputies decided to expel the deputy, even though he had already resigned, and to deprive him of his constitutional immunity.[40]

Worse was to come, for Vicente Rocafuerte now joined the struggle against Flores and the facultades extraordinarias. Rocafuerte, a prestigious Guayaquil aristocrat, world traveler, former deputy to the Cortes of Cádiz, and author of numerous works on representative government and liberal reforms, had returned to his native Ecuador from Mexico early in 1833. Bolívar had warned Flores in November 1830 that Rocafuerte would soon return to Ecuador. "This man harbors the most sinister thoughts toward you and my friends," cautioned the Liberator.

> He is the most dyed-in-the-wool anti-militarist, and quite conceited. If that gentleman sets foot in Guayaquil, you and others, God knows, will have to suffer a great deal.[41]

Fresh back from Mexico where he had been active in politics and diplomacy, Rocafuerte decided to stand for election to

Congress. With the support of the Quiteño Libre Society and other anti-Flores elements, he was elected to Congress. For Rocafuerte the issue of facultades extraordinarias evoked bitter memories of dictatorship in Mexico and of his own imprisonment there for opposing the grant of special powers to the executive.[42] Stung by the ill treatment of Deputy Carrión and staunchly opposed to the creation of a dictatorship, Rocafuerte plunged into the political fray. In an angry and vehement note written from his sickbed, he denounced the Congress and the president for having violated the constitution. He accused Flores of "wicked transgressions" and of basing his government on the "brutal use of arms." The deputies who had voted with the administration, he charged, were guilty of corruption, immorality, and subservience to an "insolent despotism." Rocafuerte concluded his wrathful letter by tendering his resignation from Congress, rather than take part in the "destruction of the Constitution and the Laws."[43]

Infuriated by Rocafuerte's provocative accusations, especially by the charges of corruption and immorality, pro-Flores deputies retaliated by ousting Rocafuerte from the legislature and depriving him of his constitutional immunity, just as they had done to Carrión. President Flores then compounded the vengeance of the deputies by ordering the former legislator arrested and condemning him to exile in Peru without trial. Rocafuerte soon found himself headed for the coast under armed escort.[44]

If Flores and his ministers believed that they had calmed the storm and saved Ecuador from anarchy by swift acts of repression they were mistaken. Flores' draconian measures further polarized opinion, alienated friends of the administration, and made rebellion inevitable.

The drama continued to unfold. Following the sensational resignations of Rocafuerte and Carrión, the government received a series of new blows as other prominent men announced their departures from public office. Among them, Drs. Luis de Sáa and Pablo Merino, both highly respected members of the president's influential Council of State, quit the administration in protest against its policies. Resignations of other appointees—all for similar motives—followed in rapid succession. The exodus of so many respected figures coming so soon after the Olmedo and Valdivieso affairs sent shock waves from the capital to all parts of the nation.[45]

Guayaquil, perennial fount of discontent and home of the lucrative customhouse, was the likely spot for an insurrection. Accordingly, on 12 October, Commandant Pedro Mena, commander of the port's small garrison, declared himself the leader of a revolutionary movement to free the people from the "extraordinary powers" of Flores. Mena quickly gained control of Guayaquil, but he was an ignorant, grasping, and cynical man who lacked the ability to organize a government and to win the support of the civilian population. At the very outset he lost the backing of the respectable citizenry of Guayaquil by his lust for money and his arbitrary seizures of wealth. In a desperate bid for popular backing Mena freed Vicente Rocafuerte from the armed guard conducting him into exile and offered him a role as civilian leader of the revolution. Rocafuerte, after some hesitation, accepted the invitation to become *Jefe Supremo* (supreme chief) of the rebel government.[46]

Rocafuerte's assumption of what he thought was the leadership of the revolt gave respectability to a movement that came to be known in Ecuadorian history as the "Revolution of the Chihuahuas," probably a wry reference to the Jefe Supremo's past services in Mexico.[47] Rocafuerte was useful to the rebel government primarily as a figurehead to provide moral stature and expertise in international diplomacy. But he was forced to spend most of his energy attempting to restrain the rapacity of Mena and his band of unscrupulous henchmen.[48]

Meanwhile, on 17 October, news of the Guayaquil insurrection reached Quito. Flores decided immediately to lead a strong force to the coast to snuff out the revolutionary fire. He departed in haste on the following day, but not without leaving instructions to put down with vigor an anticipated revolt by members of the Society of El Quiteño Libre. During the night of 19–20 October, while the president was en route to Guayaquil, a small number of rebels in Quito attempted to seize power. They were put down bloodily. Killed in the uprising were Colonel Francis Hall and several of his coconspirators. After the fighting had ended the nude body of Hall was found hanging from a post. Whether the government troops exceeded their instructions from the president in the needless killing of the dissidents is not known, but historians have inclined to hold Flores responsible for the savage suppression of a minor revolt that probably posed no serious threat to the state.[49] There is no evidence to prove that the president either ordered or approved of the brutal homicides, but his harsh policies led to the tragic outcome of the Quiteño Libre affair, even if Flores did not order the killings.

As the government forces advanced on Guayaquil, Commandant Mena showed greater zeal in extracting money from the merchants than in organizing the defenses of the city. Flores seized the port almost without a fight while Mena and his men boarded the Ecuadorian warship *Colombia* and retreated to the island of Puná, which dominated the shipping lanes into the harbor of Guayaquil. Rocafuerte, took refuge aboard a United States warship, and later managed to rejoin the Chihuahuas on the *Colombia*.[50]

The occupation of Guayaquil by government troops did not put an end to the uprising. From late November 1833 to June of the following year a military and political stalemate developed, with Flores controlling most of the coast and the Chihuahuas commanding the sea and a few centers of insurgency on the northern coast and in the interior. From his base on the strategic island of Puná Mena maintained a blockade of Guayaquil and carried out harassing raids against small coastal communities and plantations. Flores issued a decree branding the rebels "pirates," but he lacked the necessary naval power to deal with the outlaws and to break the blockade that had halted the flow of trade and customs receipts. The influence of seapower, small as the forces were, was felt keenly by Flores at this time.

General Flores was also powerless to prevent Rocafuerte from engaging in efforts of diplomacy to win the support of foreign nations, especially Peru and New Granada. The Jefe Supremo of the Chihuahuas even made a trip to Lima where he won the promise of material aid from President José de la Riva-Agüero, but the promise was not fulfilled because of civil war in Peru. A mystery surrounded Rocafuerte's dealing with authorities in Lima, for he never revealed the nature of the commitments he must have made to the Peruvians in return for promised military aid.[51]

A break in the stalemate finally came in June 1834 when the unscrupulous Mena, exasperated by Rocafuerte's interference with the military, arranged to have the Jefe Supremo turned over to Flores. With the imprisonment of Rocafuerte it appeared that the president was about to triumph over the last rebel forces. But the popularity and influence of Rocafuerte in Guayaquil continued even while the leader was imprisoned. Recognition of this fact led Flores to doubt his own ability to govern the coast effectively. Meanwhile, bad news arrived from the interior. Revolts had broken out in the far north. The rebels, many of them associated with the Quiteño Libre group, quickly took Quito and proclaimed José Félix Valdivieso as Jefe Superior of a provisional government.[52]

The loss of Quito to insurgents erased whatever hope Flores might have had to regain control of the country in the immediate future. Making a careful assessment of the situation, Flores decided that he might yet salvage things by making a compact with Rocafuerte, who commanded no troops but enjoyed great prestige in the coastal region. The captive Jefe Supremo was astounded when his captor offered to make peace with the Chihuahuas, promised not to seek reelection at the end of his presidential term (11 September 1834), and, by implication, committed himself to support Rocafuerte as next president of Ecuador. After some haggling over terms of the transaction the two leaders agreed to a formal pact that called for friendly cooperation of the signatories, amnesty for all rebels, and the convocation of an extraordinary congress to prepare for the administrative transition. In effect, Flores promised to arrange for Rocafuerte's succession to the presidency.[53]

Though liberal critics of Flores, like Pedro Moncayo, condemned the pact and attempted to persuade Rocafuerte to renounce it, the two leaders honored the agreement.[54] The pact violated the concept of freely elected governments, but it made political sense, for it temporarily reduced tensions between coast and sierra by bringing together a major leader of each region. The arrangement offered the additional advantage of bringing cooperation between two leaders of complimentary talents. The Guayaquil aristocrat offered experience in government and intellectual vision while the Venezuelan general provided military leadership and an indomitable spirit. The collaboration of these two men, as long as it might last, would provide Ecuador with the elements of stable government.

The Department of Guayas was quickly brought under the control of Rocafuerte, appointed Jefe Superior of the department by Flores, when remnants of the Chihuahua army banished Mena. But the rebellious regime of Valdivieso in Quito was another matter. Both Flores and Rocafuerte appealed to Valdivieso to join in the convocation of an extraordinary congress to settle the dispute over the presidency, but Valdivieso refused. On 10 September 1834, with the civil war still unresolved, Flores formally retired from office. At the same time a junta of leading citizens of Guayaquil appointed Rocafuerte his successor with the title of Jefe Supremo of Ecuador.[55] Thus the pact between Flores and Rocafuerte was fulfilled.

Ecuador suffered under the rival governments of Quito and Guayaquil until January 1835. Valdivieso's army managed to extend the Quito regime's authority over the southern sierra and over much of Guayas as well. As the highland forces overran a great part of the coastal region they burned one of Flores' haciendas and destroyed much property on another. In late December, at the urgent request of Rocafuerte, General Flores gathered a small army and marched into the highlands to meet the main force of the Quito regime. On 20 January 1835, in a decisive battle at Miñarica (near Ambato) Flores met and defeated the highland army. Three days later he entered Quito, and Valdivieso fled to Colombia. Ecuador was not reunited under the provisional rule of Vicente Rocafuerte.[56]

The victory at Miñarica refurbished Flores' military reputation, which had suffered from his frustrations with Mena at Guayaquil. Olmedo lavished fulsome praise on the victorious general in a new poem entitled "Oda a Miñarica." Rocafuerte, who was detained on the coast by civil disturbances in Manabí, entrusted temporary civil authority over the highlands to his military commander-in-chief.[57]

Flores governed in Quito until 20 April. As the victorious general he could have remained in power longer, but he chose to honor his agreement with Rocafuerte and go into voluntary retirement. In taking leave from public responsibilities he addressed a farewell message to the Ecuadorian people in which he affirmed his loyalty to the constitution and declared his preference for the tranquility of private life. But his numerous references to the victory at Miñarica and the recitation of his great "sacrifices" for the good of the nation gave more than a hint that he had not abandoned interest in the public arena.[58]

Flores did not express bitterness in his farewell message, but he undoubtedly felt a sting in his heart as he departed from Quito. A little over a year later the government newspaper published an article entitled "La Presidencia" which purported to express the sentiments of a military officer after serving a term in the presidency of a Spanish American nation. Many of the complaints might have been those of Flores. Everyone wants favors, said the article:

> miners want funds; émigrés, jobs; patriots, rewards; . . . lawyers, judgeships; . . . canons, bishoprics; nuns, relaxation of vows, all in the name of Protection and Promotion. Soldiers want to be corporals, corporals to be sergeants, sergeants and so forth up to general, and the generals want to be president.

Everyone who is turned down, said the anonymous writer, becomes angry with the president who had accepted the position as an honor but learned that it is far easier to face the enemy than to face his fellow countrymen.[59]

This article went on to describe how the president struggled through visits, appointments, private conferences, and public ceremonies to meet his obligations to the people and the state. His best efforts are rewarded with charges that he is "ignorant, immoral, a protector of enemies" and "arbitrary, a despot, and a tyrant." If this is the life of the president, will there be anyone who wants to govern? asked the author. He answered his own question: "Why not? There is a country where they bury widows alive, and there is never a shortage of brides."

As a private citizen General Flores devoted himself to his family and to the reconstruction of his properties that had been devastated by civil war. Living in ostensible retirement on his hacienda La Elvira, not far from Guayaquil, the ex-president kept in touch with Ecuadorian leaders and with public men in foreign countries. In letters to President Santander of Colombia Flores revealed many of his private thoughts—and doubtless concealed others. He declared that he was simply "raising chickens in order to live" and that he preferred the quiet country life of his estate on the banks of the Babahoyo River to the hectic existence of a president in the capital. "All I want now, believe me," he wrote, "is not to leave this jungle except to descend into my tomb."[60]

Though Flores asserted that he "was no longer worth anything in the political world," he carefully monitered events not only in Ecuador but in Peru, New Granada, and Venezuela. He reported to Santander that from Ecuador it appeared that the opposition party in New Granada wanted "to overturn the established government, destroy the constitution, and tear everything down that exists." Most significantly, he reported that in Ecuador, too, there were plans to bring down the government, but Flores was "resolved to support even a stick if it governed constitutionally."[61]

In the year 1835 Juan José Flores was not finished as a public figure in Ecuador, notwithstanding his protestations to the contrary. He had suffered a temporary loss of prestige and had been forced to come to terms with his adversaries. He had served out his four-year constitutional term and had relinquished power to a political opponent in a manner that had the appearance of magnanimity. Thanks to his victory at Miñarica, his military reputation was undiminished.

If Flores had not succeeded in consolidating the political institutions of the new nation during his first term, he had at least made significant progress in that direction. Responsibility for difficulties in public finance was shared by Flores with the members of Congress who had demonstrated no more wisdom in the matter than the president. His reputation for personal honesty had been soiled by journalistic exposures, but he had admitted no wrongdoing. Time would erase, or blur, the effects of the vivid accusations of Colonel Hall and company. People were usually tolerant in matters of private enrichment by men of public office, for the practice was widespread and probably aroused more envy and respect than disapproval. Surely the landowners, merchants, and lawyers who dominated political affairs understood the importance of the acquisitive instinct.

Flores was Ecuador's indispensable man. His military feats, like those of Bolívar, had been celebrated in poetry. President Rocafuerte, recognizing that he required Flores' support, named him commander-in-chief of the armed forces and took care to flatter and cajole him in frequent letters. At the age of thirty-five, Flores was still a young man. He could afford to wait a few years, confident that the passage of time would bring new opportunites.

5
CONTRAPUNTAL POLITICS, 1835– 1839: ROCAFUERTE AND FLORES

After the battle of Miñarica and the consolidation of Roca-fuerte's power over the nation General Flores, as we have learned, sought the quiet relaxation of private life on his haci-enda La Elvira, located along the Babahoyo River in the coastal lowlands about forty miles upstream from Guayaquil. Though in official retirement, Flores remained a person of national prominence. Historical records do not tell us why the ex-president chose to live at Babahoyo rather than at one of his estates in the highlands, but one probable motive was his wish to maintain close relations with the coastal merchants, planters, and politicians who wielded so much influence in national af-fairs. Perhaps, too, as a military officer he liked the strategic situation of La Elvira, which dominated the road from Guaya-quil to Guaranda and hence to Quito. Maintaining residence near the major port also afforded rapid communication with foreign countries, especially with Peru and New Granada, an advantage that permitted prompt reception of international news. Finally, a sense of courtesy and propriety may have sug-gested to the general that it would be correct to reside at a considerable distance from the capital in order to avoid possible embarrassments both to himself and to his successor in the presidental chair.

Vicente Rocafuerte, the man who assumed authority over Ecuador, first as "Supreme Chief" after Miñarica and then as president in 1835, was a wealthy and prestigious creole from Guayaquil. Born in 1783 of an aristocratic family, he possessed all of the advantages of education, travel, and worldly experi-ence that wealth and high social standing provided. In contrast with the humble origins and limited education of General Flores, Rocafuerte received a private education at home and then traveled to Europe to complete his education at exclusive schools in Madrid and Paris. While abroad he met many eminent people, among them Bolívar and the Baron von Humbolt. He became an exponent of the enlightened ideas then in vogue and returned to Guayaquil in 1807 with a firm resolve to help free his homeland from "Spanish tyranny."[1]

Rocafuerte performed significant service in the struggle for Spanish American independence, though he took no part in the fighting. In 1812 his native province of Guayaquil elected him to serve in the liberal Cortes of Cádiz, but he did not reach Spain until after the Cortes disbanded. During the next decade he worked for the cause of independence as a publicist and a diplomat, journeying to Spain as an envoy of Bolívar and to the United States as a representative of Mexican liberals to oppose the diplomacy of Iturbide's empire. After the collapse of the imperial regime in 1824 Rocafuerte served the Mexican republic as a diplomat in England where he helped secure diplomatic recognition of Mexico, made diplomatic contacts with several other nations, and worked on plans to improve education in Hispanic America. In 1830 he returned to Mexico and busied himself writing and publishing in behalf of such liberal causes as religious toleration and prison reform. After suffering three arrests and nearly losing his life in the political turmoil of Mexico, he took ship for Guayaquil, where he arrived in February 1833.[2]

The return of such an illustrious native son immediately attracted the attention of the nationalists and liberals in Quito who saw in the newly arrived guayaquileño a champion of their own cause. *El Quiteño libre* welcomed Rocafuerte in a front-page article and endorsed him for election to Congress. Once elected to Congress in 1833 Rocafuerte pleased his supporters by opposing a grant of extraordinary powers to the president, but his subsequent pact with Flores (July 1834) to end the Guayaquil revolt disillusioned many of the surviving members of the Quiteño Libre Society who believed that he had abandoned his principles in order to gain the presidency.[3]

Rocafuerte's pact with Flores was a political compromise of a practical sort which paved the way for the Guayaquil leader to assume presidential power. From Rocafuerte's perspective the controversial agreement acknowledged the fundamental fact that Flores was *the* military leader of Ecuador. Since government could not endure without the consent of the commander of the armed forces, it was necessary for Rocafuerte to obtain the support and goodwill of the man he had once scorned as a "ferocious tyrant" and whom he now addressed as "my esteemed friend."[4]

It was inevitable that Rocafuerte would eventually break with Flores, for the views of the two leaders clashed sharply. The guayaquileño was every inch an artistocrat—urbane, refined, eloquent, and aloof. His many letters to Flores reeked of didacticism and condescension, which must have irritated the general. Not given to conviviality or dissipation in any form, Rocafuerte tended to be somewhat cold, austere, and even haughty at times. Though sometimes described as intransigent in matters of political principles, he knew how to make practical compromises when cornered by adversaries or circumstances. But he did not make concessions merely for the sake of popularity or private gain. His greatest weaknesses were his impulsiveness, his hot temper, and his bluntness. His occasional outbursts and his excessive candor frequently offended and astonished many people and won him few friends. Though he was admired and respected, he was not loved by his countrymen.[5]

Rocafuerte saw himself as the champion of "the glorious struggle for liberal principles" against everything that was "backward," "feudalistic," and "gothic." He sought to remodel the colonial society of Ecuador according to "the lights of the century," as he was so fond of saying, to modernize society through selective imitation of the institutions of the leading nations of the world. In theory, if not always in practice, he believed in expanding the scope of liberty, and he declared that governments exist for the benefit of nations—not nations for governments. He favored religious toleration and restrictions on the power of the military and the Catholic Church. He wished to free the economy from the baneful influences of government monopolies and restrictive taxes, and he sought to expand and improve the public education system.[6]

As for the issue of federalism versus centralism which agitated so many Spanish American nations, Rocafuerte wisely avoided a forthright stand, preferring to address himself to the concrete problems of government rather than to stir up debates over abstract political theory. Before 1835 Rocafuerte had seen the merits of each viewpoint at different stages of his intellectual development, but in the Ecuadorian presidency his policies, like those of Flores, favored a high degree of centralism.[7]

During the period of provisional government from September 1834 to August 1835, as supreme chief of the nation Rocafuerte concerned himself less with philosophical problems than with the practical necessity of suppressing the rebellious opposition and of controlling the armed forces. Rumors of impending uprisings and revolutionary outbreaks came almost on a weekly basis, and Rocafuerte was kept in an almost constant state of alarm. The chief danger to the government came from Valdivieso who promoted invasions and revolts from his refuge in Pasto near the northern border. But there were other military chieftains who operated independently near the Peruvian frontier and in the northeastern province of Manabí. The nation was on the verge of anarchy much of the time.

Undaunted by the ardor and the determination of the rebels Rocafuerte resolved to use harsh measures to enforce his authority and to rescue Ecuador from what he called the "crater of revolutions."[8] A regime of liberty, in his opinion, could not thrive until the nation enjoyed peace and the rule of law. To restore order the supreme chief adopted a policy of having captured rebel officers executed without trial and of exiling all rebels who surrendered to authorities without fighting. The number of arbitrary executions is not known, but there were many. In addition, scores of conspirators, including the famous Manuela Sáenz (Bolívar's most famous mistress), were sent into exile. Rocafuerte freely admitted that he had adopted a policy of terror to establish order and declared in a letter to Flores that "it is necessary to do everything at lance-point."[9]

Rocafuerte's heavy reliance upon the military for repression of the dissidents gave the impression to many that the new president wished to erect a dictatorship. Walter Cope, the British consul at Guayaquil, reported that "Rocafuerte has conceived

the strange project of establishing a despotism, that he may introduce reforms, reductions in expenditures and free institutions,
unopposed." Cope believed that Rocafuerte was "as desirous to
keep up the strength of the Army as he was before to disband or
reduce it."[10] The British consul might also have pointed out that
the guayaquileño leader's harsh policies strongly suggested he
was closer in spirit to the enlightened despots of eighteenth-
century Spain than to the contemporary liberals of England so
much admired by Rocafuerte.

The Ecuadorian head of state knew well that General Flores
was the key to the achievement of domestic tranquility. Without
the support of the former president the new government could
not hope to control the restless and capricious military chieftains in the provinces. In a steady stream of personal letters
Rocafuerte lavished praise on Flores and sought his advice on
cabinet nominations. He appointed Flores' friends and in-laws
to administrative posts. He even offered Flores an opportunity
to invest in a promising venture in mining. As if these inducements were not enough, Rocafuerte conferred the title of
general-in-chief of the army on Flores and gave him emergency
powers to govern the Department of Guayas in case of invasion
or insurrection.[11]

If Flores was irritated now and then with the patronizing
tone of Rocafuerte's letters, he was doubtless pleased by much
of Rocafuerte's flattery that they contained. Though the general had ostensibly committed himself to retirement, he accepted the title of general-in-chief and the handsome salary
that went with it. He was not anxious for a year or so to return
to active participation in public affairs. In private letters Flores
expressed strong disapproval of the disorders provoked by
Valdivieso and others, indicated his refusal to support an uprising in late 1835, and rejoiced at the news of the execution of
more than thirty "bandits." He professed a moral obligation to
back the Ecuadorian government, but he also expressed reluctance to exercise the emergency powers and military authority
granted him by Rocafuerte simply to deal with outbreaks of
petty violence. He preferred to remain a private citizen and to
refuse any active military command, for it made him feel
ashamed, he said, "to appear in public only because a handful

of bandits . . . might disturb the repose of the people." But life as a private citizen, "raising chickens" at La Elvira, would soon prove too boring for a man accustomed to an active life and the exercise of power. Late in 1836 he allowed himself to be elected to the Senate and returned to public life in January 1837.[12]

Meanwhile, Rocafuerte, as Supreme Chief, did not intend to govern arbitrarily for an indefinite period. In February 1835 he issued a proclamation convoking a constituent convention to draft a new constitution and legitimize the provisional government that he headed. The proclamation quickly became the subject of controversy, for it contained clauses that prohibited clergy and military men on active duty not only from serving as deputies in the forthcoming convention but even from taking part in electing the deputies. Rocafuerte's aim, as he explained it, was to free the elections from any improper influences, but the policy provoked vigorous complaints from the military and the clergy. Flores supported his successor in the controversy, but the conservative vicar of the diocese of Cuenca considered the proclamation to be heresy and issued an edict of excommunication against anyone who read two newspaper articles that endorsed the official policy of clerical exclusion from the political process. Rocafuerte reacted angrily by shutting down a Church newspaper in Cuenca and ordering the vicar and a clerical editor into exile without a judicial hearing.[13] In letters to the ex-president, Rocafuerte explained that his high-handed treatment of the clerics was prompted by the discovery of a plan "to revolutionize the country in the name of religion."[14]

Despite clerical opposition, in late June 1835, the national convention assembled in the central highland city of Ambato. Rocafuerte presented a lengthy address to the deputies that outlined the enormous social and political difficulties facing Ecuador, lauded his own efforts to ameliorate conditions, and recommended a new constitution that would occupy a middle ground "between the two extremes of democracy and monarchy." This surprising reference to monarchical government seemed to reflect an awareness that attachments to regal institutions and autocratic rule had not disappeared in Ecuador. Pure democracy, warned Rocafuerte, could not be based on a mixed population composed of "castes and colors, most of whom . . .

groan under a shameful feudalism worse than that of Russia." He hoped that the convention would frame a "simple, clear, and concise" constitution suited to the realities of the country. At the same time he emphasized the need for a program of reforms to expand the system of public education, to promote commerce and industry, and to regulate the clergy, especially the lax religious orders. Above all he stressed the urgent need to recognize the "deplorable" system of public finance to permit the government to meet its foreign and domestic obligations.[15]

The first hint of a possible clash between Flores and Roca-fuerte appeared when the national convention began to show signs of loyalty to General Flores. Though the convention agreed to name Rocafuerte "provisional president" of the nation, it also rescinded the extraordinary powers granted to the chief executive by the Congress of 1833.[16] Then, when Flores sent a message to the convention in which he offered to submit to a legislative review of his presidential service from 1830 to 1834, the deputies not only declined to investigate his public conduct but adopted "a solemn vote of gratitude" to the "illustrious General Flores" and declared him to be "the first citizen of Ecuador, with full possession of all the rights that belong to a native-born Ecuadorian."[17] The bestowal of these honors on the first president was more than a mere courtesy, for the conferring of full citizenship rights on the general removed the possibility of excluding him from the presidency on constitutional grounds because of his foreign birth. Thus, it was clear to all that General Flores had strong support in the Congress and was, in effect, the national caudillo who could seize the reins of power once more if he wished. For the time being, however, Flores was content to abide by his pact with the enlightened leader from Guayaquil.

Still more unpleasantness was in store for Rocafuerte. On 2 August the deputies approved the Constitution of 1835, which was little more than a reworking of the Constitution of 1830— the document that Rocafuerte had criticized so severely in his address to the legislators. The only major change in the framework of the government was the adoption of a bicameral legislature to replace the former single-chambered congress—a change not requested by the provisional president. Most disappointing to Rocafuerte, who favored a vigorous executive, were the clauses restricting executive authority and establishing impeachment procedures to make the president and his ministers responsible to Congress.[18]

On the day the new constitution was adopted the convention elected Vicente Rocafuerte to a four-year term as the second president of the republic. It was not certain, however, until the last moment that the deputies would actually select the Guayaquil leader for the highest post in government. Rumor had it that most of the convention members favored Flores and that only the personal intervention of the general himself prevented his reelection to the high office.[19] Whether Flores interceded in behalf of Rocafuerte is not known, but it seems clear that he did not seek the presidency for himself, nor did he make any effort to deny the office to his rival.[20] When the votes were cast Rocafuerte received a clear-cut majority, twenty-five votes out of thirty-nine, while Flores received eight votes and the remaining ballots were scattered.[21]

The political strength shown by the ex-president in the national convention caused a small rift between the two leaders. In his frequent letters to Flores the newly elected president failed to mention that the general had been honored by the receipt of eight votes for the presidency. Flores, who received reports from many sources, noted the obvious omission from Rocafuerte's letters and wrote to the chief executive asking for confirmation of the news of the eight votes. Rocafuerte replied that the news was true and that he feared "our foreign enemies may take some advantage of the stupidity (*torpeza*) of those Deputies who voted for Flores."[22] This gauche reply—rather typical of the tactless Rocafuerte—could not have failed to wound the proud general.

President Rocafuerte, despite difficulties behind the scenes with Flores and his supporters, took charge of the executive branch of government with a clear sense of purpose and a good understanding of most of the nation's problems. However, he did not get on well with other men in government, and he failed to appreciate the importance of growing nationalist feelings in the country. Convinced that few Ecuadorians possessed sufficient administrative ability for high office, he offended many of his compatriots by selecting as his three Cabinet ministers men of foreign birth—a Chilean, a Frenchman, and a Spaniard. Within two years the president was compelled to ask for the resignations of these three ministers.[23]

To Rocafuerte's credit it must be said that he was not interested in currying favor and popularity but rather in providing the nation with effective and stable government.[24] In both domestic and foreign affairs he was determined to establish a solid foundation for an expanding economy and a better life for the people. By virtue of his education and his experience he was remarkably well qualified to carry out such a program, especially in the area of foreign trade and international relations. Though he did not succeed in all he attempted, he nevertheless managed to develop a sound and coherent foreign policy.[25]

Rocafuerte's conduct of foreign relations was premised on the conviction that Ecuador needed many years of peace to consolidate its government and build a strong economy. He sought therefore to avoid confrontations and conflicts with neighboring countries and to establish diplomatic and commercial relations with the leading maritime nations of the world. He was prepared to defend Ecuador's vital interests with force if absolutely necessary, but he preferred to exhaust the resources of peaceful diplomacy before resorting to war. Sensing that Flores might not fully agree with the policy of peace, Rocafuerte explained in a letter to the former president: "Our century is not warlike but peaceful. This is an era of peace, of the sciences, the arts, commerce, and wealth." Citing the examples of peaceful development in France, England, Germany, and the United States, he declared that from "these examples we conclude that peace, hard work, affluence, commerce, and wealth . . . ought to constitute the basis of administrative policy in the new states of America."[26]

Under the earlier leadership of Flores the scope of Ecuador's foreign policy had been limited, for the most part, to contacts with the neighboring nations of New Granada and Peru.[27] Rocafuerte moved to enlarge Ecuador's perspective to include many nations. His long association with Mexico induced him to negotiate a treaty of peace, amity, and commerce with that nation in 1838.[28] He sent an envoy to Chile and invited the United

States to send a diplomatic agent to Ecuador. The reluctance of the United States government to sanction the dismemberment of Gran Colombia, together with problems over claims of North American citizens against Ecuador, posed obstacles to a prompt acceptance in Washington of Rocafuerte's overture. Nevertheless, the invitation ultimately bore fruit, for the United States soon authorized a consulate in Guayaquil and, in January 1839, sent an envoy to Quito with instructions to negotiate a treaty with Ecuador. Though Rocafuerte left office before it could be concluded, he deserved most of the credit for the treaty that was signed with the United States in mid-1839.[29]

Among the European powers France and Great Britain merited priority in diplomacy. In his dealings with France Rocafuerte welcomed to Quito an "honorary consul-general" from Paris, granted most-favored nation status to French shipping and citizens, and commenced talks on a treaty of recognition. A formal agreement, however, was not reached during Rocafuerte's presidency.[30] The importance of British trade at Guayaquil enhanced the importance of seeking a treaty of amity and commerce with England. Ecuador's share of the Colombian debt owed to British bondholders (from loans floated during the wars for independence) posed a major obstacle to agreement. Rocafuerte took steps to acknowledge his nation's responsibility for 21.5 percent of the entire debt (Ecuador's share amounting to 1,152,271 pounds sterling) in accordance with a convention previously agreed to by New Granada and Venezuela.[31] To arrange the terms of payment Rocafuerte sent Colonel Richard Wright, one of several British officers of the Bolivarian legions who had settled in Ecuador, to London to see if British bondholders would agree to accept ownership of Ecuadorian mines and vacant lands in payment of the large debts.[32] Though the final settlement of the debt question took years, the British government responded warmly to Rocafuerte's goodwill and commenced negotiations that led to a preliminary agreement on a treaty of amity and commerce in late 1839.[33]

At about the time Colonel Wright left for England (1838) Rocafuerte entrusted a secret mission of great importance to Pedro Gual, a prestigious and experienced diplomat of Venezuelan birth and former minister of foreign relations in Gran Colombia, to seek recognition of Ecuadorian independence by Spain. The Spanish government as early as 1834 had indicated a willingness to undertake negotiations leading to the establishment of formal diplomatic relations with the former colonies. In 1836 Mexico concluded a treaty of peace and commerce with the mother country.[34] News of Spain's disposition to seek reconciliation reached Ecuador quickly and aroused widespread interest. Politically, a treaty would be advantageous because it would terminate the technical state of war with Spain and help to legitimize the government in Quito. Economic advantages would also result from a settlement, for Spain was a substantial importer of chocolate and would therefore be a good customer for Ecuador's most lucrative export, cacao.

In August 1835 President Rocafuerte secured permission from the national convention to make a settlement of the debt owed to Spain and to admit British shipping into Ecuadorian ports.[35] But in Europe Gual made slow progress in the negotiations, for the Spanish government insisted on special and exclusive commercial privileges and on a very large debt settlement. Though a treaty of recognition was not completed during Rocafuerte's term of office, Ecuador nonetheless sent two consuls and a consul-general to Spain, and the way was paved for completion of a treaty soon after General Flores' return to the presidency in 1839. Though Rocafuerte's persistent diplomacy failed to secure the ratification of an accord with any new major power during his tenure, his efforts were important in expanding Ecuador's contacts with the outside world and in pointing to a new direction in foreign policy.[36]

Opening diplomatic and commercial relations with the major maritime powers was important, but the thorny international problems posed by Ecuador's neighbors, New Granada and Peru, overshadowed all other diplomatic efforts of Rocafuerte because of the perennial danger of war. Unsettled boundaries, territorial ambitions, machinations of political refugees, and assorted international intrigues produced serious tensions among the Andean nations at this time. Rocafuerte, though often given to intemperate and impulsive actions in dealing with his fellow countrymen, exercised remarkable restraint and prudence in seeking friendly relations with Ecuador's neighbors.

The government of New Granada under President Francisco de Paula Santander feared that Ecuador, having failed to ratify the Treaty of Pasto, would revive its claims to the Cauca region. Santander not only refused to recognize Ecuador but undermined the strength of Rocafuerte's government by permitting Valdivieso's rebel forces to operate freely along the northern border from sanctuary in New Granada. The Ecuadorian president adopted a very conciliatory tone in all his dealings with Santander, persuaded the national convention to approve the Treaty of Pasto, and even agreed to accept Ecuador's share of the Gran Colombian debt according to the terms of an agreement worked out by Venezuela and New Granada without the participation of Ecuador.[37] His acceptance of a foreign debt obligation of more than a million pounds sterling provoked much criticism of Rocafuerte, but he accepted the onus as the inevitable price of peace with Colombia and as a step toward improved relations with Great Britain.[38]

The reduction of tensions resulting from his policy of conciliation allowed Rocafuerte to seek still friendlier understandings with New Granada. He pressed Santander to halt the political machinations of Valdivieso, initiated negotiations for a treaty of amity and commerce, and even proposed a defensive military alliance with New Granada. Though Santander did not agree to any of these proposals, relations between the two nations gradually improved to the point that war no longer threatened.[39]

The surprising suggestion of a military pact with New Granada was actually a clever defensive strategem on Rocafuerte's part to protect Ecuador from a new menace coming from the south. In 1836 General Andrés de Santa Cruz, an ambitious and aggressive Bolivian leader, managed to form the Peru–Bolivian Confederation and put a temporary end to civil wars in the region. Santa Cruz not only governed in a very autocratic fashion but apparently hankered for a crown and craved many high-sounding titles, such as "Invincible Grand Marshal" and "Supreme Protector and Invincible Pacificator." In the manner of monarchs he proclaimed his own saint's day a national holiday. He even arranged to have his bust stamped on gold and silver coins.[40]

In Guayaquil General Flores followed the news of Santa

Cruz's activities and took note of the Bolivian leader's love of regal splendor. In a letter to President Santander Flores remarked:

> General Santacruz [sic] has invested himself with all the pomp of a monarch, and has yielded to many weaknesses which denigrate and make him look ridiculous, such as to claim that Bolivia is a new Macedonia and he a new Alexander, to assert that his star guides him, to have arranged to have his son born under the national colors of Bolivia, to proclaim that his cranium is similar to that of Napoleon . . . , and in short, many other wretched things which reveal the political path which he has taken.[41]

A few months later Flores returned to the same theme, noting: "every day Santacruz receives new kinds of flattery. . . . The policy of conquerors [in Peru] is well known: a new form of government. Everything is regal."[42]

General Flores' antipathy toward Santa Cruz soon put him at odds with President Rocafuerte, who repressed any misgivings he might have had about the dictator in order to maintain friendly and peaceful relations with Peru. What began as a mere divergence of opinion between the general and the president, however, soon turned into a major disagreement when, in 1836, Santa Cruz's aggressive foreign policy provoked a war between Chile and his confederation.

The Chilean government immediately sought to enlist the aid of other South American nations, most notably Argentina and Ecuador. Dictator Manuel Rosas of Argentina was easily persuaded to side with Chile in the hope of securing his northern border and of acquiring territory at the expense of Bolivia. But President Rocafuerte steadfastly refused to yield to Chilean blandishments. Even before the arrival in Quito of Chile's special envoy, Ventura Lavalle, Rocafuerte had approved a draft treaty of amity and commerce with the Confederation of Peru and Bolivia, thus presenting a stern negative to any overtures that might come from Santiago.[43]

Chargé Lavalle, knowing that General Flores' opinions counted almost as much in Ecuador as did the president's, sounded out the general and found him to be warmly in favor of joining Chile in her war on Santa Cruz's confederation. The

Ecuadorian general's enthusiasm for war was whetted by hints from Lavalle that Chile would entrust supreme command of an invading army in Peru to Flores. The Chilean diplomat speculated in his reports to Santiago that Flores was motivated by a "great desire for glory," a strong wish to defeat the hated Santa Cruz, and an eagerness to gain new territory for Ecuador.[44] Lavalle's analysis was correct as far as it went, but it omitted the fact that Flores' concern went beyond personal glory, for he believed that General Santa Cruz threatened Ecuadorian independence through a secret plan to incorporate Ecuador into a Pan-Andean confederation—a nineteenth-century recreation of the ancient Inca empire.[45]

Though Flores was flattered by attention from Chile, he was also courted by Peru. In a clever bid for the ex-president's support Santa Cruz sent García del Río, Flores' former finance minister, to Babahoyo for the purpose of persuading the general to cooperate with the confederation. Flores' rejection of this overture, as well as other inducements from Santa Cruz, suggested that he was quite convinced that the Confederation of Peru and Bolivia threatened the security of Ecuador.[46]

General Flores' disagreement with the administration's policy toward Peru developed simultaneously with the appearance of widespread discontent in Ecuador with many of Rocafuerte's domestic policies. Even if the president's program had been carried out with utmost tact and discretion, it would have aroused opposition from the conservative vested interests. Rocafuerte sought nothing less than to modernize Ecuador, to expand and improve public education, to free the economy from governmental restrictions, to renovate the judicial system, to repair roads and build new ones, and to reform the system of public finance and taxation. As a man who had resided in the United States, England, and the Continent, he saw his native land as a backward country in desperate need of progress. His struggle to bring enlightened institutions to Ecuador was admirable in many ways, but it was very controversial in the traditional society of this Andean nation. Never doubting his own intellectual superiority and the validity of his own views, Rocafuerte frequently made enemies by scolding his opponents for what he regarded as their stupidity, egotism, and immorality.[47]

Improvement of the educational system was one of the most important goals of reform. The national convention of 1835 gave broad authority over public instruction to the chief executive, and Rocafuerte quite wisely chose to emphasize the expansion of elementary schools.[48] He issued a national curricular plan and approved the Lancasterian system of instruction that was so popular at the time. To fill the shortage of textbooks he established a press devoted exclusively to the printing of texts.[49] Schools for Indians received less attention than under Flores, but Rocafuerte opened some important new institutions such as an elementary school for girls, a school of obstetrics, an agrarian institute in the university, and a nautical school in Guayaquil. In July 1838 he inaugurated a military academy in Quito modeled on West Point, for the purpose of turning out better trained and disciplined officers.[50]

The results of Rocafuerte's energetic crusade for better education was disappointing. The president complained bitterly at the end of his term that the "vigorous resistance to the progress of enlightenment" by the wealthy but obscurantist elite thwarted most efforts at improvement.[51] Most prominent among the opponents of educational reform were members of the clergy, who objected to the secularization of Church schools and to the introduction of non-Catholic philosophical ideas into the curriculum. Rocafuerte's appointment of William Wheelwright, a Yankee Protestant, as director of schools in Quito stirred up a clerical storm of opposition. When Wheelwright required school children to read a Protestant translation of the Bible, the bishop of Quito demanded an investigation. Rocafuerte not only defended his appointee but ordered the press to print nothing about the dispute.[52]

For most of the Catholic clergy the Wheelwright incident was the culmination of a series of affronts to the Church and its servants. Not only did the second president deprive the clergy of electoral rights and shut down a clerical newspaper, but he criticized the lax morals of ecclesiastics and was known to favor the separation of church and state. What is more, at the end of his presidential term, Rocafuerte recommended abolition of two bulwarks of traditional Church privilege and power, the compulsory tithe and the ecclesiastical fuero.[53] Though Flores was not a staunch friend of clerical privilege, his more moderate views on Church issues caused the hierarchy to look at him as a shield against the reformist policies of Rocafuerte.

In his efforts to stimulate and modernize the economy the second president aroused less opposition than in matters of education and religion. Though he favored freeing the economy from the fetters of the government-run estancos,[54] he acquiesced in legislative measures that periodically suspended and reestablished the various monopolies.[55] Like Flores before him, he recognized a need for more and better roads, and he attempted to promote their construction without cost to the national treasury by creating provincial commissions empowered to build roads. The system worked badly and few roads were built because of the lack of funds.[56]

Attempts to promote mining and agriculture were not very fruitful either. Rocafuerte encouraged the formation of a semi-private company to rehabilitate the old Pillzhum mines near Cuenca, but the enterprise failed to yield substantial quantities of precious metals.[57] With regard to agriculture, the president hoped that his newly established Agrarian Institute would provide the scientific and technical knowledge needed to modernize farming methods, but the institute proved short-lived and ineffective. Similarly, Rocafuerte's attempts to attract foreign settlers to colonize vacant lands were a failure. Nevertheless, the value of agricultural production, after falling somewhat in the first three years of his tenure, rose rather sharply during his last three months in office. This delayed improvement was probably attributable to relatively peaceful conditions in the countryside and to higher cacao prices.[58]

Always a believer in low tariffs, and encouraged by brisk foreign demand for the cacao bean, Rocafuerte decided early in 1836 to seek rapid commercial expansion through the reduction of customs duties by 40 percent. He justified this measure on the ground that a reduction in import taxes would actually increase government revenues by making contraband activities less profitable. Fearing that Congress would not agree with his proposal to lower the tariff, he decided to do it by executive decree, even though the constitution granted the president no such authority.[59]

The question of tariff rates was only part of a larger problem of public finance, which had grown worse as a consequence of the civil disturbances of 1833–1834. According to the president's official report, the army garrison at Guayaquil in 1836 "was dying of hunger, the navy abandoned, the government employees in misery, and anarchy raising its haughty head." The traffic in libranzas, despite earlier prohibitions, continued unabated, and usurers, Rocafuerte asserted, managed to devour the entire proceeds of the customhouse (1.5 million pesos) in the year 1835.[60] In addition, sporadic revolts and occasional incursions of Valdivieso's forces from New Granada caused periodic drains on the treasury until the latter part of the second presidential period.

Like Flores before him, Rocafuerte struggled mightily to balance the budget and to commence payments on the national debt. When the national convention of 1835 rejected his proposals for financial reforms Rocafuerte decided to undertake a program of fiscal measures without legislative sanction. For example, to pay the troops, a matter of utmost importance, the president ordered a forced loan of eight thousand pesos and imposed a fine of fifteen thousand pesos on the rebellious José Félix Valdivieso.[61] Such expedients helped the government meet its payroll for a month or two, but they did nothing to solve the long-term problem.

In October 1835, after consultation with General Flores, Rocafuerte named Colonel Francisco Eugenio Tamariz to the post of minister of finance. Though Tamariz proved to be unpopular, partly because of his Spanish birth, the new minister was knowledgeable in matters of finance. Like García del Río under Flores, Tamariz seized the reins quickly and fired off orders to governors of provinces, treasurers, and tax collectors instructing them to tighten up procedures, to render clear and detailed accounts, and to cease issuing and receiving libranzas.[62] At the same time the president issued a decree ordering a new classification of the public debt, and declaring a system of priorities for the payment of the debt.[63] Though well intended, these administrative actions had little if any effect on the problem. During the following months the nation sank deeper into a fiscal quagmire. Contrabandists and usurers continued to ply their trades. The government lacked money to buy even paper and pens. Troops went unpaid on the northern border, where the threat of rebel invasions was great. Finally, in January 1836, the situation became critical when it was learned that the province of Guayaquil lacked funds to pay the army garrison there and the navy.[64]

To forestall a possible military revolt in Guayaquil and to put the nation's fiscal system on a sounder footing Rocafuerte issued three controversial decrees that came to be known as the "Decrees of 10 February." The first one not only reduced import duties by 40 percent, as previously noted, but required payment in cash (not paper) and ordered administrators of the customhouse and tax collection offices to watch employees carefully for any infractions of the law. The second and third decrees provided for the issuance of new government notes to replace all the old treasury paper and for a system of paying off the various types of debts by earmarking specified revenues for this purpose.[65] Contrabandists and usurers could not have been pleased, for the decrees took much of the profit out of smuggling and terminated the exorbitant interest rates that had become almost customary.

It is difficult to say how effective the fiscal reforms of 1836 would have been if they had remained in effect for more than a year. The president, in requesting that Congress approve all of the executive decrees on finance, declared that his policies had been so successful that there were no more *libranzas,* taxes were collected properly, troops were paid in full, and other government employees were receiving half of their pay on a regular basis. What is more, he said, the public debt of 1.2 million pesos had been reviewed and validated and the government had begun to pay it off.[66]

It cannot be denied that Rocafuerte and Tamariz worked with great energy and zeal to put the treasury on a sound basis. By the end of 1836 they believed that they had made significant progress. However, the chief executive and his minister of finance, in reporting to the Congress of 1837, claimed far greater success in fiscal matters than was actually the case.[67] It would be ingenuous to believe that an executive campaign lasting only a year could have eliminated the time-honored corruption, fraud, and inefficiency among government employees.[68] The president without doubt strained the government's resources to pay the troops regularly and in full, but Rocafuerte admitted privately that he was not entirely successful. In the provinces of Imbabura and Loja the troops were unpaid at the very moment when the president declared they had been paid in full. A few months later the important Second Battalion at Cuenca was reported to be restless because it had received neither pay nor rations.[69]

Yet another serious fiscal problem, glossed over by Rocafuerte in his effort to convince the Congress of the striking success of his reforms, was the enormous foreign debt. While admitting that the foreign obligations amounted to 13 million pesos—more than ten times the domestic debt—the president assured the legislators that it was a small sum that could easily be handled with the benefit of the great amount of gold and silver soon to be produced at Pillzhum and elsewhere. Unfortunately the precious metals did not pour forth from the mines and the British bondholders showed little interest in the government lands and colonization projects offered to them. As a result the government could not meet its obligations to foreign creditors.[70]

The Congress of 1837 that listened to the president's defense of his policies met in a political atmosphere charged with excitement. Most of the legislators resented Rocafuerte's policies and were determined to turn matters around. They regarded the Decrees of 10 February as an unconstitutional arrogation of power, and they strongly condemned the administration's policy of friendship toward the dictatorship of Santa Cruz in Peru. Though political parties had not yet formed in Ecuador, the opponents of Rocafuerte had voiced their discontent to each other, and many wished to take drastic action against the president. General Flores, now a member of the Senate and in Quito once more, was elected president of the upper chamber and quickly assumed the role of leader of the opposition.[71] The stage was thus set for a confrontation between the general and the president.

Some of Rocafuerte's harshest critics begged Flores to oust the president by force, but the general declined invitations to lead an uprising on the grounds that the use of violence would damage his reputation and set a bad example for the nation. After rejecting a forceful solution Flores agreed to a plan for a "legal revolution" that called for the impeachment and removal of the chief executive and his ministers, the voluntary resignation of the vice-president, and the installation of an unnamed person as the new president. In all probability, if the "legal revolution" had been executed, the new chief of state would have been General Flores.[72]

President Rocafuerte, who got wind of the cabal, at first seemed to play into the hands of his enemies. In an ill-tempered address to the Congress the chief executive portrayed himself as the champion of virtue, accused the legislature of harboring agents of corruption, and depicted the Ecuadorian people as incredibly backward, ignorant, and superstitious. Congressmen naturally took umbrage at the president's ill-chosen words, and the Senate sent a formal reply to Rocafuerte expressing surprise and regret over the "unusual and alarming remarks" and warning that the upper chamber would not submit to a diminution of its "dignity or firmness."[73]

Sensing that he faced overwhelming opposition to his administration and that he might be removed from office, Rocafuerte decided to back away from the confrontation by making concessions. Before Congress had completed a week of deliberations the president announced that he had accepted the resignations of his ministers of war and finance.[74] This action probably saved Rocafuerte from being removed from office by the "legal revolution," but it did not save his program. Congress rescinded the controversial decrees of 10 February, rejected the draft treaty of amity with the Confederation of Peru and Bolivia, and directed the chief executive to attempt to mediate in the war between Chile and Peru.[75] The Senate then impeached the former minister of finance, found him guilty of unconstitutional and illegal acts, and deprived him of citizenship rights for a period of two years. In the lower chamber similar charges were brought against the president, only to be dropped without ultimate impeachment.[76] Congress passed a bill reestablishing the earlier tariff rates, approved a new law on amortization of national debt (passed over the president's veto), and disapproved an executive decree creating a national lottery.[77] In other antagonistic moves Congress forced the president to grant safe-conducts to Valdivieso and other political exiles and adopted a decree law sharply limiting the exercise of extraordinary powers by the chief executive.[78]

It was clear by 1837 that President Rocafuerte had suffered such serious reverses that his power and prestige were in jeopardy. He had, however, outmaneuvered his bitterest enemies on the issue of impeachment and had managed to cling to office. That Rocafuerte would be allowed to serve out his term was conceded by General Flores when he declared to the Senate his prayer that "Providence would grant him [Flores] a long life in order to see a regular alternation in the administrations of the Republic and to demonstrate that he was always firm in his principles."[79] These carefully chosen words not only acknowledged an end to impeachment plans, but also served as public notice that General Flores intended to return to the presidency in two years to carry out a "regular alternation" in the executive office.

In later years Rocafuerte would accuse Flores of "base intrigues" and revolutionary conspiracy in the political events of 1837. The charge of conspiracy was somewhat exaggerated, for the opposition to the administration was quite outspoken. Flores not only openly disagreed with the president but, at a banquet attended by many of the most highly placed persons in government, even engaged in a very heated argument with the chief executive over policy toward Peru.[80] Leaders of the opposition doubtless discussed their strategies and tactics secretly, thus giving a conspiratorial appearance to their activities, but opposition groups, like administrative leaders, frequently require privacy for strategic planning.

Flores explained his role in the events of 1837 by insisting that he had defended the constitution and legal order while rejecting entreaties to lead a military revolt. Though he could truthfully assert that he had not crossed the blurred line of legality, the methods adopted for attempting to oust the president were devious and the tactics were politically disruptive, almost as disruptive as if he had chosen violence. Flores helped to perpetuate fiscal mismanagement in Ecuador by wrecking the treasury reforms of Rocafuerte and Tamariz, reforms that held at least some promise of improving the budgetary situation of the government. Furthermore, the general undermined the president's prudent policy of peace and friendship with Peru. Though a war with the confederation might have provided the general with an opportunity to enhance his military glory, it would have drained the economic and human resources of Ecuador.

General Flores was guilty of opportunism and some degree of irresponsibility in his leadership of the opposition to the administration, for his actions on fiscal problems played into the hands of usurers, contrabandists, and grafters. But Rocafuerte was not above criticism either. As president he behaved in a high-handed manner, issued decrees without authority, and exercised extraordinary powers without congressional approval. His arrogance carried him to the point of seriously considering a dissolution of the Congress of 1837, even though the constitution did not allow for such action by the executive.[81] A more effective leader would have tried to work with the legislature to achieve compromises, but Rocafuerte chose instead to scold the congressmen angrily and then to sulk. Though he was a brilliant man whose enlightened ideas were far ahead of his times, his abrasive manners and his lack of restraint made it impossible for him to work with the Congress to carry out his program of reforms.

Although Rocafuerte managed to fulfill a four-year presidential term, he suffered such a severe loss of respect as a result of his conflicts with the Congress in 1837 that he accomplished little during the balance of his tenure. Deprived of his chief advisers and thwarted in his legislative program, the president presented a forlorn figure in the waning months of his administration. He stayed on as chief executive only because General Flores declined to sanction a military revolt.

Discontent was so widespread in Ecuador that Rocafuerte was obliged to be on almost constant alert against uprisings. In such a political climate it was natural that Flores would be the subject of many rumors. The president sent a steady stream of letters to the general, always addressing him as "my dear friend" or "my dear *compadre*," for the purpose of preventing another rupture with the powerful caudillo. On one occasion Rocafuerte wrote to the general that there were reports of new intrigues to make Flores "lifetime President and . . . to elevate your family to the rank enjoyed by the Medici in Florence."[82] Though the president scoffed at the rumor, the mere mention of the matter served as a warning to any plotters that their conspiracy was not a secret from the government.

Though nothing came of the rumors of a plot to create a lifetime presidency, the episode was significant nonetheless. Assuming that there was some basis in fact to the rumors, the episode revealed that in the late 1830s some Ecuadorians were toying with the idea of establishing an aristocratic regime under a perpetual executive. It was natural that conservatives harboring such aspirations would think of Flores who had championed monarchy during the last years of Bolívar's rule. Ideas of monocratic government were still alive in Ecuador.

General Flores had evidently decided to abide by constitutional procedures and to wait for his opportunity in 1839 to be properly elected by Congress to a second presidential term. Though his personal relations with the president had cooled considerably, he continued to give public support to the administration. When a serious military uprising occurred in Riobamba in March 1838, the general showed his loyalty by taking command of a military force and marching to the highlands. Though the revolt was suppressed before Flores arrived, the general seized the occasion to denounce the rebels as "criminals" and to praise the administration for its good deeds, and its reconciliation of factions.[83]

Shortly after the Riobamba revolt General Flores decided to pay a visit to the nation's capital and, in his capacity as general-in-chief of the army, to make an inspection tour of new military units. Public demonstrations of enthusiasm greeted the general wherever he went, and his review of troops turned into a triumphal march through the nation.[84] In a private letter to General Santander describing his national tour Flores remarked that he encountered strong discontent with the government, but that the people

calmed down with the hope that in the next term they will have what they want. You cannot believe the protestations of friendship that everyone has made to me.[85]

When Congress assembled in January 1839 Rocafuerte knew that it would soon elect Flores as the next president. Nevertheless, the chief executive decided to present a new and ambitious legislative program of reform, once more according to "the lights of the century." In characteristic form, his address lectured the congressmen on the economic and social problems of the nation. The judicial and financial systems, he said, should be completely overhauled and centralized, and new civil and penal codes ought to be adopted. To bring the military under control, he said, the president should be empowered to remove all officers of the rank of colonel and above, and the separate legal system of the military fuero should be abolished. He also recommended drastic reforms of the Church that included revocation of the ecclesiastical fuero, the gradual elimination of religious orders, and a new law to guarantee the freedom of worship.[86]

It is not easy to ascertain Rocafuerte's purpose in offering such an ambitious and controversial program on the eve of his departure from government. Perhaps he wished to stir up difficulties for his successor. If he had an understanding with Flores that there would be another "alternation" of administration in 1843, he may have been announcing four years in advance his next presidential program. Or, perhaps he simply wished to present a utopian view of an ideal, reformed nation. In any case, most of the legislators, no doubt irritated by many tactless and sarcastic remarks contained in the presidential address, rejected any serious consideration of the presidential proposals.

Bitter and frustrated over his failure to achieve many of his goals in government, Vicente Rocafuerte prepared to vacate the presidency and return to his home in Guayaquil.

6

AN ADMINISTRATION OF
NATIONAL UNITY, 1839–1842

When the Congress of 1839 met in January General Juan José Flores knew that everything was arranged for his succession to the presidency. Predictably, on the last day of the month, the members of Congress cast ballots to select a new chief executive for a four-year term lasting until 1843. General Flores received twenty-nine of thirty-eight votes cast. The weakness of the political opposition to the national caudillo was measured by a scant nine ballots scattered among six minor candidates.[1]

A minimum of controversy attended the selection of Ecuador's third president. The outgoing executive accepted the electoral results and was content to relinquish command. Most members of Congress were favorably disposed toward the general and welcomed his return to the presidential palace. And yet, beneath the surface of presidential politics, trouble was brewing—the result of a hitch in the election of a new vice-president. Vicente Ramón Roca, a merchant and active public figure of Guayaquil, believed that he had a commitment from Flores to be elected to the second highest post in the government, but Congress, for reasons not entirely clear, voted instead for Francisco de Aguirre, a loyal *floreano* (supporter of Flores) from Quito. Roca, a proud and ambitious man who was destined to become president later on, was so offended by the breach of faith that he became an implacable opponent of the new administration.[2]

The selection of Aguirre rather than Roca for vice-president was the product of behind-the-scenes maneuvering over which Flores probably had little control. It is likely that the new president found it necessary to abandon his earlier commitment to

Roca in order to placate highland leaders at the expense of the coast. In any case, the incident served as a reminder of the complexities and the dangers that lurked in presidential politics.

General Flores did not need the Roca episode, however, to remind him of the many problems to be faced. During the preceding four years he had had ample opportunity to meditate on the difficulties confronting a president of Ecuador. In semiretirement he was able to compare his earlier successes and failures as chief executive with those of Rocafuerte. He must have been aware that the second president's broad vision of a reformed and enlightened society surpassed his own rather narrow and limited concepts of the goals of government. There was much to admire in Rocafuerte's proposals to modernize society according to the "lights of the century," but Flores could see, too, that the program of his successor was too ambitious and too controversial for a nation so conservative and contentious as Ecuador. And most of all, he saw that the Guayaquil leader's abrasive and tactless dealings with other leaders in public life stirred up needless strife and often defeated his own proposals.

General Flores' reflections on Ecuador's first eight years of independence prompted him to minimize discord and to emphasize conciliation and accommodation in his new administration. Quite wisely he decided to use the gentle art of persuasion, to avoid giving offense whenever possible, and to attempt to harmonize the various conflicting interests of the nation. National unity became the central theme of the new administration as Flores embarked on his second presidential term.

After taking the oath of office President Flores sounded the keynote of his administration in a brief message to the Congress. Carefully refraining from specific policy proposals, the new chief of state called upon Ecuadorians in public life to put aside hatreds and resentments, and he promised to inspire the confidence of the legislators by his own moderate, frank, and impartial behavior. He would govern strictly in accordance with the constitution, he promised. He would "revere Religion," respect the other branches of government, and guarantee the public credit.[3]

To allay any suspicions of secret plans for a military dictatorship, the new president called upon his comrades in arms to respect "liberal institutions" and to support "the civil authority." More importantly, he declared that "the time had come to resolve the problem of whether Ecuador could be governed without recourse to extraordinary powers." He pledged firmly to respect freedom of the press, to make no arbitrary arrests, and to refrain from exiling citizens without due process, even though the constitution permitted banishment by executive order. Emphasizing his desire for a government of national unity, Flores urged the citizens of the nation to enlighten him with their good counsel and to guide him with "dispassionate criticism."[4]

This soothing rhetoric, though a relief from the caustic presidential messages of the previous four years, could not achieve political harmony unless suitable actions followed. Flores knew that he had many adversaries who would scoff at his generous promises and stir up trouble at the first opportunity. Fortunately for the new administration the opposition was not formed into an organized or cohesive political party, but instead consisted of scattered factions that followed diverse leaders. Some of the opponents occasionally formed into fragmented political clubs and societies. To prevent the fusion of these factions into a united opposition Flores promised a magnanimous policy of appointments to public office based solely on "the merits, aptitudes, and probity" of the candidates. Translated into practical policy this promise meant that the president would use the power of patronage to win the support of many of his foremost opponents. To the astonishment of many, Flores appointed as minister of war a charter member of the Quiteño Libre Society, the aristocratic General Manuel Matheu, longtime political enemy of the new executive. Another major surprise was the selection for the post of minister of finance of Luis de Sáa, a supporter of the Valdivieso revolt of 1833 and a distinguished patriot from the Independence movement of 1809. Francisco Marcos of Guayaquil, minister of the interior and foreign relations, was the lone floreano stalwart in the ministry.[5]

The policy of conciliation and national unity was evident in a number of other administrative actions. José Félix Valdivieso, Flores' first minister of state in 1830 but a formidable opponent and political pariah since his rebellion in 1833, received a safe-conduct to Quito and was welcomed back into the fold. Once elected to the presidency of the Senate in 1841, Valdivieso loyally supported the administration and, in turn, was rewarded with high appointments in the executive branch.[6]

Yet another act of conciliation was the restoration of civil rights to Francisco Eugenio Tamariz, Rocafuerte's first minister of finance, who had been impeached and stripped of his legal rights during the "legal revolution" of 1837. President Flores not only restored the "good fame and reputation" of Tamariz but won his cooperation by offering him attractive posts in the government. The former finance minister accepted the governorship of the province of Cuenca.[7]

Vicente Rocafuerte, of course, was the person of most importance to a successful policy of national unity. Even though the outgoing president had forfeited most of his influence over the Congress, he was still a political figure of consideration. By force of intellect and high social standing Rocafuerte, if he chose, might rally large numbers of citizens to the banners of liberalism and nationalism against a government headed by Flores, a foreign general of obscure social origins. If counted among the government's opponents, the fiery and articulate Rocafuerte was not only capable of inflaming the passions of the people of Guayas against Flores but also of providing leadership of a rebel movement. If friendly to the administration, however, the ex-president would be very useful in maintaining the loyalty of the ever fickle and dangerous coastal region.

The political alliance of Flores and Rocafuerte was based upon mutual need, not friendship. They were an unlikely pair who were pushed together, not drawn together, by their ambition to preside over the government of Ecuador. While in the presidency Rocafuerte had needed the military leadership of the Venezuelan general to control unruly troops. Flores now needed the social prestige and the intellectual grasp of the Guayaquil aristocrat. This uneasy partnership had been dissolved briefly during the tense days of the "legal revolution" in 1837, but it was renewed a few months later by an exchange of letters between the general and the president that reflected their mutual desire to forget the hard feelings of the impeachment crisis and work together once more.[8]

A private understanding to take turns in the presidency was probably at the center of the Flores–Rocafuerte alliance. Historical documents do not reveal the existence of a written agreement between the two men to alternate in power, but strong evidence of such an understanding is to be seen in the actions of both leaders.[9] Rocafuerte's cooperation in the smooth transition to the second Flores administration gives some support to the notion of a private understanding. Additional evidence is provided by General Flores' decision in 1838, just before the commencement of his second presidential term, to have Rocafuerte "elected" to the provincial governorship of Guayas. The governorship of his home province gave the outgoing president a power base during the four-year interim, at the end of which he might expect to return to the highest executive post.[10]

The spirit of "national unity" seemed to flourish as both leaders cooperated and showed marked courtesy toward each other. Rocafuerte, for example, agreed to accept the post of governor only as proof of his "affectionate friendship" for the general, and he expressed regret that Flores had inconvenienced himself to such a degree in order to arrange the gubernatorial election in Guayas. Flores in his inaugural address praised his "illustrious predecessor" and begged him to "enlighten me with his advice and to help me with his cooperation."[11] A few weeks after the inauguration President Flores took the trouble to accompany Rocafuerte a few miles along the road to Guayaquil and to entertain him with a lavish farewell banquet at a large country estate.[12]

From 1839 to early 1843 the Flores–Rocafuerte collaboration continued, though somewhat unsteadily at times. Remaining true to form, Rocafuerte produced a spate of letters to the president in which he lectured his ally on the evils besetting the nation, recommended candidates for appointments, and offered paternal advice on national policy. He reported on his efforts to eliminate fraud from the customhouse at Guayaquil, scolded Flores for ordering expenditures that exceeded the meager revenues of the port, warned that clergymen of Cuenca, Guayaquil, and Quito were plotting against the government, and urged the president to avoid war with New Granada and Peru over border disputes. Though there were occasional disagreements, especially regarding a renewed dispute with New Granada over Pasto, the two leaders got along surprisingly well during the first half of the presidential term. General Flores, intent on his policy of national unity, showed remarkable patience and tolerance in his dealing with the complaints and dire warnings from the governor.[13]

One of the most interesting discordant notes marring the harmony between Flores and Rocafuerte concerned the possible need to exercise extraordinary powers. The "liberal" governor of Guayas argued repeatedly that the president should rule autocratically "like the Spaniards." "Only a firm and vigorous authority," warned the governor, "can contain the aspirations of ambition."[14] "The only way to maintain a government in America," Rocafuerte asserted, "and to save the people from the bloody claws of the ferocious restorers of liberty and the fatherland is with clubs, clubs, and more clubs."[15] On yet another occasion the Guayas governor recommended the "energetic government" of Chile and the bloody dictatorship of Juan Manual Rosas of Argentina as suitable models, even though they bordered on "despotism or ferocious tyranny."[16]

Rocafuerte reasoned that dictatorship in Ecuador was necessary because of the conspiracies and machinations of fanatical opponents who would stop at nothing to overturn the government. The "popular masses," he said, were "too weighed down with vices and ignorance" to be ready for the enjoyment of liberty. Only a regime that would impose discipline and development could prepare Ecuador for a truly liberal government in the future, argued the governor of Guayas.[17]

President Flores' actions make it clear that he rejected this counsel of despair, for he preferred to exercise only the normal and regular powers granted by the constitution and wished to refrain from autocratic rule if possible. It was ironic that the liberal and cultivated civilian leader of the coast should have urged monocratic rule upon a professional military leader who only a decade or so earlier had been a spokesman for monarchism under Bolívar. Though Flores no doubt received Rocafuerte's calls for a government of force with a fair degree of sympathy and understanding, he was not yet ready to accept such advice. Despite the continued suggestions of monocracy and monarchy, Flores had committed himself to support the liberal institutions established under Ecuador's constitutions since 1830. He wished, at least for the nonce, to give republicanism a fair trial.

Flores apparently believed that the promotion of national unity through the conciliation of rival factions and the forgiveness of former adversaries would achieve political harmony. To a limited extent the president's magnanimity toward old foes and his cooperative spirit seemed to promise a new era of good feelings after the strife and tensions of the first two administrations. But there was no way to soothe all of the politicians and to conciliate all of the rival regions, institutions, and interest groups. In choosing to work with specific public men, such as Rocafuerte, Valdivieso, and Matheu, the president, for example, not only turned Roca permanently against the government but alienated an influential mercantile group in Guayaquil. The appointment of Rocafuerte as governor of Guayas antagonized the clergy who had counted on Flores for protection but now feared that the new administration would carry out Rocafuerte's most radical proposals to separate church and state and to abolish the clerical fuero.[18]

As the governor of Guayas Rocafuerte sent frequent reports to the president of dangerous activities carried on by the government's opponents. He cautioned that there were some "very suspicious persons" who had been aroused by libelous rumors disseminated from Quito. It was whispered about, wrote Rocafuerte, that the government planned to expel all of the regular clergy, seize the property of the monasteries and convents, and legalize divorce. In the governor's opinion, these false reports were the work of a secret society intent upon undermining the government.[19]

Flores was not inclined to take the warnings of conspiracy at face value. He replied to the governor that all was quiet in the highlands and that he anticipated undisturbed rule for at least two years. Rocafuerte saw no grounds for such optimism. "In the political societies now forming in Quito, Cuenca, etc. I see only new fields of intrigue open to ambition and unbridling of passions," the governor declared, "a new freemasonry without secrets or wry faces, and new clubs of our modern Jacobins."

Ecuadorians in exile planned to return to engage in subversive politics, in Rocafuerte's opinion, and other political adversaries hoped to arrange a clandestine intervention in Peruvian affairs. As for the Congress that had just placed Flores in the presidency once more, Rocafuerte warned that the legislators had laid a trap by empowering the chief executive to solve the problems of budgetary deficits without at the same time authorizing him to dismiss dishonest government employees.[20]

As usual, Rocafuerte exaggerated the dangers of the opposition. It was true, of course, that many Ecuadorians had rejected the olive branch tendered by the president, but the country was relatively tranquil. The governor's warning against a snare set by Congress was quite misleading, for it would have been unconstitutional for the legislators to grant the president authority to remove government employees arbitrarily.[21]

Quite possibly Rocafuerte wished to stir up trouble between Flores and the lawmakers. If so, he did not succeed, for the president pursued a policy of cordiality toward the Congress of 1839 which was remarkably effective in producing a climate of goodwill. Shunning his predecessor's aggressive approach to legislation, Flores chose to ignore Rocafuerte's sweeping reform proposals and to suggest new laws only in the most general terms. By submitting few specific requests to the Congress he reduced the chances for friction and bad feelings.[22] Unfortunately this easygoing policy produced relatively little legislation.

If the price of political harmony was to be legislative stagnation, President Flores was not prepared to refrain indefinitely from exercising more dynamic leadership. The treasury was empty. The economy of the coast was improving somewhat, but highland agriculture and industry languished. Public education, the armed forces, and the oppressed Indian population, in the opinion of the president, also presented problems requiring the urgent attention of the government.

Flores, therefore, prepared an ambitious and controversial agenda for the new Congress that convened in January 1841. In his address to the senators and representatives the president laid out a broad program of recommendations. Among the less controversial items were requests to add a fifth justice to the Supreme Court (to avoid tie votes), to improve the police force, and to balance the budget. A proposal to expand and strengthen the public elementary school system was more polemical because of its cost and its expected effect upon the Catholic Church.[23]

Still more controversial were two major proposals to modify the basic tax structure of the nation. The first of these requested the enactment of a higher tariff to protect highland agriculture and manufacturing, a measure that was bound to arouse antagonism between coast and sierra.[24] The second proposal called for a fundamental overhaul of the tax structure to do away with the "monstrous inequity" of Indian tribute. Flores urged the congressmen either to abolish the special tax on Indians and to replace it with a tax on wealth, or to extend the head tax to all citizens so that Indians would no longer carry a disproportionate burden. It was not fair, declared the president, to force the neediest part of the population to pay a heavy tax while almost half of the people "neither pay nor contribute anything."[25]

To propose a fundamental social and fiscal reform such as the abolition of Indian tribute required considerable courage, if not temerity, in the conservative social climate of Ecuador in the 1840s. Both Flores and Rocafuerte had failed during the preceding administrations to modify the tribute system significantly, partly because the treasury required the revenues and partly because whites and mestizos regarded tribute as an important symbol of the Indian's inferiority.[26] Thus, any proposal to modify the ancient tax on Indians was certain to stir up vigorous opposition both in Congress and among the politically active elements of society at large. In proposing to reform both the tribute and the tariff systems at once President Flores put himself on a collision course with the lawmakers.

Whether the chief executive could have succeeded in putting his program of reform through Congress in 1841 will never be known. Probably he would have failed on the major issues. But a test of wills between the executive and legislative branches did not take place, because the Chamber of Representatives failed to muster a quorum and could not conduct legislative business.[27]

Profoundly disappointed over the dissolution of Congress for lack of a quorum, the president withdrew somewhat from public life and tended to neglect presidential responsibilities in the middle years of his second term. Flores developed the habit of absenting himself from Quito for prolonged periods, sometimes to take command of the troops, but also for unspecified reasons at other times. Under article 63 of the constitution executive authority was to be delegated to the vice-president or his designee when the president was absent.[28] As a consequence Vice-President Aguirre served as acting president for many months in 1840 and 1841. Quite possibly General Flores was following the unfortunate example of Bolívar, who habitually occupied himself with military affairs and ceremonies of state while delegating responsibility for day-to-day operations of government to subordinates. Perhaps, too, like Bolívar, Flores wished to place himself in a lofty position, above the political fray and removed from the ordinary functionaries, so that he might enjoy the splendor and the adulation associated with supreme office.

Though President Flores did not exercise rigorous executive leadership, he did at least attempt to carry out some of the general program that he had outlined in his address to Congress on assuming high office in 1839. In the field of public education, for example, he issued a series of executive decrees and orders intended to improve the public education system. He placed the elementary schools under a separate administration, created a new normal school, imposed the Lancasterian system of mutual instruction on all primary schools, and directed that schools be established in all cantons of the nation.[29]

The Flores administration gave continued financial support to the military academy created by Rocafuerte, and took steps to improve the university. Flores reestablished the chairs of chemistry and botany (which had been vacated under Rocafuerte) and secured authority from Congress to bring to the university three foreign professors "of sciences, arts, and professions." He also helped establish a school of obstetrics to train midwives and ordered the conversion of an army barracks into a school of mechanical arts and crafts.[30] As a sidelight on intellectual developments of this period, it should be noted that historical knowledge was advanced in 1841–1842 by the publication of Juan de Velasco's important three-volume work, *Historia del reino de Quito*. Though the government did not directly subsidize publication of the work, the official newspaper encouraged private subscriptions to help pay the costs.[31]

At the close of his second term the president claimed great progress had been made in education, but his remarks on this subject were so brief and vague that one could guess at the melancholy truth. Most of Flores' educational program consisted of presidential decrees and orders that proclaimed great improvements but achieved relatively little. The "school of arts and crafts" apparently existed only on paper. The military academy had few students and had managed to graduate only two officers in one year. Enrollments in the secondary schools of Quito and in the university were so low that the government had to order reorganization and reductions of the educational system.[32] No doubt some new schools were opened in various towns here and there, but specific information on the number and quality of these schools is lacking. In mid-1840 the condition of the schools in the northern city of Imbabura was so bad that the minister of the interior ordered an investigation and reorganization of the schools, but the results of the order were not published. The city of Ambato complained in 1842 that it had no schools at all and asked for aid from the national government.[33] In 1843 the parish priest of Alangasí founded a primary school for Indian children of the little village, but this was a rare and isolated development that only underscored how little progress the Flores administration had made in the enormous task of providing educational opportunity for the largely illiterate and unschooled population of Ecuador.[34] The obstacles to educational progress were enormous in Ecuador, but greater improvement might have been achieved if the president had been willing to push his administration toward an actual implementation of the many decrees and orders that he signed. At the very least, General Flores might have exerted himself sufficiently to rescue the military academy from neglect and decay. But he did nothing to revive this ailing institution, which closed its doors shortly after Flores fell from power in 1845.[35]

The second Flores administration also made some efforts to promote the general welfare through the application of scientific knowledge and new technology. One such effort was a presidential order to the chief of police in Quito to install two hundred street lights in the city for the purpose of reducing the high crime rate.[36] After a series of damaging earthquakes shook the sierra in November 1840 the government asked Dr. William Jameson, a Scottish naturalist in Quito, to investigate a possible link between the tremors and the great volcanoes of the highlands. Though the results of this study have not come to light, Dr. Jameson carried on botanical research that led to the eventual publication of a major work on the plants of Ecuador.[37] The government also initiated a vaccination program for smallpox in which emphasis was placed on inoculating children, but the government had difficulty obtaining enough vaccine for large numbers of people.[38]

Yellow fever, however, posed a far greater threat to Ecuador, and especially to the city of Guayaquil, than smallpox. Unfortunately there was no vaccine and very little medical knowledge for coping with a severe epidemic of yellow fever which broke out in Guayaquil and its environs in 1842. The port city, notorious for its tropical afflictions, had experienced eruptions of this disease in 1825, 1829, and 1835, but none of them on the scale of the catastrophic scourge of 1842.

Crewmen of a ship from Panama apparently introduced yellow fever into Guayaquil in September. The disease spread rapidly, striking down victims of all social classes by the thousands. The death rate rose quickly to about forty-five per day. As the death toll reached the thousands, panic seized most of the people of Guayaquil. Half of the population fled the disease-ridden city either to the highlands or to the island of Puná in the estuary of the Guayas. Shops and warehouses were boarded up. The streets were emptied of their normal traffic. Commerce came to a standstill except for a few ships that dropped their cargoes at Puná and hastened away to avoid the quarantined harbor of the ravaged city.[39]

Governor Rocafuerte, to his enduring credit, demonstrated heroic dedication and valor during the crisis that gripped the coastal province. Shunning the temptation to flee to the safety of the highlands, he remained at his post to supervise the care of victims and to fight the epidemic as best he could. He established four emergency hospitals for the stricken city, and provided them with doctors, nurses, and medicines, all paid for out of the government treasury.[40] He removed most of the army garrison from the danger area, instituted special police patrols in the partially deserted city, and arranged for carts to carry bodies to the cemetery. In the erroneous belief that burning the personal effects of victims would prevent the disease from spreading, the governor had mattresses and bedroom furniture carted out of the city for incineration. Even though personal relations between Flores and Rocafuerte were not good at this time, the emergency spurred the president to send provisions and medicines and to offer to go to Guayaquil in person if the governor should be taken ill with the fever. The president and his wife also organized a charity fund to provide aid for the families of the victims.[41]

Given the state of medical knowledge of the times, Rocafuerte and Flores could do little against the disease other than to comfort the victims. The epidemic simply ran its course until it finally disappeared in 1845. Its effects were measured not only in the high death toll but also in the disruption of the economic and political life of the normally thriving and dynamic port city. Commerce declined sharply as a result of the absence of most merchants and foreign vessels. The lucrative exports of cacao and other products fell off and imports were curtailed. Customs revenues declined markedly, putting pressure on the national treasury.[42]

Acting on the advice of Governor Rocafuerte and borrowing a practice of Spain in the eighteenth century, President Flores urged citizens of the principal cities to form private associations called Sociedades de Amigos del País (Societies of Friends of the Nation). By means of these societies Flores hoped to stimulate the "spirit of association" that in turn would effect material progress through local and private initiative.[43] In the highlands the experiment worked badly. With most capital tied up in land, and without any banks, it was difficult to mobilize venture capital in the sierra for expanding the road system and developing manufacturing. But on the coast, especially around the dynamic commercial city of Guayaquil, it was another story. In this region, with the active support of the national government and of Governor Rocafuerte, Ecuadorian and foreign businessmen promoted a very significant economic expansion, dampened only by the short-lived yellow fever recession. The coastal prosperity was based upon a thriving trade in cacao and upon the application of steam power to economic purposes.

In 1841 the first steamship constructed on the Pacific coast slid into the River Guayas from the Guayaquil shipyards. A short railroad was constructed at Chonana, and steam power was introduced to bale cotton, grind sugar cane, and operate a saw mill. Governor Rocafuerte helped establish a lighthouse in the estuary and began improvements in Guayaquil's water-front.[44] In October 1841 the first ship of William Wheelwright's Pacific Steam Navigation Company arrived at Guayaquil, thus providing Ecuador with regular steamer service to all major west-coast ports.[45]

The arrival of the Steam Age in Ecuador coincided with a major expansion of foreign trade spearheaded by a surge in the exports of cacao. Increased shipping on the west coast and rising cacao prices accounted for much of the upswing in Ecuador's international commerce, but the Flores administration could justly claim some credit for the advance by virtue of the new commercial treaty signed with Spain early in 1840. Reestablishment of trade ties with the mother country brought rapid growth of exports to Spain, especially of cacao. This new demand for the chocolate bean raised the prices from two pesos to four (and even to five pesos for a short time) per *carga* (eighty-one pounds) between 1839 and 1844, bringing a bonanza to the planters of the Guayas region. Though the yellow fever epidemic and a poor harvest in 1844 caused a brief downturn in exports, the coast enjoyed unprecedented commercial prosperity under Flores' second administration.[46] However, efforts by the national government to spread the prosperity to the north coast by declaring the small maritime community of San Lorenzo a free port failed because the government did not succeed in building a projected cart road from the northern port to Quito.[47]

Though the declared value of exports and imports doubled between 1839 and 1846, customs receipts did not keep pace with the rising volume of trade. Collections rose by about 33 percent from 1839 to 1842, but by 1846 they had fallen to 78 percent of the 1839 figure.[48] A major reason for the poor performance of the customhouse was the large amount of smuggling that went on. Contrabandists' activities, which dated back to the earliest days of Spanish rule, were not only costly to the treasury but difficult to stop. Governor Rocafuerte reported to Flores on the widespread nature of illicit commerce of the Guayas region and attempted to make customs collections more efficient, but he could not stamp out the abuse. Rocafuerte believed that better management of the customhouse and greater vigilance would increase government collections by about forty-eight thousand pesos per year. If it is assumed that such measures would have eliminated about one-half of the contraband, then the annual value of revenue losses in Guayaquil must have amounted to about one hundred thousand pesos, or approximately one-quarter of customs collections.[49] Unfortunately, the national government's decision to develop the northern port of San Lorenzo aggravated the problem by providing contrabandists with a ruse to evade tariff payments legally. Since San Lorenzo was a free port without a road to the interior, shippers landed their cargoes at the northern port free of duties and then transshipped them to Guayaquil. Though President Flores issued a decree prohibiting this abuse and others, smuggling continued more or less as before.[50]

The loss of potential customs receipts through contraband was only a modest part of the general problem of the national treasury which had plagued Ecuador since independence and which still showed no signs of abating in the 1840s. When Flores took command in 1839 he appointed the highly respected Luis de Sáa to preside over the ministry of finance and to cope with the perennial problems of attempting to balance revenues and expenditures. Large sums of taxes were unpaid and delinquent taxpayers escaped the law. A severe shortage of funds not only made it impossible to pay full salaries to the military and civil servants, but prevented urgently needed repairs to dilapidated jails and hospitals.[51]

Responding to a presidential request for emergency action on the budgetary crisis, Congress authorized the chief executive to reduce government expenditures, to pay one-third of government salaries in paper bills rather than coin, to reform the troublesome estanco system, and to require that a greater por-

tion of customs duties be collected in cash. Armed with this
authority, Flores reduced expenditures by cutting salaries of
some civil servants, eliminated some positions entirely, reestablished the tobacco monopoly, and ordered provincial governors
to economize. Though these measures were not drastic, they
did permit the government to weather the fiscal crisis inherited
from the previous administration.[52]

Congress and the president also approved a new Basic Law
of the Treasury that included reforms in accounting methods,
but none of the changes adopted between 1839 and 1843
brought either fundamental or substantial improvements. Provincial treasury people and governors, with the notable exception of the upright Rocafuerte, often proved to be useless in
implementing reforms. Lax methods of tax collection, irregularities in accounts, and illegal issues of the forbidden libranzas
continued as in the past. There were occasional crackdowns,
but they produced no long-term benefits. Little had changed in
the fiscal operations of the government since 1830.[53]

The circulation of counterfeit money and the bootlegging of
aguardientes were two more problems that bedeviled the nation
during Flores' second administration. In May 1840 the government began a program to stamp out illicit liquor sales, but the
highland bootleggers were as evasive and as resourceful as the
smugglers in Guayaquil. At the end of a year and a half of exertions to wipe out contraband liquor traffic, the minister of finance learned that almost all distillers in the province of Cuenca
were still bootlegging at least a part of their liquor production.[54]
The executive branch also attempted to eliminate counterfeit
money, but with no more success than in the case of bootlegging.
Spurred by shortages of legitimate coinage and the absence of
banks to facilitate credit, the evil proliferated in many parts of
the nation, but most alarmingly in Guayaquil. Governor Rocafuerte warned that false coins had become so important in the
financial transactions of the port city that it would be dangerous
to eliminate their use. Nevertheless, the president and his finance minister persisted in their efforts to combat counterfeiting, but even the threat of capital punishment did not deter the
criminals.[55] Ultimately Flores yielded to Rocafuerte's suggestion
that counterfeit pesos be legitimized to avoid a financial panic,

but when the government issued two hundred thousand new paper pesos to cover the redemption of counterfeit currency the new paper bills were promptly counterfeited.[56]

Years later when Rocafuerte was exiled in Peru he denounced Flores bitterly for wild extravagance and fiscal mismanagement.[57] Undoubtedly there was some truth in the charges, for the second Flores administration was responsible for waste in some instances, such as the addition of a large number of inactive army officers to the payroll. However, the president offered the plausible argument that this action was taken to conciliate military leaders who might rebel if denied gainful employment.[58] Rocafuerte also charged that General Flores became extremely wealthy in office by intriguing with "usurers, corregidores, and tithe collectors." The former president pointed out that Flores built himself luxurious houses in Quito, one popularly called the Villa of Pleasure (Quinta del Placer) and the other Robber's Palace (Palacio del Robo), both at public expense. Rocafuerte also claimed that Flores used public money to import costly furniture and paintings for his residences and expensive machinery for his haciendas. Although Rocafuerte's anger at Flores doubtless led him to exaggerate his criticisms, there must be much truth in this picture of presidential graft and high living at public expense.[59]

In the absence of detailed treasury records of the period there is no way to determine just how much money was diverted from the treasury by the greedy president. There is one instance, however, of treasury accounts published in the official newspaper in 1846 which reveal that in 1840 Flores arranged to receive an eighty-thousand-peso rebate clandestinely from the settlement of a Spanish claim of almost one hundred fifty thousand pesos which was honored by the Flores administration. Although the accounts were published by a regime hostile to Flores, and the treasury records in question are no longer available for examination, the evidence is so detailed and credible that it is very difficult to believe in the president's innocence. A bribe of eighty thousand pesos was an enormous sum of money at that time, as can be seen from the fact that the president's official salary was twelve thousand pesos per year, a very handsome income in itself. Flores' secret profit from this transaction amounted to almost 7 percent of the national budget.[60]

Since Flores appears to have been the leading grafter, it is obvious that his administration was not as efficient in rooting out graft as it might have been. But honesty alone would not have balanced the government's books, for Rocafuerte, whose integrity in financial matters was very high, had demonstrated in his presidential term how difficult it was to overcome institutionalized corruption and inefficiency. It was unfortunate, of course, that President Flores did not earnestly continue the struggle initiated by Rocafuerte. Even so, the second Flores administration achieved modest improvements in finance over previous years. Though the national debt was not materially reduced and no payments were made to foreign creditors, the treasury managed to make cash payments of two-thirds of government salaries in 1840 and 1841, a healthy advance over the fifty-fifty payments in cash and paper money of earlier years. Improved fiscal conditions permitted President Flores to boast to Congress in 1841 that his administration had been able to wage a military campaign in Pasto without resorting to extraordinary exactions of any kind. We know that the government's credit recovered somewhat because the discount on treasury bills declined from 70 to 60 percent. The yellow fever epidemic, however, reduced revenues from commerce and put a squeeze on the treasury during the last year of Flores' second term.[61]

Relations between the state and the Church posed yet another difficulty for the Flores administration. The issue here was not the personal integrity of the president but rather the political question of how to dispel a climate of suspicion and ill will between the clergy and most of the nation's political leaders. Church–state relations had not been good during Flores' first presidential term, but they were much better than relations under his successor, Rocafuerte, who provoked the clergy into organizing an active opposition to the government. It was generally recognized that General Flores, though a Mason, was more moderate and flexible in his views toward the Church than was the second president, but Flores' open collaboration with Rocafuerte persuaded the more intransigent clergy that there was little to choose between the two leaders.

Ecclesiastical leaders appear to have overlooked the fact that most of Flores' policies toward the Church were benign. Flores did not seek to separate church and state, to abolish the religious orders, or to terminate the clerical fuero. He hoped to establish harmonious relations with the prelates, though he disapproved of the disorderly and licentious behavior of a great part of the Ecuadorian clergy. The bishops ignored the president's goodwill and focused instead on his insistence on guarding the patronal rights of the state. Defense of the patronato led President Flores to engage in a lengthy quarrel with the Papacy over the appointment of a new bishop in Cuenca. This dispute provoked widespread clerical hostility toward the government over the issue of alleged state intervention in ecclesiastical affairs.[62]

More friction occurred when the Flores administration, with the active support of Congress, attempted to reform the decadent monastic orders of Ecuador. Laws were adopted setting limits on the number of members permitted in the religious orders, requiring the regular clergy to reside in their monasteries, forbidding alienation of monastic property, and establishing procedures for the renunciation of vows.[63] Though such legislation was indeed a form of state intervention in ecclesiastical affairs, it was largely symbolic. To enforce the new laws the government called upon the bishops to carry out investigations (*visitas*), which produced no tangible improvements in monastic discipline, largely because the bishops did not wish to reform the corrupt orders.[64] The government shut down one small religious order that lacked funds for proper communal life, seized the property of some friars who refused to pay taxes, and briefly imprisoned a handful of monks who had sent an insulting message to Congress.[65] These actions and a few others taken against the regular clergy did not reflect a strong anticlericalism on the part of Flores. A request from the executive branch to the Senate in 1843 to study the possibility of readmitting to Ecuador the previously banished Jesuits showed that the president was willing to permit the return of the most active and influential religious order—hardly a sign of hostility toward the Church.[66]

Flores' moderation toward the Church was not appreciated by the priesthood, chiefly because the clergy resented any governmental intervention at all in the problem of ecclesiastical abuses that had been institutionalized during the long colonial period. As tensions between church and state grew, a number of zealous priests began a movement to build an organized political opposition to the government. Though political activity by the priesthood appeared in many parts of the country, the conservative and pious city of Cuenca became the center of the most zealous opponents of the government.[67]

The climate of hostility between ecclesiastical and secular authorities worsened with the appearance of several opposition newspapers that worked to arouse public opinion against the government. Governor Rocafuerte, always ready for a fight with the Church, became alarmed and persuaded the president to provide secret funding for an ostensibly private newspaper, *La Balanza,* to defend the administration and attack its critics. As editor of the subsidized paper Rocafuerte selected an itinerant publicist of Guatemalan origin, Antonio José de Irisarri.[68]

Irisarri's pen, declared the governor of Guayas, would defend the administration with more force than "a regiment of lancers."[69] The Guatemalan writer was a talented and experienced person, but his selection as the editor of *La Balanza* proved a disaster for the president's policy of national unity. Irisarri's love of controversy and his penchant for attacking the enemy frontally led him into journalistic polemics that alienated readers and sometimes embarrassed the government. The most damaging of these controversies occurred when the columns of *La Balanza* excoriated the clergy of Cuenca for intervening in national politics. This attack provoked Fray Vicente Solano, an irascible clerical publicist, to reply to Irisarri with great vigor. A lengthy and clamorous polemic ensued, often couched in unbecoming language and replete with personal insults. Since it was an open secret that *La Balanza* enjoyed governmental support, both Rocafuerte and Flores were hurt by the journalistic wrangle. Not surprisingly, Irisarri's newspaper folded after government funding was withdrawn.[70]

Though the disaffected clergy constituted a major force within the political opposition, there were also secular leaders who possessed enough strength and money to found newspapers and to develop serious electoral challenges to the administration. When the opposition organized a political offensive for the primary elections of late 1839, the government defended itself by founding yet another proadministration paper, *El Poder de los principios,* and by using the journalistic power of the existing *Gaceta del Gobierno.* When the government's publicity campaign appeared incapable of preventing possible victories by the opposition, the Flores administration then decided to enfranchise the troops and march them to the polls to vote wherever needed.[71]

The political opposition learned from this experience late in 1839 that Flores' policy of national unity did not mean that the government intended to allow fair play in elections. The government was determined to win by fair means or foul.[72] Of course, the managed election of 1839 was not novel, but the opposition was nonetheless infuriated by the hypocrisy of an administration that pledged strict adherence to the constitution and then combatted its political adversaries with secretly subsidized newspapers and illegal votes.

Personal criticism of the president by the opposition press added to the hard feelings generated by the electoral campaign late in 1839. Articles in the antiadministration *El Popular* referred to Flores as a "foreigner" and raised the touchy subject of the assassination of Marshal Sucre. Nothing could arose the president's ire more quickly than reminders of his Venezuelan origin and of his possible involvement in Sucre's killing. Though Flores claimed that he suffered "defamations and libels" of this sort "with patience and resignation," he evidently ordered the editors of the *Gaceta* and *La Balanza* to reply to the partisan attacks on him. Both newspapers not only defended the chief executive but assailed the offending *El Popular* for lack of "morality." The journalistic discussion of the Sucre affair must have caused tongues to wag all the more, for both *La Balanza* and the *Gaceta* continued to publish articles and editorials which implicated General Obando in the infamous crime.[73]

In defending the president from partisan criticism *La Balanza* and *El Poder de los principios* addressed themselves to the larger issue of the role of the political opposition in a republic. Both papers accused opposition editors of libel and "abuses of liberty." *El Poder de los principios* set forth the interesting opinion that in a monarchy "under which the magistrate possesses titles of hereditary legitimacy," a systematic opposition may be permitted with-

out danger to public security, but in "democratic republics" like
Ecuador such opposition is unacceptable because "it weakens . . .
the authority of the executive."[74] This assertion was debatable,
but the signifance of the statement lay in the fact that a spokesman for the administration was arguing publicly that monarchical government was superior to republicanism in that it could
better tolerate political opposition because the prestige of a legitimate monarch is much more secure than that of a republican
president. Here was a hint that people in the administration,
perhaps the president himself, had begun to compare the relative strengths and weaknesses of monarchies and republics.

An editorial in *La Balanza* adopted a somewhat different tack
by assailing the "spirit of party" as unacceptable. Partisan spirit,
declared the Guayaquil paper, "is always unjust when the party
is not tolerant or reasonable." "Parties," went on *La Balanza*,
"produce nothing but animosity, rancor, and vengefulness."[75]
Irisarri's newspaper was thus warning the opposition, in a
slightly indirect manner, that the administration was not disposed to permit the development of an organized, vocal party
that might challenge the government at the ballot box.

Journalistic warnings, however, did not intimidate the anti-
Flores groups. During the year 1840 clerical leaders and the
followers of Vicente Ramón Roca in Guayaquil worked assiduously behind the scenes to build support for antiadministration
candidates in the congressional elections to be held late in the
year. Reviving the 1837 slogan of a "legal revolution," they
aimed at winning control of the national legislature scheduled
to meet in January 1841.[76]

The administration, aware of the continuing danger posed
by its adversaries, mustered its own forces in a determined effort to maintain control of the new Congress. The advantages
of incumbency were considerable, and the Flores regime did
not scruple to use its position of power to assure electoral victories. Military commanders and provincial governors loyal to the
administration could be counted on to use their strong influence to gain a favorable outcome. Intimidation of voters and
candidates, violation of the secrecy of voting, and improper
manipulation of electoral assemblies were among the methods
used by the government to maintain control. Of course, the

political opposition was not immaculate in its methods either, for its leaders were accused of trying to permit illiterate Indians to vote, of having priests preach politically partisan sermons, and of creating disorders in the electoral assemblies. Apparently the worst abuses occurred in the conservative city of Cuenca where the clerical party was well organized and very active.[77]

At the conclusion of the voting it was clear that the government had won a substantial majority in both houses of Congress, but, surprisingly, opposition candidates dominated in the highland provinces of Pichincha and Imbabura, and the elections of Cuenca were in dispute.[78] However, the administration's victory was precarious, because quarrels over electoral methods and ballot-counting soon led to a legislative paralysis and to the worst political crisis since the Revolution of the Chihuahuas. The first indication of trouble brewing came in December 1840 when the administration attempted to convene an extraordinary meeting of the new Congress to deal with urgent business such as the consideration of a pending treaty with Spain. Opponents of the government managed at this time to prevent the attainment of a quorum, thus blocking the extraordinary session.[79] When members of Congress assembled in January 1841, this time in ordinary session, it appeared at first that the impasse could be broken. But the opposition, led by clerical forces, challenged the credentials of the congressmen from Cuenca on the grounds that the government had manipulated the elections by fraud and intimidation. Evidence of wrongdoing was so strong that both chambers, though dominated by nominally proadministration majorities, voted to annul the Cuenca elections.[80]

Cancellation of the elections in Cuenca immediately produced a legislative crisis, because it left both chambers without a quorum.[81] For more than a month pro-Flores senators and representatives attempted to achieve a quorum, but opposition legislators, some of them from Pichincha Province, declined to fill the quorum by attending. The president, for his part, turned aside a request from the legislature to order new elections in Cuenca as a means of supplying the numbers needed for a quorum. General Flores offered elaborate legalistic reasons against ordering new elections, but his arguments sounded hollow in view of the fact that he had condoned the obviously illegal votes of illiterate soldiers.[82]

When the Congress of 1841 finally disbanded without having mustered a quorum, political opponents blamed President Flores for the "scandal" and strongly implied that his continued rule was unconstitutional.[83] Flores responded that the demise of Congress was the result of the unfortunate cancellation of the Cuenca elections, which he had opposed.[84] Thus, he implied that it was a case of legislative suicide, not murder by the executive. Amid charge and countercharge a dispassionate observer might have noted hypocrisy and intransigence on both sides.

One of the charges circulating by word of mouth was that General Flores had engineered the legislative collapse in order to perpetuate his personal rule in Ecuador. Fearful of an adverse public reaction, Flores announced his "determination not to retain command for one day more than the presidential term." As proof of his "obedience and submission" he pledged to quit the presidency on 10 September 1843.[85] This solemn promise, though uttered in apparent sincerity, would not be honored when the president's term of office drew to a close.

The dissolution of the legislature in 1841 was a major setback for the Flores administration. Not only did it demonstrate the failure of the president's policy of national unity, but it also raised serious questions in Flores' mind about the efficacy of representative government. But his disappointment with political developments did not lead him to establish a dictatorship during the remainder of his term. Though critics, among them Rocafuerte, would later accuse Flores of dictatorial rule at this time, there is no evidence to support such charges. Rather than resorting to a government of force, the president broadened the base of consultation within the executive branch by creating new "auxiliary commissions," by appointing prestigious citizens to high posts, and by convoking an extraordinary meeting of Congress in 1842. These actions were certainly not indicative of a president bent upon making himself the military dictator of Ecuador.[86]

Flores' attempt to convene an extraordinary Congress in

1842 was no more successful than the failed effort of the preceding year. A quorum could not be attained because the membership of the Congress remained unchanged, and the earlier political problems were still unresolved.[87] The failure for a second time in a year of the legislative branch to function raised serious questions about the suitability of the Constitution of 1835 and even, in the mind of the president, about the usefulness of respresentative government.

Flores' doubts about republicanism, harbored by him since the late 1820s, now began to assert themselves once more. Though the president has left no journal or other record expressing his private thoughts during the governmental crisis, enough information about his thoughts and actions has survived to make it clear that his earlier belief in monocratic government was revived by what he regarded as the failure of Ecuador's constitutional system in 1841 and 1842. A new meaning could now be seen in the president's declaration in his inaugural address of 1839 that "the time had come to resolve the problem of whether Ecuador could be governed without recourse to extraordinary powers."[88] Flores considered his second term in the presidency an experiment to determine "whether Ecuador could be governed" in a normal, constitutional fashion. Though his own crude mistakes in manipulating elections and refusing to yield to demands for new elections, and his lack of financial integrity, caused some of the most serious difficulties, he did not recognize his own failures. Rather, he convinced himself that republican institutions had failed and that Ecuador's government required drastic changes.[89]

7

THE FRUSTRATIONS OF FOREIGN
AFFAIRS, 1839–1843

In foreign affairs, as in domestic, President Flores began his second term of office with sanguine expectations. To the Congress of 1839 he declared that he sought peace and international understanding. "I shall cultivate frank and faithful relations," he said, "with all the nations that deign to appreciate our friendship." Though these words may have been uttered sincerely, Flores' conduct of foreign policy was anything but "frank and faithful." The goodwill and friendship he vowed to cultivate eluded him because he engaged in aggressive policies aimed at territorial aggrandizement and in secret plots to overthrow the governments of sister republics in South America.

It was ironic that Flores would soon embroil Ecuador in dangerous quarrels with other Spanish American nations, for the prevailing sentiment in Ecuador in 1839 favored fostering close ties with the sister republics formerly under Spanish rule. Ecuadorians had come to feel that their small nation was at the mercy of the great trading nations of the world and that the weak and struggling republics of Hispanic America needed to protect themselves from the great powers. Though the terms "Pan-Hispanic" and "Third World" had not yet been coined, the sentiments emerging in Ecuador clearly reflected the sort of beliefs later associated with movements by small nations to defend themselves against domination by great powers. President Flores gave voice to the views then current when he declared in his inaugural address that "all nations are morally equal" and expressed a desire for harmonious relations with the neighboring nations, "with whom we are linked by natural sympathies, by common principles, and by the ancient and glorious memories of those great deeds of history."[1]

The Ecuadorian Senate, responding to the president's concern about the weakness of small nations, endorsed a resolution authorizing the chief executive to invite other South American governments to an assembly of plenipotentiaries.[2] A little over a year later Flores' minister of foreign relations, Francisco Marcos, responded favorably to an invitation from Mexico to participate in a Pan-Latin-American congress of ministers-plenipotentiary. Marcos offered Guayaquil and Quito as possible sites for the projected meeting. Nothing came of the Mexican proposal, but hints of nascent Pan-Latin-American sentiments cropped up from time to time as the threat of United States aggression against Mexico grew more serious in the early 1840s.[3]

British consul Walter Cope took the trouble to report to his government on the growing antipathy in Ecuador toward "the European powers," and on General Flores' participation in "the prejudices which are becoming the fashion."[4] This view was seconded by James C. Pickett, a diplomat from the United States who arrived in Quito at the outset of Flores' second term. Pickett observed that Ecuadorians "talk much of a S. American system" which, he predicted, "will come to nothing." Pickett went on to say that there was "a feeling decidedly friendly to Spain, and not to other European nations." Some Ecuadorians, he reported, opposed treaties with any non-Hispanic nations, "and if there should be an exception in favor of the United States, it will be because they are regarded as belonging to the American family."[5]

James Pickett's report of Ecuador's friendliness toward Spain was significant, for the Flores regime adopted a policy of rapprochement with the mother country.[6] A treaty of diplomatic recognition between the two countries, long stalled by Rocafuerte's refusal to grant Spain's demands, was signed a year later. It was President Flores' willingness to make special tariff concessions and to recognize the debts of the Audiencia of Quito which made possible the final agreement. The recognition of Ecuador's independence ended the technical state of war between the two nations and fostered an expansion of maritime commerce, especially the cacao trade already noted.[7] The Spanish treaty also brought forth expressions of Pan-Hispanic sentiments. The government newspaper in Quito, probably at the behest of the president, published rhapsodic articles about the common bonds of language, culture, and tradition which linked the nations of the "Spanish race."[8] President Flores sought personally to encourage the spirit of reconciliation with Spain by referring to the treaty of recognition as a "family compact" that united the two nations with "the bonds of blood."[9] Such talk of cultural and racial links to Spain proved to be a prelude to a strange and surprising plan, developed by Ecuador's president in great secrecy, to establish a Spanish-backed monarchy in Quito and to join the two nations dynastically—a plan that would have shocked most Ecuadorians had it been made public.[10]

Spain was not the only European nation that the Flores administration sought to draw closer to. Though Ecuador's president professed to distrust the great world powers, his administration deliberately cultivated harmonious relations with these very nations. The fact that France had recently engaged in aggressive military actions against both Mexico and Argentina did not deter Flores from receiving Jean-Baptiste Washington de Mendeville as the French consul-general. Nor did he hesitate to sign a commercial treaty with France which granted tariff concessions on cacao and other Ecuadorian exports.[11]

A major test of the anti-great-power sentiment was offered by Great Britain, the superpower of the century and the major trading nation at Guayaquil. Once again feelings hostile to great European powers yielded to economic pragmatism when the Flores administration signed two major accords with the British consul. The first of these was a treaty of amity and commerce which was signed only six months after Flores took office, though ratification was long delayed by England because of differences over supplemental articles in the document.[12] The second agreement was a treaty to abolish the Ecuadorian slave trade. Though President Flores approved the pact, which permitted British vessels to detain and search ships suspected of carrying slaves into Ecuadorian ports, it was not ratified for several years because the Ecuadorian legislature of 1843 declined to give its approval.[13] The delays in ratifying both treaties showed that relations with Great Britain were not entirely harmonious, but certainly it could not be said that the Flores administration was antagonistic towards the world's leading maritime power.

The chief obstacle to the establishment of Anglo-Ecuadorian cordiality was not the slave trade—important as the subject was to England—but the debts owed to British bondholders by Ecuador. The acceptance by the preceding administration of a portion of the Gran Colombian debt, amounting to more than a million pounds sterling, placed a staggering obligation on the penurious treasury in Quito. British patience was strained severely when Ecuador assumed large obligations to Spain, and President Flores recommended that preference be given to Spanish creditors over the British. Lord Palmerston, the British foreign secretary, complained bitterly about "defrauding the British creditors" and instructed Consul Cope to warn the Ecuadorian government that failure to meet its financial commitments "might compel H M's Govt. to interfere in a more active manner to obtain redress for H M's subjects." This vague threat was translated into nothing more serious than a letter of complaint from Consul Cope to the Ecuadorian foreign minister. The question of the British bondholders would rankle for many years, but meanwhile Ecuador's trade with Great Britain would grow in volume.[14]

Though the United States probably did not qualify as a "great power" in the late 1830s, its menacing posture toward Mexico had aroused antipathy in Ecuador by the time General Flores assumed the presidency for the second time. Nevertheless, the Flores administration proceeded to negotiate a treaty of amity and commerce with James Pickett, an American diplomatic agent on temporary assignment in Quito. The only delay in reaching an agreement was caused by the United States' insistence on a most-favored-nation clause, which would have denied Flores' desire to grant special commercial privileges to Spain. The problem was soon resolved when Pickett agreed to a qualified most-favored-nation clause that permitted Ecuador to make special concessions to Spain. The North American diplomat had no way of knowing that the provision for a special relationship between Spain and Ecuador would become part of an international monarchical plot that would pose a challenge to the Monroe Doctrine. The treaty with the United States was signed on 13 June 1839 and ratified in April 1842.[15]

Flores' largely cordial and successful transactions with the European powers and the United States were in sharp contrast to his bellicose and frustrating dealings with his closest neighbors, New Granada and Peru. As events were to prove, Pan-Hispanic-American sentiments did not provide sufficient basis for harmony among the Andean nations at this time. The chief obstacle to friendly relations was the persistence of troublesome boundary questions that former President Rocafuerte had wisely chosen to leave unresolved. But General Flores, always the ambitious military man, eager for dramatic action, could not resist the temptation to exploit opportunities to reclaim territories lost in earlier skirmishes with Ecuador's more powerful neighbors to the north and south. If either New Granada or Peru showed evidence of weakness, such as civil strife or foreign difficulties, General Flores was ready to seize the moment to expand Ecuador's borders.

The first opportunity presented itself when disorders erupted in New Granada's southern province of Pasto as a result of the closing of some minor monasteries by authorities. The Bogotá government managed at first to quell the largely religious revolt in 1839 but, when the restless General Obando joined the Pasto rebels in mid-1840, New Granadan authorities had more trouble on their hands than they could handle.[16] General Pedro Alcántara Herrán, in charge of the government's forces in Pasto, decided to invite President Flores to lend Ecuadorian assistance. Herrán knew that it was risky to encourage the entrance of Ecuadorian troops into the region, because it might be difficult to persuade them to leave. Nevertheless, the New Granadan general believed the civil war to be so serious that the gamble was worth taking.[17]

As early as September 1839 General Herrán made his first overture to Flores about possible joint efforts to control the "rebellion of fanaticism" that, he said, might spread into Ecuador. Apparently Flores did not feel that New Granada had yet been weakened enough by civil war to justify a military move, but when Obando joined the fray the Ecuadorian president decided that the right moment had arrived. After ordering a general mobilization in July 1840 he led a force of fifteen hundred troops northward and helped to defeat Obando and his rebels in Pasto.[18]

In a lengthy communiqué President Flores proudly announced the military victory in Pasto and then hurried back to Quito where he was honored by a triumphal welcome and a solemn Te Deum mass in the cathedral.[19] The rejoicing in Quito over the return of the president did not conceal, however, the disagreeable fact that, except for a jeweled sword bestowed upon him by General Herrán, Flores had returned empty-handed. The government of New Granada, bolstered by the defeat of the rebels, felt strong enough to refuse any territorial concessions at all. Flores was furious, for General Herrán, both in correspondence and in face-to-face negotiations, had agreed, albeit reluctantly, to seek approval from the New Granadan congress of a cession of part or all of Pasto. But after their victory over Obando, General Herrán and President Mosquera ignored the commitment, which they probably had never intended to carry out and, in any case, would have been refused by the New Granadan congress.[20]

Though Flores had clearly been outwitted by his northern neighbors, an opportunity for revenge presented itself in 1841 when the troublesome Obando managed once more to raise the standard of revolt in Pasto. Flores rushed northward again with Ecuadorian troops, this time ostensibly to cooperate with Granadan authorities, but with a firmer determination to secure territorial concessions. Resorting to techniques learned a decade earlier, Flores secretly arranged with disaffected citizens of Pasto and Túquerres to publish pronunciamientos requesting annexation of their territory by Ecuador. After occupying the city of Pasto, Flores issued decrees that clearly implied that his government was sovereign in the region.[21] But this effort to seize the region by political cunning and military force failed, for the government of New Granada quickly emerged triumphant over Obando and then confronted the Ecuadorian invaders with superior forces. Flores had no choice but to retreat to Quito. Though the Congress of New Granada subsequently approved an expression of gratitude to General Flores for his "important cooperation" in quelling the insurrection in Pasto, the Bogatá government sternly refused to make any territorial concessions at all.[22]

On behalf of Flores it should be stated that there were some circumstances in the Pasto affair which mitigated his ineptitude somewhat. Insurrections in ill-defined border regions, such as Pasto, make for great nervousness in adjoining nations because of worrisome troop movements near the frontier and because of the tendency of rebels to seek haven and support in the country next door. The danger of contagion was real, for clerical agitation in Pasto against the Bogotá government spread into Ecuador when New Granadan monks and friars fled southward. Soon there were rumors that the discontented clerics were plotting to have Ecuador annex Pasto. There were also reports that enemies of Flores were plotting to use the chaos on the northern frontier to stir up trouble inside Ecuador. Flores' two campaigns in the north did at least help to put an end to such difficulties.[23]

Even so, Flores' forays into Pasto in 1840 and 1841 were costly and humiliating mistakes. The modicum of political stability attained by the suppression of Obando and rebel friars was scarcely worth the cost to the hard-pressed treasury in Quito and the damage to Flores' own reputation. His failure to gain either the promised territorial or monetary recompense severely undercut the president's prestige. Though General Flores had hoped to figure as the military hero of Pasto, he emerged as the artless general who had been twice duped by the faithless leaders of New Granada.

Flores' blunders in the north were compounded by yet another major miscalculation in foreign policy, this one relating to Peru and the problem of Ecuador's southern boundary. At issue were the provinces of Jaén and Maynas, effectively occupied by Peru in the 1830s and 1840s but long claimed by Ecuador on the basis of Gran Colombia's treaty of 1829 with Peru. The accord assigned the disputed region to Gran Colombia. Ecuadorian independence in 1830 caused the region to fall under Quito's sovereignty thereafter. This claim, however, was weakened by a subsequent draft treaty (never properly ratified) between Ecuador and Peru which recognized Peruvian sovereignty in the area. Even though President Flores had his hands full with the Pasto affair, he chose in 1840 to renew Ecuador's claims to Jaén and Maynas and even to risk possible war with Peru, a nation of much greater population and resources than Ecuador.

In the year 1840 Peru and its neighbor Bolivia were unstable nations, debilitated by the recent war between Chile and the Peruvian–Bolivian Confederation, by internal civil strife, and by rivalry between the two governments that had just emerged from the collapse of the confederation. Rumors of revolts and of impending strife between Peru and Bolivia circulated with great frequency, giving the impression that the regime of President Agustín Gamarra in Lima (since the breakup of the Peruvian–Bolivian Confederation in 1839) was nearly impotent and that Peru verged on anarchy. A tottering government in Lima seemed to offer an opportunity for Ecuador to regain the lost provinces of Jaén and Maynas.[24]

President Flores' assessment of the strength of the Gamarra government appears to have been attributable in large part to the advice of Bolivian general and former Protector of the Peruvian–Bolivian Confederation, Andrés de Santa Cruz, who fled to Ecuador early in 1839 soon after his defeat by Chile. His arrival in Guayaquil with a large party of followers quickly aroused suspicions in Lima (well justified, as it turned out) that the erstwhile Protector hoped to win the support of the government in Quito for a plan to seize power in Peru once more.[25] Though General Flores had been opposed to the Protector's policies before the destruction of the confederation, he extended both courtesy and protection to the exiled former head of state. Courtesy was soon transformed into intimacy and very confidential relations. Santa Cruz even entered into a business arrangement with the president when he rented a mill on one of Flores' private estates.[26]

The Ecuadorian president would have been well advised to keep his distance from the unscrupulous and scheming ex-Protector who simply wished to use Ecuador and its president for his own purposes. Santa Cruz was angry with Chile over the breakup of the confederation, and he was bent upon returning to power as soon as possible. By using friends and allies left behind in Bolivia and Peru he intended to stir up revolts and to produce enough confusion to permit him to seize power once more. The exiled general was willing to use whatever means and methods that might give him hope of success. He would misrepresent political conditions in Peru in order to give the impression that the government was about to collapse and that all Peruvians and Bolivians would welcome him back enthusiastically. He would also make wild promises of cessions of Peruvian territory to Ecuador in order to win support for his schemes— not that he intended to honor territorial commitments once he was back in power.[27]

President Flores appears to have been dazzled by the lures held out by the wily exile, especially by the offer of coveted territory. Unfortunately, Flores' decision to collaborate in the conspiracies of Santa Cruz deprived Ecuador of a chance for harmonious relations with Peru. President Agustín Gamarra, at the head of a somewhat unstable government in Lima, after an initial display of friendliness toward Flores, turned cold and sullen when he saw that the Ecuadorian chief executive was becoming an accomplice of the scheming exiled leader.[28]

Late in 1839 General Flores revealed his complicity in the ex-Protector's intrigues by proposing to Chile, now the dominant naval power on the Pacific coast of South America, a plan to divide Peru into two separate nations and to cede northern Peru to Ecuador. Chilean authorities, who saw that weakening Peru would be harmful to international equilibrium in the region, declined to support the proposal.[29] A partitioned and impotent Peru would be easy prey for Santa Cruz.

The rebuff by Chile was a blow to their plans, but the two schemers went ahead just the same with a war of nerves against the Lima government. Santa Cruz plotted uprisings in both Peru and Bolivia and made preparations in Guayaquil to invade the former confederation once he had stirred up enough turmoil there. Flores, for his part, demanded the cession of Jaén and Maynas and sent diplomatic agents to Peru to help coordinate the program of internal disruption aimed at weakening and intimidating the government at Lima. But the Peruvian regime, even after the death of President Gamarra, managed not only to reject Flores' territorial demands but to repulse two successive filibustering expeditions by Santa Cruz.[30]

To the great distress of General Santa Cruz, Flores declined to commit Ecuadorian troops to the campaign against Peru, partly because his main forces were tied down in Pasto in 1840 and 1841.[31] But in January 1842, just after the failure of Santa Cruz's second filibuster, Flores decided at least to warn of the possible use of armed force to occupy Jaén and Maynas if Peru did not yield the disputed territory peacefully. Peruvian leaders, emboldened by their second defeat of the one-time Protector, felt strong enough to call Flores' bluff by rejecting the Ecuadorian ultimatum.[32]

Relations with Peru remained tense and menacing throughout the year 1842. Diplomatic discussions took place, but no progress was made toward a settlement. Peruvian leaders demanded that Santa Cruz be expelled from Ecuador for having plotted the "dismemberment and enslavement" of Peru and Bolivia while enjoying asylum. But President Flores, still believing that Santa Cruz was useful to his foreign policy objectives, refused to withdraw Ecuador's hospitality to the ex-Protector.[33]

The continued presence of Santa Cruz in Ecuador was profoundly disturbing to the Peruvian government not merely because of the filibusters and the territorial demands but because Peruvian intelligence had picked up reports of a mysterious "grand project" concocted by the two conspirators in Ecuador to create a new Andean political entity, perhaps a new monarchy, or several monarchies. Just how much the Peruvians knew of the Flores–Santa Cruz schemes is not clear, but their information, some of it improperly seized from an Ecuadorian diplomat, led them to believe that the plot called for overturning the existing governments in Lima and La Paz, the restoration of Santa Cruz to power, and the granting of territorial concessions to Ecuador. The Peruvian intelligence, as far as it went, was fairly accurate, for documents of the period, including General Santa Cruz's private letters to Flores, reveal that the former Protector and his associates were indeed planning to reconstitute the Peru–Bolivian Confederation, perhaps under the monarchical form of government, and to reward Ecuador with Peruvian territory. One secret plan presented to Flores by Santa Cruz and his followers envisioned the inclusion of Ecuador in a grand Andean confederation, a sort of revival of the ancient

Inca empire in territorial scope. Though the plan proposed to make General Flores the head of the new government, it may be safely assumed that the wily ex-Protector was merely dangling bait in front of Flores. Once the plan was implemented Santa Cruz himself would most likely have taken charge.[34]

Even though the authorities in Lima did not possess the full details of the machinations of the two generals, they knew enough to recognize that Peru was under a serious threat from the north. They also recognized that Peru, even when weakened by civil strife, was a large and strong nation that was fully capable of handling a small nation like Ecuador. It followed from this premise that Peru would eventually prevail if it firmly resisted Flores' demands. This estimate of the situation proved correct and paid off handsomely in October 1843, when General Santa Cruz led a third filibuster into Peru, was captured, and sent off to Chile.[35] With the former Protector removed from the scene, Peru soon overcame the problems of political instability that had been so debilitating.

Even before the capture of Santa Cruz it was becoming evident that President Flores' aggressive policy toward Peru had not only failed but had exposed Ecuador to possible retaliatory moves by angry and resentful authorities in Lima. The danger was not small, because Ecuador had no navy worthy of the name and no allies. In attempting to force both New Granada and Peru into granting Ecuador's territorial demands, Flores' succeeded only in provoking the wrath of his more powerful South American neighbors. Thus, Ecuador's president, who early in his second term dreamed of great triumphs in foreign affairs, was faced with defeat, frustrations, and looming international dangers.

Flores' aggressive policies toward New Granada and Peru also had unfortunate effects inside Ecuador by stirring up criticism and opposition among citizens who feared war and its consequences. Opposition in Quito to the Pasto adventure worried Flores,[36] but the greatest problem of antiwar sentiment arose in Guayaquil. Most citizens in the port city, where the president's collaboration with Santa Cruz was an open secret, reportedly opposed the war of nerves against Peru and the president's complicity with Santa Cruz. The merchant community was most distressed by the prospect of the probable imposition of emergency taxes and by the fear of a Peruvian invasion of the Ecuadorian coast, with great property damage and disruption of commerce a likely consequence.[37]

Governor Rocafuerte, as could be predicted, made himself the champion of the peace party in Guayaquil. In letters to the president he cautioned against war with both New Granada and Peru, but also urged preparation of Ecuador's defenses against Peruvian attack. In April 1840, after a lengthy interview with the former Protector, Rocafuerte advised the president to avoid any entanglement with the exiled leader because it would "doubtless bring discord" with Peru.[38] A crisis in the relations between the governor and the president arose in December 1841 on the eve of the ex-Protector's second military expedition against Peru. Flores hurried down to Guayaquil, and rumor had it that the president was about to commit Ecuadorian troops to the project—a step that would have meant war with Peru. In a conference of the three leaders in Guayaquil Rocafuerte vehemently opposed Flores' proposal to support Santa Cruz's filibuster with Ecuadorian forces. An angry president reminded the governor that the latter had earlier opposed the Pasto campaigns on the grounds that there were better opportunities for boundary settlements in the south, but now the governor was seeking to foil a project to achieve the kind of settlement he earlier claimed to favor. But Rocafuerte stood steadfastly for peace and even threatened to resign the governorship of Guayas if Ecuadorian troops were sent to Peru. Though Flores confided to others that he suspected Rocafuerte wished to deprive him of brilliant military victories, the president nevertheless recognized that an open break with the governor would pose grave political difficulties for his administration. Rather than risk a complete and open rupture with his political ally in Guayaquil, with the attendant possibility of an antiwar uprising on the coast, Flores chose the side of "prudence and moderation" by deciding not to go to war with Peru at this time.[39]

The near rupture between the president and the governor over foreign policy illustrated the intricate interrelationships between foreign and domestic policies. During the crisis over possible war with Peru, Guayaquil and other cities of Ecuador were suffering from the ravages of counterfeit money—a matter seemingly unrelated to foreign policy. Yet the ill will between Flores and Rocafuerte generated by the Santa Cruz affair made for continuing tension between the two leaders and contributed to a strong disagreement over the best policy for dealing with the monetary problem. Flores' reluctance to yield to Rocafuerte on the money issue caused the irascible governor to threaten once more to resign.[40]

Thus, in late 1841 and early 1842 President Flores had good reason to feel deeply disheartened. The gloomy picture of failures in foreign policy was not relieved by any cheery news on the domestic scene. With the rise of a vocal political opposition, the dissolution of the Congress of 1841, and now the menacing behavior of the preeminent leader of the mercantile community and governor of Guayas, Flores could see that his policy of national unity was a failure. For a military man like Flores, who aspired to brilliant accomplishments, it was deeply discouraging to face such frustration both in foreign and domestic affairs.

As Flores passed the midpoint of his second term he was confronted with serious internal and foreign challenges that forced him to take stock of the nation's condition and to reflect on what must be done. His conclusion, as demonstrated by subsequent events, was that Ecuador was gravely ill and needed strong medicine. Rather than accept personal blame for having helped bring on the national predicament by his own errors of judgment and by faulty presidential policies, Flores chose to indict the political system, that is to say, the republican form of government. Given the president's diagnosis of the illness, the prescription was obvious: Ecuador must change its form of government. Monarchy, backed by the power and prestige of a European nation, was the answer.

8

REX EX MACHINA

The problems in foreign and domestic affairs that culminated in the years 1841 and 1842 were serious and required careful handling. But President Flores convinced himself that these problems constituted a grave crisis that called for drastic measures. In reality, the difficulties, which were largely of his own making, were much less severe than he imagined.

In foreign affairs, for example, accommodation with Peru and New Granada was within easy reach. Relations with the Bogotá government were already returning to normal late in 1841 as a result of indications from the Flores administration that it would acquiesce in continued Granadan control of Pasto. If Ecuador's president had also been willing to retreat from his territorial demands against Peru and to put a stop to Santa Cruz's flagrant abuses of asylum in Guayaquil, then the dangerous confrontation with Peru would have ended quickly. An international crisis of sorts did in fact exist in 1841 and 1842, but President Flores had created it, and he had the power to resolve it by means of judicious diplomacy.

The internal conditions of Ecuador, both political and economic, were much more complex than the international. It would not be true to say that the president had the power simply to dispel domestic difficulties by a change of course. If Flores had done more to combat corruption and if he had allowed clean elections, he would have lessened somewhat the fiscal and political dangers to his government. But such actions would not have been enough to quell the partisan strife of ambitious politicians, nor would they have ended the menacing rivalry of the major geographic regions of the country. However, the fact that Flores could not solve the problems by a simple change in policy does not mean that extreme measures were needed. A close look at the difficulties reveals that they were not so grave as to require a change in the form of government.

Aside from the chronic poverty of the national treasury, which could not be cured by creating a throne in Quito, the most serious internal difficulty was the lack of a legislature between 1841 and 1843. The dissolution of Congress in 1841, brought on by partisan strife and governmental manipulation of elections, was the joint responsibility of the administration and its critics. But the absence of a national legislature, while embarrassing to the executive branch, was not so grave as to necessitate anything more extreme than temporary executive rule and perhaps an amendment to the constitution to provide acceptable methods for dealing with a legislative hiatus.

Unfortunately, President Flores chose to believe that the dissolution of Congress demonstrated that the government of Ecuador was so "fragile and defective" that it could "not fulfill its primary purpose of preserving social order." Ecuador had become a victim of the "pernicious abuse of a systematic opposition to the government" which, the president told members of the national convention in 1843, "produces alarms and persecutions, demoralizes the people, impairs the laws, weakens public order, and finally, produces upheavals and calamities." "Only in hereditary monarchies," he concluded, "which have sufficient strength to resist and to preserve public order, could a systematic opposition be permitted."[1]

Flores' arguments were obviously alarmist. There was, of course, much political discontent in Ecuador at this time, but the nation was not on the verge of civil war. The president openly admitted this when he stated to the same convention that "the Republic has enjoyed domestic peace and unalterable tranquility."[2] Here was a most curious contradiction: the country was calm and peaceful, said the president, but the republican government was incapable of maintaining public order. The explanation of these contradictory assertions is to be found in Flores' secret decision to transform the government into a monarchy, or failing that, into an autocracy under his personal rule. He dared not reveal the secret for fear that public knowledge of his intention would stir up such a storm that his government would fall. It was necessary, therefore, to maintain firm control while attempting to persuade the legislators and the citizens that representative government in Ecuador had proved a failure.[3]

The motives of President Flores' decision to abandon republicanism will never be fully understood because of the secrecy with which he proceeded. Nevertheless, many of the reasons for the president's change of mind may be inferred from his public and private statements, from his actions, from the views of his closest political advisers and associates, and from the general circumstances of Ecuador in the early 1840s.

We know, for example, that General Flores had been an exponent of monocratic government in the late 1820s, that he had been one of the "faithful friends" of Bolívar, and that he had championed various schemes for a Bolivarian dictatorship and the creation of a hereditary monarchy in Gran Colombia.[4] His acceptance of the presidency of Ecuador had required him to set aside his monocratic preferences and to accept, at least for the time being, the form of representative government specified by the Constitution of 1830, and later by that of 1835. But, given Flores' military background and his early preference for monarchy, and given also the authoritarian spirit of Ecuadorian society and government inherited from Spanish rule, it was not surprising that Flores should have maintained a private skepticism toward republicanism. As he came to experience the many frustrations of presidential responsibilities, he must have recalled more than once Bolívar's gloomy declaration that "America is ungovernable."[5]

The loss of personal prestige by President Flores was another factor that undoubtedly influenced his thinking in favor of monarchy. Flores' standing in the aristocratic society of Ecuador had always been precarious, despite his marriage into a select family, because of his humble origins in coastal Venezuela. His unsure social footing made it doubly important for him to achieve notable success in the presidency. But the collapse of the Congress in 1841, the fruitless Pasto campaigns, and the stern refusal of Peru to surrender Jaén and Maynas were such obvious failures that Flores' stature suffered significantly.

Perhaps the worst blow to the prestige of the president, and to his sense of honor, was public discussion of the assassination of Marshal Sucre. Political opponents first raised the issue of Flores' possible involvement in the crime late in 1839 during an electoral campaign. The subsequent publication of articles in the official and semiofficial press defending the chief executive served only to stir up more talk about the president's possible complicity in the notorious killing. Matters grew worse between 1840 and 1843 when General Obando, the most probable culprit in Sucre's assassination, led the Pasto rebellion and was subsequently brought to trial and convicted in New Granada. News of the sensational trial and the evidence presented relevant to the assassination inevitably reached Ecuador, and more news stories appeared in the press. Though the reports were favorable to Flores, the mere fact that the question of Sucre's murder was being discussed caused much new speculation and gossip about the rumored role of Flores in the killing. The effect was very damaging to the honor and reputation of the president.[6]

The loss of prestige by Flores seriously affected government in two ways. First, it angered the president and caused him to become more intolerant and resentful of political opponents who he believed were bent upon destroying his all-important honor. Second, the diminished esteem of the president resulted in a serious loss of executive power in a political system that relied rather heavily on the charismatic leadership of the president. Though the framers of Ecuador's two constitutions had hoped to create a broad-based representative government with three separate branches, the chief executive overshadowed all other elements in the system. Three centuries of Spanish rule, to say nothing of native government before the Conquest, had accustomed the Ecuadorian people to look to the authoritarian figures of viceroys and audiencia judges, appointees of the king. With the achievement of independence the president of the republic inherited most of the respect and aura of authority formerly associated with viceroys and judges, though the aristocratic members of Congress and governors of provinces also enjoyed much public esteem.[7]

A basic problem in the new government, however, was that it

lacked the sort of unquestioned authority that the king of Spain had always enjoyed. Legitimacy, that concept of sanctioned prerogative or rightful power inherent in monarchy, was a quality that in a republic had to be earned and maintained through the trust of the people. The promulgation of constitutions with great ceremony, Te Deum masses, and public oath-taking helped to promote respect for the new government. And so did the charismatic appeal of General Flores, primarily because of his popular standing as a military leader and former associate of Simón Bolívar.[8]

Though Juan José Flores lacked intellectual sophistication, he was sufficiently informed in the theory of government to understand the importance of legitimacy to the success of a republic. He sought to promote respect for the new regime in a variety of ways, one of which was to inscribe on Ecuadorian coins the words "Power in the Constitution"—a superficial measure, of course, but indicative of his desire to promote legitimacy.[9] On turning over the reins of government to Rocafuerte in 1835 Flores stressed the importance of "supporting the *legitimate* government" (emphasis added), and he made the same point in private correspondence.[10] He was keenly aware that gossip about the murder of Sucre was damaging to his public stature and, consequently, to the government. And he believed that the political disarray caused by the dissolution of Congress in 1841 left the chief executive "without title of legitimacy," as he declared in a manifesto to the nation in 1842 and then later in his formal address to the national convention of 1843.[11]

Flores' concern with the loss of governmental legitimacy was a major factor in his decision to establish monarchy in Ecuador. It was naive of him to think that legitimacy could be produced by the simple expedient of creating a throne in Quito. Apparently Flores chose to believe that the problem of public sanction of governmental authority could be solved almost miraculously by dragging onto the political stage a deus ex machina, or in this case, a rex ex machina, so to speak. Yet Flores must have known that the restoration of monarchy would provoke vigorous opposition in many quarters, for he realized that it was necessary to keep his decision secret until the last minute. The impossibility of openly preparing public opinion for a major change in the form of government made the whole enterprise extremely risky.

Another important aspect of the president's thinking which had to be kept from the public was his desire to perpetuate himself in power. Just what role he intended to play under the new monarchy is not clear, but probably he expected to command the armed forces and to act as chief adviser or prime minister of the foreign prince. And, to extend the period of his rule, Flores decided to have himself elected to a third term in the presidency. Since this aim was contrary both to the Constitution of 1835 and to his public vow to quit the presidency at the end of his second term, it was necessary to maintain silence about his decision to stay on. It was evident that personal ambition for power was such a strong motive in the president's thinking that he was willing to break his public promises, ignore a private understanding with Rocafuerte, and set aside the constitution in order to satisfy his hunger for power.

Flores' preference for monarchy was also encouraged by some of his close advisers and associates. The secrecy in which the plan unfolded makes it impossible to identify all of the advocates of monarchy in the presidential circle, but a few of them may be discerned. One such influence was the itinerant statesman and publicist from New Granada, Juan García del Río, who had earlier served as an adviser to both Bolívar and San Martín, and then had held the post of minister of the treasury in Ecuador during the latter part of Flores' first administration. Afterwards he went to Peru where he was appointed minister of the treasury in 1835 by Santa Cruz. With the fall of the Peruvian–Bolivian Confederation in 1839, García del Río returned to Ecuador with the party of the Protector's followers who fled Peru into exile. García del Río was intelligent, cultured, and articulate. His long-held monarchist views were a matter of public record, and it is quite likely that he used his intellectual talents behind the scenes to persuade the uncultivated Santa Cruz of the potential benefits and the feasibility of monarchy in Spanish America. It is also more than likely that he used his intimacy with Flores to put the scheming exiled Protector on good terms with the Ecuadorian president. If so, then

García del Río was of key importance in helping to generate the "grand project" of Santa Cruz and Flores. That he was privy to it, and even a participant in the plan, is strongly indicated by the fact that in 1841 the Ecuadorian government sent him to Peru on a secret diplomatic mission, which Lima authorities strongly believed was connected with a plot to overthrow the government there. It is not possible to measure the degree to which this Granadan gentleman shaped the "grand project," but he was an important monarchist intellectual and a master of the art of persuasion. He was in close contact with both Flores and Santa Cruz. His influence on behalf of monarchy was probably considerable.[12]

Another person who advised Flores and helped to shape his thoughts was Antonio José de Irisarri, that polemical Guatemalan who was employed by Rocafuerte and Flores to publish a series of newspapers, most notably *La Balanza,* to defend the administration from its critics. The growing importance of Irisarri with the Flores regime became evident in 1843 when he was appointed director of the government press, editor of the *Gaceta del Gobierno,* and publisher of a new semiofficial weekly paper called *La Concordia.* As the government's chief propagandist Irisarri enjoyed influence over the president.[13]

When Irisarri arrived in Ecuador with Santa Cruz's party of exiles from Peru he brought with him no firm commitment to any particular form of government, but he quickly became a member of the inner circle associated with the "grand project" and began to publicize political viewpoints favorable to monarchy.[14] In a series of articles in *La Balanza* entitled "Letters on Revolutions" he interpreted the history of Ecuador and other Spanish American republics since independence as a depressing story of "human frenzy, of contradictions, of deceits, of uprisings, of crimes, and of public calamities." The excesses of republican government, said Irisarri, caused conditions bordering on anarchy, which in turn produced a "mania for revolutions" that prevented the new nations from making material and social progress.[15]

Foreshadowing President Flores' address to the national convention of 1843, Irisarri blamed the "continual upheavals among our peoples" on the visionary republican constitutions that were so unsuited to social realities. The charters of government were too democratic, he said, for a people not schooled for democracy. The result was "a democracy without a people, an aristocracy without nobles, an oligarchy of many, who are succeeded by fewer and fewer, which becomes a monarchy without a monarch, which is a despotic government."[16]

In his "Letters on Revolutions" Irisarri limited himself to pointing out governmental deficiencies and refrained from offering solutions to the problems. But on 11 July 1840 he published a translation of an article, taken from a North American newspaper, that agreed with his own views on the inappropriateness of republican constitutions in Spanish America and criticized the results of democracy in the United States. The article concluded that liberty, security, and progress could better be fostered and protected by monarchical governments, such as those of England and France, than by republics styled after the United States. "The republican form has been fatal," declared the article, "for the Republics of South America. Liberty for them has been converted into weakness and anarchy. . . . These states, just emerging but already old, . . . will come to an end shortly . . . by suicide."[17]

Thus, by using the words of an unidentified foreign writer Irisarri managed to disparage republicanism and to promote monarchism without committing himself or the government to the royalist cause. Flores must have approved of Irisarri's journalistic labors, for he subsequently promoted the Guatemalan publicist to positions of greater responsibility and even asked him to undertake a secret mission to Peru in 1843 to help in the scheme to restore Santa Cruz to power there. Though Irisarri later denied any complicity in the monarchist plot, two of his letters to the Ecuadorian president demonstrate his personal involvement conclusively.[18]

Vicente Rocafuerte, though a staunch opponent of monarchy, also contributed to Flores' decision to transform the governmental system. While in the presidency the guayaquileño had shown great impatience with constitutional restraints and had resorted to vigorous repressive acts of dubious legality. In his many letters to Flores Rocafuerte often recommended autocratic methods to deal with political opponents. He frequently expressed the same sort of pessimism regarding the effectiveness of government in Ecuador and Spanish America as that of Irisarri in his "Letters on Revolutions." On one occasion Rocafuerte warned Flores that "the revolution marches forward in giant steps, and the worst of it is that the revolution is aimed at you personally." As a cure for the political malady the former president recommended the manipulation of public opinion through a controlled press and the repression of opponents by the exercise of extraordinary powers—in other words, by dictatorship.[19] Rocafuerte certainly did not wish to persuade the president to collaborate with Santa Cruz or to establish a throne in Quito, but his warnings about dangers from the opposition, his pessimism about the trend of events, and his espousal of political manipulation of the people and of authoritarian methods lent support to Flores' own disillusionment with republican institutions and to his determination to strengthen the government through a substantial augmentation of executive authority.

Rocafuerte's influence on Flores' thinking was not exercised through friendly persuasion, for the two men continued to dislike each other for reasons already explained. But the president's admiration for the guayaquileño's superior intellectual capacity must surely have caused him to give serious consideration to Rocafuerte's political assessments and recommendations, especially when they coincided with Flores' own notions. Rocafuerte's suggestions did not persuade Flores so much as they justified him in his inclination toward authoritarian and monocratic government.

The most important personal influence on the Ecuadorian president was the exiled Protector of the former Peru–Bolivian Confederation. General Santa Cruz had much in common with Flores. Both were men of humble social origins who had risen to high rank in the armed forces during the wars against Spanish rule. Both had little formal education, but great ambition. Both were well schooled in the politics and intrigues of military officers and were inclined to use Machiavellian methods in statecraft. It was not surprising that the two generals got on well with each other once the ex-Protector had managed to ingratiate himself by means of a series of flattering letters, followed by intimate conversations about politics and Peru.[20] Before long the exiled leader unfolded his "grand project" to the gullible president, a scheme to create a new Andean confederation, under monarchical government if feasible. Santa Cruz knew how to appeal to Flores' ambition by offering territorial concessions to Ecuador and by claiming vast influence with foreign diplomats. He appears to have persuaded Flores that an agent of Santa Cruz in London had won official British backing for the restoration of the confederation, possibly under monarchy.[21]

Part of Santa Cruz's "grand project" was unveiled to Flores in an interesting document entitled "Political review of Peru and means that should be adopted to wipe out evils," written by Luis Orbegoso, a Peruvian confederate of Santa Cruz. The opening paragraph of the essay pictured Peru in the chaos of civil war brought on by "criminal and ignorant" leaders of "parties without principle" who had destroyed the great Peruvian—Bolivian Confederation. A "vast plan" was needed, said the "Political Review," to form "a reciprocal union of the Republics of Ecuador, Peru, and Bolivia." The exact nature of the "reciprocal union" was not specified. The document simply declared that "our mutual exigencies and affinity of feelings and customs impel us to unite our nations by close bonds." To accomplish this great task a "genius," a man of "wisdom and tact, together with great valor," was needed. The person chosen for this "lofty mission" of rescuing the Andean nations from anarchy and promoting "the advance of civilization" was, of course, General Flores "whose heroic career is written in brilliant letters in the pages of history."[22]

This simple-minded yet clever appeal to Flores' vanity, ambition, and fear of political opposition had the effect desired by Santa Cruz and his followers. Flattered by the praise of his "heroic" abilities and persuaded by the distorted picture of spreading anarchy and lawless opposition to virtuous governments, Flores agreed to the proposal of a conspiracy to create a new Andean confederation. Just what role Santa Cruz intended to assign to the Ecuadorian president in the event of success is not known, but Flores was willing to gamble on the outcome. Perhaps he expected to become "protector" of the new political entity until a foreign prince could be found. Or, perhaps he believed he would remain as "protector" and preside over king-lets to be placed on separate thrones in Quito, Lima, and La Paz. Though the "Political Review" made no mention of monarchy, it is clear from subsequent events, especially from Flores' communications with foreign diplomats, that he and Santa Cruz planned to establish monarchy, under European protection, as the form of government of the projected Andean union.

It was naive of the Ecuadorian president to join in the grandiose plans of the exiled Protector, for the project of uniting three nations under monarchy stood little chance of success. Too many things could go wrong with such an ambitious program. Strong opposition in Ecuador both to absorption into an Andean union and to the imposition of monarchy was predictable. Similiar difficulties in Peru and Bolivia should have been foreseen. Emerging nationalist sentiments in the three countries would surely have stirred up disruptive forces within the Andean confederation, especially if the union were accomplished with the backing of a European nation such as Spain or Great Britain. And finally, the great personal ambitions of both Flores and Santa Cruz would almost certainly have caused these two leaders to clash at some point, with unfortunate consequences.

The chief significance of the "grand project" was that it committed Flores to pursue a plan to impose monarchy in Ecuador. Presidential advisers and associates had contributed to his decision to move in this direction, but Flores' own assessment of social and political conditions must also have figured prominently in shaping his thought at this time. Flores was aware that the social structure of Ecuador was stratified and highly aristocratic and that it seemed more suited to a traditional monarchical regime than to a republican form based on the notions of popular sovereignty and evolution toward democracy.[23] Only a small fraction of the population participated in the political process, while the bulk of the population, submerged in poverty and ignorance, played no active role in republican procedures at all. Republicanism was a foreign importation that had little to do with governmental traditions and the social makeup of Spanish America in general and of Ecuador in particular.

The contradiction between republican political theory and social reality was apparent to many. Irisarri pointed to the inconsistency in his "Letters on Revolutions," and in other writings he denounced the unfortunate imitation of the United States and questioned the suitability of republican institutions in Spanish America.[24] North American visitors in Ecuador like Dr. Adrian Terry noted the lack of social foundation for a republican form of government. "Would not a limited monarchy have been more conducive to the happiness and prosperity of the people of Gran Colombia," he asked, "than a republican government?" "The mass of the people," he continued, "are too ignorant to govern themselves and . . . under a republican form the government is essentially a military despotism."[25] Walter Cope, the experienced British consul in Guayaquil, made similar observations about political and social conditions, though he refrained from recommending the restoration of royal rule.[26]

Friedrich Hassaurek, United States minister in Ecuador in the early 1860s, focused attention on the same condition, which had not changed in two decades:

> Our neighbors in Ecuador have established a republican form of government without being republicans. They cling to their aristocratic traditions. . . . The descendants of the old noble families still cherish their ancient titles of nobility. They look with great veneration on the pomp and splendor of European monarchies, and distinguish those of their own number who can boast of a count or a knight among their ancestors.

And he concluded: "Shall we be surprised, therefore, if monarchical ideas are gaining ground in those countries?"[27]

Disillusionment with the results of republicanism in the late 1830s and 1840s was not confined to Ecuador, but rather swept through most of Spanish America, affecting primarily the wealthy creole classes who deplored republican turbulence and began to long for the peace and order of the Spanish regime.[28] Chile was perhaps the first to respond to the new stirrings in its conservative revolution of 1830 and the establishment of the "monarchical republic" under the conservative constitution of 1833. News of the events in Chile quickly reached Ecuador, in part through the journalistic efforts of the tireless Irisarri. Rocafuerte, while president, had commented to Flores that the

Chilean system was "the most positive means of organizing these backward regions."[29]

The winds of conservatism blew not only from the south but also from the north where Mexico was experiencing horrendous political difficulties, complicated by a dangerous confrontation with the great republic of the United States over the Texas question. The Mexican crisis, which gave rise to a monarchical project in that nation, was widely reported in South America and attracted much interest in Ecuador.[30]

In the latter part of 1842 there was much talk in Bogotá of monarchist stirrings in Mexico, and it was generally believed that General Antonio López de Santa Anna not only sought to overthrow republican institutions in Mexico but wished to spread the monarchist movement to South America. Rumor had it that General Tomás Cipriano de Mosquera and his brother, the archbishop of Bogotá, both favored bringing a European prince to New Granada.[31]

In the midst of this royalist ferment, a Mexican diplomatic emissary, Manuel Crecencio Rejón, arrived in Quito for the purpose of secretly promoting "the establishment of constitutional monarchies, imitating the example that Santa Anna would provide," according to the Spanish chargé in Quito.[32] Only a few months earlier President Flores had received word from his diplomatic envoy in Bogotá that the government of New Granada had concluded a draft treaty with the British chargé which provided for the establishment of a British protectorate over the nation and pledged all of the customs revenues to the payment of the Colombian debt to British bondholders.[33]

In their nostalgia for political tranquility Spanish Americans naturally turned their attention to the monarchies of Europe. Though England was a Protestant nation and of very different cultural background, the English monarchy stood for stability. Moreover, British merchants, who were more active than those of any other nation in Spanish America, helped lend prestige to the English model. France under the rule of Louis Philippe, "king of the bourgeoisie," also attracted the admiration of the wealthy classes of Spanish America. Though French commerce was less important than British, the Spanish-American elite classes admired France more than any other country. "The wealthy Ecuadorian families send their children to France to be educated there," wrote Hassaurek in 1861, "and the young men go there to learn manners and in search of amusements." Their admiration of French culture was so strong, said Hassaurek, that "the desire to see Ecuador as a province of France is avowed by many without reservation."[34]

The American minister wrote at a later date, of course, when the government of Gabriel García Moreno was attempting to establish a French-backed monarchy in Quito, but social and cultural values had changed little, if at all, since the early 1840s. Ecuadorians tended to look to Europe for intellectual and cultural leadership. The ratification of the treaty of recognition with Spain focused new attention on Spain and Spanish culture, stimulated in part, of course, by the Flores administration. Ecuadorian esteem of European monarchies was reflected in an article in the *Gaceta* about the youthfulness of the reigning monarchs, most of whom had been crowned since 1830.[35]

It would be an exaggeration to conclude that most politically active citizens in Ecuador and New Granada had abandoned republicanism for monarchy in the early 1840s. Attachment to republicanism was still strong, but disappointment with the results of independence was widespread, and many leaders, especially conservatives, were entertaining thoughts of European dynasties and foreign protectorates as the means of avoiding a possible collapse of government and a frightening descent into anarchy.[36] Since a return to kingship, even under constitutional guarantees, would have been vigorously opposed by liberals and the champions of republicanism, most monarchists felt constrained to keep their views and plans secret. To trumpet dynastic plans to the Ecuadorian public in 1842 and 1843 would undoubtedly have provoked not only political opposition but violent efforts to bring down any government seeking to establish a throne in Quito.

President Flores understood the need for secrecy in his plans when he made a hasty trip from Quito to Guayaquil in late November 1841. He journeyed to the port city ostensibly to deal with political unrest on the coast and to mollify the discontented merchant community there, but his real purpose was to promote the "grand project" of Santa Cruz.[37] When Governor Rocafuerte blocked Flores' proposal to send troops to Peru (as we have seen), the president decided to seek European support for the Peruvian project. His first move was to hold private conversations with British consul Cope and with Belford Huston Wilson, the British chargé at Lima, who happened to be in Guayaquil en route to London. Encouraged by these gentlemen, or at least not disuaded by them, President Flores drafted a confidential proposal to Foreign Secretary Palmerston to be delivered at the Foreign Office by Chargé Wilson. This proposal was the opening move by Flores in a covert plan to establish a European monarchy in Ecuador.

In his letter to Palmerston, dated 31 December, 1841, the Ecuadorian president used money as the chief bait to ensnare the English government. Flores professed a desire to pay Ecuador's debt to the British bondholders, but payment was made difficult by the large sums of money necessarily expended on an army to defend Ecuador from its neighbors. The chief danger came from Peru whose aggressive leaders, he said, had already invaded Bolivia and were plotting an attack on Ecuador. "Although Ecuador would like to be a disinterested observer of this contest," Flores declared, without mentioning his complicity in General Santa Cruz's plots against Peru, "it cannot disarm itself without compromising its own security." Flores' letter next called attention to "the frequent revolutions which are deplored in almost all of the new states of Spanish America." These insurrections were caused, he said, by the adoption of fragile political institutions ill suited to the peculiar circumstances of Spanish America.[38]

President Flores conceded, in his letter to Palmerston, that some Latin American nations, whose constitutions were more flexible than most, had achieved stability. "But, since it is not easy for all of the new Republics to reform their constitutions without exposing the people to great upheavals," he argued, "it is necessary to look for firm support in powerful and well-grounded Governments." Flores then asked the British foreign secretary to accept a set of proposals entitled "Bases of the Project" which he enclosed with his letter. The specific propositions were:

First.   The Ecuadorian Government will pay its British creditors
            with lands of the Florean Islands [Galápagos] and with
            the remaining vacant lands and values of which it dis-
            poses, without excluding payment of the same from the
            surplus of public revenues once domestic peace has been
            guaranteed.

Second.   For the purpose of assuring the domestic and foreign
            peace of Ecuador, as well as protecting the interests of
            British subjects, the English Government commits itself to
            guaranteeing the interior and foreign peace of Ecuador.

Third.   To such an end, Her Majesty's Government will use its
            influence as it may deem convenient to establish a durable
            state of affairs which will guarantee the independence of
            Ecuador and Bolivia.[39]

President Flores chose at this time not to make a candid and
complete proposal for the establishment of a British-backed
monarchy in Ecuador. His reticence is explained, in the light of
his subsequent negotiations with Spain, as a tactic aimed at in-
ducing British leaders to suggest the desirability of monarchy.
This approach, if word of these secret negotiations should get
out, had the advantage of permitting Flores to deny that he had
plotted to restore monarchy.

Flores' proposal to Lord Palmerston contained some clever
elements. To turn the huge debt owed to Britain into a possible
asset required a lively imagination, an ability to see potential
benefits in burdensome liabilities. His offer of the Galápagos
Islands though vague in its terms, was doubtless tempting to the
leaders of the world's greatest maritime power, the nation that
had only recently acquired the Falklands (Malvinas) in the
South Atlantic and might find it advantageous to secure a naval
base on the Pacific Coast as well.[40] Finally, Flores flattered the
British by inviting them to play a tutelary role, "as the government may deem convenient," in the political affairs of the quar-
reling and unstable Andean nations. Flores, of course, hoped
that Palmerston would deem monarchy as the best form of
government "to establish a durable state of affairs."

No amount of cleverness on the part of the Ecuadorian president, however, could conceal the obvious fact that the British
government was being asked to establish a protectorate not only

over Ecuador but over Bolivia as well. The acquisition of a naval base in the Galápagos would increase Britain's military power in the region by deployment of forces on the Pacific Coast, but to assume a commitment to "guarantee the independence" of two beleaguered nations halfway around the globe was a dubious proposition. Furthermore, to suggest that England should "use its influence as it may deem convenient to establish a durable state of affairs" was an unattractive invitation to meddle in the sensitive domestic and international relations of the Andean nations. The Foreign Office was quite well informed regarding the tangled problems of the Pacific Coast nations, and it was difficult to see how a political intervention in the region would profit either the exchequer or British investors and merchants.

It was not surprising that Lord Palmerston and his successor, Lord Aberdeen, did not reply to the Ecuadorian proposal. Belford Wilson, who had agreed to present the confidential letter personally to the foreign secretary and to explain Flores' ideas in greater detail than appeared in the letter (doubtless the monarchical aspects), apparently decided merely to drop off the communication in the Foreign Office and avoid acting as a spokesman for the proposal.[41] But, even if Wilson had carried out his promise to Flores to lobby for the protectorate scheme, it is doubtful that either Palmerston or Aberdeen would have accepted such a commitment on the Pacific Coast. The Foreign Office probably feared not only that England would be enmeshed in South American politics but that Flores wished to use the prestige of England and her naval power merely to carry out his own designs and those of General Santa Cruz. Though Flores pursued the protectorate idea with the British during the ensuing three years, the foreign secretaries declined to support it.[42]

The president of Ecuador was doubtless disappointed at the indifference of English authorities to his overtures, but he was a resourceful man who did not give up easily. Before long a new opportunity presented itself. On 10 August 1842, while Flores was still hoping to interest the British in the Galápagos, Sr. Luis de Potestad, Spanish chargé d'affaires, arrived in Quito. Potestad brought with him, as aide to the legation, Juan Pío Montúfar, the grandson of the famous Ecuadorian Marqués de Selvalegre, precursor of the independence movement in Quito.[43] Flores offered a warm reception to the Spanish envoy and saw to it that the *Gaceta* publicized the event prominently: "The favorable disposition of our government and the sympathy merited by the personal character of Sr. Potestad," entoned the government paper, ". . . promise that the relations between two peoples of common origin will grow closer and closer for their happiness and good fortune."[44]

The lyrical news coverage given by the *Gaceta* to the establishment of formal diplomatic relations with Spain reflected the Ecuadorian president's wish to cultivate much closer ties with Spain than anyone suspected. Less than a week after Potestad's arrival in Quito the president gave a private audience to the new chargé and offered confidential assurances that the Spanish legation "will always be the preferred one" in Quito. Flores went on to declare that even though he might leave the presidency he would continue to have enough influence as "perpetual commander-in-chief of the armed forces" to guarantee a preferential policy toward Spain. Potestad felt that the confidential assurance of special treatment for Spain was so important that he reported it in cipher to the foreign minister in Madrid.[45]

If Potestad wondered what Flores meant by a preferred status for the Spanish legation, he did not have to wait long to learn. Early in September, before the Spanish chargé had completed a month's stay in Quito, President Flores granted him another private audience. This time the Ecuadorian executive unveiled more of his secret plans and invited the Spanish government to tell him what form of government it would prefer to have established in Ecuador. "I commit myself to it as well as to an alliance with Spain," he declared.[46] Thus, the meaning of "preferred" status for the Spanish monarchy was a proposal by the president to permit the mother country to choose a new form of government for Ecuador and to guarantee the political transformation through a military alliance. In short, since Flores knew in advance the nature of Spain's most probable choice of governmental form, he was actually proposing a Spanish-backed monarchy.

Potestad understood the president's meaning instantly. In a lengthy dispatch filled with naive enthusiasm, he reported the entire conversation to the government in Madrid. Flores had confided, reported the envoy, his discouragement over the slow progress that had been made by Ecuador since independence. The president attributed the lack of success to three major problems: domestic rivalry over who would command the government; the evil "influence of the clergy and the friars"; and the foreign menace of Peru, "which has Ecuador in a continual state of alarm."[47]

In order to solve the problem of political instability, said Potestad, General Flores had determined to modify the constitution, "a matter which has already been arranged beforehand," to extend the presidential term to ten years, and to permit reelection for an additional term.[48] It had been agreed, the chargé continued, that Flores would be elected president for a third term. Once the new government was well established under the new constitution the chief executive planned to unite his nation with Bolivia "in order to form a power with preponderance in this part of America." In addition, Flores proposed to reform the religious orders and to nationalize all the properties of the monasteries and convents.[49]

To carry out these ambitious plans General Flores told Potestad that he would need "the moral support of a naval force of something like two warships." Both England and France, in the hope of gaining commercial privileges, had offered the necessary aid for his project, Flores alleged, but he preferred to turn to the mother country so that "in the future Spain might recover her former prestige." "Tell your government," he said, "that it can count on me for whatever it may wish." Flores went on to indicate his desire for a close alliance with Spain, which he said would be useful to the mother country in the event of insurrection in the Philippines. The Ecuadorian president warned that "the Philippines had been the object of ambitions of some of the [Spanish] American governments" in the past, but with an alliance Spain could count on the aid of the Ecuadorian army.[50]

Luis de Potestad was apparently dazzled both by General Flores' personal charm and by the startling proposals that seemed to offer an unexpected opportunity to fulfill the diplomatic instructions under which the chargé was supposed to op-

erate in Ecuador. Before departing from Madrid the foreign
minister had cautioned him to work "to reestablish the former
prominence of Spain in the country" and "to take advantage of
every occasion to bring the Ecuadorian and Spanish peoples
closer together." The minister's instructions also made reference to the existence of royalist parties in America which favored "restoring monarchical forms by establishing princes of
European royal families" on New World thrones. The chargé
was directed to send "detailed news" to Madrid about any stirrings of monarchism.[51] With instructions of this tenor, the enthusiasm of the inexperienced and ingenuous Spanish diplomat
for Flores' proposals was understandable.

In reporting to Madrid Potestad did not conceal his unrestrained admiration of the Ecuadorian president, nor did he
withhold enthusiastic endorsement of the offers to establish a
military alliance and dynastic ties between Spain and Ecuador.
"General Flores, who has been in all of the Central American
campaigns," wrote the chargé, "commanding the armies of Colombia, Bolivia, Venezuela, etc. . . . , has a great following in the
entire continent." Though confused about the geography of
Spanish America, Potestad was sure that Flores was "the great
Captain of America," "a highly enlightened man of proven virtues" who had gained the respect of all people. General Flores,
according to the chargé, was the "only man" capable of establishing peace and order in Ecuador and other nations of the region, rather a sweeping assessment for a callow diplomat who
had been in South America for only a month. "Spain could
count on Flores' friendship and favorable disposition . . . , and
in any case," he urged, "it would be useful to have the presence
of a Spanish warship in these waters." Potestad closed his dispatch by asking for "opportune orders" as soon as possible.[52]

In the following months General Flores met frequently with
the Spanish chargé for the purpose of revealing details and
particulars of the "grand project." He introduced General
Santa Cruz to Sr. Potestad in order to acquaint the Spanish
envoy with the plot to topple the government of Peru, to restore
the Protector to power, and to establish monarchy in the former
confederation, as well as in Ecuador. The revelation that these
two leaders were stirring up revolts in Peru and planning an

armed invasion, which might have alarmed a sober diplomat, did not dissuade Potestad from supporting the plan, for he was easily convinced that such activities were necessary in order to save Peruvians from anarchy and "annihilation." Potestad's only regret was that the projected invasion could not take place so long as the Chilean navy remained dominant on the Pacific coast, as Flores had explained it to him. Only the presence of a small Spanish naval squadron in the Pacific waters would permit the monarchical plan to go forward.[53]

President Flores easily persuaded the gullible Potestad that the sole purpose of the project was to rescue Spanish American nations from the decay and ruin that had been brought on by the Independence movement and the adoption of republican institutions. As a first step to prepare the way for monarchy in Ecuador, Flores told the chargé, arrangements had been made to hold a constituent convention in January 1843 for the purpose of extending the presidential term of office from four to ten years. Everything was arranged, Flores confided, for his continuance in the presidency for at least a decade, and perhaps for two. The purpose of the constitutional revision, as the chargé later explained to his government, was "to prepare the spirit of the nation for the establishment of a system of government which, while preserving the name Republican, moves as close as possible to a Constitutional Monarchy."[54]

President Flores capitalized on the credulity of the Spanish chargé and managed to manipulate him almost at will. When Flores mendaciously told Potestad that both France and England were eager to cooperate in the "grand project" but said that he preferred the support of Spain, the envoy grew anxious and urged his government to speed a favorable decision lest the opportunity be lost. When the commander of Flores' military guard, Colonel Antonio España, asked Potestad to request that Spain confer upon the Ecuadorian president the Cross of Carlos III, the Spanish envoy readily complied in order to please Flores and keep in his good graces. Upon learning that a Mexican diplomat was seeking to spread monarchism through Spanish South America, Potestad reported to Madrid that "the republican party here is reduced to a very small number of individuals without prestige or support. . . . The idea of establishing monarchies

spreads more widely every day." The Spanish diplomat's enthusiasm for the "grand project" had so warped his judgment that he
believed that monarchist sentiments were in the ascendancy.[55]

Potestad's warm endorsement of the monarchical scheme
and his many reports on conditions in South America would
eventually help persuade the authorities in Madrid to participate in the plan, but a decision was not made quickly. Meanwhile, a worried and impatient President Flores decided to com-
municate directly with Madrid. On an unknown date, probably
in mid-1843, he sent to the Spanish government a document
presenting three possible courses of action. First, he proposed
the creation of "one or two monarchies in the Republics of
Ecuador and Peru, to be ruled by a prince or princes of the
Royal family of Spain, or by a regency, in the absence of the
princes." After repeating his earlier suggestion of an alliance
between Spain and Ecuador and his request for two Spanish
warships to aid in the conquest of Peru, Flores held out the
hope that Santa Cruz would regain control of Bolivia and unite
that nation with Peru under the newly established throne. The
president did not make clear whether Ecuador was to be united
with Peru and Bolivia, but he offered Guayaquil and its shipyard as a naval base for Spain to protect the Philippine Islands.
Second, as an alternative plan, Flores proposed Spanish naval
protection of an invasion of Peru in order to ensure Peruvian
payment of debts owed to Spain and to give protection to Spanish subjects there. Third, if Madrid did not accept either of the
first two proposals, Flores recommended a simple treaty of alliance and the stationing of a Spanish warship at Guayaquil "if it
should be needed."[56]

This three-tiered proposal was sufficiently flexible to accom-
modate varying levels of Spanish commitment. Realizing that
authorities in Madrid might show less enthusiasm than Potestad
for the scheme of dynastic union, the Ecuadorian president
offered several scaled choices of risks and benefits tailored to
suit the mood and spirit of the men in Madrid. Even the first
option of one or two monarchies for Ecuador, Peru, and Bolivia
represented a retreat from the more ambitious project presented to Potestad in late January 1843, which called for three
thrones, one for each of the three Andean nations. In his ear-

lier, more ambitious plan, Flores had also expressed the hope of bringing Juan Manuel Rosas of Argentina into the dynastic plan. Evidently the president had decided to reduce the scope of the project because he believed that Spanish leaders were withholding approval out of fear that the plan was too ambitious and too risky.[57]

The inclusion of Peru and Bolivia in Flores' monarchical proposal showed the strong influence of Santa Cruz in the whole matter.[58] The notion of combining the three principal Andean nations, which constituted the heartland of the ancient Inca Empire, suggests the possibility that the two leaders of the project had in mind the idea of creating a latter-day Tahuantinsuyu, as the Indian empire had been called before the Spanish Conquest. Though Flores apparently did not mention this idea to Potestad, it would have been wise to refrain from mentioning Tahuantinsuyu, for the diplomat would not have cared for references to an Indian rather than an Iberian inspiration of empire. The earlier inclusion of Argentina as a possible component of the monarchical scheme adds some support to the Tahuantinsuyu idea, for the Inca Empire embraced the Argentine northwest.[59] However, Flores may simply have believed that the autocratic Rosas might have been receptive to a monarchical proposal.

A careful reading of President Flores' three-tiered propositions presented to Spain in 1843 reveals that the president's most important goal was to gain a military alliance with a European nation and to secure naval protection. The third option, which included an alliance with Spain and the provision of a warship at Guayaquil, was the bare minimum of support needed to deter Peru from attacking Ecuador while allowing Santa Cruz and Flores to promote military uprisings in Peru and Bolivia. Even if he failed to establish thrones in the Andes, Flores hoped to topple the governments of Ecuador's southern neighbors and to allow the ex-Protector to regain his former position of power.

Though General Flores lied to the Spanish chargé when he said that England and France wished to support the project, he did make attempts to enlist the backing of both these major powers. In the event that Spain declined to participate in the enterprise, it was expedient to have other options available. Since Great Britain was the leading maritime nation of the world and the most influential power in Latin American affairs, Flores did his utmost to secure British participation in the project. Following up on his earlier overture to permit the establishment of a British protectorate and to change the form of government, the Ecuadorian president tried repeatedly to convince the British leaders to take possession of the Galápagos Islands as partial payment of Ecuador's debt to English bondholders. The British government, surprisingly enough, showed only modest interest in the suggestion and ultimately rejected it on the grounds that the islands were not sufficiently valuable to justify the risk of a possible confrontation with the United States and France.[60]

In his dealings with the French government General Flores apparently adopted an approach similar to that used with the British.[61] In December 1843 the Ecuadorian chief executive initiated a series of friendly overtures, lavishing praise on King Louis Philippe and promising the French consul to maintain much closer relations with France. Next, Flores sent personal greetings to the French monarch, via Consul Levrault, hinting at his own lack of attachment to republican forms, and declaring that he would receive suggestions from France with "the liveliest interest."[62] When the French government delayed a response, Flores proceeded to make additional overtures that bore a marked resemblance to those used with the Spanish chargé. The Ecuadorian president offered to conclude a generous trade treaty with France and suggested the possibility of French colonization in the Galápagos Islands. And he even managed to insinuate a request to be awarded the "Star of the Great Office of the Legion of Honor." Flores apparently impressed the French consul very favorably, because the latter's dispatches reflected a strong bias toward the president. Nevertheless, Levrault failed to convince the Paris government, for approval of the monarchical project was not granted.[63] In the latter part of 1844 Flores made a final, desperate attempt to arrange for a French-backed throne in Ecuador by suggesting the selection of the imprisoned Louis Napoleon for the Ecuadorian crown, but Louis Philippe refused to release the candidate from prison.[64]

Only the Spanish government gave favorable consideration to the "grand project," but even the Spaniards, though intrigued by the prospects of establishing dynastic ties with daughter nations, were cautious about accepting the plan. The reasons for their delay are not known, but Spanish authorities were probably worried about several aspects of Flores' scheme. The Spanish navy was small and the military risks in the planned invasion of Peru were considerable. If the plan should fail, there would be not only military but political losses that would do irreparable damage to Spain's prestige in Spanish America, which was still weak and fragile as a result of the wars of Independence.[65] The broad scope of the plan, embracing three nations, must also have given pause to cautious men. Finally, Flores' plan to confiscate the properties of the religious orders was bound to raise eyebrows, for Spaniards understood very well that an attack on the Catholic Church would cause political problems by antagonizing the Ecuadorian clergy and the most conservative groups—the very elements most likely to support the establishment of a throne in Quito under favorable circumstances.[66]

Nevertheless, after weighing the potential risks and benefits, the government in Madrid found Flores' project too tempting to resist. Flattered by the invitation to place princes of the royal family on Andean thrones, and excited by the prospect of regaining influence over former colonies on the Pacific Coast, the ministry decided in April 1843 to approve the proposals and to send two ships of the royal navy to provide the "moral support" requested by the Ecuadorian president.[67] Though the formal communication of acceptance of the plan did not reach Quito for almost a year, Flores must have anticipated a favorable reply, for in late November 1843, Chargé Potestad hastily returned to Madrid for consultations.[68] The envoy's return to Spain could be taken as a rather good sign that the government wished to confer with its diplomatic agent before making a final commitment to the plan. Nevertheless, Flores was extremely pleased when Juan Pío Montúfar, acting for the absent Potestad, informed him that Her Majesty's government had approved his proposals (apparently the most ambitious ones) and was ready to send the requested naval support. The Ecuadorian president responded that he too was ready to carry out his commitments and suggested that the negotiation of a treaty between their two countries was the best way to carry out the completed change in the form of government. He informed the acting chargé that the port of Guayaquil would provide the Spanish warships with excellent accommodations and that his plans for Peru and Bolivia would be executed soon after the arrival of the Spanish ships.[69]

Thus, in April 1844, it appeared that the "grand project" would finally go forward. A Spanish naval force could be expected soon in the waters of the Guayas estuary—or so Flores believed. With this augmentation in sea power it would be possible to carry out the plan that Flores and Santa Cruz had been dreaming of for several years. But the plan was a complex one that depended on the successful execution of several coordinated moves. Not only was it necessary to acquire naval supremacy off the coast of Peru, but General Santa Cruz would have to regain power in either Bolivia or Peru—or, preferably, in both countries. In addition, the power of the chief executive in Ecuador had to be expanded sufficiently to permit the president to carry out the transformation of the government from republic to monarchy. Flores did not neglect the necessary preparations. In fact, even before receiving formal approval from Spain, he had already begun to overhaul the constitution in a fashion designed to make way for monarchy.

9

THE "CHARTER OF SLAVERY," 1843–1845

When President Flores issued an executive decree on 21 October 1842 convoking a national convention to meet on 15 January 1843, word spread throughout Ecuador that the Constitution of Ambato—Rocafuerte's constitution—would be replaced. It was also said that Flores intended to perpetuate himself in power.[1] Surprisingly, however, there were no rumors of a project to introduce monarchy, for this part of Flores' plan remained a dark secret.

There was scattered but muffled discontent with the president's move. The only outspoken opposition to the idea of a constituent congress came from the members of the municipal council of Quito who issued a protest against the proposed convention. The troublesome councilors were quickly hailed into court for "subversion" by the governor of Pichincha.[2] Most of the opponents of the administration chose to withhold criticism of the national convention and to await its outcome. After all, as the president had made clear, the dissolution of the Congress of 1841 had revealed serious flaws in the existing constitutional system. Even Rocafuerte, long an admirer of Chile's conservative Constitution of 1833, conceded the need for a convention to make amendments to the nation's political charter. Indeed, there was strong sentiment in Ecuador in favor of revising the constitution, in accord with what seemed to be a wave of rewriting government charters in nearby nations.[3]

When Flores convoked the national convention in late 1842 he also issued a decree setting forth the rules under which the deputies would be elected.[4] In most respects the regulations followed the conservative and aristocratic patterns already estab-

lished in earlier Ecuadorian elections by requiring indirect elections and by setting substantial property requirements for the
office of deputy.[5] But article 24 of the decree was exceptional,
for it permitted all members of the executive branch except the
president to serve as members of the forthcoming convention.
This seemingly innocuous provision, buried in the middle of
the regulations, provided the key to control of the elections, for
it allowed the president and his party to name most of the
candidates from the ranks of the executive branch, thus assuring a preponderance of proadministration views. Flores did not
admit publicly the improper purpose of article 24, but, as we
have seen, he confided to the Spanish chargé in Quito that the
election was "a matter already arranged beforehand."[6] Though
Flores exaggerated his ability to determine the membership of
the constituent congress, the elections resulted in a convention
heavily dominated by the executive branch. Not only were generals, colonels, and provincial governors elected, but even the
vice-president, ministers of state, and justices of the Supreme
Court served as deputies. Although no one charged that there
were irregularities in the elections, it was obvious that the selection of the representatives in the constituent congress was managed by the administration.[7]

Flores' success in controlling a substantial majority of the deputies made him too confident of his ability to impose his views and
manipulate events. Among the delegates were public figures of
independent mind like José Joaquín de Olmedo, José Modesto
Larrea, Colonel José María Urbina, and Vicente Rocafuerte,
some of whom would turn against the government and conspire
to oust Flores from power.[8] But Flores underestimated the potential influence of such adversaries and overestimated his own
power. As a consequence of his lack of clear political perception,
the president committed a series of crucial mistakes that not only
played into the hands of his adversaries but ultimately provoked
a successful rebellion against his administration.

The most important error of judgment was Flores' failure to
consult adequately with Rocafuerte and other coastal politicians
about his plans for constitutional revision and his own reelection to the presidency. Without substantial support from
Guayaquil the government would find itself in serious difficul-

ties. Another mistake was the alienation of the powerful clerical hierarchy by insistence on policies that displeased Church leaders. Yet another blunder was the hasty imposition of tax reforms, which, though meritorious in some respects, proved to be so unpopular that they touched off angry and dangerous protests. The government's faltering attempts to cope with its irate adversaries revealed the basic weakness of the regime.

The first sign of a strain between church and state came with the president's promulgation of election rules for the convention. Article 24 of the regulations excluded all men of the cloth from the forthcoming constituent assembly. Since clergymen had served in past congresses, this innovation was offensive to the clergy, who constituted one of the most conservative and articulate power groups in the nation. Flores recognized the importance of the clergy, for he declared privately that "the influence of the priests and the friars" was one of the chief causes of Ecuador's backwardness, "as much because of their wealth as because of the fanaticism that they seek to perpetuate in the lower classes of the people." After the adoption of a new constitution he proposed "the reform of the friars by confiscation of their properties, along with various other improvements."[9] Such views, if sincere, would make it difficult to win the support of the church. Thus, Flores not only passed up an opportunity to weld together a strong conservative alliance but assured himself of the hostility of most of the clergy.[10]

The national convention met in Quito on the appointed day, 15 January 1843. Vicente Rocafuerte, one of only six deputies not in attendance, was detained by the yellow fever epidemic in Guayaquil and by the complications of an embarrassing incident in which he had intemperately accused the whole judicial branch of "protecting crime rather than defending virtue." The fiery governor of Guayaquil would arrive in Quito to take his seat later, but only after apologizing to the justices of the Supreme Court.[11]

President Flores initiated the business of the constituent assembly by presenting a lengthy address that offered the customary boasts of accomplishments by the executive but which emphasized the need for quite drastic changes in the constitution. Though he mentioned the new diplomatic ties with "the Spanish

Monarchy" and urged payment of the Spanish debt "in the short-
est time possible," he did not breathe a word of the secret monarchical plan that was afoot. He chose instead to educate the deputies to the necessity of sweeping governmental reforms. He
pointed critically at Ecuador's "fragile and defective institutions," and he illustrated the nature of changes needed by draw-
ing lessons from the history of the great republics of western
civilization.[12]

In reviewing examples of the past Flores described the great
variety of republican institutional forms and emphasized the
importance of shaping the political constitution of a nation to
fit the particular nature of its society. He dismissed the governmental systems of ancient Greece as alien to Ecuador, but he
pointed approvingly to the office of archon with lifetime tenure and to the Athenian Areopagus, that peculiar institution
which so fascinated Bolívar. Flores' reference to the Areopagus suggests that he was subtly recommending the Liberator's
short-lived constitution of Bolivia of 1826 which provided a
governmental structure midway between a monarchy and a
republic.[13] The Ecuadorian president admired the "conservative Senate of Rome," which "assured . . . domestic order," and
he called attention to a number of European republics that
provided for long terms of office or lifetime appointments of
magistrates and legislators. He concluded his survey of republican institutions with some critical remarks about the Constitution of the United States, which he regarded as unworthy of
imitation, even though, in his opinion, that document embod-
ied more conservative principles than Latin Americans generally recognized.[14]

Flores saved most of his scorn for the Ecuadorian Constitution of 1835, about which he voiced many complaints. He
charged that the legislature was improperly constituted, so that
the two houses tended to unite against the president, who
lacked effective veto power. Periodic elections of legistlators, he
said, caused "upheavals, domestic commotions, and . . . perpetual restlessness." A pernicious tendency toward irresponsible
political opposition, Flores charged, was undermining the effectiveness of the government in a most alarming manner. "Only
in hereditary monarchies," said the president, "which have

strength of their own, and sufficient resources to resist, . . . can a systematic opposition be permitted."

Flores seemed to be on the verge of recommending monarchy at this point, but he refrained from it. Though he remarked that civil liberties were less meaningful in republican Ecuador than in monarchical England, he did not openly endorse kingship as a solution for the nation's governmental problems. Rather than making requests for specific reforms, the president espoused general principles that were sometimes articulated somewhat vaguely. Though Flores hinted at a need for a longer presidential term, which he most certainly wanted, he refrained from recommending such a change in order to avoid giving the impression that he wished to perpetuate himself in power. He declared that he favored "a healthy, rational, enlightened reform [that would] conserve liberal principles," but he did not explain how this goal might be achieved except through the formation of a "conservative Senate."[15]

Behind the scenes President Flores was not coy about the specifics of constitutional reform. In fact, with the aid of his closest advisers he prepared a draft constitution for presentation to the convention. Flores even sought the counsel of the prestigious New Granadan statesman Don Pedro Gual, who prepared a draft charter for Ecuador which included some of Flores' pet notions, such as lifetime terms for senators. But, to the disappointment of Flores, Gual did not approve of a presidential term of more than six years, and Gual's draft appears to have been adopted only in part.[16]

From his confidential disclosures to the Spanish chargé we know that Flores intended not only to extend the presidential term to ten years but to permit immediate reelection. He also wished to extend the terms of members of congress, with senators holding office for life. At the same time the president proposed to weaken the influence of the legislature within the government by permitting it to meet only infrequently.[17] The purpose of the projected charter, as disclosed by Flores to the Spanish envoy, was "to prepare the spirit of the nation for the establishment of a system of government which, although preserving the republican name, would approach a constitutional monarchy as far as possible."[18]

The convention's first draft of a new charter of government apparently followed the president's suggestions very closely, for it provided for a very conservative government with a greatly strengthened executive branch. It extended the presidential term to eight years, permitted immediate reelection of the president, and augmented executive power in several ways. With regard to the legislature, senatorial tenure was changed from four years to lifetime, and the new congress was turned into a weak and ineffective body by provisions that permitted it to meet only once in four years for a period of no more than four months. The presidential veto power was bolstered by a provision requiring the vote of three-quarters of the members of both legislative chambers to override an executive objection.

General Flores must have been quite pleased with most aspects of the preliminary version of the new charter, though he was probably unhappy with a presidential term of only eight years, rather than ten, and with an article taken from the Constitution of 1835 which declared that the Ecuadorian nation "is not, and cannot be, the patrimony of any family or person."[19] There was nothing to be done about this anti-monarchical clause, for any open objection to it would have been interpreted as a possible move toward monarchy. The troublesome article remained in the document, because Flores did not dare to broach the issue even with the most-trusted leaders in the convention.

Most of the business of the constituent assembly went smoothly until the arrival of Governor Rocafuerte in mid-February. Not unexpectedly, the outspoken and strong-minded guayaquileño quickly stirred up a stormy debate over the draft constitution and the issue of reelecting the incumbent president. An anonymous writer, probably Flores himself, later charged Rocafuerte with hypocrisy for having earlier urged the president to seek reelection and to establish "a military dictatorship for twenty-five years." Personal ambition, according to the anonymous writer, prompted Rocafuerte to break with Flores and to seek power for himself.[20]

Frustrated ambition was probably one of the governor's motives in opposing the president's plans, but Rocafuerte was also convinced that Flores was a corrupt and evil leader who was causing much damage in Ecuador. Mustering all of his energy and cogency, Rocafuerte launched a vehement attack on the draft constitution under consideration by the convention. His arguments were so persuasive that he managed to win acceptance of several important amendments by the pro-Flores assembly. Among his parliamentary victories were the rejection of lifetime terms for senators, a prohibition of immediate reelection of the president and the vice-president, and the exclusion of the clergy from service in the congress (a point favored by Flores but omitted from the first draft). But the irate governor met defeat in his proposals to institute jury trials in criminal cases, to abolish the death penalty for political crimes, and to disestablish the Roman Catholic Church. More importantly, he failed in an attempt to strengthen the role of congress by providing for biennial sessions rather than one meeting every four years, as stipulated in the draft constitution. Rocafuerte also failed, not surprisingly, to win assent to his suggestion that all members of the convention be barred from holding any government office or post during the next presidential period.[21]

The new Constitution of 1843, approved by the convention on 31 March, was a mixture of many ideas and tendencies. Rocafuerte later denounced it as excessively "aristocratic," but careful analysis of its contents does not confirm this charge.[22] Restrictions on suffrage and office-holding through property, income, and literacy requirements, though part of the new constitution, were not innovations any more than the provisions for indirect election of congressmen.[23] The lengthening of terms of office for senators and representatives to twelve years and eight respectively was a conservative move, but it did not increase the influence of the upper classes. Thus, it would seem that the new constitution did not inaugurate aristocratic government in Ecuador, but rather continued it.

The distinguishing characteristic of the fundamental law of 1843 was not a provision for elitist control but the creation of a vigorous executive branch, strengthened at the expense of the legislature. The bicameral congress was to meet only once in four years for no more than ninety days. The veto power of the president was nearly absolute, for a three-quarters majority was necessary in both houses to override a veto—a virtual impossibility. Though the senate was empowered to elect a "Permanent Commission" of five senators to advise the president when the Congress was not in session, this provision was a flimsy substitute for frequent meetings of congress, and it did not make up for the legislature's loss of an effective response to executive vetoes.[24]

The new constitution expanded presidential authority in a number of other important ways. It delegated to the chief executive almost unlimited power of appointment and removal. Absolute executive control over removal of appointed officials, not permitted in earlier constitutions, gave the president unchallenged supremacy over the entire administrative machinery of the nation, reaching from the highest levels down to the local cantons and parishes.[25] In addition, the president needed only the consent of the Permanent Commission of the Senate to declare war, and he could assume direct command of the armed forces without relinquishing the presidential office. Only the president was authorized to convoke an extraordinary session of the congress.[26]

Though the presidency was greatly invigorated by the new charter of government, the new powers did not turn the chief executive into a constitutional dictator. The president was not only elected by the congress, but he and his ministers were accountable to the legislators and were subject to an impeachment process similar to that in the Constitution of the United States. In addition, the ministers were required to appear before congress to present reports on the budget and other matters.[27] The charter also contained the usual articles that permitted the exercise of extraordinary powers in the event of foreign invasion or domestic revolution, but these powers were narrowly circumscribed. Even arrests and detentions for alleged conspiracy were subject to a three-day limitation, after which regular legal proceedings were required.[28] The president was limited to a term of eight years, could not be reelected, and could not suspend or dissolve congress. A sort of bill of rights forbade censorship of the press, outlawed entailed estates (mayorazgos) and titles of nobility, and guaranteed the right of due process to all Ecuadorians.[29]

On 24 March, just a week before the new constitution was

approved in its final form, an angry Vicente Rocafuerte took the floor of the convention to condemn the projected charter of government as "a political abortion." These strong words provoked indignation among most of the deputies. General Guerra, a staunch supporter of Flores, had to be restrained from making a physical attack on the governor. In the midst of great disorder in the chamber, Rocafuerte threatened to walk out of this "meeting of slaves," but was persuaded by a few friends to remain.[30]

But the worst was yet to come, for the fiery deputy returned on the following day to deliver a prepared speech that made his remarks of the previous day sound moderate by comparison. The draft constitution, Rocafuerte declared, was "null and void" because the members of the convention had not been granted power by the people "to turn the [nation's] institutions upside down." In discarding the Constitution of Ambato and concocting a new charter, the deputies had created, in the words of Rocafuerte, "a political monstrosity." The purpose of the new constitution, said the indignant deputy, was to "abet the aspirations, the avarice, and the ambition" of General Flores. "This new Constitution," scolded Rocafuerte, perhaps with more truth than he realized, "is the result of skillful and complicated intrigues to reelect General Flores to the presidency, much to the dishonor of the nation and to the detriment of its public revenues."[31]

Not content with these accusations against the convention and the president, the deputy from Guayaquil went on to establish a rationale for revolution against the Flores regime. The new constitution, with its "aristocratic principles," said Rocafuerte, "tends to prepare the way for tyranny." Soon there will be a conflict between the old constitution and the new "which will produce torrents of disorder and rebellion." Responsibility for violation of the fundamental contract of government, declared the irate deputy, rested on the shoulders of the president. "It is a great calamity," Rocafuerte concluded, "that General Flores governs."[32]

Rocafuerte later declared that one of the purposes of his caustic remarks was to provoke the president into resigning from office and into refusing to accept reelection.[33] If so, his plan worked badly, for Flores remained in office while Rocafuerte felt compelled to withdraw from the convention. After attempting unsuccessfully to organize a revolution in Guayaquil, Rocafuerte took ship to Peru. While living in voluntary exile he worked tirelessly to bring down the government of his rival in Ecuador.[34]

Though Rocafuerte failed to block the adoption of the new constitution, his influence on events in Ecuador from 1843 to the fall of the Flores government in 1845 can scarcely be exaggerated. His vehement speech of 25 March at the convention was profoundly disturbing to Flores and the president's supporters. Even though the guayaquileño leader had lost much of his popularity during his term in the presidency, he was still widely respected. Moreover, his mastery of the language of political denunciation was unexcelled, and he knew it. During the year 1843 Rocafuerte wrote a series of fourteen essays entitled *A la nación*, the first of which he published in Guayaquil and the rest in Lima. These polemical essays, which appeared in book form in the following year, portrayed Flores as a dissolute, vulgar, tyrannical ruler. "Ravenous adventurer," "political strumpet," "traitor," leader of a "band of Ethiopians," and "Janizary" were a few of the rhetorical appellations lavished on the Ecuadorian president by the venomous pen of the political expatriate.[35] Apparently it was Rocafuerte, too, who invented the colorful term "Charter of Slavery" to refer to the constitution of 1843, a phrase that soon caught on in Ecuador and helped to undermine whatever respectability the new fundamental law might have had.[36]

General Flores attempted to respond in kind to the damaging attacks by accusing the Guayaquil leader of "childish vanity," "crass ignorance," and "arrogance." In an essay likewise entitled "A la nación," Flores charged that Rocafuerte was "the Proteus of Ecuador who changes his forms and colors according to his convenience and ambition: a tyrant when he governs and an anarchist when he is out of power."[37] But the president's countercharges were much less effective than the powerful invective of Rocafuerte.

In the sixth essay of *A la nación* the guayaquileño pursued the interesting theme of the logical consequences of an alleged aristocratic domination under the new constitution. Though Rocafuerte knew nothing of the plans for Flores and Santa Cruz to establish monarchy in the Andean nations, he nevertheless detected what he believed to be a strong tendency toward monarchism. He charged that the new "monstrous" regime imposed upon Eucador an "aristocracy more humiliating and shameful than that of Genoa and Venice." The Senate, with its twelve-year terms of office and the possibility of reelection, constituted, in Rocafuerte's opinion, "a lifetime aristocracy" similar to the aristocracies of England, France, and Brazil. He also noted that the convention had adopted a legal formula for the promulgation of laws and decrees (using the regal *nos*) which smacked of "the authority and rule of kings, princes, and prelates." Under this "negroid, military aristocracy" commanded by Flores, the Guayaquil leader concluded, Ecuador could expect within eight years to have a "lifetime presidency."[38]

Rocafuerte's charge was very close to the mark, for Flores, who on 31 March was reelected president for a third term, probably intended to hold office indefinitely in the event that he failed to erect a monarchy in Quito. The new constitution was important in his plans, for it provided the means of making a transition to a monocratic regime either under a Spanish prince or a lifetime president. In order to promote respect for the new fundamental law, promulgated on 16 April 1843, President Flores arranged for an elaborate ceremony in the cathedral of Quito in which all high officials of church and state swore allegiance to the new charter and listened to a solemn Te Deum mass.[39]

Elaborate ceremonies, however, could not heal the wounds that had been opened by the work of the national convention. A majority of the clergy joined with the friends of Rocafuerte in their open opposition to the new government. This became evident during the oath-taking when the secretary of the bishop read a reference to the controversial article of the constitution which reserved patronal rights to the state and permitted private worship by non-Catholic religious groups. These provisions deeply offended the clerical hierarchy, and the offense was not mitigated by another constitutional provision that excluded priests from serving in the Congress.[40]

Attempts by the government to "clarify" the offending articles pacified some of the agitated spirits, but in conservative

Cuenca troops were alerted for possible antigovernment demonstrations by priests and the devout. Though violence was averted at the oath-taking ceremonies, authorities worried about widespread anticonstitution murmuring and the founding of an antiadministration newspaper under the editorship of the perennial gadfly, Father Solano. Outspoken clerical opposition to the government soon spread from Cuenca to Guayaquil and Quito.[41]

Ultimately most of the clergy agreed to swear to uphold the constitution, but many took the oath with reluctance and under duress. A minority, among them the prestigious coadjutor of Quito, Dr. José Miguel Carrión, refused to pledge their loyalty. As a consequence, President Flores ordered that all clerics who refused the oath be removed from their ecclesiastical benefices.[42]

As President Flores commenced his third term he was aware that his efforts to achieve institutional stability were not yielding good results. He had so provoked Rocafuerte and his followers that the spirit of rebellion was lurking in many quarters, especially on the coast. An angry priesthood also presented a serious challenge that threatened the orderly march of government. To cope with the menacing situation Flores decided to turn conciliatory, to attempt to disarm his opponents once more by the superficial device of selecting men of diverse viewpoints for the high posts in government. The most important choices were the aristocratic and independent-minded José Modesto Larrea as minister of government; Francisco de Aguirre, veteran floreano and publicist of Guayaquil, as minister of finance; and Colonel Juan Hipólito Soulín as minister of war and navy. But the leading power among the president's advisers was a newcomer on the political scene, Benigno Malo, whose contradictory name and surname must have prompted many humorous comments among the administration's adversaries. Though Malo was a mere *suplente,* or substitute deputy, from Loja in the recent national convention, he soon rose to the position of minister of government and foreign affairs, replacing the prestigious Larrea. The young and able Malo carried the heaviest burden in the new ministry, working assiduously to molify the dissident clergy and to harmonize the clashing interests of the nation.[43]

The political atmosphere was so poisoned with animosity that it was very difficult to clear the air. Nevertheless, the new administration, under Malo's leadership, endeavored to conciliate the opposition, especially the clergy. The executive branch undertook negotiations with the Vatican in a vain attempt to arrive at a concordat with the Papacy. In yet another move, the administration indicated publicly a willingness to permit the return of the Jesuits, who had been expelled in 1767 by Spain. Though neither of these initiatives produced significant change, these friendly gestures toward the Church showed that the government earnestly wished to mend fences with the clerical hierarchy.[44]

Relations between the executive and the legislature (still the national convention in 1843) were quite harmonious, largely because most of the deputies had been hand-picked by the administration. The two branches collaborated on a program of legislation that included measures to institute one year of military service for white and mestizo youths, to forbid censorship of the press, to forbid seditious and obscene publications, and to improve the roads.[45] In a bid to establish better understanding with England, the government approved a new law ostensibly prohibiting the importation of slaves and granting freedom at age twenty-five to all children born of slave mothers. However, a loophole, similar to one in the earlier law of 1830, permitting special licenses to import slaves for mines and agriculture, so weakened the measure that the British government refused to ratify a treaty with Ecuador ending the slave trade.[46]

The most important political issue facing the executive and the legislature in 1843 was neither slavery nor press freedom, but rather a developing financial crisis resulting from large treasury deficits. The president and the convention worked without friction to find a solution to the problem, but the government blundered so badly that it aroused a dangerous political storm. Though the legislators had a hand in the controversial fiscal legislation, it was primarily the policies of the president which caused the violent opposition to the government.

To meet an emergency in which the treasury could no longer pay many of its employees,[47] the president proposed major tax reforms. In the light of his unfortunate experience in 1831 with the temporary abolition of Indian tribute and the imposition of the short-lived contribución ordinaria Flores should have known that major changes in the taxation system were very difficult to accomplish.[48] It was therefore surprising that in 1843, when beset by angry political opponents, Flores chose to gamble with a major plan to overhaul the tax system. Obviously the president had not gauged the temper of his opponents or the mood of the nation.

In fairness to General Flores it must be said that an increase in revenues was imperative and that the burden of taxation in Ecuador was very low, averaging less than one peso a year per inhabitant.[49] Furthermore, Flores' proposed tax program was balanced and humanitarian, especially with regard to the over-burdened Indian. Nevertheless, the tax reforms of 1843 proved to be highly unpopular among the white and mestizo people of Ecuador.

In requesting legislative approval of new taxes the chief executive proposed first that either the inequitable Indian tribute (contribución personal) be abolished and be replaced by a general levy on all Ecuadorians, or that tribute be extended to all adult males. Second, he recommended that import duties be raised in order to "promote the spirit of enterprise" and bring greater prosperity to agriculture and industry.[50]

Both proposals generated lengthy debates in the convention. The tariff proposal provoked all the old antagonisms between coastal and highland interests, while the general head tax aroused fears of popular resistance to the imposition of a new general tax. The deputies, apprehensive over the public's possible reaction to such major reforms, delayed action for five months. Finally, in early June 1843, the reluctant congressmen dutifully approved the administration's tax measures, one raising the tariff and the other imposing a new tax called the "general contribution."[51]

The general contribution was a complex measure that actually comprised two taxes. The first was a business, professional, and urban property tax, which was graduated upward according to the ability to pay. For example, physicians and pharmacists on the coast were to pay twenty-four pesos annually, while their counterparts in the highlands were assessed only twelve pesos, on the assumption that incomes were smaller in the interior than on the coast. Similarly, coastal merchants were to pay three-tenths of one percent of the value of their capital, and highland merchants only one-tenth of a percent. Priests were assessed a flat four pesos annually without regard to the region of their residence. The second levy of the general contribution was a head tax of three and one-half pesos on all adult males. Exempted from the general contribution were Indians, soldiers, and members of religious orders, but Indians were to continue paying tribute of three and one-half pesos, which was identical to the new head tax on whites and mestizos.[52]

President Flores apparently expected some degree of opposition to the new levy, for his decree of implementation warned that persons failing to pay the new obligation would be conscripted into the army.[53] But he was scarcely prepared for the vehement reaction which swept through the nation. Up and down the Andes, from the town of Tulcán in the north to Azogues in the south, angry demonstrators gathered to shake their fists and to shout their determination to resist any authorities who might try to collect the tax or to draft them into the army. "Death to the three pesos!" became the cry of the outraged citizens.[54]

Opponents of the general contribution objected most strongly to the fact that the new tax imposed on white and mestizo populations an obligation similar to Indian tribute, a tax associated only with the servile Indian people. It was not surprising, then, that Ecuadorians viewed the new levy as tantamount to tribute and commonly called it the "contribution of whites" to distinguish it from the "personal contribution" of Indians. Most whites and mestizos felt that the imposition of "tribute" upon them was an act of social degradation that equated them with the miserable Indians.

The anti-head-tax riots and uprisings of 1843 broke out in small towns and villages of the highlands both to the north and the south of Quito. It was not the larger cities but rather the small, rural communities (such as Chambo, Licto, Punín, Guano, Cayambe, Cotacache, and Tabacundo) that witnessed the first acts of resistance and violence. The first disorders appeared to be completely spontaneous outbursts of anger that, for the most part, lacked leadership, organization, and planning. Apparently most of the rioters did not seek to overturn the government, for their typical cry of "Death to the three pesos!" was accompanied by the shout of "Long live the government!" Dissident priests reportedly incited revolt in some of the parishes, and Ecuadorian political exiles in New Granada took advantage of the disorders to cross the frontier and take part in some of the fighting. But authorities found no evidence of an organized conspiracy against the regime.[55]

Many of the disorders were little more than vociferous protests, but some of them turned violent and menacing, such as the riot in Cayambe, a town only thirty miles northwest of Quito. There an angry mob killed a wealthy landowner and tax collector, Colonel Adolphe Klinger, and dragged his body through the town square. President Flores responded quickly to the emergency by dispatching the much-feared General Juan Otamendi to pacify the Cayambe-Otavalo region in the north and by sending General Bernardo Daste southward with troops to maintain order in the restless province of Chimborazo. The generals and provincial governors were instructed to exercise restraint and moderation, but Otamendi's troops killed about forty rebels. Fearing continued outbreaks of trouble, President Flores requested and obtained use of extraordinary powers from the Permanent Commission of the Senate. The storm of protest was quieted, however, not by the use of broadened executive authority but by the president's decision to cancel the general contribution.[56]

The official newspaper of Ecuador reported in September that all revolts had been quelled and that order had returned in all parts of the nation. In fact, however, unrest continued to simmer and in October General Daste was sent to the province of Chimborazo once more to put down a new rebellion that had broken out in the city of Ambato. The renewal of resistance to authority in October was alarming to the government, because the rebels for the first time showed signs of organization under the leadership of Colonel Felipe Viteri. The latter raised the banner of "Religion and Rocafuerte" (an incongruous slogan) in an effort to arouse sentiment against Flores and the new constitution. Dr. Francisco Montalvo (brother of the later famous Juan Montalvo) and other opponents of the president were arrested for involvement in the October uprising. Montalvo was exiled to Peru and Colonel Viteri was imprisoned in the Galápagos after his defeat by General Daste.[57]

The revolts of August and October 1843 revealed the underlying weakness of the Flores regime in the period immediately following the adoption of the new constitution. Villagers and townspeople of the small highland communities who normally had little or no connection with national politics were suddenly swept into a widespread movement of rebellion against the aggravation of a new tax. The impulse to resist national authority appears to have sprung from the lower classes rather than from the anti-Flores elements among the prosperous landowners, businessmen, and professional people who were hit the hardest by the general contribution. Most descriptions of the disorders indicate that it was the lower-class whites and mestizos—whose economic and social proximity to the Indian made them acutely sensitive to measures that tended to equate them with the Indian—who reacted with indignation to the "contribution of whites."

Government reports of the uprisings said nothing of a war of classes, perhaps because the administration did not want to spread panic among the well-to-do. But a spirit of class conflict, or rivalry of socioeconomic groups, was evident in some of the disorders. The killing of Colonel Klinger was in part an act of aggression on the part of white and mestizo peasants against a wealthy landowner. Several large haciendas were sacked and looted in the antitax violence that swept through the highlands.[58] The French consul, Leonice Levrault, who followed the revolts with avid interest, reported that the "peasants" were engaged in an armed rebellion that threatened to overturn the government of Flores. "The revolution," he wrote, "if it should take place, would be a social revolution rather than a political one. . . . Its object is to destroy the aristocracy." He believed that a "caste war" with a "tendency toward social disorganization" was a clear possibility if General Flores could not bring the rebels under control.[59]

The official newspaper of Ecuador, not unexpectedly, sought to give the impression that the government had acted swiftly, decisively, and humanely to resolve the crisis. But Consul Levrault reported that "public opinion reproaches the Government for not having taken suitable measures to avoid the shedding of blood." Levrault warned that political dissidents would be quick to take advantage of "the weakness of the Government which is represented as incapable of taking energetic measures."[60] Though the French consul hoped that President Flores would be able to rally the upper classes to his support, he reported that "the general opinion . . . blames all the ills that devastate this unhappy country on the chief executive." Levrault believed that Flores was surrounded by people who were "largely in agreement with his enemies," who gave him bad advice, and who were seeking to convince him that he ought to resign from the presidency.[61] British consul Walter Cope analyzed the situation in somewhat similar fashion, concluding that "an alarming crisis is approaching."[62]

In August and September, during the early stage of the highland disorders, the people of Guayaquil took no part in the antitax movement. At first glance this quiescence of the Guayas region, normally so prone to restlessness and protest, seems strange. Not only was the general contribution levied upon the coast and the interior, but it imposed much higher rates of taxation on property and professions for the guayaquileños than for the highlanders. Nevertheless, there were no reported rebellions in the coastal region against the "tribute of whites," probably in part because the absence of dense Indian populations made the people less sensitive to the social leveling implicit in the new tax. The relative quiet in Guayas was also to be explained, in the view of the British consul, by the fact that people of the coast "are little disposed to popular commotions, and are more under the control of the Commercial Body by whom such measures are viewed with alarm." The merchant community, though strongly in disagreement with the government, chose to express its dissatisfaction by "a more legal and orderly mode."[63]

Though guayaquileños disliked the new "tribute of whites," what they really hated was an upward revision of the custom duties, promulgated on the same day as the head tax. The issue of the tariff, of course, had caused political division in the nation since independence. Guayaquil's preference for low duties and the interior's insistence on protection were contrary impulses that could not be reconciled easily. As recently as April 1840 Guayaquil merchants had attempted, without success, to win reductions in the tariff on textiles.[64] In 1843 the national convention, acting on the request of the president, adopted a new law on customs duties which raised the rates on some types of fabrics as well as on a variety of alcoholic beverages and other items. The new law was a complex measure designed to favor some economic interests of the coast, such as sugar, cotton, coffee, and salt producers.[65] But the basic purpose of the new law was to provide greater protection for the national economy, especially for the highlands, and this fact was not lost upon the merchant community of the port city. Of course, many guayaquileños had been turned against the government by Rocafuerte before he departed for Lima. News of the highland revolts against the general contribution provided the merchants with an opportune moment to assail the government by means of a strongly worded petition.

In late October a group of merchants petitioned the Flores administration to convoke an extraordinary meeting of the Congress to enact a reduction in the customs rates. This request was quickly followed by a second petition, this one signed by almost two hundred of Guayaquil's most prominent citizens, among them the poet-statesman José Joaquín de Olmedo and a future president of Ecuador, Diego Novoa. The second petition, though couched in polite language, denounced the Flores regime rather harshly. It declared, for example, that the Constitution of 1843 lacked "popular sanction" and had been "tacitly disapproved by a majority" of the people. After pointing out that Guyayaquil had not been properly represented in the constituent convention because of the yellow fever epidemic, it demanded the convocation of a new convention and guarantees of honest elections, free from "intrigues and personal interest."[66]

The menacing protests from Guayaquil, which arrived in Quito just as the last highland rebellion was being quelled, put the national government in a new state of alarm. The Council of Government decided that the petitions were "notoriously subversive" and recommended that those who signed the disrespectful documents should be prosecuted.[67] General Flores, however, decided that forceful repression was not the answer to the problem. In early November, sensing that the crisis called for conciliation, the president hastened to Guayaquil to deal with the problem personally.

Soon after his arrival Flores managed to calm some of the agitated spirits and to work out an arrangement that appeared to satisfy the discontented guayaquileños. He agreed to issue a decree that in effect reinstated the earlier and lower customs duties. In addition, he promised to call an extraordinary meeting of Congress to deal with the outstanding political controversies. Whether the president actually intended to convoke the Congress is not known, but he failed to fulfill this pledge before losing power. Nevertheless, the modification in the tariff regulations satisfied the merchants for the moment and permitted Flores to return to Quito and to renounce the extraordinary executive powers in the belief that he had pacified the nation.[68]

In reality, the problem of political discontent had not been resolved at all. Flores' concessions on the tariff and his cancellation of the general contribution had temporarily calmed the opposition and had bought some time to work out long-term solutions, but the loss of revenues from the new taxes deepened the fiscal crisis. The national treasury was now in worse shape than ever because of the cost of putting down the recent revolts. The French consul in Quito reported that in early 1844 the problems of the treasury were mounting not only because of the disorders but because of the reappearance of yellow fever in Guayaquil, which reduced commerce and "deprives the Government of its principal resource." The same observer stated that corruption in the treasury continued on a large scale in spite of the efforts of the administration to enforce discipline and honesty on the tax collectors and other fiscal agents of the government.[69]

Further evidence of the deterioration of the Flores administration was seen in the public controversy provoked by Rocafuerte's anti-Flores campaign in Peru, which was so effective that it provoked Ecuador's president to reply. The effect of the unseemly polemic that resulted between the chief executive and a political exile was to diminish the stature and dignity of Flores at a time when he desperately needed to improve his image.[70]

Meanwhile, unsettling rumors spread that Rocafuerte was plotting in Lima to foment revolution in Ecuador.[71] In addition, dissident priests led by Bishop Carrión continued to oppose the government and, according to some reports, to conspire against it.[72]

Thus, by 1844 it could be seen that President Flores' efforts to stabilize the government by means of authoritarian rule and to prepare Ecuador for monarchy were far from successful. Yet Flores did not abandon his grand design to create thrones in Ecuador, Peru, and Bolivia. Not only did he actively pursue confidential talks with Spanish, French, and British diplomatic agents (as described earlier), but he continued to conspire with Santa Cruz.

Not long after the adoption of the Constitution of 1843 the two conspirators agreed on a new plan to recapture power for the ex-Protector in Peru and Bolivia. In August, just when the tax revolts erupted in the highlands, Santa Cruz and a small party of followers secretly boarded a Peruvian vessel in the estuary of the Guayas and headed for the southern coast of Peru. He had been invited to return by the Peruvian president, General Manuel Ignacio de Vivanco, who wished to replace President José Ballivián of Bolivia with Santa Cruz. Vivanco's motives and goals in this murky affair are far from clear, but his well-known monarchist sympathies suggest that he may have been a party to the clandestine project of Flores and Santa Cruz.[73] Though the ex-Protector attempted to shroud his actions in secrecy, his opponents in Peru and Bolivia maintained surveillance of his movements. When he landed on the coast south of Arica he learned that President Vivanco had abandoned the plan to intervene in Bolivia. Instead of being welcomed as a returning hero Santa Cruz was promptly captured and turned over to his worst enemies, Chilean authorities, who whisked him off to imprisonment in southern Chile. He was kept under guard until 1846, when the Chilean government allowed him to depart for Europe.[74]

The capture and internment of Santa Cruz was a severe setback for the "grand project."[75] But the monarchical plan suffered a worse blow in December 1844 when the Spanish ministry, hard-pressed by the need to patrol Spain's own coasts because of internal disorders and overcommitted by a decision to send warships to the Río de la Plata region to protect Spanish subjects there, was obliged to delay the assignment of a naval force to Guayaquil. Though the foreign secretary in Madrid assured General Flores of Spain's continuing friendship and cooperation, the postponement of naval assistance came at a bad time for the embattled Ecuadorian president.[76]

By the close of the year 1844 it was clear that the secret monarchical project could not be carried out. Without naval support and without General Santa Cruz, Flores could not proceed against Peru. Nor could he hope to establish thrones in Lima and La Paz. As for a throne in Quito, this too was out of the question, for the Ecuadorian president's political position was far too precarious to permit him to change the form of government. Framing a new constitution and reelecting Flores by means of a rigged convention, far from consolidating the government and providing stability, had aroused widespread opposition that threatened at any time to overturn the government. Even if naval support from Spain had been forthcoming early in 1845, it seems highly unlikely that the monarchical project could have been consummated. In Ecuador, as in the rest of Spanish America, hatred and distrust of Spain, kindled by the wars of Independence, had not subsided sufficiently to permit the creation of Spanish thrones without provoking strong opposition.[77] Nor was it likely that a squadron of only three Spanish naval vessels would have been capable of handling the Chilean fleet and the military power of other Spanish American nations that were bound to oppose the monarchical project.[78]

President Flores miscalculated badly in his "grand project," not because monarchy was inherently wrong or necessarily unacceptable, but because he placed confidence in the mercurial and unreliable Santa Cruz and in the weak, vacillating, and unpopular government of Spain. Compounding these fundamental errors, Flores chose to embark on his monarchical adventure at a time when his presidential leadership was gravely weakened. General Flores believed, no doubt, that his policies would produce stunning political successes that would yield governmental stability and enhance his own popularity. But he badly misunderstood the nature of Ecuador's difficulties in the 1840s, in part because he failed to distinguish between himself and the state. He convinced himself that his own difficulties as president were proof that the form of government required modification. He believed that Ecuador was ungovernable under existing forms merely because *he* could no longer govern effectively.

If Flores had worked more effectively to solve the fiscal problems of Ecuador, especially the corruption in the tax collection system, he would have eliminated the greatest source of governmental instability. Moreover, had he been willing to step aside at the end of his presidential term in 1843, as the constitution required, the people of the coastal region would have had an opportunity to elect one of their own to the presidential office, thus assuring an alternation in power. But Flores, who was viewed more and more by Ecuadorians as a foreign military adventurer, chose to perpetuate his personal rule, thus exacerbating the difficulties of the nation.

During the year 1844 President Flores made efforts to restore his own prestige and to achieve political harmony in the nation. In an effort to publicize the government's views he installed the polemical Irisarri as editor of the government newspaper, *Gaceta,* and arranged to have the Guatemalan writer bring out a new weekly with the significant title *La Concordia.*[79] But the public relations program failed to calm the nation, in part because the controversial Irisarri was by this time utterly detested not only by the clergy but by the leading citizens of Guayaquil.[80] Flores' reliance on Irisarri was yet another miscalculation.

By the beginning of the year 1845 the collapse of the Flores regime was at hand. Most of the prominent citizens of Guayaquil were opposed to the government, and a revolution was in the planning stage. Out of fear that army units on the coast could not be trusted, the government made the mistake of sending arms to people in the small towns of the Guayas region and to Guaranda, on the edge of the highlands.[81] Many of these weapons fell into the hands of people who turned against the government. In the latter part of February word reached Quito that Vicente Ramón Roca, a merchant-politician of Guayaquil, was organizing a large-scale revolt involving most of the leading citizens and important military units of the Guayas region. The president tried to avert disaster by ordering the arrest of Roca, but this action failed to prevent the outbreak of the insurrection, which occurred on 6 March 1845.[82] Guayaquil once more demonstrated that it was, in the words of the government newspaper, the "forge of . . . civil war, the workshop of revolutions, and Pandora's box of calamities."[83]

After appointing José Félix Valdivieso as acting president, Flores headed for the coast with three or four hundred men to join the loyal General Otamendi and his troops at the president's hacienda La Elvira on the upper Guayas River. He hoped to rally enough support to overwhelm the forces of the port, but by the time he arrived it was too late. The rebel's gained strength with each passing day. General Carlos Wright, commandant-general of Guayas and ostensibly loyal to the government, quickly capitulated to the revolutionary forces for reasons not fully understood. Colonel José María Urbina, governor of the coastal province of Manabí, threw in his lot with Roca and was promptly promoted to the rank of general. Rocafuerte, still in Lima and hoping to become president once more, secured Peruvian recognition of the provisional government and arranged for the shipment of more than a thousand rifles and other war matériel to Guayaquil.[84]

The revolutionary forces, under the command of General Antonio Elizalde, longtime foe of Flores, enjoyed the advantages of superior naval power, communication by sea with the outside world, and the rainy season that kept the lowlands flooded and hampered the operations of Flores' small army of highlanders. The president's fate was sealed by his immobility, which forced him to remain at La Elvira for weeks, while suffering devastating attacks by land and water. As the siege of Flores' camp dragged on, the revolution gradually spread to all parts of the nation. Finally, when it seemed useless to prolong the killing and suffering, on 17 June 1845 President Flores yielded to his adversaries.[85]

Though General Flores was obviously defeated by the insurgents, he contrived to make his failure appear to be merely a statesman's agreement to stop the bloodshed. The accord worked out between the two parties to end the civil war consisted of two documents entitled "conventions" (*convenios*), which would later be referred to as the Treaties of La Virginia, as if they were a formal agreement between two sovereign powers. Flores apparently insisted on using the language of diplomacy, and when he signed the documents he referred to his approval as a "ratification." According to the terms of the agreements, the new regime was to assume responsibility for all debts incurred during the fighting, to respect the honors and pensions of all military officers, and to refrain from persecuting anyone for his opinions and actions in the war. For his part, General Flores undertook to absent himself "voluntarily" from Ecuador for two years, though, curiously, he did not resign the presidency. The provisional government, in return, agreed to permit Flores to continue as general-in-chief of the armed forces with full salary and payment of back salary, half of which was to be paid to Flores' wife, who was to remain in Ecuador. Additionally, the provisional government promised to pay Flores a sum of twenty thousand pesos to cover his expenses in Europe and to guarantee the security of his private properties during his absence. At the end of two years General Flores was to be permitted to return "without any impediments."[86]

Neither General Flores nor the members of the revolutionary government felt honor-bound to observe the terms of the Treaties of La Virginia. After Flores' capitulation the new administration arrested Acting President Valdivieso, General Daste, and many other floreanos, and extorted large "extraordinary contributions" from them in exchange for their liberty.[87] Many military officers were exiled and others were retired, only to have their pensions cut off. A national constituent convention later revoked the "treaties" on the grounds that General Flores had not abided by their provisions.[88]

The deputies of the convention were right, of course, in charging Flores with bad faith. Evidently the defeated president viewed the peace settlement with his adversaries as little more than a means to buy time. The ink was scarcely dry on the conventions when Flores, according to evidence later gathered by the new government, secretly began efforts to bribe insurgent military officers and to stir up opposition to Roca and his followers.[89]

When his efforts to turn the tables on the victorious insurgents failed, Flores wrote a confidential letter to the acting Spanish chargé, Juan Pío Montúfar, which partially revealed his intentions. In this letter, written on the eve of his departure for Europe, the former chief of state asked the Spanish diplomat to write the first secretary of state in Madrid on Flores' behalf requesting arrangements for a friendly reception in Spain. Flores expressed the hope of gaining entrée into the "inner circle of government" in the Spanish court. Montúfar, mindful of the monarchical project that had failed, responded to the request enthusiastically. He called the attention of his superiors in Madrid to "the repeated proofs of friendship and deference that General Flores has always shown toward the Government [of Spain]."[90]

Flores' confidential request of the Spanish chargé makes it clear that the former president, even after his government had fallen, had not abandoned hope of carrying out his monarchical scheme. Though it is not certain that General Flores had already decided at the time of his expulsion from Ecuador to return in force with a Spanish prince in tow, his letter to Montúfar, together with his subsequent activities in Europe, strongly imply that he wished to keep the monarchist option open. General Flores was a tenacious man who did not take defeat lightly. He had enjoyed the exercise of power and had convinced himself that his personal leadership, preferably under the aegis of a European prince, was indispensable for the welfare of Ecuador. He was wrong, of course, not because monarchy was intrinsically inappropriate, but because Flores' time in Ecuador had passed and because the idea of a Spanish-backed monarchy seemed to be an attempt to reverse the historic accomplishments of Bolívar and San Martín. General Flores' refusal to accept defeat and his subsequent insistence on reactivating the "grand project" would have disastrous consequences both for Flores and the struggling young nation of Ecuador.

10

THE SPANISH PROJECT, 1845–1847

As General Flores sailed north from Guayaquil, bound for Europe via Panama, Kingston, and London, he left behind a nation in complete disarray, with a provisional government in Guayaquil and another government in Quito under José Félix Valdivieso. The violence and destruction of the recent civil war, the high cost to the treasury of the military operations, and the intensification of political and regional rivalries brought on a temporary economic paralysis and widespread public uncertainty. Foreign diplomatic agents judged the country to be in crisis. In the opinion of the Spanish chargé d'affaires, Ecuador was in danger of being devoured by anarchy.[1] The British consul, though somewhat more restrained in his assessment, reported in July 1845 that the provisional government of Guayaquil was having great difficulty pacifying the departments of the interior and that the country at large was "in a state of agitation and alarm, as each party commands a force of nearly equal importance."[2] A diplomatic agent of the United States, Delazon Smith, informed his superiors in Washington that "every department of the Government is, if not deteriorating, at a perfect standstill." Smith expected at any moment "a fresh revolution between the Citizens of Guayaquil and those of Quito."[3]

The coastal insurgents managed to put together a provisional government, a triumvirate consisting of Vicente Ramón Roca, José Joaquín de Olmedo, and Diego Novoa, the latter a wealthy Guayaquil merchant and landowner. Though the rebels claimed that each member of the triumvirate represented one of the three major departments of the nation, all three were guayaquileños, a fact that made it difficult to inspire the confidence of highlanders. The situation resembled that of 1835 after the "Chihuahua Revolt," for the revolution in both instances had been carried out by the forces of the coast, thus imposing the will of Guayaquil on the nation.

The triumvirate, after removing Valdivieso from the acting presidency in Quito, convoked a constituent convention to meet in the southern highland city of Cuenca in October 1845. Citizens of Quito took umbrage at the slight given to the capital by the selection of the southern city, but *quiteño* deputies swallowed their pride and attended the convention rather than allow guayaquileños to dictate the new constitution.[4] The National Convention of Cuenca managed to draft a new governmental charter, but the Constitution of 1845 was undistinguished in most ways. It corrected the imbalance between the executive and the legislative branches by providing for annual meetings of a bicameral congress, by permitting the legislature to overturn executive vetoes with a two-thirds vote, and by reducing the presidential term of office from eight years to four. Property and literacy requirements for voting, however, continued the aristocratic and oligarchical concept of government that had predominated from the inception of Ecuadorian nationhood. To conciliate the Church the new constitution prohibited the practice of any religion but Catholicism, even in private.[5]

Though the chief goal of the national convention of 1845 was to legitimize and stabilize the new regime, the work of this assembly did little to achieve its purpose. The promulgation of yet another constitution, the fourth in fifteen years, tended to demean rather than enhance the concept of constitutional rule. In addition, the Constitution of 1845 contained a fatal flaw in its rules for the election of the president. Article 65 required that the president be elected by no less than a two-thirds vote of all members of Congress, a difficult number to obtain in Ecuador, given the reluctance of political factions and regional leaders to make compromises.[6] The difficulties imposed by article 65 would prevent the election of a president in 1849 and provoke a lengthy crisis that provided a sort of open invitation to the exiled Flores to meddle in Ecuadorian politics.[7]

To make matters worse, the insurgents who toppled the Flores regime revealed very quarrelsome tendencies from the beginning. At the Convention of Cuenca, a bitter contest erupted over the selection of a presiding officer. Vicente Ramón Roca, a politician of mediocre talents, won the high office, but not without provoking hard feelings on the part of his numerous opponents. Rocafuerte, who returned from exile to take part in the deliberations, coveted the presidency, but ended up supporting the great Guayaquil poet, Olmedo. Roca's victory over Olmedo gave rise to charges of unfair and dubious political tactics by the victorious side. Rocafuerte, never a good loser, declared bitterly that the convention had preferred "the staff of merchant to the Muse of Junín [Olmedo]."[8]

Though the partisan rancor weakened the Roca government, the effects of political division were offset to some extent by the upsurge of nationalism that accompanied the ouster of Flores. Ecuador's first president had attempted to play down his Venezuelan origins as we have seen, but the revolt of 6 March brought forth a torrent of xenophobic denunciations of the "foreign adventurer" who had governed the nation most of the time since 1830. The spirit of nationalism could be discerned in the debates of the Convention of Cuenca and in the Constitution of 1845 which declared that only native-born Ecuadorians were eligible for the presidency. This new spirit tended to reduce the importance of political rivalries and regionalism and thus to strengthen the national government.[9]

Nationalist enthusiasm, however beneficial it might have been to the Roca administration, did nothing to solve the horrendous economic and financial problems of Ecuador. The civil war that brought down the Flores government had lasted more than three months, draining the treasury, disrupting normal tax collecting, and paralyzing the economy. Flores left the treasury without a peso, according to the charges of his adversaries.[10] The new minister of finance, Manuel Bustamente, was no more successful, and perhaps less so, than his predecessors in balancing the budget. The government resorted to the same vexatious methods of the past to make ends meet, such as special "voluntary" loans, forced loans, collection of Indian tribute in advance, and delayed payment of salaries. The Roca regime also suspended the salaries of military officers opposed to the Revolution of 6 March and extorted large sums in the guise of fines from former floreano appointees. Persecution of affluent

floreanos was so widespread that it interfered with the economic activities of this important productive social class, according to the British consul at Guayaquil.[11] Economic matters were
also made worse by Flores' machinations in Europe, as will be
seen, which forced the government to maintain military readi-
ness to deal with internal revolts and with a possible foreign
invasion.

As if these problems were not enough, the Roca government
managed to provoke a dangerous quarrel with New Granada
which resulted in a diplomatic rupture and nearly caused a war
between the two nations. The dispute related to Ecuador's secret collaboration with General José María Obando, who was
seeking to overthrow the Bogotá government. Roca apparently
wished to use Obando as a weapon against President Mosquera,
who was suspected of favoring Flores in 1845. Though the
squabble was settled early in 1846, reconciliation came only
after a general military mobilization had taken place.[12]

Meanwhile, in September 1845, General Flores arrived in
London and commenced his sojourn in Europe. The mid-1840s
were a period of democratic ferment and uneven economic
progress in the Old World. Political leaders in England were
deeply concerned with the demands for political democracy put
forth by the Chartists and with the arguments for free trade
made urgent by the failure of the potato crop in Ireland. In
France the corrupt government of Louis Philippe, the Citizen
King, sought desperately to maintain itself in the face of mounting opposition from republicans, Catholics, and popular elements. Spain at this time was a demoralized, second-rate power,
struggling to achieve political stability and a measure of economic development after the conclusion of the early Carlist
Wars in 1843. Though nominally under the rule of Isabella II,
Spain was governed by a succession of inept ministries under
the regency of the headstrong and dissolute mother of Isabella,
María Cristina de Borbón.

Though the internal conditions of England, France, and
Spain did not appear auspicious for winning European backing
for a monarchical project, General Flores soon busied himself
with activities that looked suspiciously like the preliminaries of
an expedition to recapture power in Ecuador. While in En-

gland, he visited some of the manufacturing cities and, with the assistance of the former Ecuadorian consul in London, Colonel Richard Wright, he talked with businessmen about some newly conceived plans to build a railroad from Guayaquil to Quito and to promote immigration into Ecuador. Such talk must have sounded innocent to most of his listeners, but "immigration" would later serve as a cover for an invasion force of foreign mercenaries. Flores also sought to ingratiate himself with British authorities, whose goodwill was essential to the success of a filibustering expedition to South America. Thanks to the intervention of Colonel Wright Flores obtained an interview with the foreign secretary of the Tory government, Lord Aberdeen. In his conversation with Aberdeen the Ecuadorian expatriot asserted that "as a man of honor and principles" he would have to avenge himself if the government of Ecuador revealed its "imprudence and madness" by annulling the Treaties of La Virginia. Since Flores had already received word that the Ecuadorian government might not honor the agreement, he was offering not just a hint but a justification of plans for an invasion of Ecuador.[13]

There is no record of Lord Aberdeen's response to the general's remarks, but it mattered little, for Aberdeen was soon replaced by Henry John Temple, third Viscount Palmerston, when the Whigs took control of the government in early 1846. Though Flores later claimed that he did not decide until May or June 1846 to ready an expedition against Ecuador, his activities in England nine months earlier indicated that he began laying the groundwork for the project almost immediately after setting foot on English soil.[14]

Just before leaving London for the Continent Flores received notice of his nomination as Grand Officer of the Legion of Honor, which had been authorized by Louis Philippe a year or so earlier. In Paris he was entertained by the king himself, and he received an invitation from Spain to visit the queen mother and regent, María Cristina. For reasons that are unclear he chose to go to Rome before accepting the important invitation from the regent of Spain. Perhaps he wished to have the blessings of the pope, for he secured an audience with the Holy Father and received a rosary as a gift, which he later displayed as proof of his intimacy with the monarch of the Church. While in Rome Flores also paid a call on the Duque de Rivas, a prestigious Spanish intellectual then serving as Spanish ambassador in Italy. After disclosing to the ambassador a plan to establish monarchy in several South American nations, Flores received letters of introduction to ministers in Madrid from the influential Rivas.[15]

In May 1846, while traveling from Italy to Spain, General Flores received a report of the Ecuadorian government's rejection of the Treaties of La Virginia and of the persecution of his friends and followers. Receipt of this bitter news, according to the exiled general, caused him to make an angry decision to vindicate his honor by organizing an armed expedition to land on the shores of Ecuador to strike a blow against the faithless government of Roca.[16] This, at least, was Flores' version of events. It seems likely, however, that the news of the rejection of the treaty and the persecutions, which had been brought on by floreano plots against the Roca regime, provided a pretext rather than a motive for the preparation of an expedition. But whether Flores made his decision in England or in France to lead a filibuster is of less importance than the fact that Flores proceeded to develop a large plan to assemble an expeditionary force to strike at South America.

In Spain the ex-president gained easy access to the highest circles of government. The precise content of his conversations with Regent María Cristina and the ministers of the queen is not known, but it may be assumed that Flores reminded his Spanish hosts of the earlier monarchical plan that had failed in part because of Spain's failure to send a naval squadron to Guayaquil. It is likely, also, that he spoke of republican "anarchy" in South America and of the need for the stabilizing influence there of monarchy. Flores' personal charm and self-assurance doubtless added strength and credibility to his arguments for Spanish support of a filibustering expedition.

Spain's recent loss of most of her empire in the New World and her decline as a world power had caused Spanish leaders to ponder the means of expanding commerce and regaining Spanish influence in the world. General Flores understood the Spanish eagerness for prestige and position in the world, and he exploited it by offering to expand Spain's dominion by establishing monarchies in South America. The Ecuadorian general knew that for more than a decade Spain had been engaged in a program to achieve reconciliation with her former colonies and that this program had begun to bear fruit in the form of diplomatic recognition of Mexico and Ecuador. Flores knew, too, that the Madrid government had accepted his own proposal in 1843 to establish a throne in Quito, but he did not know that Mexico had just recently won approval of a plan to erect a throne for a Spanish prince in Mexico City. The fact that the government in Madrid was committed to a policy of fostering dynamic ties with the New World made it relatively easy for General Flores to persuade María Cristina and others to lend official support to his plan.[17]

The former president of Ecuador was also aided by the fortuitous arrival in Bordeaux, France, of General Santa Cruz, who in April 1846 was allowed to go to Europe by the government of Chile.[18] Just when Flores learned of the arrival of his fellow monarchist-conspirator is not known, but soon the two expatriots were collaborating in the projected expedition.[19] The support of Santa Cruz was important, for his participation reinforced Flores' arguments and helped convince Spanish authorities that monarchist sentiments were widespread in South America. In addition, Santa Cruz's longtime associate, José Joaquín de Mora, was editor of the progovernment newspaper *El Heraldo.* Mora would prove to be very useful to Flores, not only as a person of influence in Spain but as an experienced diplomat with important connections in the English government.[20]

Some of the secret aspects of the Flores project will probably never be known, but from a variety of sources, especially diplomatic dispatches, newspaper accounts, and the unpublished memoir of Flores' chief of staff, Colonel Senén de Buenaga, the basic outline of the story can be pieced together. Though Flores and members of his family subsequently denied that the expedition aimed at establishing monarchy, it is a fact that the project was monarchist.[21] The prince designated to occupy the throne in Quito was probably Juan, the ten-year-old offspring of María Cristina in her morganatic marriage to the Duke of Riánzares.

It was widely rumored that Flores was to serve as regent of the new kingdom during the minority of the prince. According to Colonel Buenaga, Flores revealed aspects of his restorationist scheme to the French ambassador in Madrid and declared to him that he favored either a Spanish or a French prince, whichever seemed best once the exiled general had regained power in Ecuador. A similar revelation to the British minister suggested the possibility of an English dynastic link.[22] Flores was obviously dangling bait before the diplomats in order to enlist the support of their governments.

Whether the monarchical plan of 1846, like that of 1843–1844, embraced Peru and Bolivia is not known for certain, but the particpation of Santa Cruz and Mora strongly suggests that it did. Rumors that New Granada and Venezuela were also to be included were probably unfounded, but Flores may have spoken loosely to María Cristina and others of the need for monarchy in all of Spanish America.[23]

The first public hint of something afoot in Spain came in a series of articles on the life and achievements of General Flores, published in a Madrid newspaper, *El Tiempo,* in early July.[24] The author of the biographical sketches was the prestigious Rafael María Baralt, who must have acquired most of his information directly from Flores himself. Baralt portrayed the former president as a hero of Independence and a prudent ruler who was driven from his country by evil and faithless men. Though Baralt was later to condemn the expedition, his first articles seemed to justify Flores in attempting to wrest power from the "demogogic" usurpers in Quito.[25]

Though the ex-president of Ecuador encouraged favorable publicity for himself in the Spanish press, he sought to conceal his scheme to lead a pack of filibusters to South America. However, keeping such a large enterprise secret proved impossible. In Spain alone the project was so large in scope that the preparations were bound to attract attention and generate rumors. The Spanish government granted Flores large sums of money, perhaps as much as thirty million pesos, to finance the project, and to permit the use of Spanish army barracks and depots in the northern provinces.[26]

At the outset Flores hoped to recruit three thousand men in Spain and five hundred or so, with the help of Colonel Wright, in Ireland, but he was obliged to settle for a total of about two thousand troops, three-quarters of them enlisted in Spain and the rest in Ireland. To encourage rapid recruitment of men Flores offered a promotion and a bonus of one hundred pesos to each man on enlistment, double pay compared to the Spanish armed forces, and sixteen acres of land and livestock in Ecuador to those who enlisted for five years and remained in service for the full period. Officers were to receive four hundred sixty acres of land. Most of the recruits came directly from the Spanish army, with the encouragement of the minister of war. The chief of the secret police in Madrid, upon hearing that Flores was having difficulty recruiting enough men, offered to impress five hundred men from the poorest-class neighborhoods, but Flores turned down the offer.[27]

Some recruitment took place in the Canary Islands and in Bordeaux, but the chief organizational activity outside Spain took place in the British Isles. Under the leadership of Colonel Richard Wright Flores either purchased or leased three ships of British registry, one a sailing vessel of twelve hundred tons, the *Glenelg*, and two smaller steamships, the *Monarch* and the *Neptune*, to be used as warships. Colonel Wright, pretending still to be Ecuador's consul-general, arranged for arming the steamships, secured supplies and munitions, and recruited several hundred volunteers, most of them hungry Irishmen fleeing from the incipient potato famine. A few English officers also joined Wright's force.[28] The activities of Flores' agent in England and Ireland could scarcely have escaped the attention of the British government. Though Wright's actions clearly violated the Foreign Enlistments Act, the authorities looked the other way. In August and September 1846, Foreign Secretary Palmerston received letters from José Joaquín de Mora and General Santa Cruz informing him somewhat vaguely of the projected expedition and seeking his support for it. Lord Palmerston declined to endorse the project, but he carefully refrained from opposing it.[29] The foreign secretary took no steps to stop Wright's preparations other than to deny a request by Wright to purchase "Six Mountain Howitzers with Carriages and other Equipment" from the Royal Ordnance Department.[30]

To the British foreign secretary the affairs of Ecuador must have seemed trifling in comparison with the weighty matters of Europe, the Near East, the boundary dispute between the United States and Canada, and the question of suppressing the slave trade throughout the world.[31] Yet Palmerston could not ignore Flores' offers of commercial privileges, his promise to pay the British bondholders Ecuador's share of the Colombian debt, and his tempting offer to turn over to Britain the strategically important islands of the Galápagos. Through General Leonard Stagg, Flores managed to keep the Galápagos offer under active consideration in 1845 and 1846.[32] For these reasons the foreign secretary may have decided to acquiesce in Flores' project and to permit Colonel Wright's activities, while carefully avoiding any official act of encouragement or approval. Whatever his motives may have been, Lord Palmerston pretended to have no knowledge of Wright's energetic preparations until he was forced to take cognizance of them by the clamorous protests of Spanish American diplomats and British merchants.[33]

In northern Spain the organizing work went forward with the main body of troops during the months of July and August 1846. Utilizing regular army barracks and depots near the cities of Orduña, Durango, and Vitoria, Colonel Buenaga mobilized nearly two thousand troops and gathered supplies for the growing force. Weapons, ammunition, musical instruments for a military band, and fancy dress uniforms, evidently designed by General Flores, were also procured. But there were difficulties of many kinds, especially in recruiting troops and in managing financial matters. Despite the generous inducements to attract enlistments the expedition did not reach the desired number of men. Many of the officers, according to Buenaga, were quarrelsome and dishonest in handling money. Carlist officers who were supposed to organize a battalion of Spanish emigrés in Bordeaux, succeeded in attracting very few volunteers.[34]

The seriousness of the difficulties became apparent to Colonel Buenaga in late August after he had written to General

Flores repeatedly urging him to come north to resolve urgent problems that were beginning to mount up. But the leader of the expedition refused to leave Madrid. Buenaga learned through private correspondence that the house of General Flores was in "horrible disorder," that he was wasting immense sums of money, and that he was surrounded by incompetent advisers who were contributing to the confusion.[35]

In desperation Colonel Buenaga went to Madrid in September and found the situation to be much worse than he had imagined. Flores had given himself up to a life of pleasure, living with a "public woman" called "Micaela the Stammerer," whose "favors had been bought by everyone for five francs." A few worthless individuals had insinuated themselves into Flores' favor by procuring women for him. As a consequence the Ecuadorian general had completely lost the respect of his subordinates. Buenaga was shocked to see that Flores, ignoring Spanish custom, dealt with his officers on a basis of great familiarity. The commander of the expedition was so discredited, in the opinion of his chief-of-staff, that his advisers quarreled in his presence and talked openly of the filibustering plan, causing all kinds of rumors to circulate in Madrid about Flores and his enterprise. After remonstrating to the commander-in-chief of the expedition and receiving unsatisfactory replies, Colonel Buenaga resigned his position and quit the project. To protect his good name Buenaga sent copies of his letter of resignation to friends in the north, thus provoking the resignations of several other prestigious officers.[36]

The departure of Colonel Buenaga was a severe blow, but the most damaging development was the loss of secrecy that was so important for the success of a filibuster. It was impossible, of course, to enshroud such a large-scale enterprise in complete clandestinity. In a nation with some degree of press freedom, such as Spain at that time, the recruitment of two or three thousand men could hardly be accomplished without any publicity or comment. But some of Flores' confidants were grossly indiscreet, and the general himself attracted too much attention to his activities by his lavish display and his womanizing. Worst of all, perhaps, was Flores' failure to tend to business when urgent matters required his presence. If he had abandoned his circle of courtesans and flatterers and had gone north when he was needed, he might have succeeded in putting the expedition together rapidly. But he did not, and the newspapers of Madrid began to print the news that would soon wreck the whole plan.

First word of the Flores expedition appeared in early August. The news might have leaked out even earlier if some newspapers had not exercised restraint and if others had not bowed to pressure from the government. Flores reportedly spent twenty-four thousand reales, in an effort that was only partially successful, to buy off the press.[37]

On 6 August an opposition newspaper of Madrid, *El Clamor público,* broke the journalistic silence on the public secret of the Flores expedition with the publication of a brief article reporting the military preparations of a "foreign general" to carry out some undisclosed plan against a "republic overseas." Once the news was out, brief as the report was, there was no way to hold back the opposition press from uncovering the whole story. A progovernment paper, *El Popular,* lamely defended the projected expedition with the risible claim that the government of Spain was not involved and that it was "good that Spaniards do something, that they become accustomed to expeditions, and that they come out of that isolation in which some people wish to keep them." But *El Católico, El Imparcial,* and *El Nuevo espectador* quickly joined *El Popular* in printing more news and rumors and in denouncing the Flores enterprise.[38]

Two opposition newspapers, *El Tiempo* and *El Eco del comercio,* which joined the fray somewhat belatedly, did the most damage to Flores' plans. *El Tiempo,* in whose pages the Venezuelan writer, Baralt, had earlier published high praise of the former president of Ecuador, began on 13 August a devastating series of six articles by the same author. Perhaps Baralt was stung and embarrassed by the deception practiced on him earlier when Flores persuaded him to write articles portraying the exiled general as a South American hero. At any rate, the Venezuelan writer attacked the plan to invade Ecuador with Spanish mercenaries as the "most unjust, the most impolitic, the most scandalous step" taken by the conservative regime of Spain. He pointed out that the expedition was aimed at a nation whose independence had been recognized by Spain under treaties that had been "fulfilled religiously" by Ecuador. The government of Spain, said Baralt, was guilty of consenting to "aggression against an allied power." He rejected Flores' claim to be the legitimate president of Ecuador and suggested instead that the ex-president was proposing to conquer Ecuador like "an unpopulated or savage country." Then the Venezuelan writer posed the following rhetorical question:

> Is Flores a filibusterer who goes on his own account to conquer a patrimony; or is he an envoy of Spain who, with soldiers and orders from the former mother country, carries the charge to recover the colonies whose independence she has recognized?

As for rumors of plans to establish monarchies in Ecuador, Peru, and Mexico, Baralt charged that such plans would convert Flores into "the Monk of monarchical restoration" and provoke the Spanish American republics into severe retaliatory actions, such as the suspension of diplomatic relations and the expulsion of Spaniards from their nations. Baralt's remarks in *El Tiempo* proved prophetic.[39]

If the columns of *El Tiempo* were candid and critical, those of *El Eco del comercio* were fierce and incisive. While the scholarly Baralt had criticized the project as improper, the editors of *El Eco* attacked the Spanish government itself for bad faith in its dealings with a foreign nation and with the Spanish people: "That expedition of General Flores is not the simple project of a private citizen . . . ; that expedition . . . was authorized, legitimized, and approved by the Spanish government." *El Eco* went on to condemn "the disloyal conduct of our ministry" which was permitting and supporting "the enlistment within our territory of any army, large or small, against the duly constituted power of another nation" recognized by Spain.[40] After *El Eco* published a second editorial condemning the government for making Spain a "co-participant" in a "projected war against a friendly state" by encouraging enlistments of Spanish officers and troops, the government seized the next issue of the paper, temporarily halting the slashing attack on the Flores project.[41]

Though *El Eco del comercio* was silenced for a short while, other newspapers continued to print the news of preparations for the invasion of Ecuador and to comment upon various aspects of the developments. In a feeble effort to counter the adverse publicity the Spanish government encouraged friendly newspapers to defend the ministry against the damaging attacks in the opposition press. It was not surprising that *El Heraldo* of Madrid, edited by the secret agent of Flores and Santa Cruz, José Joaquín de Mora, published a series of articles strongly supportive of the Flores expedition. Mora, undoubtedly the author of the articles, declared that South Americans are governed by men rather than laws and institutions. In Ecuador it was General Flores who, as "guide and master of the nation," had taught Ecuadorians "to be free and independent." All respectable people of that country, said the editorial, looked to General Flores as "the only guardian on whom the nation can count to reject anarchy and turbulence." It was, therefore, the duty of the exiled general to respond to the will of his compatriots to return to his homeland and reclaim the presidency. To do this it was necessary to organize an armed expedition strong enough to overcome any possible resistance. "The expedition is not an enterprise of violence, aggrandizement, and conquest," the editorial declared, "but rather a mission of reconciliation and peace." To those like Baralt, who had warned that the invaders would be looked upon as foreign conquerors, *El Heraldo* replied that an armed force of Spaniards and Englishmen would be viewed with great favor in Ecuador, because foreigners, especially foreign military officers, are highly respected in South America. On the subject of a projected throne in Quito for a Spanish prince the editorial was silent.[42]

If the leaders of the Madrid government believed that favorable comment in the press would help the cause of Flores' project, they were badly mistaken, for the security of the enterprise depended not on favorable publicity but rather on no publicity at all. Widespread disclosure of the military preparations in northern Spain and the British Isles set in motion a train of events that overwhelmed the project. In Madrid political opponents of the Moderado cabinet raised the issue of the Flores affair in both chambers of the Spanish Cortes (parliament). Deputy Antonio Ros de Olano spoke of the reports of the preparation of an expeditionary force "to march against one of the republics of America" and asked if it was not true that the Spanish government was giving its protection to the expedition of "the illustrious General Flores." Ros de Olano warned that Spain's involvement in the project would cause her to lose the goodwill and the expanding commerce which she had been laboring to encourage in recent years.[43]

In the Senate General Francisco Serrano angrily declared that it was "a very curious thing" that the members of the cabinet pretended ignorance of the manufacture of saddles and uniforms and of the recruitment of soldiers from the Spanish army, because it was possible that this small army could be used for an insurrection within Spain. But General Serrano knew that the Flores project was aimed at Ecuador, and he told the Senate that there were strong indications that the South American republics would react energetically against the expedition: "I know that the diplomatic representatives of Peru and Chile have sent notes to the Minister of State protesting against that expedition," he declared, and "that all of America will rise up against it; the interests we have in those countries are going to be confiscated." He concluded his attack by demanding that the ministry take the measures necessary to halt the expedition.[44]

Responding to criticism from the government's opponents, the minister of war made a cautious denial of military involvement in the Flores project. When this disclaimer failed to quiet the adversaries, Francisco Javier Iztúriz, president of the Council of Ministers, declared before the Senate that "the Government is completely alien to the expedition of General Flores."[45] Iztúriz's deceptive statement succeeded in silencing the criticism in the Cortes for several months. But in January 1847, when new reports of Flores' activities appeared, several members of the Cortes were emboldened to launch a second and more sustained assault on the Iztúriz ministry. Parliamentary orators decried the government's obvious complicity in the Flores project, its violation of treaty obligations with a friendly nation, and its adoption of a policy that was sure to provoke the hostility of Spain's daughter nations in the New World. Though Iztúriz continued to deny the charges, the attack succeeded in bringing down his ministry. With the collapse of the government all official Spanish support of the Flores project came to an end.[46]

Even before Spain gave the coup de grace to the monarchist plot the British government had taken action to halt Flores' preparations in England and Ireland. Lord Palmerston, as has been seen, was not at first disposed to interfere with Colonel Wright's activities, but he was finally persuaded to put a stop to the preparations when he received anxious and angry protests from South American diplomats and from British merchants who feared an interruption of profitable commerce in the New World.

News accounts in Madrid newspapers and private correspondence alerted several Spanish American agents to Flores' preparations in Spain and the British Isles. The Ecuadorian government, evidently suspicious of the intentions of the exiled general, appointed Francisco de las Rivas as Ecuadorian consul-general in Madrid for the purpose of keeping an eye on Flores.[47] The new consul-general managed to supply the Ecuadorian government with detailed reports on Flores, but he was not so instumental as the agents of Argentina, New Granada, Peru, and Chile in stopping the project. As early as August 1846 the New Granadan minister in London and Paris learned of the filibustering preparations and informed his Argentine counterpart of the alarming developments. The news traveled quickly to other South American agents in Europe and across the Atlantic to Buenos Aires, Santiago, Lima, Bogotá, and Quito.[48] Diplomatic representatives of New Granada, Chile, and Peru, whose nations felt threatened by the projected expedition, warned the Spanish government that it risked war with Spanish America if the Flores enterprise was not halted. The warnings fell on deaf ears in Madrid, but in London they had a decisive effect.[49]

Lord Palmerston could no longer pretend ignorance of the military preparations after receiving protests from Spanish American foreign ministers and diplomatic agents in London, one of whom was the prestigious Latin-Americanist, William Parish Robertson, then serving as consul of Peru in the English capital.[50] Too much was now known of the small naval squadron being fitted out to transport Wright's Irish volunteers to the north coast of Spain for a rendezvous with Flores' army and thence to the Pacific coast of South America. Rumors of Flores' plans to attack not only Ecuador but several South American republics and to implant monarchy in most of the region had caused such a frenzy in the governments of Hispanic America that the protests submitted to Palmerston contained thinly veiled threats of drastic action, including economic retaliation and even war. The foreign secretary knew, of course, that the British fleet could handle any emergency on the Pacific coast, but talk of commercial reprisals and suspension of debt payments had a strong effect on Palmerston's thinking. Owners of British commercial firms doing business in the affected region, warned by South American diplomats of possible war and interruption of trade, put pressure on the foreign secretary to seize Flores' ships and to prosecute the project's leaders in Britain for violating the Foreign Enlistments Act.[51]

Palmerston did not respond immediately to the numerous complaints and protests, but in late November 1846, just when the *Glenelg,* the *Monarch,* and the *Neptune* were about to leave the Thames for Spain, orders were given to customs officials to detain and search the three vessels in question. After discovering that the ships were armed and that a large number of British subjects, mostly Irishmen, were on board, all three ships were seized and charges were brought against the leaders for violation of the Foreign Enlistments Act.[52] The confiscation of Flores' flotilla was a crushing blow, for it deprived the expedition of its only means of transporting troops to Ecuador and of attacking the fortifications of Guayaquil.

While Spanish newspapers and politicians were denouncing the Flores project and while Lord Palmerston was reacting to South American protests, General Flores tarried in Madrid, enjoying the abundant pleasures of the Spanish capital. Ignoring reports from the north of desertions and a revolt among his troops, Flores preferred the easy life of Madrid to the Spartan existence of military encampments. On one occasion he took the trouble to write letters to the presidents of Chile and Peru declaring his intention to regain the presidency of Ecuador by force and asking for the neutrality of Chile and Peru when his expedition should arrive on the Pacific coast.[53] These letters served only to confirm the worst fears of the South American leaders.

Finally, on 9 November Flores left Madrid and headed north for the port of embarkation, Santander.[54] In Orduña, where some of his soldiers were quartered, he ordered a full-dress military review. As the general watched from his carriage and a military band played martial music, the solidiers paraded through the main street of the town. In Santander, as the expedition awaited the arrival of the ships from London, there were military drills, more parades, and great festivities, which permitted Flores and his officers to show off their fine dress uniforms. Making no effort to conceal his presence in the northern port, Flores and his general staff attended mass, accompanied by their troops, all in gala uniforms. After mass there was yet another parade and review, followed by a rousing speech by General Flores in which the commander promised victory and future happiness for his followers in the friendly nation of Ecuador.[55]

If spirits were raised by the stirring oratory, they were soon dashed by news from England of the embargo of the expedition's three ships. General Flores understood immediately the crushing importance of the British action. Without ships there could be no expedition at all. He quickly set in motion efforts to secure the release of the ships and to acquire other vessels in Spain or France. However, the bad news from England quickly spread gloom among Flores' officers, recruits, and creditors who could see that there was little hope of recovering from the loss of the flotilla on the Thames. Flores strove to hold the expedition together, but his endeavors came too late to counter the forces of disintegration. Troop desertions began to occur on a daily basis. Worse still, many officers, who had earlier been dismayed by Buenaga's resignation, decided to quit. Creditors, seeing disaster looming, refused to make more provisions available until they were paid. City authorities quarreled with Flores over tax liabilities. By the latter part of December the expedition was on the brink of extinction.[56]

Faced with impending collapse in Santander, Flores decided that the expedition could not be saved without the retrieval of his ships or the acquisition of new ones. On Christmas Day, 1846, he left Santander and headed for Bordeaux, Paris, and

London in the hope of securing a naval force. Soon after his
departure a "committee of authorities" in Spain resolved to
seize all of the expedition's property and to sell it in order to
pay the creditors. In mid-January 1847 the government of
Spain dissolved what was left of the leaderless mercenary
army.[57]

A Spanish observer in Santander summed up the demise of
the Flores project as follows:

> Thus ended the famous expedition to Ecuador, which attracted so
> much attention of Spaniards and foreigners, and by means of which
> they sought to found an empire or kingdom, whose head would have
> been Quito and whose arms would have reached out to Chile and
> Venezuela. It left no more traces in this city than a large number of
> sick men in the hospital, four unfortunate ones in the cemetery
> (killed violently), and three men in jail who expect to be taken to the
> scaffold for the murders of those in the cemetery. If the thirty mil-
> lions invested in this expedition, the greater part of it in England,
> had been used wisely in this country, how much good would have
> redounded to the benefit of our exhausted homeland?[58]

The results of Flores' ill-fated enterprise were certainly unfortunate for Spain. Government funds were wasted on a large
scale; a ministry was brought down; creditors lost considerable
sums of money; and Spain's relations with her daughter nations
in the New World suffered a setback. The projected expedition
also caused damage in South America. Receipt in Quito of the
first reports of the filibuster plans jolted the Roca administration and caused a sensation among Ecuadorians. Up and down
the southern continent, from New Granada to Chile and Argentina, the governments of the Spanish American republics reacted in fear and anger to the news of the threatened monarchist invasion. General Flores suffered a decline in his personal
reputation as he was branded the "Prince of the Reconquest"
for his central role in the affair.[59]

In Ecuador, not surprisingly, the reaction was the most vigorous and profound. The government of Vicente Ramón Roca at
this time was in a precarious situation as a result of its inability to
solve pressing financial problems and its failure to promote a
spirit of reconciliation after the overthrow of Flores. Efforts to

establish firm rule were punctuated by at least three revolts in the year following the Treaties of La Virginia. Discontent was reported to be widespread, and the government failed to win general popularity.[60] Elections for Congress in mid-1846, though largely managed by the Roca administration, resulted in the election of many who wished to see Roca ousted from office. According to rather detailed information gathered by the Spanish chargé in Quito (not a friend of Roca), the opposition planned to impeach the president for alleged unconstitutional acts and to replace him with none other than Vicente Rocafuerte, who was elected president of the Senate in September.[61] Arrival of the sensational news from Spain, however, caused the opponents of Roca to abandon their plan and to work for national unity in order to ward off the expected invasion of mercenaries. The Ecuadorian president, taking full advantage of the sudden change in the political winds, named Rocafuerte special diplomatic emissary to seek the cooperation of Peru, Bolivia, and Chile. It was a shrewd ploy, for Roca managed to utilize the considerable talents of Rocafuerte in the field of diplomacy while strengthening his own hold on the presidency.[62]

The sense of danger felt in Ecuador caused the government to move rapidly and energetically to place the nation on a war footing. President Roca already enjoyed the exercise of extraordinary powers, thanks to the crisis with New Granada.[63] Congress now authorized a considerable expansion of the army. Militias were called up in the various provinces. Retired officers were placed on active duty. And a war steamer and other vessels were fitted out in Guayaquil. Through diplomatic channels the government attempted to secure the naval protection of the Pacific Squadron of the United States. Instructions went out from Quito to provincial governors ordering them to act quickly against the slightest sign of rebellion. Known floreanos were hastily sent into exile, and a forced loan was decreed for an indefinite period, to pay for the increased military expenditures.[64]

Fearing that Flores might use his wealth in Ecuador to finance revolts, the government seized, but did not confiscate, his landed properties during the emergency. In addition, all livestock on the ex-president's haciendas was confiscated and sold at auction, and all of Flores' slaves and freedmen (*libertos*) were drafted into the army. The government also ordered Flores' wife and two of his daughters into exile, but they refused to leave.[65] Sentiment against Flores and his expedition was so strong that two newspapers appeared in Quito, founded for the sole purpose of combatting the projected invasion. One of the editors was the future dictator, Gabriel García Moreno. These short-lived papers whipped up hatred of Flores and Spain, and called upon Ecuador's sister republics for aid in resisting the expected attack from Europe.[66]

The Roca administration waged a vigorous campaign on the diplomatic front against the expedition. In a sharp protest to Spain, Ecuador demanded that the filibustering project be stopped immediately. At the same time it ordered the Spanish chargé in Quito, Montúfar, to present explanations. The latter, who was either not well informed or pretended not to be, replied in evasive language. This moved the Ecuadorian minister of foreign relations to demand a more candid and satisfactory response. Montúfar's subsequent refusal to make a formal and categorical denial of Spanish complicity made him the target of mounting hostility on the part of the Ecuadorian government and the public.[67] The press demanded that he be expelled, and the Roca administration took a number of steps that placed Ecuador and Spain on the brink of war. Ecuadorian ports were closed to Spanish shipping and Spanish subjects were denied entry into the republic. All debts owed to Spaniards by Ecuadorians were canceled. Chargé Montúfar denounced the measures, warned that Ecuador was risking war, and demanded his passport. In formal correspondence with his home government the Spanish diplomat reported that he feared for his life and requested that two warships be sent to Guayaquil. On 18 January 1847, just when the Spanish government was liquidating the remnants of Flores' expeditionary force in Santander but before news of the collapse had reached Ecuador, Sr. Montúfar departed for Spain, thus severing diplomatic relations.[68]

Long before the Spanish chargé fled from Quito the Madrid government had learned from a variety of sources that the Flores project had put the greater part of Spanish South America in a state of alarm and that New Granada, Peru, Bolivia, Chile, and Argentina were joining in a common effort to repel the anticipated invasion. This united opposition to the Flores project was generated in part by the strenuous diplomatic campaign of the Ecuadorian government, conducted by the very able minister of foreign relations, Manuel Gómez de la Torre.[69] But it was also the result of a spontaneous response of Spanish American republics to the foreign threat to their national security and form of government. Rumors of a monarchist plot and the certain knowledge that the expedition was being readied in Spain aroused fears that Spain sought to deprive her daughter nations of their independence and to convert them into new-style colonies. The fact that the enterprise was headed by General Flores, whose military talent was widely respected, served to heighten anxieties in South America.

Nations distant from Ecuador tended to pay relatively little attention to the whole affair. Paraguay, Uruguay, Venezuela, and the Central American republics barely took notice of the expedition. Mexico was so fully occupied in its war with the United States that it took no part in the protests.[70] The Brazilian government, under the monarchical rule of Dom Pedro II, was so distracted by disputes with Argentina and Great Britain that it paid only halfhearted and belated attention to the Flores matter.[71]

Ecuador's main concern was to win the support of those nations that were strategically important in defeating the expedition if it should cross the Atlantic and attempt to reach Ecuadorian shores. According to this concept the most important nations were the United States, Argentina (for control of the Strait of Magellan and the Horn), and the Pacific Coast countries of Chile, Peru, and New Granada. Though the United States, under the guiding policy of the Monroe Doctrine, might have been expected to pledge quick and forceful action against a European intrusion in the hemisphere, it did little to help. Perhaps because of slow communications with Quito, and because of the war with Mexico, the United States was slow to send any assuring word to Ecuador, and when it did, the U.S. secretary of state's first response went to Peru rather than to Ecuador. The Quito government's request for the support of the United States' Pacific Squadron went unheeded.[72]

Ecuador was much more fortunate in receiving the prompt

and enthusiastic cooperation of Argentina, New Granada, Peru, Bolivia, and Chile. All of these nations had good reasons to fear the Flores project. The collaboration of General Santa Cruz with Flores raised the specter of the possible reestablishment of the old Peruvian-Bolivian Confederation that had caused so much trouble in the 1830s by disturbing the power balance of the South American continent. Argentine dictator Rosas not only feared the return of Santa Cruz but was also currently engaged in a maritime struggle with Spain, along with France and England, over shipping in the Río de la Plata and other matters. If the projected expedition took the route around the Horn or through the Strait of Magellan, it would most likely need to stop at west-coast ports before reaching Ecuador, thus posing a potential threat to other nations. And there were rumors, undoubtedly incorrect, that the expedition would go by way of Panama, crossing overland and placing New Granada in jeopardy. Both New Granada and Peru, with bitter memories of border disputes with Flores, had reason to oppose his return to power in Quito. And, of course, none of the governments of these nations wished to see monarchy imposed in South America by Spain. Thus, it appeared that there was an ample basis for a concert of Spanish American republics to oppose the Flores expedition.[73]

The government of Peru was one of the most aggressive nations in seeking collective action to defend the Pacific Coast from the expected invasion of mercenaries. On 9 November 1846 Foreign Minister José Gregorio Paz Soldán extended an invitation to most of the governments of Spanish America, and to Brazil and the United States, to attend a congress of ministers plenipotentiary in Lima for the purpose of forming a hemispheric alliance to repel outside aggression. Since the proposal fitted perfectly with Ecuador's goals, Foreign Minister Gómez de la Torre in Quito and Minister Plenipotentiary Vicente Rocafuerte supported Peru's initiative with their own efforts to organize a united defense of the South American continent. The Lima congress of American republics of 1847–1848 proved a disappointment, however, for few countries bothered to attend. Argentina, Venezuela, and Brazil begged off. The United States showed no interest in the meeting at all. Only five nations—

Bolivia, Peru, Chile, New Granada, and Ecuador—bothered to take part.[74]

The five republics in attendance at the Lima congress felt seriously threatened by one or more aspects of the rumored intentions of Flores and Santa Cruz. Bolivia, fearing the machinations of the ex-Protector, pledged that "all of the resources at its command" would be committed "at any point in America to maintain with honor the brilliance of the arms of Ayacucho."[75] Chile, no less anxious about the Flores–Santa Cruz challenge to South American stability, promised to participate in the common defense with land and naval forces and with monetary aid.[76] New Granada was equally vociferous in its official opposition to the expedition because of the difficulties it had had with Flores in the past.[77] And, of course, Peru showed greater preoccupation with the threat of invasion than any other nation except Ecuador itself.[78]

Yet, despite the strong motivation for cooperation and self-defense, the ministers of the five republics at the Lima congress had great difficulty reaching any meaningful agreements. It took them nearly three months of wrangling to settle on the terms of a mutual defense pact. Peru took advantage of Ecuador's weakness to insert a clause into the treaty of alliance which strengthened the Peruvian claim to territory then in dispute with Ecuador. Perhaps the greatest disappointment for the Quito government was the rejection by the other four nations of Ecuador's reasonable proposal that the five "confederated republics" refuse asylum to General Flores in their respective territories. Such a commitment was important, for the former Ecuadorian president had arrived in the Caribbean region by the time of the Lima congress and was already at work plotting to overthrow the government in Quito. Yet the ministers of New Granada, Peru, Bolivia, and Chile declined to adopt the suggestions, with the flimsy excuse of lack of specific instructions.[79]

The Lima congress ended its deliberations on 1 March 1848, with the announcement of the completion of four documents: a treaty of "confederation" (actually a defensive alliance), a commercial treaty, a consular convention, and a postal agreement. None of the accords was important, least of all the one that purported to establish a confederation or alliance. The Ecuadorian government took little notice of the work of the congress, and the five nations failed to ratify the alliance.[80]

Although the Lima congress proved ineffectual, other diplomatic efforts of the South American republics were more effective in blocking the Flores expedition. The vigorous protests by the foreign ministers and diplomatic agents of New Granada, Argentina, Peru, Chile, and Ecuador deprived Flores of his fleet in England and caused severe troubles in Spain. In addition, Ecuador, Chile, and Peru, acting in concert, closed their ports to all Spanish shipping. This united action appears to have made a profound impact on Spanish public opinion and to have helped convince the government to abandon the Flores project.[81]

It is clear that General Flores' scheme to regain power and restore monarchy in Ecuador was ill-conceived, badly planned, and poorly prepared. Flores' shoddy leadership destined the project to failure. The idea of monarchism might have found some support in Ecuador and elsewhere in Latin America, but an invasion by Spanish and Irish mercenaries was bound to provoke a strong nationalist reaction against what looked to Ecuadorians like an attempt at reconquest by Spain.[82] Finally, the participation of General Santa Cruz in the project, and the rumored inclusion of Venezuela, New Granada, Bolivia, and Peru in the restorationist scheme, helped to assure a vigorous, though far from monolithic, collective response by South American nations.

The effect upon Ecuador of the projected filibuster was drastic and enduring. Though the startling news of the expedition momentarily strengthened the hand of the weak and unpopular President Roca, the long-term effect was to undermine stable government in Ecuador. Beset with pro-Flores revolts and rumors of revolts, the Roca regime became preoccupied with national defense and political survival, and thus it neglected important domestic matters. A kind of paralysis set in as the government devoted most of its energy to the surveillance of General Flores and his partisans. Though Flores always maintained that his purpose was to save Ecuador from misrule, the methods he chose condemned this hapless Andean nation to many years of tension, strife, and uncertainty.

11

KING OF THE NIGHT, 1847–1855

General Flores reacted to the total collapse of his projected expedition against Ecuador with a stubborn refusal to surrender hope of returning to South America at the head of a military expedition. He would repeatedly defend his plan as a crusade to wrest the presidency from usurpers who had forfeited legitimacy by violating the Treaties of La Virginia (which Flores himself had violated by organizing his expedition in Europe). Honor required him to return to Ecuador, he maintained, to drive from power the illegitimate rulers in Quito.[1]

General Flores professed to be the legitimate president of Ecuador and the would-be savior of the nation. But leaders of the government in Quito referred to the ex-president as a pirate, a bandit, a tyrant, and a traitor. These epithets did not miss the mark by much, for Flores had in fact become a renegade and a filibuster in the mold of William Walker, Narciso López, and other adventurers of the age who connived with foreign governments, raised private armies, and plotted to gain power by any means.[2]

It is impossible to determine how much popular support Flores continued to command in Ecuador, but probably he could count on little more than a small minority of partisans and friends. Flores' popularity, however, was less important than the attitude of President Roca, who was staunchly opposed to the return of the ex-president. As a consequence Flores recognized the need to use force to regain power. For this reason, when he left Spain for England in late December 1846 he thought only of salvaging the expedition by freeing his ships from the British government's embargo, but Lord Palmerston turned him down. He would have to look for support elsewhere.[3]

His relentless pursuit of power would take the general on a long and circuitous route through part of Europe, the United States, the Caribbean, Central America, and finally South America. Early in 1847 he went to Paris where he made his home a gathering place for military officers and for much talk of organizing a new expedition. Though he claimed to have close ties with the French court, he won no official support for an armed expedition. After a hasty and fruitless trip to Belgium, Flores abruptly left Paris in late July 1847 and took ship for New York.[4]

Accompanied by Colonel Richard Wright, General Flores arrived in New York in September 1847 when the United States was engaged in the final military operations of its war against Mexico—not a propitious time for a South American to seek backing for an armed expedition against Ecuador. Perhaps Flores sought only to ingratiate himself with President James K. Polk and Secretary of State James Buchanan for the purpose of securing North American neutrality in the event of an invasion of Guayaquil by Flores' forces. His true purpose will never be known, for his request for an audience with Polk was not answered.[5] Perhaps it was fortunate for the exiled general that he won no sympathy in Washington, for sponsorship of a filibustering expedition by the aggressor against Mexico would surely have aroused fear and resentment in the southern continent.[6]

Early in November 1847 General Flores turned up in Kingston, Jamaica, where he began a relentless campaign to overthrow the government of Ecuador by means of intrigue and conspiracy. His prestige and influence with Ecuadorian officers made it possible for Flores' agents to persuade military leaders to attempt uprisings. If friendship and loyalty did not suffice then he and his envoys would promise money and promotions. Even before Flores' arrival in Jamaica, there took place in Ecuador five attempted floreano coups, followed by a lull, then a new rash of plots and uprisings after Flores turned up in the Caribbean. Most of the plots involved only a few officers and civilians. Doña Mercedes Jijón de Flores helped organize one of the revolts. It is estimated that there were nineteen to twenty-three plots and rebellions, most of them connected with Flores, between 1846 and the end of 1848. The Quito government was kept in an almost constant state of alarm.[7]

In promoting so many uprisings General Flores was exploiting the political weakness of Ecuador at midcentury. The political picture of Ecuador and her sister republics resembled the European monarchies and principalities of the Renaissance when rulers and nobles engaged in endless intrigues and conspiracies against one another. Flores' Machiavellian intrigues threatened at times to provoke chaos in his adopted country. British consul Cope, a careful observer, declared that the Roca administration was "in great measure paralyzed and the finances deranged." Cope feared that Guayaquil would secede from Ecuador, and he concluded that "it is a matter of wonder how a Government can be carried on under such circumstances." The only positive note in the consul's appraisal was the observation that some opponents of the unpopular Roca administration had come to its support "through a common sense of danger" caused by the threat of General Flores.[8]

To pay for increased military expenditures the Roca regime resorted to forced contributions (always very unpopular) and to collection of Indian tribute in advance, thus provoking native unrest and the flight of peasants from the highlands.[9] President Roca, exercising extraordinary powers, banished without trial suspected conspirators, including Flores' wife and all her children. Shortly afterward Congress approved a decree making Flores an outlaw, forbidding him to enter Ecuador, and declaring forfeit all property of those who attempted armed invasion or revolution.[10] The minister of the interior declared that Flores' machinations had brought the nation to the brink of "a frightful chaos."[11] But chaos was not yet imminent, and the Roca government managed to withstand the conspiracies.

Meanwhile, in Jamaica Flores decided to visit Venezuela, his native land. His arrival in that country occasioned a rash of rumors that the ex-president was scheming to resurrect the former state of Gran Colombia (Venezuela, New Granada, and Ecuador) and that he was plotting with General José Antonio Páez against José Tadeo Monagas. The rumors probably had little basis in fact, but it is very likely that Flores was seeking support for an expedition against Ecuador. If so, he was not successful in his quest.[12]

If General Flores was attempting to advance the cause of monarchism in Venezuela (which is not certain), his activities received a setback in April 1848 with the receipt of news of the fall of the French monarchy of Louis Philippe. The wave of democratic enthusiasm that spread across much of Europe prompted the Ecuadorian consul in Caracas to predict that the fall of the Orléans dynasty and the rise of the "democratic impulse" spelled the end to the Flores projects.[13] The consul read too much into the fall of Louis Philippe, however, for monarchism was not yet dead and Flores' plots would continue.

It should be borne in mind that General Flores, even though he continued to support monarchism, was not absolutely wedded to that system. Rather, he favored the broader concept of a monocratic regime, preferably under the rule of a king, but under a strong executive in any case. After the failure of the Spanish expedition he publicly denied his monarchist views and began to emphasize conservatism. He sided with Páez in Venezuela as the representative of the "propertied and select" class of citizens against Monagas, representative of the lower classes and *descamisados* [the shirtless ones]. He presented himself as an aristocrat who strongly opposed the disorders and instability caused by democratic tendencies.[14]

From Venezuela Flores returned briefly to Jamaica where he apparently attempted to organize an armed expedition but was stopped by the British government.[15] Unable to advance his cause in Kingston, Flores sailed to Panama, then a province of New Granada. His arrival early in 1848 on the Isthmus, which placed him on territory touching the Pacific Ocean, stirred a wave of anxiety in South America as far south as Peru. Ecuadorian protests and journalistic reaction to the ex-president's presence prompted the New Granadan government to expel him in June 1848.[16] The unwanted general departed for Costa Rica.

Flores' selection of the small republic of Costa Rica, with a population of no more than ninety thousand, was probably influenced by its location on the Pacific Ocean, which afforded rapid maritime communication with Ecuador. The Roca government was quick to suspect that the scheming ex-president expected to launch a "new crusade" against Ecuador from Central America.[17] No doubt Flores wanted to do just that, but he failed to win support for a filibuster during his three-year stay in Central America.

Soon after arriving in mid-1848 in the small Costa Rican capital of San José Flores set about the task of cultivating friends in high places and quickly insinuated himself into the good graces of President José M. Castro. The Ecuadorian general soon became one of the president's most-trusted advisers and was named "Illustrious Citizen of Costa Rica" by presidential decree.[18] Within a few months General Flores was deeply involved in a secret plan with President Castro to establish a British protectorate over Costa Rica and to remodel the government along monarchical or monocratic lines.

In 1848 Central America was experiencing severe tensions caused in part by boundary disputes and the rivalry of the United States and Great Britain for control over any future interoceanic canal in the region. In the international power struggle Honduras, Nicaragua, and El Salvador tended to favor the United States, while Guatemala and Costa Rica identified with Great Britain.[19] Flores quickly saw that his own conservative, pro-British leanings were well suited to the Costa Rican situation and to the inclinations of President Castro.

Between October 1848 and December 1849 the Ecuadorian general wrote a series of letters and papers to Colonel Wright (now back in England) and to Lord Palmerston proposing the creation of a British protectorate over Costa Rica and the transformation of its government into a monarchy or a moncracy. Britain was to assume control of the treasury and the customhouse and to provide a small naval squadron and a military occupation force, which Flores offered to command. To lend political stability to this new British dominion Flores at first proposed that President Castro be declared "President for Life," but later he suggested that, to combat the menace of the United States in this region, monarchies should be established in Mexico and Central America.[20] President Castro appeared to be enthusiastic about the project, for he instructed his minister in London to make a similar protectorate proposal to the British government.[21]

In his efforts to win British backing and to shape the destiny not only of Costa Rica but of the rest of Central America and Mexico, General Flores devoted great energy to the protectorate scheme. He sought to develop an "English party" in the country and he cultivated the influential British consul-general in Central America, Frederick Chatfield, but he failed to win approval of the proposed protectorate. Chatfield credited Flores with sustaining the Castro government and with pro-British views, but he remarked that General Flores

> is not a man of the day; he belongs to a past period, which makes it hopeless for him to recover a political station in the Equator. He indulges impracticable theories, and does not perceive the necessity of adapting himself to the times.

Chatfield concluded that Flores should "cease to meddle in the politics of the country" since he "already finds the ground sinking beneath him."[22]

It was true that Flores' position was deteriorating. He had hoped to ingratiate himself with both President Castro and the British government, in the fervent hope of securing support of one or both governments for a filibustering expedition against Ecuador. But he failed to persuade the Foreign Office that the risks of a Costa Rican protectorate were worth taking. To make matters worse, President Castro fell from power in late 1849, leaving Flores with waning influence. The final blow to the protectorate–monarchy scheme was provided in 1850 by the signing of the Clayton–Bulwer Treaty between the United States and Great Britain. This treaty, which provided for joint control by the two powers of any Central American canal, greatly reduced international tensions and undermined the rationale for a Costa Rican protectorate.[23]

Not wishing to anger General Flores or turn him against England, the British foreign secretary wrote a soothing letter to the ex-president of Ecuador and thanked him for his letters. Palmerston also instructed British agents in Central America and Ecuador to render "every unofficial assistance in your power to General Flores and his family." This official instruction would later prove helpful to Flores in his campaign against the government of Ecuador.[24]

If Flores' fortunes in Central America were waning in early 1850, they were waxing in Ecuador as a result of the failure of the Congress in late 1849 to choose a successor to President Roca, whose term had expired. The congressional deadlock over the presidential succession produced a period of great instability which lasted for a year and eight months, during which time two inept politicians attempted to exercise executive power but found themselves checked by the restless and ambitious General José María Urbina. The ship of state drifted. Civil servants went unpaid. It was rumored that Ecuador would soon be partitioned between Peru and New Granada.[25]

The ever-vigilant British consul, Walter Cope, reported that Ecuador was in a state of anarchy and that the wealthiest citizens were

> turning their attention to General Flores who . . . seems to be the best calculated to control the Passions and Pretentions of the conflicting parties & to restore a regular form of Government; but the tide of popularity is not yet sufficiently turned to admit a public demonstration in his favor, tho' I will venture to say that if he could be brought back to the Equator and protected on his first arrival, there would be little or no opposition to him afterwards.[26]

The political and economic deterioration of Ecuador in the period 1849–1851 was noted by other diplomatic envoys, most especially by the callow and impulsive Colonel John Trumbull Van Alen, chargé of the United States in Quito. Van Alen, lacking experience in diplomacy and knowledge of Ecuadorian politics, decided that Ecuador could be rescued from ruin only by General Flores. "This country must fall speedily into a state of anarchy," he reported to Washington, "or it must recall General Flores, and give him arbitrary power."[27]

Apparently some floreanos had filled Colonel Van Alen's ears with high praise of the ex-president, for the American chargé was not acquainted with Flores. Van Alen proceeded, without instructions from Washington, to involve himself with the Spanish chargé in an effort to encourage General Flores to return to

Ecuador. If Van Alen had informed his government of his political activities in behalf of Flores, it is very likely that the secretary of state would have disapproved because of Flores' pro-British and anti-Yankee activities in Central America. Perhaps the headstrong chargé withheld information on his behind-the-scenes efforts to restore Flores to power precisely because he feared that Washington would put a stop to them. In any case, without instructions and without funds he could do very little to help his chosen candidate for the presidency to outfit an expedition in Central America.[28]

Effective assistance to Flores was not forthcoming from other quarters either. The sympathy of the Spanish chargé was of little use, for Spain lacked the power and the will to back Flores once more. No Central American nation would assist him either. General Flores told Consul-General Chatfield at this time that he was actually preparing an expedition, but Chatfield reported to London that the general "had neither men, money nor arms," and he predicted disaster if a Flores filibuster took place.[29] Evidently the exiled leader was lying to Chatfield, for there was no filibuster.

Suddenly, in May 1851, Flores' fortunes took a turn for the better when he received an invitation from Peru to go to Lima where he would be granted asylum and help by the Peruvian government. In early July he arrived in Lima, ready to cooperate with Peruvian authorities in return for their support of an expedition against Ecuador.[30] The government of Peru at that time was in the hands of General José Rufino Echenique, who was so conservative that many of his advisers were said to be monarchists and his supporters had been dubbed the "Spanish Party."[31] Flores could not have hoped for more congenial company.

In Ecuador news of Flores' arrival in Lima coincided with a successful military revolt by General Urbina (vigorously anti-Flores) against the fumbling administration of Diego Novoa, who was alleged to be pro-Flores. The Ecuadorian government immediately demanded that Peru refrain from granting asylum to the former president, only to receive evasive replies followed by an admission that asylum had been granted as a "humanitarian gesture." But Peru gave assurances that the government would be vigilant to prevent Flores from leaving Lima.[32]

Ecuadorian fears were well founded, for the Echenique regime did in fact plan to use General Flores in its international policy. Echenique was deeply suspicious of the "advanced ideas" disseminated from Europe after the revolutions of 1848, and he feared that "socialism" might spread to Peru via Ecuador from the "red" regime of José Hilario López of New Granada.[33] The conservative Flores could be useful in containing the spread of radicalism to Ecuador. In addition President Echenique had dreams of territorial expansion and hoped to annex Guayaquil and nearby provinces.

Flores was probably not fully informed of Echenique's intentions, but he was familiar with Peru's long-standing territorial aspirations and he had to know that the Lima government intended to use him for its own purposes. No doubt Flores believed that after he had regained power in Ecuador he could deal successfully with an aggressive Peru. In any event, shortly after his arrival in Lima the exiled general began to accept a generous stipend from the Echenique administration which permitted him to cut a wide swath in society and stimulate conversation about the gold spurs he wore when paying calls. (Flores was penniless when he arrived.) Some of the surplus funds he received were apparently used in an attempt to bribe army officers in Guayaquil, for the Urbina administration discovered a floreano plot there in late September 1851.[34]

By late November it was an open secret that the Ecuadorian general was recruiting officers and men in Lima and attempting to procure ships for an armed expedition. Peruvian authorities denied complicity in the project, but Flores told the British chargé that he had official assistance.[35] Though Flores would continue to advocate monarchy into the 1860s, he appears not to have made any arrangement with the Peruvians to establish a throne in Quito. For the time being Flores aimed only at seizing power and installing a conservative regime to block the spread of "socialism."

News of the expedition in preparation reached Quito quickly and caused a reaction bordering on panic. The government arrested all suspected floreanos, imposed huge forced contributions on most of them, and expanded the army by the customary impressment of hapless Indians and mestizos. President Urbina was reported to be so desperate and angry that he sent a would-be assassin to Lima to put an end to the Flores menace.[36]

No attempt at assassination occurred, however, and Flores was able to complete his preparations by early March 1852. He claimed to have recruited an army of sixteen hundred men, most of them Ecuadorians, Chileans, and Peruvians, with a scattering of Germans, Englishmen, Frenchmen, and forty Californians (scheduled to rendezvous with the expedition in Ecuadorian waters). The actual size of the force was probably about half the number claimed. The troops were to be transported aboard five armed sailing vessels and an "old but serviceable" steamer. On 12 March the main contingent of the expedition sailed north under the flag of Ecuador.[37]

As soon as the Ecuadorian government learned that Flores' hostile force was about to depart from Callao its minister of foreign affairs, José Villamil, announced that "vandals" who intended to invade Guayaquil were pirates with "no right to use the flag of Ecuador" and that the ships of the expedition were "subject to capture by ships of any nation." In a communication to Courtland Cushing, chargé of the United States, Villamil declared that his government had

> reason to believe that this criminal enterprise is the continuation of that projected by Flores in Europe in 1846 with the wicked design of making monarchies of independent republics which were formerly Spanish colonies.

Villamil believed there was "a secret plan of monarchization which is developing under the appearance of an isolated attempt of Flores against Ecuador." Appealing indirectly to the Monroe Doctrine, Villamil stated that Ecuador wished to negotiate a "treaty of guarantee" with the United States "to uphold the principle common to both against the grave dangers which encompass them."[38]

The invitation to form an alliance with Ecuador took Cushing by surprise. He responded that the United States would not "view with indifference" any attempt on Ecuador's independence, but it was the policy of his government to avoid "entangling alliances." Cushing assured Villamil that the United States would not be an "idle spectator" of foreign interference with the sovereignty of an American republic.[39] Though Cushing adopted a posture of strict propriety and restrained friendliness, he did all he could to oppose the expected invasion. Acting without instructions, Cushing wrote to the commander of an American warship in Guayaquil harbor urging him to remain in those waters to deal with "the atrocious acts of man-stealing, robbery and plunder" of the Flores expedition.[40]

Intervention by the United States navy proved unnecessary, however, for the expeditionary force ran into serious difficulties soon after its arrival in Ecuadorian waters. Flores, always eager for more recruits, sent one of his vessels to visit an Ecuadorian prison colony on the Galápagos Islands, only to have the prisoners there seize his ship and put twenty-two men to the knife.[41] After this setback Flores decided to delay an attack on the coast. Rather than risk his small force in a frontal assault on Guayaquil, he chose to occupy the island of Puná, which commanded the sea roads to the port. By early April 1852 the invaders controlled the island, and Flores began to threaten Ecuador's foreign shipping and to conduct a war of nerves against the Urbina regime. Apparently the commander of the expedition believed that the presence of his forces would bring down the Ecuadorian government, but no rebellion occured either in Guayaquil or elsewhere.[42]

General Flores may have lost his best opportunity early in 1852 by not landing his forces in Guayaquil or nearby. At least this is the conclusion that can be drawn from the reports of the British and French diplomats in Guayaquil at the time. Walter Cope declared that discontent was so widespread and the port so poorly defended that Flores would have met with little opposition if he had landed his forces.[43] The French chargé wrote that Guayaquil was open to attack from all sides, panic had spread through the country, and the military reputation of Flores "overawes the bravest."[44] Chargé Cushing was alone in predicting that the Urbina regime would "put down the Expedition without aid from any quarter."[45]

Rather than attack immediately Flores chose to wait for the arrival of more troops and supplies from Lima. After receiving supplies, a few more troops from Peru, and forty volunteers from California, Flores decided to make some raids on villages along the Guayas estuary. His purpose was to worry the government, test his soldiers, and seize livestock for food, but the raids went badly when the landing forces suffered more than one hundred casualties and many Chilean troops deserted at the first opportunity.[46]

The ominous desertion of the Chileans and news that General Urbina had convoked a constituent convention for mid-July (to legitimize his authority) forced Flores to initiate in late June his long-delayed offensive against Guayaquil. After exchanging fire with a European war steamer, one of the attacking ships blew up, killing some forty men. On 1 July the attacking naval force succeeded in silencing Guayaquil's chief shore battery, but Flores chose not to gamble by landing his troops in the city. In the opinion of Consul-General Cope this decision not to commit his forces destroyed the last hope of the filibuster.[47]

The final collapse of the expedition came when Flores resumed the hit-and-run tactics that had worked so badly before. Dropping down the estuary Flores attacked the small coastal town of Machala. Soon after landing, one hundred twenty of his Chilean troops (who were angry with their commander over his false promise to take them to gold mines in California) mutinied and took their ship to Guayaquil. All other ships quickly dispersed, and Flores was forced to flee by land to Peru.[48]

The failure of the expedition of 1852 damaged all parties connected with it. This new defeat diminished General Flores' reputation as a military commander and gave credibility to Urbina's charges that he was a "pirate" and a tool of foreign powers bent on sowing chaos in Ecuador. President Echenique of Peru also suffered badly from the bungled invasion and felt obliged to expell Flores, who gained asylum in Chile. Soon afterwards Echenique fell from power amid charges of political ineptitude and monarchist plotting.[49]

In Ecuador, too, there was severe damage. Though defeat of the expedition improved the popularity of President Urbina momentarily, a variety of difficulties soon beset his regime. The invasion crisis forced Ecuador to the brink of war with Peru, kept the nation in a state of agitation for several months, and provoked widespread discontent over arbitrary exactions and military sequestrations. Domestic problems were compounded by diplomatic quarrels with Spain and France over the support they gave to Flores. President Urbina was subsequently humbled by a French threat of intervention that forced him to apologize and pay reparations.[50]

General Flores, after taking refuge in Chile, appeared not to have learned a lesson from the collapse of the filibuster of 1852. Nor did he care about the turmoil provoked in Ecuador by his unceasing plots. Indeed, he appeared to wish to cause chaos in order to bring down the government and seize power. In 1853 Flores began efforts to organize new filibusters both in the United States and France (Chile gave no support). Relying on some of his California volunteers and other agents in San Francisco, the Ecuadorian general managed to initiate a California-based project that promised land grants and commercial privileges in Ecuador to San Francisco merchants who pledged financial backing. But the project was halted by the United States government at the request of the Urbina administration.[51]

The dust had hardly settled on the California project when alarming reports surfaced about agents of Flores in France who were promising land grants in Esmeraldas and privileges in handling Ecuador's foreign debt to French bankers in return for a large loan to finance an expedition. But the bankers backed away when Ecuadorian diplomats in Europe denounced the scheme.[52]

In March 1855 yet another plot came to light, this one in the United States. Jeremiah Clemens, a disreputable politician and Washington lobbyist, acted as Flores' agent. Clemens went so far as to form a commercial company to raise money and to prepare an expedition of twenty-one hundred men and six warships. Flores was reported to have pledged not only the familiar coastal land grants and commercial privileges, but had also promised 115,000 acres of land east of the Andes and the right to exploit guano deposits in the Galápagos. Clemens claimed that the unsettled land grants were so rich in silver deposits that they could easily produce fifty million dollars in a decade.[53]

The Flores–Clemens project of 1855 was so tawdry that its exposure by the *New York Herald* in March of that year might have sufficed to kill it. But the Urbina regime, taking no chances with the gullibility of North Americans, called on the United States government to halt the plan. The Clemens scheme disappeared without a trace after the secretary of state declared that the neutrality laws would be applied to anyone participating in hostile movements against Ecuador.[54]

The collapse of the Clemens project underlined the fact that none of General Flores' plots against Ecuador from 1847 to 1855 came very close to success; yet Flores' unremitting efforts did cause much damage. The floreano menace provoked a chronic "feverish anxiety" in Ecuador, in the words of the American chargé in Quito, and brought about a military despotism.[55] Although the government was temporarily strengthened by the creation of Urbina's military dictatorship, British consul-general Cope reported that Ecuadorian citizens were far from happy with the harsh military rule, arbitrary exactions, and confiscations of personal property. General Flores lost most of his property holdings in these years through foreclosures and government seizures, and his friends and alleged supporters were persecuted. Even after the defeat of the Peruvian expedition of 1852, Urbina continued to impose harsh rule on the nation, using the floreano threat to justify military rule.[56]

Urbina's fear of General Flores' machinations was so strong that in 1854 it prompted him to seek the establishment of a United States protectorate over Ecuador. To win North American approval of his proposal Urbina offered exclusive commercial rights to extract guano from the Galápagos. The growing world demand for fertilizers and Peru's success in granting exploitation contracts had created a guano fever that Ecuador hoped to use as an inducement to win United States protection against any future filibusters. The foreign minister succeeded in negotiating a convention with the American minister in Quito in which the United States was to lend Ecuador three million dollars and to protect the nation from "invasions, incursions, or depredations" by any nation "or adventurer or chief-tain."[57] The convention of 1854 was not ratified by the United States, in part because no profitable guano deposits could be found, but also because of a storm of protests by Britain, France, Spain, Chile, and Peru, whose governments feared North American intrusion in Ecuador.[58]

The willingness of the Urbina administration to risk criticism for creating a North American protectorate over Ecuador was striking evidence of the desperation of Ecuadorian authorities. Flores' conspiracies and filibusters had reduced Ecuador to near impotence. It was ironic that General Flores, who claimed to champion the cause of legality and good government, was willing to push his nation to the brink of dark disaster. By the mid-1850s Juan José Flores had demonstrated that he fully deserved the ironic title of "King of the Night" bestowed upon him by a Peruvian writer.[59]

12
THE EXILE'S RETURN, 1855–1864

In late March 1855 General Flores appeared in Lima, reportedly invited to Peru by a member of President Ramón Castilla's ministry.[1] The arrival of the Ecuadorian expatriate in Peru marked the beginning of the final stage of his futile efforts to recapture power in Quito. In his desperate maneuvers Flores demonstrated that he was willing to collaborate with a Peruvian president bent upon the destruction of Ecuador. He also proved that he was willing to undermine the Quito government to the point of producing anarchy. His actions in Peru helped to provoke the total collapse of political leadership in Quito, which in turn brought on one of the sternest and most conservative dictatorships in nineteenth-century South America. In the midst of the chaos he helped to create Flores would return to Ecuador to serve as commander of the armed forces and to take part in yet another doomed project for monarchy, but he would not achieve his goal of regaining the presidency.

The Ecuadorian government, informed in advance of Flores' plan to establish himself in neighboring Peru in 1855, foresaw serious trouble and attempted to persuade the Castilla administration to deny asylum to the troublesome ex-president. The subsequent discovery of a floreano plot in Quito just after Flores' arrival in Lima confirmed the Urbina administration's suspicion of the menacing intentions of the expatriate general. President Castilla, who wished to use Flores as a pawn in a chess game of power politics, not only refused to deny asylum to the Ecuadorian ex-president but also secretly extended an invitation to General Santa Cruz to return to Peru from exile in Europe. Castilla's obvious purpose was to use both exiled leaders to cause political disruption in Ecuador and Bolivia and thus to weaken both neighboring nations so that Peru might become relatively stronger. Santa Cruz did not accept the invitation, perhaps because he distrusted Castilla, but he did go to Argentina, where his presence caused consternation in Bolivia.[2]

Castilla's cold refusal to deny asylum to Flores quickly led to growing international tensions when Ecuador recalled its minister from Lima and suspended diplomatic relations. Even though diplomats from Chile and the United States warned him that his policy of asylum was apt to provoke war with Ecuador, Castilla persisted in befriending Flores.[3] Though the Peruvian president did not admit to ulterior motives in the asylum issue, he clearly wished to weaken Ecuador because of a developing boundary dispute over the Jaén, Canelos, and Maynas regions in the western Amazonian basin. In the opinion of the United States chargé in Lima, Flores' presence in Peru encouraged the Castilla administration to assert new territorial claims and to send ships and men to the Amazonian town of Loreto, which was also claimed by Ecuador.[4]

President Castilla may not have known about all of the expatriate general's efforts to subvert the Quito regime, such as the ongoing filibuster project in Washington that had been put in the hands of Jeremiah Clemens, but Castilla must have been happy in the knowledge that all of Flores' exertions to regain power would be aimed at undermining the government of Ecuador. For example, it was doubtless pleasing to Castilla to see a lengthy newspaper article, written by Flores, which denounced the Ecuadorian government for consorting with a "Yankee filibuster" and called upon Latin American nations to unite against a Yankee invasion of South America. The article temporarily cast the Urbina regime in a bad light, which suited Castilla's purposes. However, the hypocrisy of the article was soon made evident by the revelation of Flores' own efforts to prepare a filibuster in the United States. It was further revealed that Flores had made lavish promises to North Americans of land grants, gold mines, and other concessions. To cover his embarrassment Flores was forced to write another article for a Lima newspaper in which he denied that he was promoting "directly or indirectly, in the territory of Peru, any kind of expedition."[5]

Flores' weasel words reassured no one. It was an open secret that the exiled general was promoting yet another expedition. The North American chargé reported that Flores had "offered large sums of money to two foreigners to enter his service: his partisans . . . are in high spirits." The chargé went on to say that

> an individual who was one of his most active Agents in . . . 1851–2, has said, publicly, that Flores will shortly invade the Ecuador, by land, in order to avoid the intervention of the United States.[6]

President Castilla, evidently worried by the unfavorable publicity and by warnings from the American and Chilean chargés in Lima, soon put a stop to the filibuster preparations.[7] Blocked from leading a military invasion of Ecuador, General Flores shifted to the clever tactic of applying strong diplomatic pressure on the government of General Urbina, which in October 1856 was succeeded by that of General Francisco Robles, who had been hand-picked by the outgoing president. Flores' diplomatic offensive consisted of a series of accusations of faithlessness, illegality, and inhumanity on the part of the Ecuadorian government for allegedly failing to honor the "Treaties of La Virginia" and for "confiscating" all of his property. Most of the diplomats in Lima and foreign ministers abroad did not know that Flores himself had broken the terms of the so-called treaties and the Quito government was not clearly responsible for the alienation of many of Flores' properties. The general ignorance of these matters permitted Flores to proceed with a well-organized campaign to tar the Urbina–Robles administration as tyrannical.[8] By means of his agents in Europe and personal approaches to diplomats in Lima Flores managed to win support of France, England, and Spain for his demands against Ecuador.[9] Early in 1857 Flores made a hasty trip to Venezuela, his native land, where he not only won honors and a lifetime pension but also obtained official support of his claims against Ecuador.[10]

On his return trip to Lima Flores' merchant steamer made a one-day stop at Guayaquil. The unwanted presence of the ex-president in the harbor worried Ecuadorian authorities and prompted alarmists to predict an uprising. No doubt Flores hoped for a revolt in his behalf, but nothing happened, and the steamer proceeded to Lima with its important passenger.[11]

Though the Robles administration seemed relatively unscathed by the unwelcome visit, the Ecuadorian government began to feel the debilitating effects of the diplomatic offensive orchestrated by the scheming ex-president. In late 1857 and early 1858 the governments of Venezuela, Great Britain, and Spain, joined by New Granada and Peru, began to suggest, and even to demand, that Ecuador return all of the former president's properties. The foreign minister in Quito replied that his government could not comply with the requests because it had not confiscated the estates and did not own the properties in question. The Ecuadorian government explained, with lengthy documentary proofs of sales and auctions, that the ex-president had sold some of his properties and had lost others through foreclosures.[12] As a consequence, the government was unable to return property that it did not own or control.

Ecuador's stout resistance to the concerted diplomatic pressures gave the impression that General Flores' tactics were ineffective and that Robles' administration was firm and secure. Actually, however, the war of nerves had taken its toll and the government was torn apart by discord. Peru's President Castilla was quick to perceive the weakness and to exploit it. General Flores had accomplished exactly what Castilla wanted of him.

Late in 1858 the government of Peru sent Juan Celestino Cavero on a diplomatic mission to Quito for the ostensible purpose of pressing Flores' claims. However, the real purpose of the Cavero mission was to demand Ecuadorian surrender of territory claimed by Peru in the Amazonian region. The Peruvian demands, made in an angry manner by the feisty Cavero, were of grave importance to Ecuador, for they amounted to a claim on almost half of the area contained within the jurisdiction of the colonial Audiencia of Quito. In their most extreme form the claims of the Lima government included part of Pichincha province and would have put the eastern border of Ecuador "almost within sight of Quito," as the American chargé put it.[13] The Robles administration naturally refused to yield to the Peruvian demands. A surrender to Castilla's dictation would have caused the immediate collapse of the Robles government, an end that both Castilla and Flores would have welcomed.

An acrimonious diplomatic exchange, in which Ecuador accused Peru of granting "sordid protection" to Flores, heightened the tension between the two nations. In September Peru provoked a crisis by presenting a series of peremptory demands that included insistence on Ecuadorian apologies for offensive newspaper articles, the expulsion from Ecuador of a Peruvian general believed to be plotting against the Castilla regime, and the concession of the disputed Amazonian territories to Peru.[14] If Ecuador did not yield, Peru would occupy Guayaquil. There was ironic humor in Castilla's demand for the expulsion of an expatriate general, in view of Castilla's grant of asylum to Flores, but the seriousness of the situation, especially the Peruvian threat to Guayaquil, did not permit Ecuadorian authorities to see any humor, ironic or otherwise, in the Peruvian demands.[15] Steadfast in defense of its territorial claims, the Quito government began military preparations to resist an anticipated Peruvian attack on Guayaquil.[16]

Available evidence does not show clearly the extent to which General Flores collaborated with Castilla in the great confrontation between Peru and Ecuador in 1858–1859. However, the discovery in Guayaquil of a floreano plot in September 1858 to subvert the military garrison there gave more than a hint of close cooperation between Flores and Castilla. British consul Walter Cope, always a well-informed observer, reported that the arrest of a Peruvian merchant as one of Flores' agents in the plot made Ecuadorian leaders think that "under cover of demanding redress of alleged grievances" Peru sought "to reinstate General Flores in the Government of the Equator."[17] Whether Castilla really intended to install Flores as president of Ecuador may be doubted, but it is clear that the Peruvian president was using Flores to create political chaos and to seize a great amount of territory. Quite possibly he hoped to annex Ecuador, or at least the province of Guayas with its fine harbor of Guayaquil.

Castilla had chosen a good time to strike at Ecuador, for the Robles government was in a seriously weakened condition.

Flores' diplomatic offensive and the boundary dispute over the Amazonian lands had taken their toll. Weakness also stemmed from internal problems, especially the mounting fiscal difficulties caused by the abolition of Indian tribute in 1857, the usual peculations of government officers, and increased military expenditures. To make matters worse, General Robles, never a popular figure, was unable to provide vigorous leadership because of ill health.[18]

Late in 1858 the Ecuadorian government disintegrated. When President Robles convened the Congress in September he was able to win only grudging cooperation in the midst of a menacing international crisis. But the circulation of a false rumor alleging that Robles had agreed to sell the Galápagos Islands to the United States gave opponents of the president an excuse to deny congressional cooperation with the executive branch. Led by the conservative Gabriel García Moreno and the liberal Pedro Moncayo, Congress voted to deny extraordinary powers to the president in a time of extreme emergency.[19]

On 26 October 1858, even as the Congress debated, Peru went to war with Ecuador by declaring a blockade of Guayaquil. President Robles hurried down to Guayaquil, and the Congress dissolved itself for lack of a quorum. Most observers did not understand what had happened but the departure of the president from Quito and the dissolution of Congress brought on the collapse of effective government. Ecuador descended into anarchy.[20]

In January 1859 Peru followed up on its blockade with an invasion of Guayaquil. Military occupation of Ecuador's only major port quickly brought foreign commerce to a standstill and cut off the customs receipts, the largest single source of funds of the beleaguered treasury. Political disintegration became evident everywhere, as pronunciamientos and revolts erupted in the major cities of Quito, Imbabura, Ambato, Cuenca, and Loja. The uprising in Quito was most serious, for its leaders proclaimed a provisional government for the nation in opposition to Robles. The new government in Quito, which included some prominent floreanos, soon came under the domination of García Moreno, the emerging leader of conservatism in Ecuador.[21]

Robles, with the aid of Urbina, managed to defeat the rebel government in Quito temporarily and to drive García Moreno out of the country. But the latter managed to return to Ecuador, surprisingly, with the support of the president of Peru, who hoped that García Moreno would promote more chaos in Ecuador. Contrary to Castilla's expectations, however, the conservative leader quickly gained control of the highlands, began to build a strong central government, and resisted Peruvian demands.[22]

When García Moreno attempted to win control of Guayaquil and the coast he found the rebel forces under General Guillermo Franco, who was in league with the Peruvian invaders, too strong for his highland army. At this juncture García Moreno received an offer of assistance from General Flores, who had apparently fallen from favor in Peru (for unknown reasons) and was now looking for an opportunity to return to Ecuador. Though the new conservative leader in Quito had not gotten on well with Flores in the past and had reason to fear political rivalry from the ambitious ex-president, he decided, out of military necessity, to accept the offer of assistance. Late in May 1860 Flores arrived in Quito, embraced García Moreno, and accepted supreme command of Ecuador's small army. Thus ended fifteen years of exile for Flores.[23]

At the time of Flores' return to Ecuador he was about sixty years of age, an older man by the standards of the time. Nevertheless, he appeared to have lost little of his former vigor and love of military action, for he wasted no time in undertaking a campaign to capture Guayaquil and to unite all of Ecuador under García Moreno's government in Quito. He soon established his military headquarters in the village of Ventanas in the lowlands, trained his troops, and made careful preparations. In August he pounced upon General Franco's forces at Bodega. Pursuing the defeated army, Flores soon took Guayaquil with scarcely any bloodshed, though he allowed the rebel general and his top commanders to escape aboard Peruvian ships. Thanks to the brilliance of Flores' generalship the government of Ecuador was consolidated and the nation was free of both invaders and rebels by late September 1860.[24]

Though military victory belonged to Flores, political power

remained in the hands of the clever García Moreno, who kept a wary eye on the veteran general. The official bulletin, written by García Moreno himself, which celebrated the victory at Guayaquil, omitted any mention of General Flores' role in defeating the rebels.[25]

After the successful conclusion of the coastal campaign General Flores settled down to play the part of a senior statesman and military hero, always ready to make sacrifices for the national welfare. It was more than likely that he expected that power would eventually gravitate to him. Meanwhile, he would support the conservative, authoritarian regime of García Moreno. Though personal relations between the austere president and the flamboyant general were a little distant, each showed courtesy and consideration toward the other.

General Flores quickly emerged as a major figure in Ecuadorian politics. Not only was he elected to the constituent national convention of 1860, but he was chosen as the president of that deliberative body. This position permitted him to help shape important aspects of the forthcoming Constitution of 1861. Flores championed such conservative principles as centralized government, narrow restrictions on the press, and stern laws against conspiracy. The adoption of a provision for a four-year presidential term without possibility of immediate reelection no doubt pleased the general, because this stipulation seemed to promise a chance for Flores to succeed to the presidency in 1865. One of the most interesting actions of the convention was the elimination of a clause in the draft constitution which would have forbidden the president from placing the nation under a foreign dynasty. Once more the issue of monarchism had surfaced in Ecuador, and General Flores, as president of the national convention, probably played an important role in defeating the antimonarchical clause. The spirit of monarchism was still alive in Ecuador and Flores continued to champion this ultraconservative cause.[26]

The monarchist leanings of the ex-president gave him an ideological affinity with the very conservative García Moreno, who in December 1859 had secretly proposed to the French chargé in Quito the creation of a French protectorate and monarchy for Ecuador. At the time of the proposal Ecuador was torn by civil war and was partially overrun by a Peruvian invasion. García Moreno sought to achieve political stability and to secure protection from predatory neighbors by means of a pact with France. Nothing came of the monarchist proposal, however, because the French chargé thought so little of the scheme that he failed to submit it to his government.[27]

General Flores had no part in the monarchist initiative of late 1859 because he was still in Lima conspiring to regain power. Just when Flores picked up the scent of García Moreno's royalist plan is not known, but he must have learned of it no later than March 1861, when a Peruvian newspaper published García Moreno's secret letters to the French chargé. It did not take the ex-president long to make public his enthusiasm for the idea of a French-backed monarchy. In a semiofficial newspaper of Guayaquil Flores published an article expressing his now-familiar views about the weakness of republican institutions and the lack of preparation of Spanish Amerian nations for self-government. Though he had very recently helped to draft a constitution that provided for quadrennial elections of the president, Flores declared in the newspaper article that periodic elections of a chief executive produced "deplorable convulsions," and he pointed to the recent outbreak of civil war in the United States as proof of the inadequacy of republican institutions. Rumors began to circulate that General Flores was part of a government plan to place Ecuador under French rule.[28]

The rumors appear to have had some basis in fact, for in late July 1861 President García Moreno appointed Flores' son, Antonio Flores Jijón, Ecuadorian chargé to England and France with the secret mission of reviving the moribund monarchical proposal with the government of Napoleon III. The official instructions given to Flores Jijón were so similar to the earlier plans of Generals Flores and Santa Cruz in the 1840s and to Flores' projects of the 1850s that it is hard to believe that the instructions were written without the assitance of General Flores. According to the instructions, Ecuador would cede the Galápagos Islands and the Amazonian regions (still claimed by Peru) to France in return for a French protectorate over Ecuador and the establishment of a monarchy embracing Ecuador and Peru, to be called the "United Kingdom of the Andes." Further evidence of Flores' active role in the French scheme was to be seen in a personal letter from the general to Lord Palmerston, now the prime minister of England. The letter not only introduced Flores Jijón to the prime minister but sought to enlist British sympathy and support for Ecuador in its quest for international security.[29] The subsequent intercession of Colonel Richard Wright, Flores' right-hand-man in the British Isles, on behalf of the Ecuadorian cause was clear proof of General Flores' involvement in the protectorate diplomacy.[30]

As late as October 1863 there was much talk of a French-backed monarchy in Ecuador. Friedrich Hassaurek, minister-resident of the United States in Ecuador, reported that President García Moreno was unaccountably anxious to please the French chargé. The arrival of a French warship at Guayaquil caused rumors to fly about a plan for special armed protection of the existing government against revolts and foreign intrusions.[31] Hassaurek's suspicions of a monarchical scheme stemmed in part from his belief that most of Ecuador's conservatives were enemies of republicanism and covert friends of kingship. The American diplomat's private conversations with García Moreno's advisers and ministers convinced him that the government had not given up the idea of erecting a throne or establishing a French protectorate of some kind. The enthusiasm with which members of García Moreno's administration greeted French intervention in Mexico and the establishment of Maximilian's short-lived empire there seemed to confirm the monarchist temper of the Ecuadorian government.[32]

Hassaurek need not have fretted, however, for Flores Jijón's mission to France was a complete failure. There was irony in the Ecuadorian cheering for the French intervention in Mexico, because it was precisely Napoleon III's commitment to the Maximilian venture which was largely responsible for the French rejection of the Ecuadorian proposal. The monarchist undertaking in Mexico required such large financial and military obligations that France could not take on a second major commitment with unknown risks, such as the creation of a "United Kingdom of the Andes." In December 1861 the French foreign minister sent word to García Moreno that France could not involve herself in the "internal quarrels" of South America and suggested that Ecuador and her neighbors ought to work out their problems and seek unity just as Brazil had done elsewhere on the continent. Though García Moreno and Flores continued to give the impression that there was hope for the scheme, the French refusal was final. Ecuadorian monarchism was dead, without any prospect of revival.[33]

For the most part General Flores agreed with the authoritarian and conservative policies of the García Moreno administration. He stood ready at all times to defend the government against its enemies, both foreign and domestic. Flores' loyalty and support were important to President García Moreno whose regime was unstable in its early years. The British and American diplomats in Quito both reported to their governments that the president could not survive without the support of General Flores.[34]

Although Flores had personal disagreements with some of the president's policies, such as arbitrary arrests and cruel punishments of political opponents, he did no more than to express his dissent privately and to intervene occasionally to secure clemency for some of the victims of the president's wrath.[35] Early in 1863 the general was deeply offended, according to informal reports, when García Moreno reneged on a promise to accept Flores' selection of a vice-presidential nominee. Rumors spread of a rift between the president and the general, but Flores refrained from public criticism of the government.[36]

Flores' restraint was an indication that he had made a private decision to seek political power by peaceful means. He would bide his time and wait for power to come to him rather than attempt to seize it. Meanwhile, he and his family were treated quite well by the government. His prominence in public affairs permitted him to recover much of his former fame and popularity, which had suffered so much during his years of exile. If all went well, he could reasonably hope to be elected to the presidency in 1865, because the Constitution of 1861 provided that the chief executive was to serve a four-year term without the possibility of reelection. If García Moreno abided by the constitution, Flores appeared to be the most likely contender for the presidency in 1865.

Many Ecuadorians believed not only that Flores would be

the next Ecuadorian head of state but that he might replace
García Moreno before the expiration of the presidential term
of office. Friedrich Hassaurek, the United States minister in
Quito, reported late in 1862 that the García Moreno administration "would not be able to sustain itself one day" without
the support of Flores. In January 1863 Hassaurek declared
that the Ecuadorian president had "lost the support of all
classes of people" by "his arbitrary acts, his ultramontane fanaticism . . . , his bad faith . . . , his meddling in everything
that does not concern him." The American diplomat concluded that "fear alone" kept the president in power. If General Flores were to withdraw his support, said the minister,
"the downfall of the present administration becomes inevitable." The British chargé d'affaires, George Fagan, made a very
similar assessment when he declared that García Moreno had
"lost the confidence of his supporters" and might be "super-
seded by some more popular person before his tenure of office expires." Fagan went on to identify the "more popular
person" as General Flores, "to whom the Army is devoted."[37]

The views of the foreign diplomats probably reflected the
opinions of prominent Ecuadorians who talked with the diplomats about government and politics, but their predictions of
Flores' bright future were quite mistaken. Both Hassaurek and
Fagan failed to understand García Moreno's grim determination to hang on to power and the effectiveness of his ruthless-
ness in dealing with rivals and opponents. Moreover, they were
not aware that the health of the commander of the army was
beginning to deteriorate.

Meanwhile, General Flores spent most of his time in the vicinity of Guayaquil, just as he had done many years earlier when
Rocafuerte was president. Only occasionally did he make trips
to Quito to attend meetings of the legislature and consult with
members of the executive branch. He busied himself in efforts
to restore his properties and to increase his private fortune,
which had greatly diminished during his exile. Among his
many activities at this time was the purchase of a steamship in
the United States and the establishment of a steamer service
between Guayaquil and Callao. This maritime business venture
proved unprofitable, but Flores escaped from serious losses by

selling the vessel to the Ecuadorian government at a favorable price.[38]

As general-in-chief of the armed forces Flores was the dominant political force in the coastal region. The general enjoyed so much power, in fact, that the governor of the province of Guayas was a mere figurehead. Whenever plots against the government of the lowlands were discovered, or even suspected, it was the general-in-chief, rather than the governor, who snuffed out the first sparks of insurrection. Flores' zeal for law and order was so great that it led to murmuring in Guayaquil about a military tyranny.[39]

The dangers to the García Moreno regime from insurrectionary plots and filibusters between 1862 and 1864 were considerable. Generals Urbina, Franco, and Robles, all of whom enjoyed exile in Peru under the protection of President Castilla, conspired almost continually to overthrow the Quito government.[40] Had Flores been disposed to join with any of the plotters, he could easily have brought down the government, but his loyalty to Ecuador's president did not waiver. No doubt the general wished to demonstrate his dedication to the conservative regime and to place García Moreno so deeply in his debt that Flores' succession to the presidency in 1865 would become inevitable.

Flores' military reputation and his loyalty to the government caused the opponents of the government to make attempts on his life. Late in 1862 rebels tried and failed to capture the commander of the army while Flores was recuperating on the island of Puná from tropical fevers that damaged his health.[41] A few months later henchmen of Urbina and Robles hatched a second plot to kidnap Flores, but the plan was discovered beforehand. One of the conspirators later testified that the aim of the scheme was to capture the general, put him aboard a steamer, "and send him down river, snatch from him an order that the barracks should surrender, and afterward assassinate him."[42]

Serious as the threat was from expatriot generals in Peru, the most serious menace to Ecuador and the García Moreno regime came from New Granada (soon to be renamed Colombia). In 1861 General Tomás Cipriano de Mosquera gained power in Bogotá and soon proclaimed a "United States of Colombia."

Mosquera professed to be liberal, anticlerical, and eager to reestablish the boundaries of Bolívar's Gran Colombia. García Moreno, quick to see the danger to a conservative administration in Ecuador, refused to accept the proposed union with Colombia. This refusal quickly provoked a disastrous military clash at the northern town of Tulcán, in which García Moreno was defeated, wounded, and briefly held captive by Colombia.[43]

After regaining his freedom the Ecuadorian president hurried back to Quito and worked feverishly to shore up his faltering regime. The crisis of 1862–1863 was severe, for the unpopular García Moreno was threatened not only by the ambitious Mosquera in the north but also by possible filibusters from Peru. In fact, the danger in late 1862 and early 1863 of an invasion by the exiled Urbina at Guayaquil was so great that Flores could not be called away from the port city to defend the northern frontier. For a few months García Moreno was able to buy time with dilatory diplomatic negotiations, but in August 1863 President Mosquera issued a proclamation denouncing the "theocratic" regime in Quito and demanding Ecuador's incorporation into the "United States of Colombia." García Moreno viewed the proclamation as an ultimatum and took steps to prepare for war.[44]

Ecuadorians at first feared that their nation was about to be partitioned between Colombia and Peru, but García Moreno succeeded in lifting the spirits of the people to resist the external threat. Congress granted extraordinary powers to the president, authorized new taxes, and approved a rapid expansion of the army. Since the threat from the north was now much greater than the threat from the south, García Moreno summoned General Flores from Guayaquil to take command of an army being readied to resist the expected invasion by Mosquera.[45]

Once again the aging general was called upon to defend his country from foreign enemies. Flores, who at the time was not on the best of terms with García Moreno, might have found an excuse, such as poor health or lack of adequate mobilization of military forces, to decline the summons. Indeed, he would have been wise to remain in Guayaquil, because Ecuador was not strong enough to confront the Colombian army. The president's prestige was at a low point because of his humiliating defeat at Tulcán, his policy of financial austerity, and his religious zeal. The president's recent invitation to the Jesuit order, requesting it to return to the country and assume control of the school system, had aroused much criticism. The religious issue was further agitated by the negotiation of a controversial concordat (formal agreement) with the Vatican which made extensive concessions to the Papacy. The president's decision to ratify the concordat without congressional review caused a storm of opposition among the legislators, who criticized the chief executive's "blind submission to the papal court."[46] Flores' anticlerical leanings caused him to withhold his support of the administration's religious policies, and it was rumored that he might join the opposition and topple the government.[47]

Nevertheless, Flores made a fateful decision to support the government, probably because he relished the opportunity to figure once more as a military hero and savior of the nation. On 3 October 1863 he departed Guayaquil for Quito at the head of a force of twelve hundred men. Four days later he arrived in the capital where he conferred with the president and gathered more troops for the impending war with Colombia. According to one report, the general advised the president to maintain a purely defensive posture against Colombia, but allowed himself to be persuaded by the impetuous García Moreno to take the offensive.[48]

The presence of the veteran general in Quito inspired the government and the Ecuadorian people with a new spirit of confidence and optimism. Flores' familiarity with the northern frontier region, his experience in dealing with the Colombians, and his vaunted military expertise led people to believe that the ex-president would be more than a match for the menacing Mosquera. Flores quickly recruited more officers and men, gave them a few days of training, and hastily headed north with a ragtag army of perhaps eight thousand. As the Ecuadorian army moved toward the northern border Antonio Flores Jijón attempted to distract the Colombian government with diplomatic negotiations, which appeared to have been intended to provide the Ecuadorian army with time to carry out its operations.[49]

It was the intention of General Flores to carry out a surprise invasion of Colombia, to enlist Colombian conservatives in an uprising against the liberal government of Mosquera, and thus to put an end to the threat of annexation. To carry out this bold plan the Ecuadorian military chieftain counted on his intimate knowledge of the border region, his presumed influence with the people of Pasto, and the larger size of his army. His optimism was based on faulty calculations, however, and inadequate intelligence. Though his army was roughly three times the size of the opposing Colombian force and possessed a cavalry of about fifteen hundred men, the Ecuadorian troops were mostly raw recruits. Many Ecuadorian officers were short on talent and experience. Worst of all, Flores' soldiers were very poorly equipped. In contrast with Mosquera's men, who carried modern rifles, the Ecuadorians used outmoded flintlock muskets. There was little chance that the untrained and ill-equipped force under Flores' command could stand up to the superior firepower of Mosquera's army.

Upon reaching the northern border General Flores issued a proclamation calling upon the inhabitants of southern Colombia to cooperate with the Ecuadorian army. But when Flores crossed the frontier in late November 1863, Colombians ignored his appeal and withheld support of the invaders. The Ecuadorian army soon suffered a crushing defeat at Cuaspud by Mosquera's superior force. Flores, though wounded, managed to retreat and regroup his men inside Ecuador. News of the defeat at Cuaspud caused panic in Quito, but Flores managed to save the day by negotiating a peace with Mosquera which preserved the independence and territorial integrity of Ecuador.[50] This astonishing diplomatic feat, made possible by Mosquera's political difficulties in Colombia, prompted the United States chargé in Quito to remark that "Ecuador could not have obtained a more honorable peace, even if her army had been victorious."[51]

Flores' triumph in diplomacy did not obscure the obvious fact that he had suffered the most humiliating reverse of his lifetime. The Battle of Cuaspud was Flores' Waterloo. His reputation as a military leader was irreparably damaged, for his army of almost eight thousand men had been surprised, outmanuevered, and routed by an enemy force of no more than twenty-five hundred. There were excuses, of course, such as the poor weapons and raw recruits, and there were extenuating circumstances. But the fact remained in the minds of Ecuadorians that General Flores had failed the nation at a critical moment.

The general-in-chief did not abandon public life after the humiliating defeat at Cuaspud, but his influence declined rapidly. Early in 1864, when he took his seat in the Senate, he received a figurative slap in the face when his colleagues chose not to elect him once more as president of that body.[52] A few months later when Flores went to a public meeting in Guayaquil he was mortified to see everyone turn his back upon him and depart from the room.[53]

The ex-resident's spirits may have been raised somewhat in July when he received a presidential appointment as commissioner to negotiate a settlement of the United States' claims against Ecuador. However, he was not able to take part in the negotiations with the U.S. representative because of the outbreak of serious revolts in the coastal region. Though Flores had declared after his defeat at Cuaspud that he did not want to command an army again, he quickly assumed responsibility for defending the coast against insurrections. Uprisings in Manabí to the north and in Machala, some seventy miles south of Guayaquil, were attributed to the instigation of General Urbina, who was believed to be organizing filibusters in Peru. The Manabí uprising was suppressed quickly, but the Machala affair was more serious because the rebels there could receive supplies from the nearby Peruvian ports of Túmbez and Paita and because the insurgents had at their disposal a small naval force sent to them by Urbina from Callao.[54]

The naval power of the rebels forced General Flores to delay action against them until he could outfit a small maritime force and receive reinforcements from the highlands. In early September Flores headed for Machala with three ships and a thousand troops, but the strength of the rebels forced him to retreat to Guayaquil to augment his naval resources. Ignoring the advice of his physicians, who warned that his health was precarious, Flores set out for Machala once again on 26 September 1864. This campaign proved to be Flores' last. The expedition turned into a military success for the government, but the effort was more than General Flores' weakened health could with-

stand. While at Machala he became gravely ill. An attempt was
made to rush him back to Guayaquil, but he died aboard ship
on 1 October 1864. The cause of his death is not completely
understood, but a urinary blockage was a major factor. It was
reported that Flores died "calling for his family and invoking
the Supreme God of Battles."[55]

Though his victory over the rebels at Machala could not be
counted among Flores' major military successes, it was at least a
victory in the service of the government of Ecuador. Thus, the
"Founder of the Republic" gave his life for the nation that he
had helped to create and to govern. General Flores' death was
not universally lamented, but President García Moreno declared that he would

> find nothing in the world to replace the faithful, decisive, far-
> seeing, sagacious, conciliatory, intelligent, learned, and experi-
> enced friend that I have lost.[56]

The posthumous praise clearly overlooked defects in the general's character and past behavior, but García Moreno really had
few complaints to make of the fallen general, for Flores had
become a major pillar of the regime by helping to consolidate the
dictatorship and by supporting the government in every foreign
and domestic crisis. Even when he had disagreed with government policies, Flores had refrained from public criticism.

Though García Moreno and Flores differed considerably in
temperament and general outlook, both believed in strong executive rule and in conservative social principles. If the general
disapproved of the dictator's impulsiveness and his cruelty, he
nonetheless believed in the need for an authoritarian government that would rigorously repress sedition and dissent. Both
men believed that it was proper for the government to impose
its authority on the people in order to bring about material and
social progress.

General Flores, of course, had been skeptical of republican
institutions from the start. As president in the 1830s he had
attempted to conform to the prescriptions of the early constitutions and to work harmoniously with the legislative branch. He
was not a democrat in the moldern sense, but neither were any

of the other presidents of Ecuador during his lifetime. Clearly a product of the Hispanic authoritarian traditions and of the military life, he believed in government from the top down, in a regime of rulers over the ruled. Like all of the other Ecuadorian chief executives of the era he sought, most of the time, to operate within the republican framework by means of manipulation. He rigged elections (though never with complete success) and he controlled congresses with blandishments and patronage. When the techniques of manipulation failed and his political opponents became obstreperous, he decided that republicanism had failed and that political salvation lay in monocratic government. He favored monarchy if European support for it could be found, and dictatorship if it could not be found.

The idea of monarchy had proved a will-o'-the-wisp in Ecuador. Though monarchism had much acceptance among aristocrats and conservatives, it was not a feasible option once republicanism had been accepted. The unsuccessful efforts of both Flores and García Moreno had demonstrated the impracticality of erecting a throne in Ecuador. The failure of the first monarchical project in 1844–1845 probably could not have been foreseen, but Flores' persistence in the Spanish project and in various filibustering plots was wrong-headed and did serious harm to Ecuador. "King of the Night" was an appropriate sobriquet for the leader who spent a decade and a half plotting against the government of Ecuador and who refused to yield on the issue of monarchism despite the strong evidence against its practicality.

Though Juan José Flores would doubtless have wished to be remembered as the "Founder of the Republic," most Ecuadorians today do not admire him as a founding father. The negative aspects of his role in history have overshadowed the positive. It is understandable that his filibustering expeditions and his support of García Moreno's despotism have evoked criticism and disapproval. He did much damage to Ecuador by undermining the government and causing alarm and uncertainty as he sought to regain presidential power. But it is wrong to blame all of Ecuador's problems of the late 1840s and 1850s on the errant ex-president. General Urbina, who dominated the government during most of Flores' period of exile, was a crude military caudillo with few scruples who sought to perpetuate his own power, and who later plotted against Ecuador while in exile, just as Flores had done.[57] New Granada and Peru, especially the latter country, would have made trouble for Ecuador and would probably have found other Ecuadorian expatriates to use as pawns if General Flores had not been available. Peru's attempt to make use of García Moreno in 1859 is a case in point.

As for his responsibility for the establishment of the dictatorship of García Moreno, Flores' collaboration with Castilla helped to bring on the crisis of 1859–1860 that produced the authoritarian regime, but this is not to say that the ex-president was entirely to blame for the establishment of the despotism that reigned from 1860 to 1875. Castilla of Peru, Urbina, and other Ecuadorian leaders had more to do with the crisis of 1859–1860 than did Flores. It is true that General Flores offered his military talents in support of the García Moreno regime in its early years, but he viewed this regime as the only government capable of defending Ecuador's territory and sovereignty from its aggressive neighbors. Though Flores supported the conservative dictatorship, he disapproved of many of the arbitrary and autocratic policies of the regime and he sought to restrain García Moreno from some of his worst excesses. Flores doubtless believed that, if he should succeed to the presidency in 1865, he would be able to tone down the harshness of governmental policies. But he passed from the scene without recovering presidential power.

The death of General Flores marked the end of the early era of military domination in politics. Most Spanish American nations passed through a similar stage of charismatic government under the tutelage of the generals of Independence. Flores was far from the worst of these military chieftains, most of whom misgoverned and plundered their homelands. Certainly Flores was more effective and constructive than men like Agustín de Iturbide of Mexico, Manuel Isidoro Belzú of Bolivia, and Francisco Solano López of Paraguay. He governed with greater restraint, intelligence, and understanding than was to be expected of a person of obscure origins who lacked a formal education and important family connections. Much greater things were to be expected of a Rocafuerte of Guayaquil than of a Flores of Puerto Cabello.

After Flores' fall from power in 1845 Ecuador was dominated by military caudillos most of the time until the rise of the civilian caudillo, García Moreno. Though the latter was forced to make use of Flores to cope with foreign and domestic opponents, García Moreno inaugurated a new kind of regime based upon the support (or acquiescence) of most of the aristocracy, some of the educated middle classes, and the clergy. The armed forces had to be controlled, of course, but the dictator accomplished this task in a variety of ways, such as assuming personal command of the army at times, winning support of conservative generals through conservative policies, and by intimidating disaffected officers with floggings, banishments, and summary executions of rebel leaders.[58]

The decline of the military after 1865 coincided with the rise of the Catholic clergy to a new prominence. The ecclesiastical leaders did not achieve the power and influence of the generals in the early decades of independence, but García Moreno converted the Church into a mighty pillar of the state. He reformed and disciplined monks and priests, turned the educational system over to them, and excluded heretics from citizenship. Thus, the death of General Flores marked the end of the era of charismatic military rule and the onset of a period of clerical conservatism. Government was more autocratic, even despotic, than before, but García Moreno had found the classic combination of conservative political supports in Latin America to achieve a higher degree of governmental stability: landowning aristocrats, clergy, and military—the latter downgraded and under the president's personal domination. The formula worked for a decade and a half.[59]

The conservative formula for stability had eluded General Flores for several reasons. From 1830 to 1843 his political thinking was not conservative but rather eclectic and pragmatic. His control of the military was unquestioned, and most of the landowners probably supported him until he attempted to impose a head tax on whites and mestizos in order to lighten the tax burden of Indians. By 1844 Flores had become disillusioned with republicanism and had shifted to a more conservative position. But his anticlerical leanings precluded him from embracing the Church for political purposes. The roots of Flores' anticlericalism are somewhat obscure, though his early association with Freemasonry was an important influence. His deathbed invocation of the "God of Battles" suggests that Flores may not have believed in Christian theology. Rocafuerte's anticlericalism may also have had an effect on the general's thoughts, for the latter was aware of Rocafuerte's superior intellectual talents. It is likely too that the deplorable moral condition of the Ecuadorian clergy made it difficult for General Flores to see how the ecclesiastical ranks could be turned into a useful support of the state. As a consequence, Flores, after casting about for other means of shoring up the governmental system, chose monarchy, without clerical backing, as the solution for political instability.

García Moreno also accepted monarchism as a possible solution for Ecuador's troubles, especially while the country was threatened by Peru and Colombia, but he found a better, practical remedy in a combination of personal despotism and the classic conservative political alliance. With the removal of General Juan José Flores from the scene and the adoption of a new monocratic formula Ecuador passed into a new stage of development under García Moreno in which both military caudillismo and monarchism had become irrelevant.

But even the traditional conservative formula proved incapable of resolving Ecuador's political problems in the long term. As a consequence García Moreno relied increasingly on brutal repression to control his opponents. This "perpetual dictatorship," as it was called, gave the appearance of stability, but it lasted only a few years.

The brutal assassination of García Moreno in 1875 precipitated Ecuador into another period of conflict and instability during which conservatives and liberals vied for power in a lengthy struggle that seemed almost meaningless at times. This political strife of the late nineteenth century demonstrated the failure not only of Juan José Flores but of all of the nation's leaders to cope with the conflicting forces that made it so difficult to govern Ecuador. For a brief period, from 1888 to 1892, when Flores' eldest son Antonio Flores Jijón served as president, it appeared that a spirit of enlightened moderation might pacify the contending forces of the strife-torn nation. Unfortunately, Flores Jijón's relatively peaceful administration was soon followed by new tumults and violent political battles which stretched into the twentieth century.

In retrospect it is relatively easy to diagnose the ills from which Ecuador suffered: regional rivalries, economic backwardness, corruption, and social injustice. But prescriptions to cure the illness were difficult to come by. Liberalism, conservatism, monarchism, and ecclectic moderation were all tried or attempted, and found wanting. Juan José Flores cannot be credited with finding a solution for Ecuador's problems, but, given the enormous difficulties, it was little wonder that he failed.

Notes

1. BOLÍVAR'S MAN IN QUITO, 1824–1830

1. Jay Kinsbruner, *The Spanish American Independence Movement* (Hinsdale, Ill., 1973), 75–79; Tulio Halperín-Donghi, *The Aftermath of Revolution in Latin America* (New York, 1973); and Simon Collier, *Ideas and Politics of Chilean Independence, 1808–1833* (Cambridge, Eng., 1967), 129–286. After the first citation all works are cited by author's last name and short title.

2. Captain Gabriel Lafond de Lurcy, quoted in Jorge E. Villacrés Moscoso, "El General Flores y su proyectado protectorado francés para el Ecuador," *Cuadernos de historia y arqueología* 8: (Quito), 36–37; and Adrian R. Terry, *Travels in the Equatorial Regions of South America in 1832* (Hartford, Conn., 1834), 171–172.

3. Pedro Moncayo, *El Ecuador de 1825 a 1875: Sus hombres, sus instituciones y sus leyes* (Santiago, Chile, 1885), 8.

4. Pedro Fermín Ceballos, *Resumen de la historia del Ecuador desde su origen hasta 1845*, 5 vols. in 3 (Lima, 1870), IV: 196. Ceballos was a witness of the early national history of Ecuador, which he recorded. A totally negative portrait of Flores is presented by Roberto Andrade, *Historia del Ecuador*, 7 vols. (Guayaquil, 1934–1937), V: 1720–1721.

5. Ceballos, *Resumen*, V: 96.

6. Elías Laso, *Biografía del General Juan José Flores* (Quito, 1924), 2, gives 24 July 1800 as the date of birth, but Lafond de Lurcy states that Flores was twenty-six years old in 1828 (Villacrés Moscoso, "Flores," 22–24). Few of Flores' acquaintances agreed on his age. For a full discussion of this topic see Luis Robalino Dávila, *Nacimiento y primeros años de la República* (Puebla, Mexico, 1967), 338–344, esp. n. 1, 338.

7. Laso, *Biografía*, 2; Terry, *Travels*, 172; John Trumbull Van Alen (U.S. chargé at Quito) to John M. Clayton (U.S. secretary of state), dispatch no. 27, Quito, 1 February 1850, in William R. Manning (ed.), *Diplomatic Correspondence of the United States: Inter-American Affairs, 1831–1860*, 12 vols. (Washington, D.C., 1832–1839), VI: 265; and Delazon Smith (U.S. special agent) to John C. Calhoun (secretary of state), Quito, 10 August 1845, in ibid., 251. For more discussions of Flores' racial origins see Robalino Dávila, *Nacimiento*,

338–340; and Luis Martínez-Delgado, *Berruecos: Asesinato del gran mariscal de Ayacucho* . . . (Medellín, 1973), 54–58.

8. Oil portraits are in the Flores library at the Catholic University and at the home of Gustavo Vásconez Hurtado.

9. Laso, *Biografía*, 2.

10. Flores to Bolívar: Quito, 16 June 1826, and Guaranda, 25 March 1829, in Simón B. O'Leary (ed.), *Memorias del General O'Leary*, 32 vols. (Caracas, 1879–1888), IV: 6–7, 171–173.

11. Flores to Santander, Quito, 19 September 1826, in Roberto Cortázar (comp.), *Correspondencia dirigida al General Francisco de Paula Santander*, 10 vols. (Bogotá, 1964–1968), V: 449. Flores' letters of the 1820s reveal his lack of cultural sophistication, but they also contradict charges of illiteracy and total lack of education which have been leveled against him.

12. Laso, *Biografía*, 2, 30; Robalino Dávila, *Nacimiento*, 375–377; Isaac J. Barrera, *Historia de la literatura educatoriana*, 4 vols. in 1 (Quito, 1960), III: 593–596; and Vicente Rocafuerte, *A la nación*, no. 10, in Rocafuerte, *Colección Rocafuerte*, 16 vols. (Quito, 1947), XIV: 157–158.

13. *Gaceta del Gobierno del Ecuador* (Quito), 8 May 1842, (hereinafter cited as *Gaceta*) printed the news of the doctoral award and defended it; Robalino Dávila, *Nacimiento*, 381–382. For ridicule of Flores and the honorary doctorate, see Rocafuerte, *A la nación*, nos. 4, 5, and 11, *Colección*, XIV: 57, 62–64, 167. For an example of Flores' superficial learning, see his letter to Bolívar of 16 June 1826, O'Leary, *Memorias*, IV: 6–7.

14. For more on Rocafuerte's administration, see chap. 5 below; and Robalino Dávila, *Rocafuerte* (Quito, 1964); and Kent B. Mecum, *El idealismo práctico de Vicente Rocafuerte* . . . (Puebla, Mexico, 1975), 171–199.

15. Laso, *Biografía*, 40–41; and letter from Juan León Mera to Manuel Cañete, Ambato, 12 January 1887, in Mera, *Ojeada histórico-crítica sobre la poesía ecuatoriana* . . . , 2d ed. (Barcelona, 1893), 472–473, which describes Flores' intellectual and social charm in the 1860s.

16. Laso, *Biografía*, 2–5; Flores, *El General Flores a los ecuatorianos* (Bayonne, 1847), 1–4. Flores' claim of participation in the battle of Carabobo is hotly disputed by the anonymous author of *Flores, o el panejirista de sí mismo* (no publication data, but probably Lima, 1846), 5. However, Vicente Lecuna, *Crónica razonada de las guerras de Bolívar*, 3 vols. (New York, 1950), III: 47, lists Flores as a participant, which would seem to settle the matter.

17. Bolívar to Col. Basilio García, Trapiche, 23 May 1822; Bolívar to Santander, Pasto, 9 June 1822; and Bolívar's correspondence from

6 December 1822 to 14 January 1823, in *Cartas,* III: 34–37, 120–138. Salvador de Madariaga, *Bolívar* (London and New York, 1952), 417–418, 421–423, and 446. On the problem of Pasto, see Bolívar's letter to Sucre, 28 October 1828, in *Cartas,* VIII: 99; and Flores' letters to Gen. Bartolomé Salom from 17 May 1823 to 3 July 1824, in O'Leary, *Memorias,* IV: 261–271; and Flores' letters to the intendant of Quito for the years 1823–1824, Archivo National de Historia (ANH), Quito, "Correspondencia del General Juan José Flores, 1822 a 1848," vol. 668. For an excellent account of the Pasto troubles see Roger P. Davis, "Ecuador Under Gran Colombia, 1820–1830: Regionalism, Localism, and Legitimacy in the Emergence of an Andean Republic," Ph.D. dissertation, University of Arizona, 1983 (facsimile copy available through University Microfilms International), 104–122. Andrade, *Historia,* V: 1706–1713, presents a very partisan, anti-Flores, account of the Pasto affair which ignores the fact that Bolívar, not Flores, set the policy of bloody oppression. Andrade also fails to note that the guerrilla tactics of the loyalists were treacherous in the extreme. Flores barely escaped an assassination plot.

18. Moncayo, *Ecuador,* 7–8.

19. Ibid., 9.

20. Flores to Santander, 6 October 1825, in Cortázar, *Correspondencia,* V: 442–443.

21. Laso, *Biografía,* 9–11; Ceballos, *Resumen,* IV: 181; Andrade, *Historia,* V: 1714–1728. The date of his promotion was September 26, 1826; see Santander's letter to the president of the Senate, Bogotá, 5 July 1827, in Roberto Cortázar (comp.), *Cartas y mensajes del general Francisco Paula Santander,* 10 vols. (Bogotá, 1953–1956), VII: 257. The department with Quito as its capital will be called "El Ecuador" in this work to distinguish it from the nation of Ecuador.

22. The other two departments were known as Azuay (its capital in Cuenca) and Guayas (capital in Guayaquil).

23. Flores to Bolívar, Guayaquil, 3 April 1827, in O'Leary, *Memorias,* IV: 18–19; and Davis, "Ecuador," 209–210.

24. Madariaga, *Bolívar,* 431–434, 456–458. The anonymous author of *Flores, o el panejirista de sí mismo* claims that Flores was never in command at Pasto. Flores claimed that he was in command (*El General Flores,* 4), and his letters of 1823 to 1824 certainly give this impression. Andrade, who hated Flores, admitted that he was in command at Pasto but claimed that Bolívar did not trust Flores; see Andrade, *Historia,* Vol. V, 1706–1728.

25. Ceballos, *Resumen,* Vol. IV, 154; and Madariaga, *Bolívar,* 451, 455–458. On the rebellion of the Araure Battalion in Ecuador, see

Flores' letter to Bolívar, Quito, 22 August 1826, in O'Leary, *Memorias,* Vol. IV, 8–9.

26. Sucre to Santander, 21 October 1822, quoted in Madariaga, *Bolívar,* 451; Bolívar to Santander, Cuenca, 13 September and 23 September 1822, in *Cartas,* III: 84–87 and 93–96. Bolívar complained bitterly of the lack of support from Ecuadorians, but he admitted that he used extreme measures to secure men and money; see Bolívar to Santander: Quito, 5 July and 21 July 1823, in *Cartas,* X: 422, 426; Flores' letters for the years 1823–1827, in ANH, "Correspondencia del General . . . Flores," vol. 668; and, most informative, a letter from the intendant of Quito to the Jefe Superior del Sur, Quito, 7 April 1825, in ANH, "Libro 2° de la correspondencia que lleba la Yntendencia de Quito . . . ," ff. 141–142; and see Davis, "Ecuador," 161–199.

27. José Manuel Restrepo (secretary of interior) to Captain Montúfar, Bogotá, 5 September 1826, doc. no. 2862, in José Félix Blanco and Ramón Azpurúa (comps.), *Documentos para la historia de la vida pública del Libertador de Colombia, Perú y Bolivia,* 14 vols. (Caracas, 1875–1878), X: 568–570. Restrepo's letter cites Montúfar's letter of 29 August 1826 and summarizes its contents.

28. Letter from the Municipality of Guayaquil to José Manuel Restrepo, 20 April 1827, doc. no. 3129, in Blanco and Azpurúa, *Documentos,* XI: 237–240.

29. Flores' letters to Bolívar of 22 August to 29 October 1826; November 1827 (no date); and 6 May, 14 July, and 21 October 1828, in O'Leary, *Memorias,* IV: 8–9, 11–13, 31, 82–83, 115–116, 126, and 152–153. Flores' correspondence with Bolívar has also been published recently by the Archivo Juan José Flores: *Correspondencia del Libertador con el General Juan José Flores (1826–1830)* (Quito, 1977). Citations are in the better known O'Leary unless there is a special reason for citing the newer work.

30. José María Córdoba to Santander, Quito, 20 May 1827, in Academia Colombiana de Historia, *Archivo Santander,* 24 vols. (Bogotá, 1914–1922), XVII: 38–39. See also letters from Flores to Bolívar: Cuenca, 29 October 1826, and Guayaquil, 6 May 1828, in O'Leary, *Memorias,* IV: 82–83; and Juan Illingrot (i.e., Illingworth) to Bolívar, Guayaquil, 22 July and 7 August 1827, in ibid., IV: 314–315, 318.

31. Robalino Dávila, *Nacimiento,* 100, and 351–354. Among the godparents of Flores' children were Francisco de Paula Santander and Vicente Rocafuerte.

32. Jorge Basadre, *Historia de la República del Perú,* Vols. I–X, 5th

ed. (Lima, 1863–), I: 149–162, 231–244; Francisco Andrade S., *Demarcación de las fronteras de Colombia,* Vol. XII of Academia Colombiana de Historia, *Historia extensa de Colombia,* 28 vols. projected (Bogotá, 1964–), 287–290; Madariaga, *Bolívar,* 541–553, 579–580; and Pedro Gurgeitio to Santander, Ibarra, 17 July 1827, *Archivo Santander,* XVII: 125–127.

33. Flores' correspondence with Bolívar, from his undated 1827 letter (probably late April) to 17 October 1827, in O'Leary, *Memorias,* IV: 20–28; the extensive documentation in Blanco and Azpurúa, *Documentos,* XI: 190–479; and Davis, "Ecuador," 179–191.

34. Flores' letters to Bolívar, 17 October 1827 to 11 January 1829, in O'Leary, *Memorias,* IV: 26–168; Flores' letters of 1827–1828, ANH, "Correspondencia de . . . Flores," vol. 668; Ceballos, *Resumen,* IV: 327–342; and José Le Gouhir y Rodas, *Historia de la República del Ecuador,* 3 vols. (Quito, 1920–1938), I: 127–134.

35. Laso, *Biografía,* 17–20; Bolívar's numerous letters in *Cartas,* VII: 11–26, 68–85, 91–137, VIII: 22–30, 83–94, 256–351; and Flores' letters to Bolívar from 14 March to 25 March 1829, in O'Leary, *Memorias,* IV: 168–174. For the "Prince of Tarqui" remark of Sucre, see Caracciolo Parra-Pérez, *La monarquía en Gran Colombia* (Madrid, 1957), 393.

36. Bolívar to Flores, Garzal, 5 October 1829, in *Cartas,* IX: 160–161.

37. Louis Peru de Lacroix, *Diario de Bucaramanga: Estudio crítico . . . ,* ed. Nicolás E. Navarro (Caracas, 1935), 34–35; Bolívar's correspondence, especially to General Salom, 24 January 1824; to Santander, 8 October 1826; to O'Leary, 22 October 1828; and to Flores, 12 September 1827, 8 October 1828, and 5 October 1829, in *Cartas,* IV (40), VI (85), VII (18–19), VIII (83–84, 92–93), IX (160–161); and, on Flores' promotion to prefect general, Davis, "Ecuador," 221.

38. Flores to Bolívar: Quito, 7 September 1826, and Ambato, 18 March 1829, in O'Leary, *Memorias,* IV: 10, 170–171. Throughout his life Flores continued to worship the Liberator; see Flores, *Discurso que leyó el General Flores en la inauguración de la estatua del Libertador Simón Bolívar, el 9 de diciembre de 1859* ([Quito], 1859).

39. Flores to Bolívar, Quito, 7 May 1826, in O'Leary, *Memorias,* IV: 5–6. The lady in question was almost certainly Manuela Sáenz, but Flores discreetly omitted her name from his letter.

40. On Bolívar's personality, see Peru de Lacroix, *Diario,* 327–331; Madariaga, *Bolívar,* 69–83, passim; and Gerhard Masur, *Simón Bolívar,* (Albuquerque, 1969), 37–44, passim. On Flores' womanizing, see

letter from Lafonde de Lurcy to Flores, Paris, 7 October 1842, Archivo Jijón y Caamaño (AJC, hereinafter), J. J. Flores, Archivo (in brown binding), Vol. IV.

41. Flores to Bolívar, Quito, 26 June and 7 July 1826, in O'Leary, *Memorias,* IV: 6–8. On the background to the Bolivian constitution and the lifetime presidency, see: Basadre, *Historia,* I: 113–149; and Madariaga, *Bolívar,* 517–527.

42. Parra-Pérez, *Monarquía,* 113, citing a letter of Santander to Rieux (Col. Luis Francisco?); Benigno Malo, *Escritos y discursos* (Quito, 1940), I: 428–429.

43. Historians sharply disagree on the issue of whether Bolívar approved of monarchy and attempted to establish it in Spanish America. The hero-worshipping attitude of many biographers of Bolívar has closed their minds to the possibility that the man who defeated the Spanish monarchy in northern South America may have attempted to reestablish monarchy during the last years of his life. For interpretations supporting the view that Bolívar turned monarchist, see: Carlos A. Villanueva, *La monarquía en America,* 4 vols. (Paris, 1912–1913), which broke new ground by utilizing European diplomatic correspondence to shed light on monarchist activities behind the scenes; and Madariaga, *Bolívar,* esp. 493–628. Among the most important biographers who reject the notion of Bolivarian monarchism are the following: Victor Andrés Belaúnde, Vicente Lecuna, Guillermo Ruiz Rivas, Caracciolo Parra–Pérez, J. L. Salcedo-Bastardo, and David Bushnell.

44. Parra-Pérez, *Monarquía,* 3–15, 96–110, 401, passim; Madariaga, *Bolívar,* 528–531, 600–604; Bartolomé Mitre, *Historia de San Martín y de la emancipación americana,* 4 vols., 2d ed. (Buenos Aires, 1890), III: 145–152, on García del Río. On Sucre and O'Leary and monarchy, see Parra-Pérez, *Monarquía,* 293, 305–306, 309, 396–399, and 480; and Madariaga, *Bolívar,* 529, 601, and 608. Sucre's involvement in the monarchical project is made clear by Flores' letter to Bolívar, Guayaquil, 6 January 1830, in O'Leary, *Memorias,* IV: 234. The best study of Bolívar's rule, 1827–1830, is David Bushnell, "The Last Dictatorship: Betrayal or Consummation?" *The Hispanic American Historical Review* (hereinafter *HAHR*) 63(February 1983): 65–105.

45. Flores to Bolívar, Quito, 7 September 1826, in O'Leary, *Memorias,* IV: 10; Acta de la municipalidad de Quito, 6 September 1826, doc. no. 2863, Blanco and Azpurúa, *Documentos,* X: 570–572; Madariaga, *Bolívar,* 528; and Bolívar's letters of 6 to 8 August 1826, in *Cartas,* VI: 35–45.

46. Quotation from Flores' letter of 15 November 1827, in O'Leary,

Memorias, IV: 37. See also his other letters of this period, in ibid., IV: 11–35.

47. Flores to Bolívar, Quito, 6 January 1828, in O'Leary, *Memorias,* IV: 46–49. Apparently the elections were held under the intimidating influence of Flores and other officers loyal to Bolívar. Gen. Illingworth even refused to allow a deputy from Guayaquil to attend the convention because his loyalty to Bolívar was in doubt; see letter from Illingrot (Illingworth) to Bolívar, Guayaquil, 14 April 1828, in O'Leary, *Memorias,* IV: 329. For good summaries of the Convention of Ocaña episode see David Bushnell, *The Santander Regime in Gran Colombia* (Newark, Del., 1954; reprint, Westport, Conn., 1970), 353–357; and Bushnell, "The Last Dictatorship," 75–85.

48. Flores to Bolívar, Guayaquil, 21 February, 6 March, and 6 April 1828, in O'Leary, *Memorias,* IV: 57–58, 61; Peru de Lacroix, *Diario,* 327–331; and Gen. Mariano Montilla to Flores, Cartagena, 21 November 1828, AJC, Cartas a Flores, I: ff. 795–797.

49. Flores to Bolívar, Guayaquil, 6 April, 6 and 13 May 1828, in O'Leary, *Memorias,* IV: 73–74, 83–87; and Petition of the Army of the South, May 1, 1828, doc. no. 3670, Blanco and Azpurúa, *Documentos,* XII: 411–413. This petition was probably written, at least in part, by Flores, for it contains phrases used by Flores in letters to Bolívar. For Santander's view of Flores' political activities, see his letter to Flores, Ocaña, 10 May 1828, in Cortázar, *Cartas,* VII: 417–419.

50. Flores to Bolívar, Guayaquil, 14 March 1828, in O'Leary, *Memorias,* IV: 64.

51. Flores to Bolívar, Guayaquil, 21 March, 5 and 28 July 1828, in O'Leary, *Memorias,* IV: 71, 112; *Eco del Azuay* (Cuenca), 2, 9, 16 March 1828. See also Victor Manuel Albornoz, *Fray Vicente Solano: Estudio biográfico-crítico* (Cuenca, 1942), 113–114.

52. Bolívar's response to Flores is not extant, but Flores refers to it in his letter of 28 July 1828, in O'Leary, *Memorias,* IV: 119–125, in which he acknowledges receipt of letters from Bolívar dated 3 and 22 June, and 3 July 1828. See also Bolívar's marginal notes on Flores' letter of 21 March 1828, in ibid., 71. Concerning Bolívar's disingenuous tactic of publicizing the monarchical proposal while blaming it on his adversaries, see Bolívar's letter to Urdaneta, Bucaramanga, 18 May 1828, in *Cartas,* VII: 283–284; and Madariaga, *Bolívar,* 562.

53. On Bishop Lasso de la Vega, see Parra-Pérez, *Monarquía,* 126. On aspirations for titles of nobility, see the letter from José María Maldonado to Santander, Guayaquil, 2 January 1827, in *Archivo Santander,* XVI: 135.

54. In July 1828, Flores reported a suggestion from Vice-President Nicolás Bravo of Mexico which hinted at the creation of a vast Spanish American empire under the scepter of Bolívar; see Flores to Bolívar, Guayaquil, 17 July 1828, in O'Leary, *Memorias,* IV: 117. Flores later suggested the inclusion of Peru in the empire; see his letter of 14 November 1829, in ibid., 217. On Bolívar's dreams of continental rule and supranationalism, see Madariaga, *Bolívar,* 510–516, esp. 516; and Simon Collier, "Nationality, Nationalism, and Supranationalism in the Writings of Simón Bolívar," *HAHR* 63(February 1983): 37–64. For more on Bravo and Mexico, see Parra Pérez, *Monarquía,* 276–281.

55. Madariaga, *Bolívar,* 596–612; Parra-Pérez, *Monarquía,* 251–409.

56. Flores to Bolívar: Guaranda, 25 March 1829, and Vinces, 16 May 1829, in O'Leary, *Memorias,* IV: 172–173, 198.

57. Charles Bresson (French diplomatic agent) to French minister of foreign affairs, 29 August 1829, cited by Madariaga, *Bolívar,* 604. Flores was also involved at this time in plans to make Bolívar "Emperor of Peru"; see letters from Bolívar to Páez, Quito, 25 March 1829, in *Cartas,* VIII: 266; and Flores to Bolívar, Guayaquil, 14 November 1829, in O'Leary, *Memorias,* IV: 217. On Flores' management of elections and the election of monarchists, see Flores' letters to Bolívar, Guayaquil, 24 October, 7 November, and 28 November 1829, in O'Leary, *Memorias,* IV: 208–209, 215, and 221–222.

58. Bolívar to Flores, Popayán, 28 November 1829, in *Correspondencia del Libertador,* 274–275 (this letter is incomplete in *Cartas,* IX: 200); and Flores to Bolívar, Guayaquil, 21 December 1829, in O'Leary, *Memorias,* IV: 229–231. For the Liberator's comments on García del Río's "Cuarta meditación," see his letters of 28 to 30 November 1829, in *Correspondencia del Libertador,* 274–275 and *Cartas,* IX: 197–205. Bolívar's ambivalence, and perhaps his duplicity, in the monarchical project can be seen clearly in his letters of November and December 1829; *Cartas,* IX: 202, 205, 210. For behind-the-scenes activities see the letter of Alejandro Vélez to Santander, Bogotá, 4 March 1830, in *Archivo Santander,* XVIII: 214–219. For Bolívar's attribution of the monarchical project to Flores, see Bolívar's letter to O'Leary, Babahoyo, 28 September 1829, in *Cartas,* IX: 114.

59. Flores to Bolívar, Guayaquil, 28 February 1830, in O'Leary, *Memorias,* IV: 249–251.

60. Masur, *Bolívar,* 471–475; Madariaga, *Bolívar,* 620–624; Carlos Restrepo Canal, *La Nueva Granada: Tomo I, 1831–1840,* Vol. VIII of *Historia extensa de Colombia,* 29–30, 49–58; and José Manuel Restrepo, *Diario político y militar . . . ,* 4 vols. (Bogotá, 1954), II: 67.

61. Flores to Bolívar, Riobamba, 17 March 1830, and Quito, 27 March and 20 April 1830, in O'Leary, *Memorias,* IV: 252–256.

62. Two letters from Flores to Bolívar, Pomasquí, 6 May 1830 and 6 May 1830, in O'Leary, *Memorias,* IV: 256, 289–290.

63. José Ignacio Salazar, "Introducción," Ecuador, Congreso, *Actas del Congreso Constituyente del Ecuador (año de 1830)* (Quito, 1893), iii–xvii. (Hereinafter the *actas* of the various congresses will be cited as *Actas,* followed by the year of the congress). Flores used the title of *Jefe Superior,* the same designation used by the commanders-in-chief appointed by Bolívar for the southern district and also used by Páez in Venezuela.

64. Robalino Dávila, *Nacimiento,* 124–132; Ceballos, *Resumen,* IV: 403–406; and Andrade, *Historia,* VI: 2089–2125. Le Gouhir y Rodas, *Historia,* I: 200–202, is one of the few works that does not present Flores as a scheming and ambitious promoter of independence.

65. José María Córdoba to Santander, Quito, 31 May 1827, in Cortázar, *Correspondencia,* V: 85–86, spreads the rumor of Flores' disloyalty.

66. Flores to prefect of Department of El Ecuador, no. 124, Quito, 22 April and 30 April 1830, in ANH, "Correspondencia de Flores," doc. no. 103, f. 103, and doc. no. 109, f. 109.

67. Bolívar to Flores, Cartago, 2 January 1830, in Archivo Flores, *Correspondencia del Libertador,* 279–280.

68. Davis, "Ecuador," 161–220; Bushnell, *Santander,* 310–313; Bushnell, "The Last Dictatorship," 85–97; and J. M. Restrepo (secretary of interior, Gran Colombia) to the intendant of Department of El Ecuador, no. 17, Bogotá, 8 March 1827, in ANH, "Correspondencia de Restrepo," II: doc. no. 195. See also: Robalino Dávila, *Nacimiento,* 88–126; and Le Gouhir Rodas, *Historia,* I: 97–208.

69. Sucre to O'Leary, Quito, 27 May 1829, in O'Leary, *Memorias,* IV: 502; Davis, "Ecuador," 220–227; and Bushnell, "The Last Dictatorship," 98–102.

70. Davis, "Ecuador," 227–228.

71. Ceballos, *Resumen,* IV: 404–405.

72. The literature on the murder of Sucre is voluminous. A convenient summary of the subject is found in Thomas F. McGann, "The Assassination of Sucre and Its Significance in Colombian History, 1828–1848," *HAHR* 30(August 1950): 269–289; and letter from Luis Martínez-Delgado to the editor of *HAHR,* and McGann's reply, *HAHR* 31(August 1951): 520–529. McGann's footnotes provide an excellent bibliography of the subject, but his article is marred by a crucial mistranslation of a passage in Spanish. The most recent polemical contribution to the subject is Martínez-Delgado's *Berruecos: Asesi-*

nato del Gran Mariscal de Ayacucho, ordenado por el General Juan José Flores (Medellín, 1973). For a judicious review of the Berruecos controversy, Robalino Dávila, *Nacimiento*, 359–374.

73. Robalino Dávila, *Nacimiento*, 359–374.

74. Rocafuerte, *A la nación*, nos. 8 and 12, *Colleción:* XIV, 130–131, 234; and Moncayo, *Ecuador*, 53–64.

75. Flores to Bolívar, Guayaquil, 13 May and 29 June 1830, in *Correspondencia del Libertador*, 529–531.

76. Bolívar to Flores, Cartagena, 1 July 1830, in *Cartas*, IX: 279–280.

77. Bolívar to José Fernández Madrid, Cartagena, 24 July 1830; Bolívar to Andrés de Santa Cruz, Cartagena, 14 September 1830; and Bolívar to Urdaneta, Barranquilla, 8 November 1830, in *Cartas*, IX: 283–284, 307, and 372–373.

78. Bolívar to Flores, Barranquilla, 9 November 1830, in *Cartas*, IX: 376–377, and *Correspondencia del Libertador*, 283–287.

79. Laso, *Biografía*, 22–24; Flores, *El General Flores*, 4; and the extraordinary session of the Congress, 19 September 1830, *Actas* (1830), 108.

2. PROBLEMS OF NATIONHOOD

1. Terry, *Travels*, 67–68, 83–84, and 96–100; Friedrich Hassaurek, *Four Years among Spanish-Americans* (New York, 1858); and Manuel Villavicencio, *Geografía de la República del Ecuador* (New York, 1858), 70–114.

2. Terry, *Travels*, 59–60; Hassaurek, *Four Years*, 1–2 and 11–12; Julio Estrada Ycaza, *El puerto de Guayaquil*, 3 vols. (Guayaquil, 1972–1974), esp. II: 65–71; and Walter Cope (British consul at Guayaquil), Return of Trade at the Port of Guayaquil (for 1834) . . . , Public Records Office (London), Foreign Office, General Correspondence with Ecuador, vol. 1 (hereinafter abbreviated as FO 25/1; numbering after slash will change with volume number). All Foreign Office correspondence cited herein is from microfilm copies of the Public Records Office, available in the Bancroft Library of the University of California, unless otherwise noted.

3. *La Balanza* (Guayaquil), 4 January 1840, carried information on Ecuadorian exports; Cope, Return of Trade at Guayaquil . . . during . . . 1839, enclosure with dispatch of Cope to Aberdeen (British foreign secretary), consular dispatch no. 8, Guayaquil, 19 February 1844, in FO 25/10 (very informative); and Hassaurek, *Four Years*, 15.

4. Terry, *Travels*, 280–281.

5. Ibid., 128–132, 139–140, and 193–194; Hassaurek, *Four Years*, 115–116; and Robson B. Tyrer, "The Demographic and Economic History of the Audiencia of Quito: Indian Population and the Textile Industry, 1600–1800," Ph.D. dissertation, University of California at Berkeley, 1976.

6. There is no thorough and satisfactory study of Ecuadorian regionalism, but see: Luis Bossano, *Apuntes acerca del regionalismo en el Ecuador*, 4th ed. (Quito, 1930); George I. Blanksten, *Ecuador: Constitutions and Caudillos* (New York, 1964), 14–31; and Martz, *Ecuador*, 16–41.

7. *Gaceta* (Quito), 3 July 1831.

8. The political clash over imports was clearly evident in the contest in the constituent congress of 1830 over a Bolivarian decree banning British textiles from the southern district. See the sessions of 17, 18 and 20 September, *Actas* (1830), 102–106, 112–113; and congressional decree of 24 September 1830, *Primer rejistro auténtico nacional de la República del Ecuador* (1830), 39–40. Debates on the tariff abound in the *Actas* of the 1830s.

9. Decrees of 26, 27, and 28 September 1830, *Primer rejistro* (1830), 56–57 and 74–76; and Terry, *Travels*, 85–87. The *estancos* became a chronic issue in the 1830s and 1840s.

10. Hassaurek, *Four Years*, 83–84. See also: Courtland Cushing (U.S. chargé d'affaires in Ecuador) to William L. Marcy (U.S. secretary of state), Guayaquil, 31 October 1853, in Manning, *Correspondence*, VI: 316; and Vicente Rocafuerte (president), Address to the Congress, 3 January 1837, *Actas* (1837), I: xxx–1.

11. Michael P. Costeloe, *La primera república federal de México, 1824–1835: Un estudio de los partidos políticos en el México independiente* (México, 1975); Charles A. Hale, *Mexican Liberalism in the Age of Mora, 1821–1853* (New Haven, Conn., 1968), 253–255; and Daniel Cosío Villegas, *Historia moderna de México*, 9 vols. (México and Buenos Aires, 1959–1972), III: 72–85. Economic and political parallels between Mexico and Ecuador may suggest that their attempts to establish monarchy in the 1840s and again in the 1860s might not have been mere coincidence.

12. Robalino Dávila, *Nacimiento*, 131–132; Flores, decree of 31 May 1830, *Primer rejistro* (1830), 3–14; Flores address to the constituent congress, 14 August 1830, *Actas* (1830), xxii–xxiii; and for background, Bushnell, *Santander*, 314–315.

13. *Actas* (1830), especially the extraordinary session of 19 September 1830, 108; and Robalino Dávila, *Nacimiento*, 129–145.

14. The Constitution of 1830, in *Las constituciones del Ecuador* (Ma-

drid, 1951), 105–123; *Actas* (1830); Ceballos, *Resumen*, V: 7–10; and Linda Alexander Rodríguez, *The Search for Public Policy: Regional Politics and Government Finance, 1830–1940* (Berkeley, Los Angeles, London, 1985), 34–36. The departments of Guayas and Azuay contained only about 37 percent of the populations but had two-thirds of the deputies in the Congress.

15. Article 35, section 5 of the Constitution of 1830, *Constituciones*, 113; and sessions of 3 and 4 September 1830, *Actas* (1830), 51–59.

16. There is much guesswork in estimates of ethnic populations of Ecuador: see Michael T. Hamerly, "Quantifying in the Nineteenth Century: The Ministry Reports and Gazettes of Ecuador," *Latin American Research Review* (*LARR*) 13(1978):149–150. On the "dangerous classes," see Torcuato S. di Tella, "The Dangerous Classes in Early Nineteenth Century Mexico," *LARR* 5(May 1973):79–105; and Fredrick B. Pike, *The United States and the Andean Republics: Peru, Bolivia, and Ecuador* (Cambridge, Mass., and London, 1977), 28–35.

17. Mark Van Aken, "The Lingering Death of Indian Tribute in Ecuador," *HAHR* 61(August 1981):429–436; John L. Phelan, *The Kingdom of Quito in the Seventeenth Century: Bureaucratic Politics in the Spanish Empire* (Madison, 1967), 43–82; and Oswaldo Albornoz P., *Las luchas indígenas en la Audiencia de Quito* (Bonn, 1976).

18. Van Aken, "Lingering Death," 446–459.

19. Hassaurek, *Four Years*, 132 and 299–303; Antonio Mata (minister of the interior and foreign relations), *Esposición* (1858), 8–9; and Ida Pfeiffer, *A Lady's Second Journey Round the World: From London to the Cape of Good Hope, Borneo, Java, Sumatra, Celebes, Ceram, the Moluccas, etc., California, Panama, Peru, Ecuador, and the United States*, 2 vols. (London, 1855), 222–224.

20. Cope to Aberdeen (British foreign secretary), no. 44, Guayaquil, 24 December 1843, in Great Britain, Foreign Office, *British and Foreign State Papers*, Vols. I– (London, 1812/14–), XXXIII: 628–630 (hereinafter cited as *State Papers*); Francisco Marcos (minister of the interior), *Exposición* (1843), cuadro A; Leslie B. Rout, Jr., *The African Experience in Spanish America, 1502 to the Present Day* (Cambridge, 1976), 226; and Alfredo Costales Samaniego and Piedad Peñaherra de Costales, *Historia social del Ecuador*, 3 vols. (Quito, 1961), I: 316–324.

21. Law of 26 September 1830, *Primer rejistro* (1830), 45–46; minutes of the legislative session of 20 September 1830, *Actas* (1830), 113; Cope to Aberdeen, nos. 44 and 45, *State Papers*, XXXIII: 628–630. Flores owned slaves.

22. Terry, *Travels,* 62 and 284–285.

23. Delazon Smith (U.S. special agent) to John C. Calhoun (secretary of state), Quito, 10 August 1845, in Manning, *Correspondence,* VI: 254; Pfeiffer, *Journey,* Vol. II, 221. For similar views in the 1860s see Hassaurek, *Four Years,* 217–218 and 144–145.

24. Estimate based on information in Bushnell, *Santander,* 186. See also Smith to Calhoun, 10 August 1845, in Manning, *Correspondence,* VI: 254.

25. Robalino Dávila, *Nacimiento,* 161–162 and 197–198; and id., *Rocafuerte* (Quito, 1964), 57.

26. Robalino Dávila, *Nacimiento,* 45–46 and 57–58; Halperín–Donghi, *Aftermath,* 42–43; and Julio Tobar Donoso, *La iglesia ecuatoriana en el siglo XIX* (Quito, 1934), 44–45, 147, 199, 211–214.

27. Articles, 8, 14, and 42 of the Constitution of 1830, *Constituciones,* 106–116; and Tobar Donoso, *Iglesia,* 256–261.

28. On Flores' connections with Freemasonry, see Tobar Donoso, *Iglesia,* 187–189; Moncayo, *Ecuador,* 8–9; and Andrade, *Historia,* V: 1719.

29. Terry, *Travels,* 77, 169–170; law of 17 April 1839, *Primer rejistro* (1839), 533–536; and Hassaurek, *Four Years,* 158.

30. Halperín–Donghi, *Aftermath,* 125–126; David Bushnell, "The Development of the Press in Great Colombia," *HAHR* 30 (November 1950): 432–452; and Carlos Enrique Sánchez, *La imprenta en el Ecuador* (Quito, 1935).

31. On Francis Hall see chap. 4 below.

32. *Constituciones,* 107, 110, and 113–120; and Bushnell, *Santander,* 313–116.

33. Terry, *Travels,* 147–148.

34. Ibid., *Travels,* 259–69; Ceballos, *Resumen,* V: 76–80; Hassaurek, *Four Years,* 216; Rocafuerte quoted in Tobar Donoso, *Iglesia,* 326; on the fiscal problem of the military, L. A. Rodríguez, *Search,* 38–41; and on the general problem in Latin America, Halperín–Donghi, *Aftermath,* 1–34.

35. L. A. Rodríguez, *Search;* Luis Alberto Carbo, *Historia monetaria y cambiaria del Ecuador . . .* (Quito, 1953), 17–27; Francisco Aguirre Abad, *Bosquejo histórico de la República del Ecuador* (Guayaquil, 1972), 246–247, 253–255, 291–297; and the annual reports of ministers of the treasury, especially Juan García del Río, *Memoria* (1833).

36. Flores, message to Congress, 1 November 1831, in *Gaceta,* 13 November 1831; Ceballos, *Resumen,* V: 17–18; and Carbo, *Historia monetaria,* 17–27.

3. FORGING A NATION, 1830–1833

1. Session of 22 September 1830, *Actas* (1830), 125–126; Ceballos, *Resumen,* V: 16; Robalino Dávila, *Nacimiento,* 144.

2. Flores, decree of 23 September 1830, *Primer rejistro* (1830), 33; José Ignacio Salazar, "Introducción," *Actas* (1830), xxx; Ceballos, *Resumen,* V: 16–17; Robalino Dávila, *Nacimiento,* 157–158.

3. See the many laws and decrees signed by Flores from 24 September to 9 December 1830, in *Primer rejistro* (1830), 35–114.

4. Jorge Pérez Concha, *Ensayo histórico-crítico de las relaciones diplomáticas del Ecuador con los estados limítrofes,* 2 vols. (Quito, 1958–1959), I: 23–24, 94; Francisco Andrade Suescún, *Demarcación de las fronteras de Colombia,* Vol. XII of *Historia extensa,* 283–293.

5. Robalino Dávila, *Nacimiento,* 286–287; Andrade, *Historia,* VI: 2219–2220; Restrepo Canal, *Nueva Granada,* 29–31; and Salazar, "Introducción," *Actas* (1831), xx–lxxx.

6. Restrepo Canal, *Nueva Granada,* 29–45, 59–63; Restrepo Canal sees Flores as the instigator of most of the trouble in the department of Cauca. Robalino Dávila, *Nacimiento,* 289–291; and Andrade, *Historia,* VI: 2222–2241. Andrade viewed Flores as a scoundrel in the Cauca affair, as did Rocafuerte in *A la nación,* nos. 2 and 10, *Colección Rocafuerte,* XIV: 27–28, 155–157. One of the earliest denunciations of Flores' Cauca policy is to be found in an article entitled "Apuntes para el Congreso," *El Quiteño libre* (Quito), 8 September 1833.

7. Pérez Concha, *Ensayo,* I: 94–95; Bushnell, *Santander,* 18–20, 26–30, 84, 94, 314–315; and Robalino Dávila, *Nacimiento,* 285–286. Colombian historians like Restrepo Canal and Andrade Suescún tend to ignore the forces that attracted the caucanos to Quito. The significance of the Andean commercial traffic has not been studied, but it was alluded to in some of the "actas" of the Cauca cities. See especially the Acta de Túquerres, 11 November 1830, in *Gaceta,* 20 November 1830; and the editorial in *Gaceta,* 20 November 1830. See also; Villavicencio, *Geografía,* 160–162. On gold mining, see Walter Cope's Report on Trade for 1843, enclosed with Cope to Aberdeen, no. 8, Guayaquil, 19 February 1844, FO 25/10; and Robert C. West, *Colonial Placer Mining in Colombia* (Baton Rouge, 1952).

8. Flores, message to Congress, 20 September 1831, *Actas* (1831), v–xv, and *Gaceta,* 13 October 1831 (reviews the development of the Cauca dispute); "Lei incorporando el departamento del Cauca al Estado del Eduador," approved by Congress on 7 October and signed by Flores on 10 October 1831, *Primer rejistro* (1831), 165–166; and minutes of Congress, night session of 4 October 1831, *Actas* (1831),

57. Criticism of the Cauca policy came only after its failure was evident, not while the policy appeared to be successful. But congressional approval of the president's Cauca policy continued even as late as October 1832, when the military situation had become hopeless for Ecuador. See letter from Salvador Ortega (president of Congress) to Flores, Quito, 1 October 1832, *Actas* (1832), xxx–xxxii.

9. Witness his advice to Bolívar in 1828 to prevent the Peruvians from attacking the District of the South, as described in chap. 1 above.

10. Restrepo Canal, *Nueva Granada*, 59, points out that President Urdaneta and his cousin, General Luis Urdaneta, were planning an effort to oust Flores and recover Ecuador as early as August 1830. An unpublished letter from President Urdaneta to Flores tends to confirm this view; see R. Urdaneta to Flores, Bogotá, 1 January 1830, in AJC, "Cartas a Flores," VIII: ff. 985–993.

11. Ceballos, *Resumen*, V: 18–21; Robalino Dávila, *Nacimiento*, 148–149, 289–291.

12. "Tratados de paz," *Gaceta*, no. 12, 17(?) February 1831 (the date of the microfilm copy of *Gaceta* at Saint Louis University is torn). See also: Robalino Dávila, *Nacimiento*, 151–152; and Ceballos, *Resumen*, V: 21–30.

13. *Gaceta*, 3 March 1831; Ceballos, *Resumen*, V: 30–37; and Andrade, *Historia*, VI: 2224–2225.

14. See the various "actas" of the Cauca cities and towns published in *Gaceta*, 20 March, 3, 17 April, and 1 May 1831; editorial in *Gaceta*, 8 May 1831; and Ceballos, *Resumen*, V: 37–42.

15. Ibid., V: 17.

16. *Gaceta*, 1 May, 13, 23 October 1831; Ceballos, *Resumen*, V: 50–56, 76–80; Robalino Dávila, *Nacimiento*, 181–182; Terry, *Travels*, 259–269. Legislators feared that the Vargas Battalion revolt signaled the imminent collapse of the nation: minutes of Congress, session of 11 October 1831, *Actas* (1831), 84–85. On the reaction of Bogotá to the military mutinies in Ecuador, see Restrepo Canal, *Nueva Granada*, 266–268. Andrade claims that there were eight mutinies from February 1831 to August 1832, but he fails to cite cases; *Historia*, VI: 2299.

17. The best account of Flores' dealings with Peru and Bolivia is in Robalino Dávila, *Nacimiento*, 314–335, based on original archival research. See also Restrepo Canal, *Nueva Granada*, 29–92; and Basadre, *Historia*, I: 283–306.

18. Robalino Dávila, *Nacimiento*, 332–335; Andrade S., *Demarcación*, 297–298; and Restrepo Canal, *Nueva Granada*, 311–313. The treaty was not approved by the Ecuadorian Congress until 1835, but the pact was treated as binding upon Ecuador by Flores from the

date of its signing. The treaty is printed in full in *Primer rejistro* (1835), 72–75.

19. Editorial entitled "La Paz," *Gaceta,* 22 December 1832.

20. *El Quiteño libre,* 8 September 1833. It is ironic that one of the editors of this opposition newspaper was Manuel Matheu who, as the president of the Congress in 1831, formally notified Flores of legislative approval of the president's Cauca policy. See the letter from Matheu to Flores, Quito, 6 November 1831, *Actas* (1831), xlix–xlx.

21. Flores, message to Congress, 25 September 1832, in *Gaceta,* 7 October 1832; and diplomatic correspondence between Ecuador and New Granada printed in *Gaceta,* 16 March 1833.

22. Letter from Flores to Santa Cruz, no date cited, but late 1831, quoted in Robalino Dávila, *Nacimiento,* 318–319 (speaks of the "verdadera decadencia" of the economy in a rather desperate tone). See also: "Decadencia pública," *Gaceta,* 3 July 1831; and "Apuntes para el Congreso: La Fuerza Armada," *El Quiteño libre,* 28 July 1833.

23. Flores, message to Congress, 20 September 1831, *Actas* (1831), iv–xix, and in *Gaceta,* 13 October 1831, and following issues; and Robalino Dávila, *Nacimiento,* 164–165.

24. For a pungent analysis of the contradictions between constitutional theory and political practice in Latin American politics of the nineteenth century, see Francisco Bilbao, *La América en peligro* (Santiago, Chile, 1941), esp. 34–40. Even before Bilbao's well-known work appeared, Vicente Rocafuerte described the problems well in his address to Congress, 15 January 1837, in *Actas* (1837), I: xxx–xlvii. For a modern analysis, see Halperín–Donghi, *Aftermath,* 111–140.

25. Ceballos, *Resumen,* V: 56–57; *Actas* (1831), 10–16, 22, for sessions of 23, 24, and 27 September 1831. Flores' minister of state, Valdivieso, was one of the officers not seated by the Congress. None of the congresses of the 1830s were rubber-stamp bodies—not even the Congress of 1833 that granted special powers to Flores.

26. Minutes of Congress, 4, 5, 15, and 17 October 1831, *Actas* (1831), 56, 65, 97, 102–104; *Gaceta,* 12 February and 18 March 1831, and 24 June and 1 July 1832; Ceballos, *Resumen,* V: 57–58; and Andrade, *Historia,* VI: 2277–2278. On provincial governors and prefects, see minutes of Congress, 8 November 1832, *Actas* (1832), 168–169.

27. Flores to José Modesto Larrea (president of Congress), Quito (no date), in *Gaceta,* 30 October 1831; Andrade, *Historia,* VI: 2278.

28. Tobar Donoso, *Iglesia,* 267–295; and Robalino Dávila, *Nacimiento,* 154–155.

29. Presidential decrees of 30 October 1830 and 1 July 1831, and

congressional decree of 9 November 1831, in *Primer rejistro* (1830, 1831), 109, 147–151, 183–184.

30. The government, without adequate public funds, frequently obliged the Church to provide financing for public schools. This government policy appears to have been dictated less by anticlerical considerations than by need. See Tobar Donoso, *Iglesia*, 281–298; congressional decree of 9 November 1831, *Primer rejistro* (1831), 183–184. On the new academies in the university, see "Instrucción pública," *Gaceta*, 29 December 1832; and Robalino Dávila, *Nacimiento*, 162.

31. Robalino Dávila, *Nacimiento*, 162.

32. Robalino Dávila, *García Moreno* (Quito, 1949), 298–300. The University of Quito was reported to be on the verge of extinction in 1833, according to *El Quiteño libre*, 30 June 1833.

33. Presidential decree of 16 January 1833, *Primer rejistro* (1833), 361–363; Valdivieso, circular to prefects, Quito, 19 April 1833, in *Gaceta*, 27 April 1833; and Victor F. San Miguel (minister of interior), *Memoria . . . 1833* (Quito, 1833), 12–13. The administration's concern about the education of Indian children was set forth in an eloquent editorial in the *Gaceta*, 9 February 1833. Lack of progress was indicated in Rocafuerte's request in 1835 for observance of the decree of 1833; see José Miguel González (minister-general of the Cabinet) to the president of the High Court, et al., Quito, 30 July 1835, in *Primer rejistro* (1835), 489. The very limited success of the program of schools for Indians was noted by Salazar, "Introducción," *Actas* (1833), v. The executive decree "suspending" the auctioning of resguardos was not published in the *Primer rejistro*, but it was issued nonetheless; see Bacilio Palacios de Urquijo (Corregidor of Quito) to prefect, Quito, 13 May 1833, in ANH, Oficios, Vol. III/17, doc. no. 69, f. 69.

34. Valdivieso, circular to prefects, Quito, 27 March 1833, in *Primer rejistro* (1833), 376–377, and *Gaceta*, 5 April 1833; Valdivieso to Gobernador del Obispado, Quito, 19 April 1833, in *Gaceta*, 27 April 1833. Parish priests enjoyed a regular income of four hundred pesos per year and did not need to charge for the sacraments. See minutes of Congress for 14 October 1831, in *Gaceta*, 17 June 1832.

35. "Lei estableciendo medios equitativos para hacer exequible la contribución de indíjenas . . . ," 5 October 1833, *Primer rejistro* (1833), 407–409.

36. Ibid.; and minutes of Congress for 23 and 26 September 1833, *Actas* (1833), 52–53, 65–66.

37. On legislative efforts to ameliorate *concertaje*, see Mariano Miño (secretary of Congress) to Valdivieso, Quito, 25 October 1832, in *Primer rejistro* (1832), 292–293, and *Gaceta*, 26 January 1833. Flores'

chief adviser, a wealthy landowner, sought to restrict the freedom and rights of Indians, but Congress blocked his efforts. See Valdivieso, "Decreto circular del Gobierno," 18 November 1831, *Primer rejistro* (1831), 225–227, and *Gaceta,* 18 November 1831; and Valdivieso to Miño, Quito, 17 October 1832. Congress, by a nearly unanimous vote, overruled Valdivieso's actions to restrict Indian rights and adopted the reform laws discussed above; see minutes of Congress, 11 October 1832, *Actas* (1832), 57–58.

38. "Ley estableciendo una contribución ordinaria," 9 November 1831, *Primer rejistro* (1831), 179–181; and "Ley adicional al decreto de 15 de octubre de 1828 sobre recaudación personal de indíjenas," 30 October (1833), 443–445. Indian tribute payments constituted about one-third of the revenues of the highland provinces. In 1835 they comprised 44.3 percent of Quito's revenues; see *Gaceta,* 20, 29, February, 30 June, and 31 July 1836. For congressional debate of the contribución ordinaria, see *Actas* (1831), 115–126. The presidential decree of 28 August 1832, *Primer rejistro* (1832), 244–246, describes the difficulties in attempting to prepare the lists of tributaries and to overcome their difficulties. On the decision to abolish the new tax and to substitute others, see Valdivieso, circular to prefects, Quito, 4 May 1833, *Primer rejistro* (1833), 387; García del Río testimony before Congress, *Actas* (1833), 116–118; congressional decree of 30 October 1833, *Gaceta,* 9 November 1833; and presidential decree of 5 March 1834, *Gaceta,* 15 March 1834. Descriptions of the conditions of Indians in the 1850s and 1860s indicate little if any improvement: Pfeiffer, *Journey,* II: 183–184, 222–224; and Hassaurek, *Four Years,* 133–135, 185–189, passim.

39. Untitled editorial, *Gaceta,* 26 June 1831. The author of the editorial did not state that he spoke for the administration, but editorials published in this official paper reflected the views of the executive branch. Subsequent events demonstrated that the editorial did in fact express Flores' viewpoint.

40. García del Río (minister of finance), circular to prefects of Departments of El Ecuador and Cuenca, Quito, 20 July 1833, *Primer rejistro* (1833), 393–394. On Gran Colombia, see Bushnell, *Santander,* 176–178.

41. José María Salazar to President of Ecuador, Quito (no date but December [?] 1833), in ANH, Oficios (Dec. 1833), Vol. IX, tomo 24 (hereinafter IX/24, varying according to volume and tomo numbers), doc. no. 148, f. 151 (reports threatened violence); Feliz Cacho, et al., of Indian community of Licto, petition to national convention, undated [1835], in Archivo del Poder Legislativo (Quito) (APL) (1835),

Legajo 7, doc. no. 25 (protests auctioning of lands); Indians of Pueblo of Pangar to governor of Chimborazo, April 1841, in ANH, Oficios (1841). A few more documents may be cited to show that Indians resisted auctions of their lands, but there were not many such protests in the 1830s and 1840s, probably indicating that few auctions were attempted.

42. If tithe collections are taken as a rough index of agricultural production, revenues from the tithes indicate that farm output declined by 45 percent and then rose gradually and unevenly, finally surpassing the production of 1831 in the mid-1850s. See the various reports of the finance ministers for the years 1831 to 1857.

43. "Ley prohibiendo imponer principales a censo a más del tres por ciento," 25 December 1831, *Primer rejistro* (1831), 190–191; "Ley promoviendo el fomento de las minas," 27 September 1830, ibid. (1830), 52–54; presidential decrees of 17 May 1831 (on coinage) and 10 June 1831 (founding a bank), ibid. (1831), 139–144; Valdivieso, circular, Quito, 7 July 1831, in *Gaceta*, 10 July 1831 (on mining); congressional decree of 17 November 1832, *Gaceta*, 29 December 1832 (on roads and bridges—many other documents could be cited); Carbo, *Historia monetaria*, 18–21 (on mint and money system). Little information is available on the Banco de Guayaquil, but it was placed under the management of the Consulado of Guayaquil: Flores, message to Congress, 20 September 1831, *Actas* (1831), xvi–xvii. *El Quiteño libre*, 30 June 1833, charges that the prefect of Guayas was involved in financial peculations with the bank.

44. Congressional decree of 8 November 1831, *Primer rejistro* (1831), 172–173. On the persistence of mercantilistic attitudes among merchants after independence, see Basil Hall, *Extracts from a Journal Written on the Coasts of Chili, Peru, and Mexico in the Years 1820, 1821, 1822*, 2 vols. (Philadelphia, 1824), II: 112–117; and Bushnell, *Santander*, 129–131.

45. *Actas* (1830), xxi–xxviii, 69, passim; congressional decrees of 28 September 1830 (dealing with three estancos), *Primer rejistro* (1830), 56–57, 74–76. Congress permitted the president discretion in the disposition of the salt monopoly. Flores abolished it. See also Robalino Dávila, *Nacimiento*, 137, 142, 161.

46. On bootlegging and the government's efforts to stop it see Flores' decree of 25 June 1831, *Primer rejistro* (1831), 146–147; and Congress' response to Flores, the law of 9 November 1831 (on *aguardiente* taxes), ibid., 185–186. For tobacco troubles, see the presidential decree of 13 December 1832, *Primer rejistro* (1832), 337–338; and Guillermo Pareja (secretary of Congress) to the minister of fi-

nance, Quito, 31 October 1833, ibid. (1833), 450–451. Licensed salt merchants charged two times the government's fixed price; see minutes of Congress, 4 October 1831, *Actas* (1831), 56. On Bolívar's earlier difficulties with the salt monopoloy in Ecuador, see Bushnell, *Santander*, 311–313; and on the perennial problem of the state monopolies, L. A. Rodríguez, *Search*, 68–69, 105–106.

47. Terry, *Travels*, 86. Bread was not an estanco item, but flour imports were licensed by the government, with the consequent creation of a near monopoly, high prices, bad flour, and nearly inedible bread: law of 19 August 1835, and decree of 27 August 1835, *Primer rejistro* (1835), 59–61, 523–524; law of 12 April 1837, ibid. (1837), 305–308.

48. Law of 9 November 1831 (on coinage), *Primer rejistro* (1831), 187; Carbo, *Historia*, 18–23. The U.S. dollar was worth 1.02 pesos. The legal relationship of silver to gold was sixteen to one, which undervalued silver; see Carbo, *Historia*, 20–21.

49. Restrepo Canal, *Nueva Granada*, 326. For discussion of Flores' early efforts to halt counterfeiting, see the minutes of Congress, 26 October 1831, *Actas* (1831), 148–149. Mexico also suffered ravages of counterfeiting; Wilfed Hardy Callcott, *Santa Anna: The Story of an Enigma Who Once Was Mexico*, 170, 176.

50. Ceballos, *Resumen*, V: 92.

51. *El Quiteño libre*, 26 May and 2 June 1833; Rocafuerte, *A la nación*, no. 8, *Colección*, XIV: 122; and Andrade, *Historia*, VI: 2295–2296.

52. Some of the measures adopted to deal with the monetary problem: presidential decree of 27 May 1831, *Primer rejistro* (1831), 138–140; Valdivieso, circular, 9 July 1831, ibid., 150–151; congressional decree of 17 November 1832, ibid. (1832), 289–290; García del Río to prefect of El Ecuador, Quito, 2 March 1833, in ibid. (1833), 369–370.

53. Presidential decree of 26 December 1832, *Primer rejistro* (1832), 347–348; presidential decree of 28 February 1833, *Gaceta*, 9 March 1833; García del Río to prefect of El Ecuador, Quito, 2 March 1833, in *Primer rejistro* (1833), 369–370; and unsigned editorial in *Gaceta*, 20 April 1833 (which reveals the government's sensitivity to press criticism).

54. Congressional decree, 9 November 1832, first opposed by Flores, then signed by him on 16 November 1833, *Primer rejistro* (1833), 406–407. In this connection it is worth noting that Roberto Andrade wrote that the pardon was granted by Congress "por la influencia de Flores, tal vez" (*Historia*, VI: 2296). Since the pardon was granted at the insistence of Congress over the objections of Flores, it is clear that Andrade's insinuation is incorrect.

55. Law of 5 November 1833 (against counterfeiting), *Primer rejistro* (1833), 453–456; Rocafuerte, "Decreto previniendo que las autoridades cuiden con mayor vijilancia del cumplimiento de las leyes sobre falsificación de moneda . . . ," 18 July 1836, 217–218; Rocafuerte, *A la nación,* no. 9, *Colección,* 133, and correspondence in *El Nacional* (Quito), 26 November 1847.

56. Session of 16 September 1830, *Actas* (1830), 94.

57. Flores to Larrea (president of Congress), Quito, 1 November 1831, in *Gaceta,* 13 November 1831; and minutes of Congress for 16 September 1830, *Actas* (1830), 94.

58. Rocafuerte, *A la nación,* nos. 8, 10, 11, and 12, *Colección,* XIV: 122, 156, 161, 164–165, 226, 230, and 240. The campaign of *El Quiteño libre* against Flores is treated in the following chapter. See also Moncayo, *Ecuador,* 80–81. Moncayo was one of the chief editors of *El Quiteño libre.*

59. The acquisition of wealth by revolutionary generals is a familiar story in Latin America and requires no elaboration. Flores purchased four haciendas at auction in February 1826; see also "Libro del Ramo Hijuela de los Deudores por ventas de Haciendas," 28 February 1826, f. 41, ANH; Flores to Bolívar, Babahoyo, 20 January 1830, in O'Leary, *Memorias,* IV: 238–239; Terry, *Travels,* 107–108 (describes Flores' plantation at Bodega); Camilo Destruge, *Ecuador. La expedición Flores. Proyecto de monarquía americana. 1846–47: Relación histórica por un viejo liberal* (Guayaquil, 1906), 21–22, 41. For perspective on the subject of acquistion of wealth by caudillos of the independence period, see the description of land acquisitions of José Antonio Páez of Venezuela in John Lynch, "Bolívar and the Caudillos," *HAHR* 63(February 1983):23–26.

60. Rocafuerte blamed Flores for the Urdaneta revolution even though Urdaneta had planned his blow against Ecuador before Flores moved against Cauca; *A la nación,* no. 10, *Colección,* XIV: 156.

61. L. A. Rodríguez, *Search,* 55–59; Bushnell, *Santander,* 76–111; Cruz Santos, *Economía,* 267–277, 279–286, 290–294, 304–343, passim.

62. Francis Hall, *Colombia: Its Present State, in Respect of Climate, Soil, Productions, Population* . . . (London, 1827), 33–35 (first edition, London, 1824); Madariaga, *Bolívar,* 531–532. On corruption in late-eighteenth-century England, see Bernard Bailyn, *The Ideological Origins of the American Revolution* (Cambridge, Mass., 1967), 83–93.

63. Minutes of Congress, 22 September 1831, *Actas* (1831), 6–11; law of 8 November 1831 (creating a ministry of finance), *Primer rejistro* (1831), 175. For evidence of President Flores' strong commitment to a

balanced budget, see his message to Congress, 20 September 1831, *Actas* (1831), xvi–xviii. He had reduced the army by more than one-half and had disarmed most of the small navy in time of war in a desperate effort to reduce expenditures.

64. García del Río, *Meditaciones colombianas,* 2d ed. (Bogotá, 1945), v–xx; Mitre, *San Martín,* III: 145–152; William Spence Robertson, *Rise of the Spanish-American Republics as Told in the Lives of Their Liberators* (New York, 1918; reprint, 1965), 196–202, 204; Madariaga, *Bolívar,* 601, 605, 640; correspondence of Bolívar in *Cartas,* VIII: 243, 265, 331, and IX: 231; García del Río to Flores, Guayaquil, 21 September 1832, in AJC, "Cartas a Flores," IX: ff. 77–79; and Restrepo Canal, *Nueva Granada,* 96–118.

65. His essay entitled "La cuarta meditación" in 1829, advocating constitutional monarchy, had circulated widely; García del Río, *Meditaciones,* 117–165; Madariaga, *Bolívar,* 640–641; and Parra-Pérez, *Monarquía,* 546–547. For evidence of García del Río's notoriety as a monarchist, see Thomas P. Moore (U.S. chargé at Bogotá) to Edwin Livingston (secretary of state), no. 63, Bogotá, 10 April 1833, in Manning, *Correspondence,* V: 477.

66. Clear proof of the offense given by García del Río's reformist zeal is contained in the letter of resignation tendered by Olmedo to the finance minister, Guayaquil, 7 April 1833, in *El Quiteño libre,* 12 May 1833. Olmedo made it clear that he was resigning because García del Río had carried his reforms too far and was too inflexible in enforcing them. Rocafuerte summed up García del Río and his service in the ministry of finance as follows: ". . . un viajero diplomático, acostumbrado al estruendo de las tormentas populares, hábil, elocuente, de instrucción variada y moderna; pero sin conocimientos locales y sin relaciones de familia y de patria. El y sus compañeros formaron un Ministerio que irritaba cada día más las pasiones y precipitaba la revolucíon." See Rocafuerte's presidential message to Congress, June 1835 (no date, but probably the twenty-second), *Actas* (1835), ccxiii–ccxiv.

67. Minutes of Congress, 22 September and night session of 10 October 1831, *Actas* (1831), 6–8, 81–82.

68. Presidential decree of 15 October 1831, *Primer rejistro* (1831), 167–169.

69. Minutes of Congress, 17 October 1831 (night session), 18 October, and 18 October (night session), *Actas* (1831), 105–113; and Flores to Larrea, Quito, 1 November 1831, in *Gaceta,* 13 November 1831.

70. Larrea (acting president), decrees of 20 and 30 March 1832, *Primer rejistro* (1832), 237–238; presidential decree of 28 August 1832, ibid., 244–246.

71. Flores, message to Congress, 15 September 1832, in *Gaceta*, 7 October 1832; law of 5 November 1832 (reducing the army), *Primer rejistro* (1832), 304–306; and resolution of Congress, 22 October 1832, ibid., 308. On economies in military expenditures, see the reports to Congress of Martínez Pallares, chief of the General Staff, dated 16 March and 15 May 1832, *Actas* (1832), xii–xliii.

72. Congressional decrees of 6 November and 17 November 1832, in *Gaceta*, 17 November 1832.

73. Minutes of Congress, night session, 10 November 1832, *Actas* (1832), 182–183; news article in *Gaceta*, 17 November 1832, which reproduces the congressional decree of 17 November 1832.

74. Letters from García del Río to prefect of Guayas (Olmedo), Quito, 26 November 1832 and 3, 4, and 28 January 1833, in *Gaceta*, 1 December 1832 and 4, 12 January and 16 February 1833. For letters to other prefects see *Primer rejistro* (1832), 327–331. A summary of García del Río's struggle for fiscal reform is contained in Salazar, "Introducción," *Actas* (1833), i–iv. The customhouse was a perennial source of loss of revenues; see Estrada Ycaza, *Puerto*, II: 45–50.

75. Presidential decrees of 30 November 1832 and 3 January 1833, *Primer rejistro* (1832), 331–332, and *Primer rejistro* (1833), 349–350.

76. These troublesome financial practices were by no means limited to Ecuador. Nor were they invented by, or peculiar to, the Flores administration. New Granada suffered from usury at about the same time; see Restrepo Canal, *Nueva Granada*, 326; and Bushnell, *Santander*, 132. On *libranzas*, see Bushnell, *Santander*, 100. Though Bushnell does not use the Spanish word *libranza*, the practice described was the same. Mexico, too, had similiar troubles; see Charles C. Cumberland, *The Struggle for Modernity* (New York, 1968), *Mexico*, 143–147; and Callcott, *Santa Anna*, 93, 127.

77. For a good description of the evil practices of the local treasurers, see "Abusos de la hacienda pública," *El Quiteño libre*, 16 June 1833; and Olmedo to García del Río, Guayaquil, 7 April 1833, in *El Quiteño libre*, 12 May 1833. For evidence of Flores' concern about usury and fraud, see his message to Congress, 20 September 1831, *Actas* (1831), xvi–xvii.

78. García del Río to Olmedo, Quito, 4 January 1833, in *Gaceta*, 12 January 1833.

79. "Abusos de la hacienda pública," *El Quiteño libre*, 16 June 1833; and "Apuntes para el Congreso: La hacienda pública," ibid., 7 July 1833.

80. See the *memorias* of the finance ministers for the period. Also:

José María Urbina (governor of Manabí) to Francisco de Aguirre (finance minister), Portoviejo, 9 December 1843, in *Gaceta,* 21 January 1844; Manuel Bustamante (finance minister), circular, Quito, 15 March 1847, in *El Nacional,* 19 March 1847; Benigno Malo, "Reformas: Hacienda" (1863), in Malo, *Escritos y discursos* (Quito, 1940), 342–351; and L. A. Rodríguez, *Search,* 59–72.

81. On the Spanish colonial treasury see Herbert S. Klein, "Structure and Profitability of Royal Finance in the Viceroyalty of the Río de la Plata in 1790," *HAHR* 53(August 1973):440–469, esp. 442–443 and 455–457. For brief treatment of the fiscal administration of the Audiencia of Quito and its long-term effects, see Ceballos, *Resumen,* II: 42–44; and Phelan, *Kingdom,* 173–176.

82. On the confused state of Ecuador's treasury system in 1832, see the minutes of Congress, 10 November 1832, *Actas* (1832), 178–179.

83. Cope to Backhouse, no. 6, Guayaquil, 28 May 1835; FO 25/1 cites García del Río's report to the Congress in 1833.

84. Article 57 of the constitution forbade dismissals without formal judicial proceedings. For Congress' rebuke to Flores, see the minutes of Congress, night session of 26 October 1832, *Actas* (1832), 120–121. Rocafuerte faced similar difficulties; see correspondence in *Gaceta,* 9 June 1838.

85. Minutes of Congress for 24 and 27 September and 10 October 1833, *Actas* (1833), 57, 69–73, and 118. Congressmen, lacking the good sense to dismiss the complaint outright, forced García del Río to appear before his accuser in Congress to defend the disciplinary action. The complaint of the offended tax collector caused much concern for the Flores administration; see letter of Flores to Santander, Quito, 27 September 1833, in Cortázar, *Correspondencia,* V: 467.

4. THE REVOLUTION OF THE CHIHUAHUAS, 1833–1835

1. Terry, *Travels,* 175–176.

2. *El Republicano* (Quito), 15 July 1832. Little is known about this early opposition newspaper. The first issue must have appeared on 1 July 1832. It probably ceased publication in late August 1832. The third number of the paper appeared on 15 July 1832. I have numbers 3 through 7 on microfilm from the collection of the Biblioteca Aurelio Espinosa Pólit. It is only briefly mentioned in Carlos A. Rolando, *Crónica del periodismo en el Ecuador . . . 1792–1849,* (Guayaquil, 1947–), I: 49.

3. Ceballos, *Resumen,* V: 104.

4. Decree of 3 January 1833, *Primer rejistro* (1833), 349.

5. Rolando, *Crónica,* I: 45–46; Camilo Destruge, *Historia de la*

prensa de Guayaquil, 2 vols., published as Vols. II and III of *Memorias de la Academia Nacional de Historia* (Quito, 1924–1925), I: 34–35; Andrade, *Historia.* VI: 2373; and Ceballos, *Resumen,* V: 124–125; Rocafuerte, *A la nación,* no. 13, *Colección,* XIV: 242; and Cope to Backhouse, no. 4, Guayaquil, 1 April 1835, in FO 25/1. Cope reported that Flores persuaded many of his Guayaquil opponents to support him for reelection, even though the constitution forbade reelection.

6. Destruge, *Presna,* I: 35; Ceballos, *Resumen,* V: 124–125; Rocafuerte, *A la nación,* no. 13, *Collección,* XIV; 242; and Cope to Backhouse, no. 4, Guayaquil, 1 April 1835, in FO 25/1. Cope reported that Flores persuaded many of his Guayaquil opponents to support him for reelection, even though the constitution forbade reelection.

7. Moncayo, *Ecuador,* 76–79.

8. On the subject of British officers in the independence movement see Alfred Hasbrouck, *Foreign Legionaries in the Liberation of Spanish South America* (New York, 1928).

9. Moncayo, *Ecuador,* 78–79; Ceballos, *Resumen,* V: 104–105; Bushnell, "The Development of the Press in Great Colombia," 441–442; Camilo Destruge, *Album biográfico ecuatoriano,* 5 vols. (Guayaquil, 1903–1905), II: 138–142; and Salazar, "Introducción," *Actas* (1833), xvi–xviii.

10. Moncayo, *Ecuador,* 76–77.

11. Correspondence between Flores and Hall of August 1827, ANH, "Correspondencia de Flores," ff. 123–124; and Flores' correspondence with Bolívar from 21 March to 14 July 1828, O'Leary, *Memorias,* IV: 71, 74, 111–112, and 116.

12. *El Quiteño libre,* 12 May 1833 (hereinafter cited as *Quiteño*).

13. Ibid., 19, 26 May, 2, 16, 23 June, and 1 September 1833.

14. Ibid., 30 June, 7 July, 11 August, and 1, 8 September 1833.

15. Ibid., 26 May, and 23, 30 June 1833; *Gaceta,* 8 June 1833; and *El Colombiano de Guayas,* quoted in *Quiteño,* 30 June 1833.

16. *Quiteño,* 16 June and 14 June 1833.

17. Quoted from "Carestía de sal," ibid., 16 June 1833. Other articles on the misdeeds of Flores appear in the issues of 26 May, 23, 30, June and 14 July 1833. Apparently Valdivieso, Flores' minister of interior, knew nothing of the president's connection with the salt monopoly, for he instructed the prefect of the Department of El Ecuador to investigate the monopoly and to take steps to bring salt prices down. Valdivieso cited the president as the authority for his instructions in the matter; see Valdivieso to prefect of the Department of El Ecuador, Quito, 13 June 1833, in *Gaceta,* 15 June 1833.

18. *Quiteño,* 14 July 1833.

19. Ibid., 14 September 1833.

20. Ibid., 26 May 1833. A charge that the government was responsible for arresting an innocent citizen arbitrarily brought forth an angry denial with documentation in the official newspaper; see *Quiteño,* 29 June 1833, and *Gaceta,* 19 July 1833.

21. The papers were: *El Amigo del orden* (Quito); *Las Armas de la razón* (Quito); *El Trece de febrero* (Guayaquil); *El 9 de octubre* (Guayaquil); and *El Investigador* (Cuenca). Apparently the two Quito papers were subsidized by Flores privately; see Ceballos, *Resumen,* V: 123–124; and Andrade, *Historia,* VI: 2360.

22. Flores' offer to Matheu is described in his letter to Santander, Quito, 12 August and 6 September 1833 in Cortázar, *Correspondencia,* V: 463 and 465. On Flores' use of persuasion, see Andrade, *Historia,* I:2360.

23. García del Río to Flores, Quito, 14 June 1833, in AJC, "Cartas a Flores," IX: ff. 99–100. For several months García del Río had been warning Flores of growing opposition. See his other letters in the same file of 22, 25 January and 14 February 1833, ff. 85–93.

24. Flores' proclamation of 29 June 1833 (Guayaquil), *Quiteño,* 14 July 1833.

25. *Quiteño,* 30 June and 9 July 1833; and undated "Manifiesto que los redactores del *Quiteño libre* hacen a los pueblos del Ecuador," published after the 30 June issue of *Quiteño.*

26. Flores to Santander, Quito, 19 July 1833, in Cortázar, *Correspondencia,* V: 462–463. Also see Flores' letters of 20 June and 6 September 1833, ibid., V: 460–461, 464–465; and his unsigned articles, "Observaciones a la esposición que ha publicado el Sr. José Félix Valdivieso," *Gaceta,* 19 July 1833. The contents of this article indicate that only Flores could have written it; hereinafter cited as Flores, "Observaciones."

27. "Juri," *Quiteño,* 21 July 1833; and *Gaceta,* 27 July 1833. The use of juries in Spanish America was neither traditional nor widespread.

28. Salazar, "Introducción," *Actas* (1833), xvii; minutes of 1, 2 October 1833; and Tobar Donoso, *Iglesia,* 292. The law defined sedition as "perturbación de la tranquilidad pública" and "debilitar el respeto a las autoridades constituidas." Such loose definitions obviously threatened to put an end to press criticism.

29. Olmedo had resigned from the vice-presidency in 1831 when Congress insisted that he reside in Quito rather than Guayaquil; Andrade, *Historia,* VI: 2258; minutes of Congress, 27 September (night session) and 30 September 1831, in *Gaceta,* 27, 30 November 1831. For background on Olmedo's resignation see García del Río's

letters to Olmedo, 26 November, 5 December 1832, and 4, 8, 15, and esp. 28 January and 2 March 1833, in *Gaceta,* 1, 15 December 1832, and 12, 26 January, 16 February, and 9, 16 March 1833. Some of these letters were also published in *Primer rejistro,* 1832 and 1833.

30. Olmedo to García del Río, Guayaquil, 7 April 1833, in *Quiteño,* 12 May 1833. *El Quiteño libre* was opportunistic in publishing Olmedo's letter, for Olmedo's views on finance did not coincide with those of the dissident paper. Olmedo felt that the minister of finance had gone too far in his reforms, rather than not far enough. But the editors used the letter just the same, because it embarrassed the Flores administration.

31. Valdivieso, "Esposición," 4 July 1833. Flores' suspicion of Valdivieso's disloyalty may have been well founded, for Pedro Moncayo, one of the principal editors of *Quiteño,* later reported that Valdivieso drew close to their dissident group over displeasure with Flores' "fraudulent tricks" and his treatment of Matheu. Moncayo was an insider in this matter and had no motive for implicating Valdivieso at the time of writing, the 1880s. See Moncayo's *Ecuador,* 79–80. For more on the affair, see *Quiteño,* 30 June and 7 July 1833; Flores' letters to Santander, 20 June and 19 July 1933, in Cortázar, *Correspondencia,* V: 460–461.

32. Flores, "Observaciones"; *Quiteño,* 21 July 1833; and Flores, decree of 11 July 1833 (removing Valdivieso from office), *Primer rejistro* (1833), 392–393.

33. Flores' letters to Santander, 19 July and 6 September 1833, in Cortázar, *Correspondencia,* V: 462–465; Flores, "Observaciones"; and minutes of secret session of Congress, 14 September 1833, *Actas* (1833), 1–6.

34. *Actas* (1833), 1–6; and Salazar, "Introducción," ibid., xvii–xix.

35. See chap. 3 above. The constitutionality of a grant of special powers was a moot point, but it was justified by its proponents under article 35, section 5 of the constitution, which authorized the president to "take necessary measures to defend and save the country in case of foreign invasion or domestic disturbances, when Congress is not in session." See *Constituciones,* 113.

36. Flores to Larrea (president of the Congress), Quito, 1 November 1831, in *Gaceta,* 11 March 1832.

37. Minutes of Congress, secret session of 14 September 1833, *Actas* (1833), 3–6.

38. Ibid., 4–5; Congress, resolution of 14 September 1833, *Primer rejistro* (1833), 396.

39. Moncayo, *Ecuador,* 84–85; Flores to Santander, Quito, 27 September 1833, in Cortázar, *Correspondencia,* V: 466; Ceballos, *Resumen,* 137–138; and Robalino Dávila, *Nacimiento,* 236–237. Arrests of sub-

scribers to the paper were reported by the British consul; Cope to Backhouse, no. 4, Guayaquil, 1 April 1835, in FO 25/1.

40. Minutes of Congress, secret session of 16 September 1833, *Actas* (1833), 7.

41. Bolívar to Flores, Barranquilla, 9 November 1830, *Correspondencia*, 284–285.

42. Rocafuerte's article entitled "Facultades extraordinarias," *El Fénix de la libertad*, 29 February 1832, reproduced in Rocafuerte, *Colección*, XI: 81–82; Rodríguez O., *Emergence*, 216–228; Mecum, *Idealismo*, 142–149.

43. Rocafuerte to the Congress, Quito, 16 September 1833, in *Actas* (1833), xix–xx.

44. Minutes of Congress, secret session of 16 September 1833, *Actas* (1833), 8–10; and congressional resolution of 20 September 1833, *Primer rejistro* (1833), 397–398.

45. Minutes of Congress, secret sessions of 16, 19, 20, and 25 September 25 1833, *Actas* (1833), 7–8, 10–12; Ceballos, *Resumen*, V: 126–128; and Salazar, "Introducción," *Actas* (1833), viii.

46. Rocafuerte, *A la nación*, no. 12, *Colección*, XIV: 249–255; Salazar, "Introducción," *Actas* (1833), xxii–xxvi; and Ceballos, *Resumen*, V: 139–146.

47. For speculation about the meaning of the term "Chihuahuas," see Robalino Dávila, *Nacimiento*, 244, n. 1.

48. For the Jefe Supremo's own account of the nightmare, see his *A la nación*, nos. 13 and 14, *Colección*, XIV: 252–278; see also Flores' letter to Santander, Guayaquil, 20 December 1833, in Cortázar, *Correspondencia*, V: 467–468.

49. Ceballos, *Resumen*, V: 146–155; Robalino Dávila, *Nacimiento*, 238–242; and Andrade, *Historia*, VI: 2397–2401. See also the official documents published in the *Gaceta* of 26 October 1833 and the editorial in the same issue. On punishments of members of the Quiteño Libre Society see the report of Carlos Chiriboga (governor of Chimborazo) to the prefect, Riobamba, 26 April 1834, ANH, "Oficios, solicitudes," Vol. II/27, doc. no. 290; and Cope to Backhouse, dispatch no. 4, Guayaquil, 1 April 1835, in FO 25/1. Flores must have felt relieved to have Colonel Hall removed from the political scene, but this is not to say that he ordered the killing. Flores was noted for his clemency toward opponents in government, as he would soon demonstrate in his treatment of the imprisoned Rocafuerte.

50. Rocafuerte, *A la nación*, nos. 13 and 14, *Colección*, XIV: 255–270; Ceballos, *Resumen*, V: 155–163; and Moncayo, *Ecuador*, 95–101. The United States did not have diplomatic ties with Ecuador in 1833

and did not intervene in the Chihuahua affair. The ship that gave refuge to Rocafuerte, the U.S.S. *Fairfield,* just happened to visit Guayaquil at the time. On this see Cope to Backhouse, dispatch no. 4, Guayaquil, 1 April 1835, FO 25/1.

51. Rocafuerte's report to the national convention of 1835 which describes the results of his Lima mission omits any mention of what he offered in return for Peruvian support. See Rocafuerte (Jefe Supremo), message to national convention of 1835, 22 June 1835, *Actas* (1835), ccxvii–ccxviii; and Flores to Santander, Guayaquil, 20 December 1834, in Cortázar, *Correspondencia,* V: 468–469; and Robalino Dávila, *Nacimiento,* 259–260. For his dealings with New Granada, see Rocafuerte's letter to Santander, Island of Puná, 8 June 1834, in Cortázar, *Correspondencia,* XI: 174–176.

52. Ceballos, *Resumen,* V: 180–191; Salázar, "Introducción," *Actas* (1835), xxi–xxxii.

53. Rocafuerte, *A la nación,* no. 14, *Colección,* XIV: 278–285; Ceballos, *Resumen,* V: 191–199; and Moncayo, *Ecuador,* 115–122.

54. Ibid., 121–122.

55. Salazar, "Introducción," *Actas* (1835), lxxv–lxxxvii, which reproduces documents of the event, including addresses by Rocafuerte and Flores.

56. The most detailed account of these events is found in Salazar, "Introducción," *Actas* (1835), clxx–cxcix. See also Ceballos, *Resumen,* V: 239–249; and Andrade, *Historia,* VII: 2449–2469.

57. Ceballos, *Resumen,* V: 249–251; Salazar, "Introducción," *Actas* (1835), cxcix–cci.

58. Flores, "El ciudadano Juan José Flores: A los habitantes del Ecuador," 20 April 1835, *Actas,* (1835), ccii–ccix.

59. *Gaceta,* 22 October 1836. Chances are that Flores was the author, for he occasionally wrote articles for the *Gaceta,* and this one expressed some of the same views he set forth in a letter to Santander; see Flores to Santander, Hacienda de la Elvira, 1 July 1835, in Cortázar, *Correspondencia,* V: 471–472.

60. Flores to Santander, 1 July 1835, Cortázar, *Correspondencia,* V: 471–472.

61. See Flores' letters to Santander from 1 July to 29 November 1835, in Cortázar, *Correspondencia,* V: 471–483.

5. CONTRAPUNTAL POLITICS, 1835–1839

1. Rocafuerte, *A la nación,* no. 11, *Colección,* XIV: 168–169; Robalino Dávila, *Rocafuerte,* 5–7; Andrade, *Historia,* V: 2362–2363;

Mecum, *Idealismo,* 15–40; and articles on Rocafuerte in *Cultura: Revista del Banco Central del Ecuador* (Quito), 6 (Mayo–Agosto, 1983): 363–475.

2. Rocafuerte, *A la nación,* no. 11, *Colección,* XIV: 169–226; Robalino Dávila, *Rocafuerte,* 11–26; Mecum, *Idealismo,* 37–190; and Rodríguez O., *Emergence,* 48–234.

3. Moncayo, *Ecuador,* 86–92, 120–122, 128–132; Andrade, *Historia,* VII: 2436, 2466–2468; Robalino Dávila, *Nacimiento,* 270–274. Some of the Quiteño Libre people joined Valdivieso's rebel group in the north and forcefully opposed the Rocafuerte administration.

4. For the "ferocious tyrant" remark, see Rocafuerte's letter to Santander of 8 June 1834, Cortázar, *Correspondencia,* XI: 174–175. Rocafuerte's letters to Flores brim over with expressions of friendship and affection. These letters were first published in *El Nacional* (Quito), 1 March to 4 April 1887, and were later reproduced in Rodríguez O., *Estudios.*

5. Robalino Dávila, *Rocafuerte,* 72–73.

6. A succinct statement of his views is found in Rocafuerte's letter to Santander, Puná, 8 June 1834, in Cortázar, *Correspondencia,* XI: 174–176. For greater detail, see his address to the national convention of 1835, 22 June 1835, *Actas,* (1835), ccxii–ccxlviii; his address to Congress of 1837, dated December 1836, and delivered on 3 January 1837, *Actas* (1837), xxx–xliii; and his address to Congress, 15 January 1839, *Actas* (1839), xxxviii–ci.

7. On Rocafuerte's policy recommendations favoring centralism, see his address to the Congress of 1837, 3 January 1837, *Actas* (1837), li–lii, in which he recommended an executive power like that of the autocratic presidency of Chile at that time. See also Rocafuerte's letter to Flores, Quito, 23 September 1835, Rodríguez O., *Estudios,* 224–225, for a discussion of federalism.

8. Rocafuerte to Flores, Guayaquil, 24 March 1835, Rodríguez O., *Estudios,* 146–147.

9. For the admission of terrorism, see Rocafuerte to Flores, Guayaquil, 17 March 1835, and Quito, 9 November 1836; and for the "lance-point" remark, see Rocafuerte to Flores, Quito, 4 November 1835, Rodríguez O., *Estudios,* 145, 281–282. For more on Rocafuerte's severity in dealing with insurrections see his other letters to Flores, especially those of 5 February, 11, 16, and 24 March, and 14, 17, 23, and 28 October 1835, Rodríguez O., *Estudios,* 197–233; and Rocafuerte's letters in *Cultura,* 6 (Mayo–Agosto), 440–475. The legal basis for the punishment of rebels and conspirators was provided by Rocafuerte's executive decrees of 25 April and 13 May 1835, *Primer*

rejistro (1835), 480–481, 484–485. See also letters of Manuela Sáenz to Flores, Kingston (Jamaica), 6 May 1834, and Paita, 20 November 1837, in AJC, *Cartas a Flores,* I: ff. 281–283, 315–316.

10. Cope to Backhouse, no. 6, Guayaquil, 28 May 1835, in FO 25/1 (on microfilm in the Bancroft Library). See John Lynch, *Spanish Colonial Administration, 1782–1810: The Intendant System in the Viceroyalty of the Río de la Plata* (London, 1958), 2–7, for a description of reformist goals of Spanish monarchs, which rather aptly describes Rocafuerte's position also.

11. Rocafuerte's letters to Flores from 5 February 1835 to 13 May 1836, in Rodríguez O., *Estudios,* 197–261. See also: Rocafuerte, "Decreto tributando una solemne acción de gracias al Jeneral en Jefe del ejército convencional . . . ," 24 February 1835, *Primer rejistro* (1835), 476–477; and Robalino Dávila, *Rocafuerte,* 58–59.

12. Flores to Santander, Guayaquil, 13 October 1835, in Cortázar, *Correspondencia,* V: 476–477. For more on Flores' view of the responsibilities of an ex-president, see his letter to Santander of 29 November 1835, in Cortázar, *Correspondencia,* V: 481–482. The picture of Flores' life in retirement as revealed in his letters to Santander is quite different from that described by Rocafuerte in his accusatory writing in *A la nación,* especially in no. 8, *Colección,* XIV: 117–119, in which Rocafuerte alleges that Flores was conspiring to destroy the government. A response to Rocafuerte's charge of ingratitude and perfidy is to be found in "A la nación," *Gaceta,* 30 April 1843 (in all probability written by Flores).

13. Rocafuerte, decree of 18 February 1835, *Primer rejistro* (1835), 477–479; Ceballos, *Resumen,* Vol. V, 252–254; Destruge, *Prensa,* I: 41–50; and Tobar Donoso, *Iglesia,* 310–319. The national convention of 1835 countermanded Rocafuerte's arbitrary actions and permitted the banished clerics to return to their posts in Cuenca; Rocafuerte acquiesced in the legislative decision. See Tobar Donoso, *Iglesia,* 311–319.

14. Rocafuerte to Flores, Guayaquil, 17 March 1835; and Ambato, 12 June and 19 June 1835, in Rodríguez O., *Estudios,* 205, 212–215.

15. Rocafuerte, address to the national convention, 22 June 1835, *Actas* (1835), ccxii–ccxxxvi, esp. ccxxxii–ccxxxv. Robalino Dávila has suggested that Rocafuerte probably meant to say "absolutismo" rather than "monarquía." But a careful reading of his address suggests that he meant exactly what he said. His references to Iturbide of Mexico, the emperor of Brazil, and a monarchical project in Buenos Aires demonstrate that he used the word "monarquía" advisedly. His proposal of a compromise between democracy and monarchy was his way of asking the convention to augment the powers of the chief executive.

16. Minutes of the national convention, 2 June [for 22 June?] and 1 July 1835, *Actas* (1835), 7 and 21.

17. Minutes of the national convention, 25, 27, 28, 29, 30 July 1835, *Actas* (1835), 11, 65, 76–79, 92–93; and national convention, decree of 13 August 1835, *Primer rejistro* (1835), 511–512.

18. Constitution of 1835, *Constituciones*, 125–152; Ceballos, *Resumen*, V: 262–266. For Rocafuerte's complaints, see his letter to Flores, Quito, 22 July 1835, in Rodríguez O., *Estudios*, 157; and Rocafuerte's address to Congress, 15 January 1837, *Actas* (1837), I: li–lii. The Constitution of 1835 also declared Ecuador to be a republic rather than a mere "state," abolished the administrative subdivisions known as "departments," and put an end to entailed estates (*mayorazgos*).

19. Ceballos, *Resumen*, Vol. V, 267, records the rumor. Note that Ceballos was a contemporary observer. Andrade, *Historia*, VII: 2485–2486, denies Ceballos' version but offers no documentation for his own view. Flores' correspondence with Santander gives the impression that he was aloof from the working of the convention; see Flores to Santander, La Elvira, 20 July 1835, in Cortázar, *Correspondencia*, V: 474.

20. Letters written to Flores in the months preceding the elections of deputies to the convention reveal that there was much pro-Flores political activity behind the scenes carried on by his friends and associates. Examples of such letters are: A. de la Guerra to Flores, Cuenca, 15 April 1835; and I. Torres to Flores, Cuenca, 15 April 1835, in AJC (photocopies provided by Kent B. Mecum). I have discovered no evidence that Flores actively sought to control the convention or to secure election to the presidency.

21. Minutes of the national convention, 2 August 1835, *Actas* (1835), 97.

22. Rocafuerte to Flores, Quito, 18 August 1835, in Rodríguez O., *Estudios*, 219–220. The nature of Flores' inquiry of Rocafuerte must be inferred from the latter's letter.

23. Rocafuerte to Flores, Quito, 18 August 1835 and 27 July 1836, in Rodríguez O., *Estudios*, 219–220, 270–271. An equivalent action in United States history would have been for President John Adams to appoint a British subject as secretary of the treasury, a Frenchman as secretary of war, and a Dutchman as secretary of state.

24. Rocafuerte, address to the national convention, 8 August 1835, *Actas* (1835), 111–112.

25. Robalino Dávila, *Rocafuerte*, 85–110, offers the best available treatment of Rocafuerte's foreign policy. It is based on archival research, but is far from exhaustive.

26. Rocafuerte to Flores, Guayaquil, 18 March 1840, in Rodríguez

O., *Estudios*, 320–322, offers the best summary of his views on foreign policy. His various addresses to Congress, 1835, 1837, and 1839, contain official reports on policies toward foreign nations.

27. Flores initiated preliminary contacts with the United States and France but failed to secure diplomatic recognition from either power; Manning, *Correspondence*, VI: 223. On negotiations with France in 1834, see minutes of Congress, 21 February 1839, *Actas* (1839), I: 96.

28. Rocafuerte, message to Congress, 15 January 1839, *Actas* (1839), I: lvii; Robalino Dávila, *Rocafuerte*, 86–87.

29. Livingston to Flores, Washington, 4 January 1832, in Manning, *Correspondence*, VI: 223; José Miguel González (Ecuadorian minister of foreign relations) to Robert B. McAfee (U.S. chargé at Bogotá), Quito, 11 July 1835, in Manning, *Correspondence*, V: 520–521; James C. Pickett (U.S. chargé to the Peru–Bolivian confederation) to John Forsyth (U.S. secretary of state), Quito, 30 January 1839, in ibid., VI: 239–340; Rocafuerte, message to Congress, 15 January 1839, *Actas* (1839), I: lix; and Robalino Dávila, *Rocafuerte*, 103.

30. Jean Baptiste de Mendeville (French honorary consul-general) to Pedro José de Arteta (Ecuadorian minister of foreign relations), Guayaquil, 10 August 1836, in *Gaceta*, 27 August 1836; congressional decree of 13 April 1837, *Primer rejistro*, (1837), 318; Robalino Dávila, *Rocafuerte*, 96–101. The president honored France by reconstructing the pyramids at the equator which had been erected in 1736 by French scientists.

31. Rocafuerte to Flores, Quito, 22 July 1835, in Rodríguez O., *Estudios*, 157; Convention of New Granada and Venezuela, 12 October 1836, reproduced in *Primer rejistro* (1837), 356–364; and Robalino Dávila, *Rocafuerte*, 101–102, 105–106.

32. Rocafuerte to Flores, Quito, 24 May and 7 June 1837, in Rodríguez O., *Estudios*, 282–284; Col. R. Wright (confidential agent of Ecuador) to Lord Palmerston (13 Tavistock Place, Russel [sic] Square), 28 February 1838, in FO 25/4; and Cope's consular dispatches nos. 6, 12, and 14, Quito, 18 February, 1 May, and 12 June 1837, FO 25/3.

33. Cope to Bidwell (unnumbered dispatch), Guayaquil, 7 August 1838, in FO 25/4, which acknowledges receipt of authorization to negotiate a treaty; extract of a letter from Rocafuerte to Cope, Quito, 15 August 1838, enclosed with Cope's dispatch no. 12, Guayaquil, 31 July 1839, FO 25/5. A variety of problems put off the ratification of a treaty until 1851, well after Rocafuerte had gone to his grave and Flores had lost power. See Cope to Palmerston, dispatches nos. 4 and 10, Quito, 5 March and 1 July 1851, in FO 25/22.

34. Mark J. Van Aken, *Pan-Hispanism: Its Origin and Development to 1866* (Berkeley and Los Angeles, 1959), 17–31; Jerónimo Bécker, *La independencia de América (su reconocimiento por España)* (Madrid, 1922), 119–195; Pedro Gual to Palmerston [London?], 13 December 1838, in FO 25/4; and Gual to Duque de Frías, no date or place given, but on cover dated 26 February 1839, in FO 25/5.

35. Minutes of the national convention, 19, 20, and 25 August 1835, *Actas* (1835), 144, 146, 155. An editorial in the official *Gaceta,* 26 March 1836, showed enthusiasm for reconciliation with Spain and rhapsodized about pan-Hispanic brotherhood: "En la península y en américa se abre una nueva época de rejeneración y de gratas esperanzas, identidad de los sacrificios que ambas han hecho . . . las convida a estrechar los lazos de su antigua confraternidad," and so forth. See also *Gaceta,* 24 September 1836, 3 November 1838, and other dates for continuing interest in Spain. Venezuela, Uruguay, and Bolivia opened their ports to Spain at about the same time.

36. Even the treaty of amity with Venezuela, not a major power, was ratified after Flores took office in January 1839. See minutes of the Senate, 21 and 28 January 1839, *Actas* (1839), Vol. I, 12–13, 30–31; and Rocafuerte's address to Congress, 15 January 1839, *Actas* (1839), Vol. I, lvi, which reviews his foreign policy accomplishments.

37. Salazar, "Introducción," *Actas* (1835), cxcvii–cxcix; Ceballos, *Resumen,* Vol. V, 247–248; Rocafuerte to Flores, Guayaquil, 5 February 1835, in Rodríguez O., *Estudios,* 197–198; Rocafuerte to Santander, Guayaquil, 30 November 1834, in Cortázar, *Correspondencia,* Vol. XI, 176–184; Rocafuerte, address to the national convention, 22 June 1835, *Actas* (1835), ccxlv–ccxlvi; Restrepo Canal, *Nueva Granada,* 311–313; and diplomatic correspondence published in the *Gaceta* late in 1835 and 1836, especially the issue of 13 February 1836, which reproduces the text of the treaty and ratifications.

38. Robalino Dávila, *Rocafuerte,* 101–102, 105–106; *Gaceta,* 16 June 1838, reproduces the text of the formal exchange of ratifications of the convention which took place on 22 February 1838; and Rocafuerte, address to Congress, 15 January 1839, *Actas* (1839), lvi–lx.

39. Rocafuerte's personal letters to Santander during the period of April 1835 to November 1836 provide basic information on the course of diplomacy with New Granada, in Cortázar, *Correspondencia,* Vol. XI, 186–216. See Rocafuerte's address to Congress, 15 January 1839, *Actas* (1839), lvi–lvii; and Robalino Dávila, *Rocafuerte,* 103–109.

40. Robert N. Burr, *By Reason of Force: Chile and Balancing of Power in South America, 1830–1905* (Berkeley and Los Angeles, 1965), University of California Publications in History, vol. 77, 35–57; Jorge

Basadre, *Chile, Perú y Bolivia independientes* (Barcelona and Buenos Aires, 1948), 125–178; Basadre, *Historia,* Vol. I, 290–296, 359–436; and Rubén Vargas Ugarte, *Historia General del Perú,* 2d ed. rev., 10 vols. (Lima, 1971), VII: 127–130. The draft treaty of Paucarpata, 17 November 1837, was reproduced in *Gaceta,* 16 December 1837.

41. Flores to Santander, Guayaquil, 4 March 1836, in Cortázar, *Correspondencia,* VI: 12. On the Protector's ambitions to emulate Alexander the Great, see Basadre, *Historia,* Vol. I, 292. On the movement to declare Santa Cruz lifetime Protector, see Luis Monguió, *José Joaquín de Mora y el Perú de Ochocientos* (Berkeley and Los Angeles, 1967), 257–258.

42. Flores to Santander, La Elvira, 18 August 1836, in Cortázar, *Correspondencia,* VI: 18.

43. Burr, *Reason,* 33–47; Vargas Ugarte, *Historia,* Vol. VIII, 139–145; and Basadre, *Historia,* I: 397–403.

44. Correspondence of Ventura Lavalle (Chilean chargé in Ecuador) to Diego Portales (Chilean minister of state for foreign relations) between 14 November 1836 and 17 January 1837, in Archivo del Ministerio de Relaciones Exteriores, Legación de Chile en el Ecuador, 1836–1840 (hereinafter AMRE, Chile). (Copies of this correspondence were furnished by Professor Robert N. Burr.)

45. Flores to Santander, Guayaquil, 13 October 1835, in Cortázar, *Corespondencia,* V: 478.

46. Flores' correspondence with Santander, 20 July 1835 to 6 October 1836, in Cortázar, *Correspondencia,* V: 473–483, VI: 7–21.

47. For an illustration of Rocafuerte's imprudent denunciation of his opponents, see his address to Congress, 15 January 1837, *Actas* (1837), I: xlvi–l. In his address to Congress in 1839 he seemed to denounce almost the entire country; *Actas* (1839), Vol. I, xxxviii–ci.

48. Congressional decree of 20 August 1835, *Primer rejistro* (1835), 43–45.

49. Rocafuerte, address to Congress, 15 January 1837, *Actas* (1837), I: lvi–lviii; and presidential decree of 20 February 1836, *Primer rejistro* (1836), 126–147.

50. Rocafuerte, address to Congress, 15 January 1837, *Actas* (1837), I: lvi–lviii; id., address to Congress, 15 January 1839, *Actas* (1839), Vol. I, liv–lv; Bernardo Daste (minister of war), "Circular ordenando el establecimiento de un colegio militar," Quito, 6 December 1837, *Primer rejistro* (1837), 416; news article in the *Gaceta,* 7 July 1838; "Instituto agrario," *Gaceta,* 17 November 1838. The Agrarian Institute attracted few students and Congress abolished it for lack of funds; see *Gaceta,* 17 November 1838; minutes of Congress, 2 March 1839, *Actas* (1839), I:

124; and decree of 27 March 1839, *Primer rejistro* (1839), 515–516. The military academy lasted until 10 April 1845, and became a casualty of the revolt against Flores in March of that year; see *Gaceta*, 13 April 1845.

51. Rocafuerte, address to Congress, 15 January 1839, *Actas* (1839), I: xxxix–xl.

52. Correspondence on the Wheelwright affair of February 1838, in the *Gaceta*, 3 March 1838; Tobar Donoso, *Iglesia*, 348–351; and Andrade, *Historia*, VII: 2527–2528. Wheelwright, who had served in Guayaquil as U.S. consul from 1824 to 1829, left Ecuador in disgust. In 1840 he established the Pacific Steam Navigation Company and later built railroads in Chile and Argentina.

53. Mecum, *Idealismo*, 181–183, 190–193; and Tobar Donoso, *Iglesia*, 354–383.

54. Rocafuerte to Flores, Quito, 2 September 1835, in Rodríguez O., *Estudios*, 221–222.

55. The bewildering actions of Congress on estancos may be found in the *Primer rejistro*, 1835–1839. In September 1837 Rocafuerte violated a law by arbitrarily abolishing the tobacco estanco, which was costing the government large sums of money. Congress took no action against the president for this illegal measure; see the circular letter of the minister of finance, Quito, 24 September 1838, *Primer rejistro* (1838), 455–458.

56. Rocafuerte, address to Congress, 15 January 1837, *Actas* (1837), I: lx–lxi; id., address to Congress, 15 January 1839, *Actas* (1839), I: xci–xcii; and Rocafuerte, "Decreto formando una junta de caminos en la capital i dando reglas para su mejora y reparo," *Primer rejistro* (1835), 99–100.

57. Rocafuerte, addresses to Congress, *Actas* (1837), I: lv, and *Actas* (1839), I: lxxxix; Rocafuerte to Flores, Quito, 28 January 1836, in Rodríguez O., *Estudios*, 241–242; *Gaceta*, 9 March 1836, 4 November 1837, and 31 January and 8 May 1838.

58. Rocafuerte, address to Congress, 15 January 1839, *Actas* (1839), I: xcii; Van Aken, "Lingering Death," 452–453, fig. 4 and Table I. On the cacao trade and prices, see *La Balanza*, 4 January 1840; and Consul Cope's returns of trade for the late 1830s, FO 25/3, 25/4, and 25/5.

59. Presidential decree of 10 February 1836 reducing import duties, *Primer rejistro* (1836), 116–117; Rocafuerte to Flores, Quito, 9 March 1836, in Rodríguez O., *Estudios*, 248–249; and Rocafuerte, address to Congress, 31 December 1836 (delivered on 3 January 1837), *Actas* (1837), I: xxxvi–xxxix.

60. Rocafuerte, address to Congress, 31 December 1836, *Actas*

(1837), I: xxxvi–xxxvii, id., *A la nación*, no. 8, *Colección*, XIV: 123–124.

61. Rocafuerte to Flores, Quito, 13 and 20 May 1835, in Rodríguez O., *Estudios*, 209, 211–212. The fine was to be collected from Valdivieso's properties in Ecuador.

62. Circular letters from Tamariz to governors, 6 to 20 October 1835, in *Gaceta*, 13 February 1836.

63. Presidential decree of 19 October 1835, *Primer rejistro* (1835), 96–98.

64. Rocafuerte's letters to Flores of 14 and 21 October 1835 and 6 and 20 January 1836, in Rodríguez O., *Estudios*, 227–230, 239–241. Flores offered to provide clothing and half-pay for the troops for one month; Rocafuerte accepted the offer.

65. Presidential decrees of 10 February 1836, *Primer rejistro* (1836); and Robalino Dávila, *Rocafuerte*, 52–53.

66. Rocafuerte, address to Congress, 31 December 1836, *Actas* (1837), xxxvii–xli. See also Rocafuerte, *A la nación*, no. 8, *Colección*, XIV: 123–126.

67. Rocafuerte, address to Congress, 31 December 1836, *Actas* (1837), I: xxvi–xliii; and Robalino Dávila, *Rocafuerte*, 59–62. The latter gives too much credence to Rocafuerte's assertions of fiscal success. For strong evidence of continuing fiscal chaos after the reforms, see: Alejandro Valdivieso (governor of Azuay) to Tamariz (minister of finance), Cuenca, 17 and 18 May 1836, in archive in the Departmento de Historia y Geografía, Ministerio de Defensa (Quito), in Azuay, Gobernación, Año 1836, no. 4.

68. Rocafuerte's policy of publishing government treasury accounts in the *Gaceta* was an admirable improvement over past practices of relative secrecy in fiscal matters, but these reports revealed that many of the provinces were badly organized and far in arrears in their accounts. Problems of sloppy and dishonest tax collectors continued to the end of Rocafuerte's term. See the circular letter of 24 April 1837, *Primer rejistro* (1838), 450–451; and minister of finance to governor of Guayaquil, Quito, 10 July 1838, in *Gaceta*, 14 July 1838 (on confusion, shortages, and disorder in Guayaquil collections and accounts).

69. Rocafuerte to Flores, Quito, 18 January, 18 March, and 17 October 1838, in Rodríguez O., *Estudios*, 294–296, 301; Manuel López y Escobar (minister of finance) to the governor of the province of Cuenca, Quito, 7 and 14 June 1837, in *Gaceta*, 25 November 1837, and later correspondence on the same matter in *Gaceta*, 2 December 1837. Tamariz admitted to Congress that troops in Imbabura and

Loja were unpaid—contrary to the president's assertion in his address
to the Congress; see minutes of the Senate, 27 January and 9 and 10
February 1837, *Actas* (1837), 60–61, 80, 183.

70. Rocafuerte, address to Congress, dated 31 December 1836,
and delivered on 3 January 1837, *Actas* (1837), I: xlii–xliii; Cope to
Backhouse, no. 12, Quito, 1 May 1837, in FO 25/3. On the continuing
problem of the British debt, see: Cope to Palmerston, no. 18, Guayaquil, 2 October 1839, in FO 25/5.

71. Rocafuerte, *A la nación*, no. 8, *Colección*, XIV: 116–121 (an
impassioned, partisan, and not always accurate account); Lavalle's dispatches, 22 November 1836 to 11 February 1837, AMRE (Chile)
Legación de Chile en Ecuador, 1836–1840; and Robalino Dávila,
Rocafuerte, 58–59.

72. Lavalle's dispatches of 22 November 1836 to 11 February
1837, AMRE (Chile) Legación de Chile en Ecuador, 1836–1840, are
the best source of information on the "legal revolution," but see also
Rocafuerte's *A la nación*, no. 8, *Colección*, XIV: 116–121. The Chilean
chargé appears to have encouraged the moves against Rocafuerte in
order to secure Ecuadorian collaboration with Chile in the war against
Peru.

73. Rocafuerte, address to Congress, 31 December 1836, *Actas*
(1837), I: xxxiii–xxxiv; and id., address to Congress of 15 January
1837, *Actas* (1837), xlvii; and message of the Senate to the president, 5
January 1837, *Actas* (1837), I: 13.

74. Ceballos, *Resumen*, V: 302–303. The ministers of war and treasury were General Bernado Daste (of French birth) and Manuel
López y Escobar.

75. On the repeal of the decrees of 10 February, see minutes of the
Senate, 20, 21, 23, and 30 January 1837, *Actas* (1837), I: 38–40, 42–
45, 47–48, and 68; and Chamber of Representatives, 25 and 28 January 1837, *Actas* (1837), II: 48–49, 54. On the treaty with Peru, see
minutes of the Senate, 24, 28, 30 January, and 4 February 1837, *Actas*
(1837), I: 54; and minutes of the Chamber of Representatives, 31
January 1837, *Actas* (1837), II: 60; and Lavalle's dispatches nos. 7 and
9, 17 January and 2 February 1837, AMRE (Chile), Legación de Chile
en Ecuador, 1836–1840.

76. Minutes of the Senate meeting, 16 and 21 March, and 2 April
1837, *Actas* (1837), I: 153, 165–167, 185–198; Minutes of the Chamber of Representatives, 24 and 25 February, and 3, 7, 13, 14, 15, and
20 March 1837, *Actas* (1837), II: 111–114, 116–117, 142–144, 162–
164, 166–169, 178. The impeachment proceedings were based on the
Law of Ministerial Responsibility of 1832, passed under the first

Flores administration; see the minutes of Congress, 4 November 1832, *Actas* (1832), 154–155.

77. For an excellent summary of these actions, see Salazar, "Introducción," *Actas* (1837), I: lxiii–lxxix.

78. Legislative decrees, 18 January and 15 April 1837, *Primer rejistro* (1837), 238, and 349–350.

79. Flores, address to the Senate, 24 January 1837 (paraphrased in the minutes), *Actas* (1837), I: 53.

80. Lavalle to minister of foreign relations, 17 January 1837, AMRE (Chile) Legación de Chile en Ecuador, 1836–1840.

81. Rocafuerte, *A la nación*, no. 8, *Colección*, XIV: 120–121; and Rocafuerte to Flores, Quito, 9 November 1836, in Rodríguez O., *Estudios*, 281–282.

82. Rocafuerte to Flores, Quito, 20 June and 5 July 1837, in Rodríguez O., *Estudios*, 222–224.

83. Andrade, *Historia*, VII: 2517–2520, accuses Flores of complicity in a military uprising in October 1837, but the accusation lacks credible evidence. On Flores' denunciation of rebels and support of the Rocafuerte administration, see his letter to Commandante José Martínez Aparicio, La Elvira, 8 May 1838, in *Gaceta*, 26 May 1838.

84. José Miguel González (minister of war) to Flores, Quito, 6 June 1838, in *Gaceta*, 23 June 1838; Flores to González, La Elvira, 14 June 1838, in ibid.; and news article in *Gaceta*, 7 July 1838. It is clear that Flores planned a trip to Quito before he received an invitation from Rocafuerte. See Rocafuerte to Flores, Quito, 28 March 1838, in Rodríguez O., *Estudios*, 236.

85. Flores to Santander, Quito, 23 July 1838, in Cortázar, *Correspondencia*, VI: 25.

86. Rocafuerte, address to Congress, 15 January 1839, *Actas* (1839), I: xxxvii–xcix.

6. AN ADMINISTRATION OF NATIONAL UNITY, 1839–1842

1. Minutes of the Senate, *Actas* (1839), I: 37–38.

2. Ceballos, *Resumen*, V: 321–322; Luis Robalino Dávila, *La reacción anti-floreana* (Puebla, 1967), 57–58; Rocafuerte to Flores, Guayaquil, 23 October 1839, 18 February and 4 March 1840, in Rodríguez O., *Estudios*, 309–310, 318–319. For a biographical sketch of Roca, see Salazar, "Introducción," *Actas* (1837), I: lxxxvii–cxxii.

3. Flores, address to Congress, 31 January 1839, minutes of the Senate, *Actas* (1839), I: ci–cii.

4. Ibid., ci–cvi.

5. Presidential decrees of 1 February 1839, *Actas* (1839), I: 479–480; Salazar, "Introducción," *Actas* (1839), I: cvi–cvii; Ceballos, *Resumen*, V: 324–325. On the opposition clubs and societies, see Rocafuerte's letter to Flores, Guayaquil, 8 May 1839, Rodríguez O., *Estudios*, 246. On the importance of Flores' conciliatory policies, see Walter Cope's consular dispatch no. 11, Guayaquil, 15 May 1840, FO 25/6.

6. Minutes of the Senate, 25, 26, and 29 January 1839, *Actas* (1839), I: 23, 29, 30; Valdivieso (president of the Senate) to Flores, Quito, 3 March 1841, in special issue of the *Gaceta* entitled *Alcance a la Gaceta*, 5 March 1841; Francisco Marcos (minister of the interior) to Valdivieso, Quito, 24 March 1841, in *Gaceta*, 28 March 1841; and announcement of diplomatic appointment, *Gaceta*, 5 December 1841. Valdivieso, though reconciled with Flores, harbored strong resentment against Rocafuerte; Ceballos, *Resumen*, V: 324, 327–328.

7. Minutes of the Senate, 15 February 1839, *Actas* (1839), I: 82–83; Senate resolution of 18 February 1839, *Gaceta*, 24 February 1839; Francisco de Aguirre (vice president) to Tamariz, Quito, 16 September 1840, in *Gaceta*, 20 September 1840; and announcement of gubernatorial appointment, *Gaceta*, 4 October 1840.

8. See Rocafuerte's letters to Flores for the years 1838 and 1839, in Rodríguez O., *Estudios*, 282–305. Flores' letters to Rocafuerte apparently have not survived or, at any rate, are not available. The content of some of Flores' letters to Rocafuerte can be inferred from Rocafuerte's letters.

9. See Flores' remarks, minutes of the Senate, 19 January 1837, *Actas* (1839), I: 53.

10. Rocafuerte to Flores, Quito, 14 November 1838, in Rodríguez O., *Estudios*, 303.

11. Flores, address to Congress, 1 February 1839, *Actas* (1839), I: cvi.

12. *Gaceta*, 24 February 1839.

13. Rocafuerte's letters to Flores, from 5 March 1839 to 25 January 1843, in Rodríguez O., *Estudios*, 305–360. For an example of Flores' amiable cooperation, see the correspondence between Rocafuerte and Luis de Sáa (minister of finance), 22 January to 4 February 1840, in *Gaceta*, 16 February 1840.

14. Rocafuerte to Flores, Guayaquil, 26 February 1840, in Rodríguez O., *Estudios*, 317.

15. Rocafuerte to Flores, Guayaquil, 20 May 1840, in ibid., 333–34.

16. Rocafuerte to Flores, 11 November 1840, in ibid., 344.

17. See especially Rocafuerte's letter to Flores, Guayaquil, 26 February 1840, in ibid., 317.

18. See letters from Rocafuerte to Flores, Guayaquil, 8 May and 23 October 1839, and 12 and 18 February 1840, in ibid., 307–309, 312, and 314–315. See also Tobar Donoso, *Iglesia*, 404–430.

19. Rocafuerte to Flores, Guayaquil, 5 March 1839, in Rodríguez O., *Estudios*, 244–245.

20. Rocafuerte to Flores, Guayaquil, 8 May 1839, in ibid., 307–308.

21. See the Constitution of 1835, Título VII, Sección I, Art. 62, *Constituciones*, 141.

22. On Rocafuerte's reform program, discussed briefly in the preceding chapter, see his message to Congress, 15 January 1839, *Actas* (1839), I: xxxviii–ci. Flores' position was stated in his inaugural address of 31 January 1839, *Actas* (1839), I: ci–cii.

23. Flores, address to Congress, 15 January 1841, in *Gaceta*, 24 January 1841; and minutes of the Senate, 21 and 22 January 1841, in *Gaceta*, 14 and 21 February 1841. The official minutes of the Congress of 1841 have not been published, probably because the Congress disbanded prematurely.

24. Rocafuerte's letters do not criticize Flores on the issue of the tariff, but the relations between the two men were cool in late 1840 and early 1841. See especially Rocafuerte's letter to Flores of 9 September 1840, and his letter to Rufino Cuervo, 19 May 1841, in Rodríguez O., *Estudios*, 341–342, 347.

25. Flores, address to Congress, 15 January 1841, in *Gaceta*, 24 January 1841.

26. Van Aken, "Lingering Death," 429–445.

27. News article entitled "Legislature," in *Gaceta*, 14 February 1841; and Valdivieso (president of Senate) to Flores, Quito, 3 March 1841, in *Gaceta*, 5 March 1841.

28. *Constituciones*, 141.

29. Flores, decree of 16 February 1839, *Primer rejistro* (1839), 482–483.

30. Minutes of the Senate, 4 March 1839, *Actas* (1839), I: 128; congressional decrees of 19 and 20 April 1839, *Primer rejistro* (1839), 543–544, 569; correspondence of the minister of the interior, *Gaceta*, 1 March 1840; *Gaceta*, 26 July 1840 and 25 December 1842 (on the military academy); and Flores, decree of 8 May 1839, *Primer rejistro* (1839), 589–590.

31. *Gaceta,* 22 August 1841. José Modesto Larrea obtained a copy of the work in Italy and arranged to have the first volume corrected by Ecuadorian specialists and to have the entire work published.

32. Marcos (minister of the interior) to the director-general of education, Quito, 1 April 1841, in *Gaceta,* 4 April 1841; *Gaceta,* 26 July 1840 (on the graduates of the military academy); and Fernández Salvador to Sáa (acting minister of the interior), Quito, 3 December 1839, in *Gaceta,* 5 January 1840 (on the school of arts and crafts).

33. Marcos to director-general of public education, Quito, 10 July 1840, in *Gaceta,* 26 July 1840; and letter from the municipality of Ambato to Flores, Ambato, 14 January 1842, in *Gaceta,* 27 February 1842. Roberto Andrade asserts that Flores did nothing of substance for education during his second term; see his *Historia,* VII: 2252–2253.

34. The founding of a primary school for Indian children at Alangasí in the north was praised by the government newspaper, and priests were urged to imitate this example elsewhere; *Gaceta,* 19 February 1843.

35. Presidential decree, 10 April 1845, in *Gaceta,* 13 April 1845 (which closed the military academy).

36. Marcos (minister of the interior) to the governor of the province of Quito, Quito, 24 January 1840, in *Gaceta,* 9 February 1840. On urban crime in Ecuador see Rocafuerte's letters to Flores, 5, 12, and 26 February 1840, in Rodríguez O., *Estudios,* 310–314, 317–318; and the very interesting letter of Antonio Ceballos (Comisario de Policía de Quito) to Flores, Quito, 14 February 1842, in *Gaceta,* 13 March 1842.

37. Marcos (minister of the interior) to governor of the province of Quito, Quito, 7 November 1840, in *Gaceta,* 8 November 1840; William Jameson, *Synopsis plantarum aequatoriensium,* 3 vols. (Quito, 1865) and 3 vols. (Quito, 1940).

38. Marcos (minister of the interior), circular to governors, Quito, 2 March 1840; and Miguel Carrión (governor of Pichincha) to Marcos, Quito, 12 April 1842, in *Gaceta,* 17 April 1842.

39. Rocafuerte to Marcos, Guayaquil, 5 October 1842, in *Gaceta,* 23 October 1842; id. to Flores, Guayaquil, 5 October 1842, in Rodríguez O., *Estudios, 354–355;* "Epidemia de Guayaquil," *Gaceta,* 6 November 1842; Cope to Bidwell, no. 22, Puná, 28 October 1842, in FO 25/8; and id. to id., no. 15, Guayaquil, 21 August 1843, in FO 25/9. The role of Governor Rocafuerte in caring for the victims of the disease has been fully described by Pedro José Huerta in his *Rocafuerte y la fiebre amarilla de 1842* . . . (Guayaquil, 1947).

40. Rocafuerte to Marcos, Guayaquil, 5 October 1842, in *Gaceta*, 23 October 1842; and id. to id., Guayaquil, 9 November 1842, in Rodríguez O., *Estudios*, 356–357.

41. Rocafuerte to Flores, Guayaquil, 9 November 1840, in Rodríguez O., *Estudios*, 356–357; and issues of the *Gaceta* in November and December 1842, especially those of 18 and 25 December.

42. For detailed information on this subject, see Walter Cope's annual reports on the trade of Guayaquil for the years 1843 and 1844, enclosed with Cope's dispatches no. 8, 19 February 1844, and no. 7, 20 January 1845, FO 25/10–11. See also Rocafuerte's letter to Flores, Guayaquil, 5 October 1842, in Rodríguez O., *Estudios*, 354–355; *Gaceta*, 12 March and 2 and 9 April 1843; and Rocafuerte, *A la nación*, no. 9, *Colección*, XIV: 132–133. Rocafuerte asserts that vandals and arsonists attempted to destroy Guayaquil during the epidemic, but vigorous efforts of the government defeated the criminals.

43. On the Sociedades de Amigos del País, see: Ceballos, *Resumen*, V: 325; Fernández Salvador to governor of Chimborazo, Quito, 17 February 1840, in *Gaceta*, 8 March 1840; and Rocafuerte to Flores, Guayaquil, 8 May 1839, in Rodríguez O., *Estudios*, 246–247. Andrade claims that Flores stole funds appropriated for building factories to manufacture paper and china, but this is strange because Congress did not appropriate any money for these enterprises; *Historia*, VII: 2553.

44. Rocafuerte to George Peacock, Guayaquil, 13 November 1841, in Peacock Papers, Liverpool, pamphlet entitled *Official Correspondence*, 62–64 (supplied by Ronald Duncan); Rocafuerte to Flores, Guayaquil 12, February 1840 (reports the purchase of a steam engine in Baltimore for the steamship); and 26 August 1840, Rodríguez O., *Estudios*, 314 and 339–341; *Gaceta*, 23 May 1841; Rocafuerte to Marcos, Guayaquil, 23 February and 30 March 1842, and accompanying documents, in *Gaceta*, 17 April 1842 (on a sawmill and a proposal to build a drydock); and an address by Rocafuerte on 9 October 1842, published in *El Correo* (Guayaquil), 16 October 1842.

45. Rocafuerte to Peacock, 13 November 1841, in Peacock Papers, Liverpool, 62–64; *Gaceta*, 23 May 1841 and 20 February 1842; Andrade, *Historia*, VII: 2688; and *La Balanza*, 19 September 1840 (concerning sale of shares in the steamship company to Ecuadorians). On Wheelwright and his economic activities in South America, see: Juan Bautista Alberdi, *Life and Industrial Labors of William Wheelright in South America* (Boston, 1887); and Jay Kinsbruner, "The Business Activities of William Wheelwright in Chile, 1829–1860" (Ph.D. dissertation, New York University, 1964).

46. Reports of the British consul Walter Cope for the years 1838,

1839, and 1843, FO 25/5–10, especially Cope's Report on the Trade of Guayaquil for the Year Ending December 31st, 1843, FO 25/10; and a detailed report of Ecuador's foreign trade in 1839 that appeared in *La Balanza,* 4 January 1840. Cope's reports on trade for the years 1840, 1841, and 1842 are not on the microfilm of the Foreign Office correspondence in the Bancroft Library.

47. Minutes of the Senate, 4 March 1839, *Actas* (1839), I: 126; and presidential decree of 11 April 1840, *Gaceta,* 12 April 1840.

48. Customs receipts for 1839 were 365,496 pesos; in 1841, the third year of Flores' second term, they reached 465,361 pesos: see *La Balanza,* 4 January 1840, and *Gaceta,* 27 February 1842. Apparently receipts dipped to approximately 390,000 pesos in 1842, but the figures were still well above the receipts of 1839. Monthly collections for January through August 1842 were published in the *Gaceta,* 6 March to 20 November 1842.

49. Various letters from Rocafuerte to Flores during the year 1842—but especially the letter of 15 June 1842, in Rodríguez O., *Estudios,* 352.

50. Rocafuerte to Flores, Guayaquil, 5, 12, 18 February, 18 March, and 9 September 1840, in Rodríguez O., *Estudios,* 310–316, 320–322, and 341–342; and *Gaceta,* 17 March and 5 July 1840, 19 September 1841, and 3 April 1842.

51. Minutes of the Senate, 20 and 23 February and 4 March 1839, *Actas* (1839), I: 92, 103, 106, and 127–128.

52. Minutes of the Senate, 27 February and 4 March 1839, *Actas* (1839), I: 115, 127, 128; congressional resolution of 5 March 1839, and congressional decree of 23 April 1839, *Primer rejistro* (1839), 493–494, 583–586; Flores, decree of 20 May 1839, *Primer rejistro* (1839), 594–586; and Sáa to governors of provinces, Quito, 22 January 1840, in *Gaceta,* 2 February 1840.

53. A new Ley Orgánica de Hacienda was adopted with new regulations for the accounting of revenues, but the law did not provide for any major fiscal reforms; see the law of 20 April 1839, *Gaceta,* 17 May 1840 (sic). For more information on finance see the *Gaceta,* 28 January and 9 February 1840; Sáa's letters of 22 January and 27 March 1840, *Gaceta,* 2 February and 5 April 1840; and L. A. Rodríguez, *Search,* 75–77. In Loja the Fiscal de Hacienda refused to prosecute tax evaders; correspondence in *Gaceta,* 17 January 1840. On tax evasion in Guayaquil see Rocafuerte to Flores, Guayaquil, 8 May 1839, in Rodríguez O., *Estudios,* 307–308.

54. Correspondence between Arteta (general accountant of the state) and Sáa, 8–14 May 1840, in *Gaceta,* 17 May 1840; letter from the

Junta de Hacienda de Cuenca to Sáa, 30 October 1841, and reply 22 December 1841, in *Gaceta,* 2 January 1842.

55. Rocafuerte to Flores, Guayaquil, 12 February 1840 and 9 November 1841, in Rodríguez O., *Estudios,* 312–313, 348; correspondence between Rocafuerte and Sáa, and related documents, in *Gaceta,* 31 July and 14 August 1842 (on the need for better machinery for laminating coins at the mint); and other correspondence of Sáa reproduced in the *Gaceta,* 5, 24 February and 27, 31 May 1840, 7 March, 27 June, and 14 November 1841, 8 May 1842, and 27 August 1843. It is worth noting that Flores was severely criticized during his first term for temporizing with counterfeit money in the very manner now recommended by Rocafuerte.

56. Sáa, circular to governors, Quito, 9 November 1841, in *Gaceta,* 14 November 1841; Sáa to Rocafuerte, Quito, 19 May 1842, in *Gaceta,* 12 June 1842; and Rocafuerte, *A la nación,* nos. 2 and 9, *Colección,* XIV: 29 and 133.

57. Rocafuerte, *A la nación,* no. 2, *Colección,* XIV: 28–29.

58. Flores, address to Congress, 15 January 1841, in *Gaceta,* 24 January 1841.

59. Rocafuerte, *A la nación,* nos. 1, 10, and 11, *Colección,* XIV: 11–12, 156–157, 164–165, and 226.

60. *El Nacional* (Quito), 1 June 1846 (*El Nacional* was the successor to the *Gaceta*); Ceballos, *Resumen,* V: 331–332; and Robalino Dávila, *Rocafuerte,* 154. For more charges of financial irregularities by Flores, see *El Nacional,* 1 June 1846. The president's annual salary in 1843 was 12,000 pesos; *Gaceta,* 6 August 1843. Total government revenues in 1842 are not readily available, but for 1838 they amounted to about 1,130,000 pesos; Salazar, "Introducción," *Actas* (1839), I: xxiv.

61. For a sanguine report on finances see Flores' message to Congress, 15 January 1841, in *Gaceta,* 24 January 1841. See also: news article in the *Gaceta,* 2 August 1840, on salaries and budget; M. Matheu (acting minister of finance), circular to governors, Quito, 26 September 1840, in *Gaceta,* 4 October 1840 (admits grave financial problems); Flores, decree of 16 February 1842 (issuing 182,000 paper pesos), *Gaceta,* 29 February 1842.

62. Tobar Donoso, *Iglesia,* 405–410, 435–445; *Gaceta,* 30 May and 21 June 1841; *La Balanza,* 15 February 1840. Though Tobar Donoso's treatment of church–state relations is the best available, it is decidedly proclerical and anti-Flores.

63. Congressional decree of 13 April 1839, and law of 17 April 1839, *Primer rejistro* (1839), 527–528 and 533–536.

64. Bishop of Quito to governor of Pichincha, Quito, 20 June

1842, and related documents, in *Gaceta,* 26 June 1842; Tobar Donoso, *Iglesia,* 520–568; and Robalino Dávila, *García Moreno,* 250–272.

65. Minutes of the Senate, 15, 16, 19, and 27 February 1839, *Actas* (1839), I: 81–115; and Sáa to governor of Pichincha, Quito, 24 February 1840, in *Gaceta,* 1 March 1840.

66. Benigno Malo (minister of government) to the president of the permanent committee of the Senate, Quito, 18 September 1843, in *Gaceta,* 24 September 1843. King Charles III expelled the Jesuits from Spanish America in 1767.

67. Tobar Donoso, *Iglesia,* 421–445; *Gaceta,* issues of October and November 1842; and many of Rocafuerte's letters to Flores, especially those of 5 March and 8 May 1839, and 26 August 1840, in Rodríguez O., *Estudios,* 305–308 and 339–340.

68. On Irisarri, see: Ricardo Donoso, *Antonio José de Irisarri: Escritor y diplomático* (Santiago, Chile, 1934); Destruge, *Prensa,* I: 61–77; and Burr, *Reason,* 49–55. On Irisarri's political troubles in Guatemala, 1827–1829, see his own account in *La Balanza,* 19 September 1840.

69. Rocafuerte to Flores, Guayaquil, 9 November 1841, in Rodríguez O., *Estudios,* 348.

70. Destruge, *Prensa,* I: 67–71; Tobar Donoso, *Iglesia,* 424–430; *La Balanza,* 18 January 1840 and following issues; Rocafuerte to Flores, Guayaquil, 12, 18 February, 4 March, and 29 July 1840, in Rodríguez O., *Estudios,* 312–316, 319, 338.

71. *El Popular* and *El Sufragante* appeared in Quito, while Guayaquil witnessed the appearance of *La Opinión* and *El Público.* All were short-lived, founded primarily as opposition papers for electoral purposes; see *La Balanza,* 12, 19 October 1839. *La Opinión* is described in Destruge, *Prensa,* I: 54–56. *El Poder de los principios* (Quito) was a weekly; some issues may be found in the Biblioteca Ecuatoriana "Aurelio Espinosa Pólit." On the elections, see Rocafuerte to Flores, Guayaquil, 23 October 1839, in Rodríguez O., *Estudios,* 309–310.

72. Few soldiers could meet the literacy and property qualifications for voting imposed by the Constitution of 1835; *Constituciones,* 127.

73. Flores to Santander, Quito, 28 November 1839 and 21 January 1840, in Cortázar, *Correspondencia,* VI: 37–38; *La Balanza,* 16 November and 28 December 1839, and 15, 22 February, 13 June, and 25 July 1840; *Gaceta,* 22 February 1840, 1 January 1843, and following issues; and Robalino Dávila, *Rocafuerte,* 165. The articles in *El Popular* were cited in *La Balanza* and *Gaceta.*

74. *El Poder de los principios,* quoted in *La Balanza,* 23 November 1839 and 11 January 1840. Flores contributed some articles to the

subsidized *El Poder;* see his letter to Santander, 21 January 1840, in Cortázar, *Correspondencia,* VI: 38–39.

75. *La Balanza,* 8, 15 February and 14 March 1840.

76. On the political opposition, see Rocafuerte's letters to Flores from 15 April to 11 November 1840, in Rodríguez O., *Estudios,* 324–345; and Rocafuerte's address to the electoral assembly of Guayaquil, 1 November 1840, in *La Balanza,* 7 November 1840, suplemento.

77. Unofficial minutes of the Senate and the Chamber of Representatives, 23, 25, 26, and 27 January 1841, in *Gaceta,* 28 February and 14 March 1841; Ceballos, *Resumen,* V: 341–344. An interesting view of the government's methods of manipulating an election in 1842 is provided by a letter from General A. de la Guerra to President Flores, Cuenca, 26 October 1842, in AJC, "J. J. Flores Archivo," 1842.

78. Rocafuerte to Flores, Guayaquil, 9, 30 September and 11 November 1840, and 24 March 1841, in Rodríguez O., *Estudios,* 341–346.

79. Presidential decree, 12 September 1840 (convoking an extraordinary meeting of Congress), in *Gaceta,* 13 September 1840; Flores, "Manifiesto del Poder Ejecutivo del Ecuador a la Nación," 12 April 1841 (on film in the Saint Louis University file of the *Gaceta*); Rocafuerte to Flores, Guayaquil, 29 July 1840, Rodríguez O., *Estudios,* 338.

80. Unofficial minutes of the Senate and the Chamber of Representatives, 23, 25, 26 and 27 January 1841, in *Gaceta,* 28 February and 14 March 1841.

81. Ceballos gives the impression that only the lower chamber lacked a quorum; *Resumen,* V: 341–344.

82. Unofficial minutes of the Senate, 28, 29, 30 January and 1, 4, 5 February 1841, and of the Chamber of Representatives, 27, 28, 29 January and 2, 3 February 1841, in *Gaceta,* 14 March to 4 April 1841; Flores, "Manifiesto," 12 April 1841, in the Saint Louis University microfilm file of the *Gaceta.*

83. For example, see Dr. Contrachana (pseudonym), "Alcance al Alcance," printed in Guayaquil, in the *Gaceta* file of Saint Louis University, to be found just after the 5 March 1841 issue of the *Gaceta.* The *Gaceta* issues of 4 and 11 April 1841, citing *La Balanza* of 5 March 1841, quote from another flyer entitled "Oposición al Congreso del año de 1841."

84. Flores, "Manifiesto," 12 April 1841, Saint Louis University microfilm of the *Gaceta.*

85. Ibid.

86. *Gaceta,* 28 March 1841, especially the letter from Marcos to

Valdivieso, Quito, 24 March 1841; presidential decrees of 27 August and 21 October 1842, in *Gaceta,* 4 September and 30 October 1842; and Rocafuerte, *A la nación,* no. 2, *Colección,* XIV: 27–33, 60.

87. Presidential decrees of 27 August and 21 October 1842, in *Gaceta,* 4 September and 30 October 1842; and Rocafuerte, *A la nación,* no. 2, *Colección,* XIV: 27–33, 60.

87. Presidential decrees of 27 August and 21 October 1842, in *Gaceta,* 4 September and 30 October 1842.

88. Address to Congress, 31 January 1839, *Actas* (1839), I: ci–cii.

89. Flores' decision was made secretly late in 1841 and in 1842. A clear indication of his trend of thought is found in his letter to Lord Palmerston (British foreign secretary), Guayaquil, 31 December 1841, FO 25/7. For more on this subject see chap. 9 below.

7. THE FRUSTRATIONS OF FOREIGN AFFAIRS, 1839–1843

1. Flores, address to Congress, 31 January 1839, *Actas* (1839), I: 41. For background on the growing movement for Spanish American solidarity, see Burr, *Reason,* 61–64.

2. Minutes of the Senate, 1 April 1839, *Actas* (1839), I: 201.

3. Juan de Dios Cañedo (Mexican minister of foreign relations) to Francisco Marcos (Ecuadorian minister of foreign relations), Mexico City, 2 April 1840, and reply of Marcos, Quito, 25 July 1840, in *Gaceta,* 2 August 1840; news article entitled "Mégico," *Gaceta,* 25 December 1842. The latter article, reprinted from *El Liberal* of Mexico, warned of the looming conflict between the Spanish and Anglo-Saxon races. See also: Luis de Sáa (acting minister of foreign relations) to James C. Pickett (U.S. chargé d'affaires to the Peru–Bolivian confederation), Quito, 8 March 1839, in Manning, *Correspondence,* VI: 240–241. Pickett was on temporary assignment in Ecuador to negotiate a treaty of amity and commerce.

4. Cope to Palmerston, no. 12, Guayaquil, 31 July 1839, with enclosures of two letters from Rocafuerte to Cope, 15 and 29 August 1838, in FO 25/5; and Cope to Bidwell, unnumbered, Guayaquil, 22 August 1839, in FO 25/5.

5. Pickett to John Forsyth (U.S. secretary of state), no. 6, Quito, 27 March 1839, in Manning, *Correspondence,* VI: 244.

6. Becker, *Independencia,* 145–146, 372–389; Van Aken, *Pan-Hispanism,* 31, and 128, n. 9; *Gaceta,* 24 February 1839, 5 July and 29 November 1840 (which publishes the full text of the treaty of commerce and navigation that was signed on 2 June 1840), and 13 March

1842. Though the sum of the debt settlement was not publicized, Flores admitted that it posed financial problems for the government; see his address to the national convention, 15 January 1843, *Gaceta*, 15 January 1843.

7. Flores was active in promoting trade with Spain even before the treaty was signed. See his undated draft decree on Spanish shipping in the *Gaceta*, 24 February 1839. See also: minutes of the Senate, 18 and 25 February 1839, *Actas* (1839), I: 88, 107–108; decree of Congress, 27 March 1839, opening Ecuadorian ports to Spanish shipping, *Primer rejistro* (1839), 514; and the royal decree of 17 February 1840, opening Spanish ports to Ecuadorian vessels, *Gaceta*, 26 July 1840.

8. *Gaceta*, 22, 29 March, 10 May, 5 July, and 29 November 1840, and 30 May 1841.

9. Address to Congress, 15 January 1841, *Gaceta*, 24 January 1841.

10. This subject is treated in the next chapter.

11. Mendeville to French minister of foreign affairs, no. 44, Quito, 19 May 1843, and the Treaty of Amity, Commerce, and Navigation, 6 June 1843, in Archives du Ministère des Affaires Étrangères (Paris) (henceforth, AMAE, Paris), Correspondance Politique, Équateur, Vol. I. Ratifications were exchanged in Quito on 9 November 1844. For the Spanish version of the treaty and exchange of ratifications, see *Gaceta*, 24 November 1844.

12. The diplomatic correspondence in the Ecuadorian file of the British Foreign Office contains little information on the negotiations leading to this treaty, and the document itself is missing from the file. However, some information is to be found in the following: Cope to Palmerston, no. 12, Guayaquil, 3 July 1839, in FO 25/5; Office of the Committee of Privy Council for Trade (signature illegible) to Backhouse, Whitehall, 4 December 1839, in FO 25/5; Cope to Aberdeen, no. 7, Guayaquil, 5 January 1844, in FO 25/10; Richard Wright (Ecuadorian commissioner in England) to Lord Canning, Enechtheum Club, 10 October 1844, in FO 25/10; I. MacGregor to Canning, Whitehall, 28 November 1844, in FO 25/10; and Cope to Aberdeen, no. 17, Quito 30 July 1845, in FO 25/11.

13. The draft treaty, signed in Quito on 24 May 1841, was published in full by the *Gaceta*, 4 and 11 July 1841. See also the correspondence between Cope and Aberdeen, 1842–1844, in *State Papers*, XXXIII: 628–636; Flores to Col. Richard Wright, Quito, 12 October 1843, in FO 25/9; and Cope to Aberdeen, no. 17, Quito, 30 July 1845,

in FO 25/11. Ecuador also received consuls representing Norway, Sweden, and Denmark during Flores' second term; *Gaceta,* 4 July and 12 and 26 September 1841.

14. Palmerston to Cope, no. 3 (draft), Foreign Office, 8 May 1840, FO 25/6; Cope to Bidwell, no. 20, Guayaquil, 31 October 1843, in FO 25/9; Cope to Aberdeen, no. 10, Guayaquil, 26 February 1844, with enclosed correspondence between Cope and Malo, in FO 25/10.

15. Correspondence in Manning, *Correspondence,* VI: 240–249; minutes of the Senate, 1 April 1839, *Actas* (1839), I: 199–200; Flores, message to Congress, 20 January 1841, *Gaceta,* 14 February 1841; *Gaceta,* Suplemento, 20 April 1842 (on the exchange of ratifications, carried out without the approval of Congress); and William Spence Robertson, "The Recognition of the Hispanic American Nations by the United States," 1 *HAHR* (August 1918):239–269.

16. Restrepo Canal, *Nueva Granada,* I: 541–595; Robalino Dávila, *Rocafuerte,* 197–202; *La Balanza,* 5 October and 30 November 1839, and 18 April 1840; *Gaceta,* 1 July 1840; J. M. Restrepo, *Diario,* III: 167–172; and Gustavo Arboleda, *Historia contemporánea de Colombia,* 6 vols. (Bogotá, 1918–1935), I: 365–374, 387–399, and 406–410.

17. On this see Herrán's letters to General Tomás Cipriano Mosquera, 14 and 30 August, 6, 24 September, and 8 and 29 October 1839, in J. Leon Helguera and Robert H. Davis (eds.), *Archivo Epistolar del General Mosquera,* 2 vols. (Bogotá, 1972), *Biblioteca de historia nacional,* Vols. CXVI–CXVII, I: 314, 324, 329, 337, 350–351, and 369; J. M. Restrepo, *Diario,* III: 171; *Gaceta,* 2 and 9 February 1840; and *La Balanza,* 18 April 1840.

18. *Gaceta,* 12 July, 23, 30 August, 6 September, and 18 October 1840; correspondence between Herrán and Mosquera, 18 July to 23 October 1840, Helguera and Davis, *Archivo,* II: 53–117; and J. M. Restrepo, *Diario,* III: 172–191.

19. *Gaceta,* 12 July, 23, 30 August, 6 September, 18 October, and 1 November 1840; correspondence of Herrán and Mosquera, 18 July to 23 October 1840, Helguera and Davis, *Archivo,* II: 53–117.

20. The best treatment of this subject is in Robalino Dávila, *Rocafuerte,* 206–208, and Arboleda, *Historia,* II: 40–45 and 48–49. See also Mosquera's letter to Flores, Cuartel General en Chuilán (? microfilm copy is blurred), 12 September 1840, *Gaceta,* 15 August 1841 (which promises to seek the cession of the province of Pasto, or at least a large part of it, to Ecuador); *Gaceta,* 27 September 1840; and J. M. Restrepo, *Diario,* III: 322.

21. Executive decrees of 19 and 25 April 1841, *Gaceta,* 15 April 1841; pronunciamientos of Pasto and Túquerres, 4 and 6 May 1841;

executive decrees of 4 and 6 May 1841, *Gaceta*, 23 May 1841; Marcos to Rufino Cuervo (New Granadan chargé at Quito), Quito, 18 June 1841, *Gaceta*, 20 June 1841; and editorial articles signed "Unos Ecuatorianos," but probably written by Flores himself, entitled "Ecuador y Nueva Granada," *Gaceta*, 5 March 1843 (admits Flores' participation in drafting the pronunciamientos). See also Robalino Dávila, *Rocafuerte*, 205–208; and Ceballos, *Resumen*, V; 355–356.

22. Arboleda, *Historia*, II: 29–32, 40–45, 48–49; decree of the Congress of New Granada, 26 May 1841, *Gaceta*, 14 November 1841. Tension between Ecuador and New Granada in 1841 was so high that a diplomatic rupture nearly occurred and war appeared likely; see Robalino Dávila, *Rocafuerte*, 208–221; and J. M. Restrepo, *Diario*, III: 268–281.

23. Sáa (minister of interior), circular to four provincials (officials of religious orders), Quito, 30 July 1839, and Sáa to bishop of Quito, Quito, 12 August 1839, in *Gaceta*, 18 August 1839; *Gaceta*, 11 August 1839; Herrán's letters to Mosquera, 14, 30 August, 6, 24 September, 8 and 29 October 1839, Helguera and Davis, *Archivo*, I: 314–351, and 369; and J. M. Restrepo, *Diario*, III: 171.

24. Robalino Dávila, *Rocafuerte*, 232; Ceballos, *Resumen*, V: 375–378; and Pickett to Forsyth, nos. 5, 13, and 14, Lima, 4 January and 13 and 27 June 1840, Manning, *Correspondence*, X: 497 and 503–505.

25. Pickett to Forsyth, nos. 3, 5, and 6, Quito, 30 January, 27 February, and 27 March 1839, in Manning, *Correspondence*, VI: 239–240, 244; Edwin Bartlett (acting U.S. chargé in Peru) to Forsyth, nos. 48 and 53, Lima, 14 March and 19 May 1839, ibid., X: 479–480 and 482–485; Gamarra to José Espinar, Lima, 1 March 1839; and id. to Prefect Astete, Lima, 4 December 1840, in Agustín Gamarra, *Epistolario* (Lima, 1952), 325–326 and 380; *La Balanza*, 5 and 12 October 1839, and 14 February 1840; Basadre, *Historia*, I: 423–424; and Juan G. Valdivia, *Memoria sobre las revoluciones de Arequipa desde 1834 hasta 1866* (Lima, 1874), 223–240.

26. Rocafuerte, *A la nación*, no. 8, *Colección*, XIV: 121; Rocafuerte's letters to Flores, 18 February, and 15, 29 April 1840, in Rodríguez O., *Estudios*, 316, 326, 329. Rocafuerte, who was favorable to Santa Cruz at first, may have played a role in initiating the cooperation between Flores and the ex-Protector; see Donoso, *Irisarri*, 228–235.

27. Letters of Santa Cruz to Flores, 9 March and 2 April 1839, 29 September, and 21 October 1840, and 19 May 1841, in AJC, "Cartas a Flores," I: ff. 131–132, 147–149, 151–153, and 195–197.

28. Gamarra to José Espinar, Lima, 1 March 1839; Gamarra, *Epistolario*, 325–326.

29. Burr, *Reason*, 64–65.

30. Pedro Moncayo (Ecuadorian consul to Piura) to Marcos, Piura, 7 June 1841 and 22 January 1842, in *Gaceta*, 27 June 1841 and 13 February 1842; Rocafuerte to minister of interior, Guayaquil, 6 June 1841, in *Gaceta*, 13 June 1841; Robalino Dávila, *Rocafuerte*, 232–234; Valdivia, *Memorias*, 223–240; Burr, *Reason*, 64–66; and Alfonso Crespo Rodas, *Santa Cruz, el Cóndor Indio* (Mexico, 1944), 323–328. The Ecuadorian government denied its complicity in the activities of Santa Cruz; see the *Gaceta* for the years 1840 and 1842, esp. 30 May and 26 September 1841; and *La Verdad desnuda*, 11 May 1840.

31. Santa Cruz to Flores, Guayaquil, 19 May and 9 June 1841, in AJC, *Cartas a Flores*, I: ff. 197–203.

32. Diplomatic correspondence and memorandums in the *Gaceta*, 14 November, 21, 5 December 1841, and 23, 30 January, 13 February, 20 March, and 22 May 1842. The best historical treatment is in Robalino Dávila, *Rocafuerte*, 232–248. See also Arturo García Salazar, *Resumen de historia diplomática del Perú, 1820–1844* (Lima, 1928), 109–121.

33. See the correspondence between General Bernardo Daste (Ecuadorian minister plenipotentiary in Lima) and Agustín G. Charún (Peruvian minister of foreign relations), 29 March to 13 April 1842, and Daste's report to Marcos, 16 May 1842, published in the *Gaceta*, 22 May 1842. See also Robalino Dávila, *Rocafuerte*, 242–247.

34. "Reseña política" (1841), attributed to Luis José de Orbegoso (an associate of Santa Cruz and former president of Peru), in AJC, *Cartas a Flores*, II: ff. 669–674, which presents a plan for union of Ecuador, Peru, and Bolivia under Flores' leadership; Santa Cruz to Flores, Guayaquil, 9 May and 8 August 1841, in ibid., I: ff. 163–164, 195–197; Pickett to Forsyth, no. 20, Lima, 24 August 1840, in Manning, *Correspondence*, X: 506–508, reported rumors of monarchist leanings in Quito in 1840; and the dispatches of Luis de Potestad (Spanish chargé at Quito), 10 August 1842 and 1 February 1843, make it clear that Flores and Santa Cruz were plotting to establish monarchy in Ecuador, Peru, and Bolivia, in AMAE (Madrid), Correspondencia, Ecuador, Legajo 1458. See also the *Gaceta*, 5 and 26 July 1840; *La Balanza*, 8 August 1840; *El Peruano* (Lima), 7, 11, 18, 21, 28 August and 2 October 1841, and 22 January 1842; diplomatic correspondence in the *Gaceta*, 22 May 1841; and Robalino Dávila, *Rocafuerte*, 241–247.

35. Pickett to Forsyth, nos. 43, 51–55, 60, and 61, 21 June 1841 to 13 May 1842; and Pickett to Abel P. Upshur (U.S. secretary of state),

no. 90, Lima, 24 February 1844, in Manning, *Correspondence,* X: 514–521 and 528–529. See also Juan Pío Montúfar (acting Spanish chargé at Quito) to the Spanish minister of foreign affairs, no. 53, Quito, 25 December 1843, in AMAE (Madrid), Correspondencia, Ecuador, Legajo 1458; and Burr, *Reason,* 68–69.

36. Troubles over political opposition to war are clearly implied in Rocafuerte's reply to a letter from Flores: see Rocafuerte to Flores, Guayaquil, 18 March 1840, in Rodríguez O., *Estudios,* 321. See also an opposition flyer entitled "Calamidad pública," 23 September 1841, in the Saint Louis University file of the *Gaceta.*

37. The best information on antiwar sentiment in Guayaquil is to be found in the reports of the French consul in that city: Leonice Levrault to French minister of foreign affairs, nos. 2 and 3, Guayaquil, 12 and 14 December 1841, in AMAE (Paris), Correspondance Politique, Équateur, Vol. I.

38. Rocafuerte to Flores, Guayaquil, 18 March and 22, 29 April 1840, in Rodríguez O., *Estudios,* 320–321, 323, 329.

39. Levrault to French minister of foreign affairs, no. 3, 14 December 1841, in AMAE (Paris), Correspondance Politique, Équateur, Vol. I. Levrault's dispatch appears to be based on a conversation with Flores himself or with someone very close to Flores.

40. Levrault to French minister of foreign affairs, no. 1, Guayaquil, 18 June 1842, in AMAE (Paris), Correspondance Politique, Équateur, Vol. I.

8. REX EX MACHINA

1. Flores, address to the national convention, 15 January 1843, *Gaceta,* 15 January 1843. For similar presidential warnings of dangerous disorders, see Flores, manifesto of 22 October 1842, *Gaceta,* 30 October 1842.

2. Flores, address to the national convention, 15 January 1843, *Gaceta,* 15 January 1843.

3. Flores managed to keep the monarchical project a secret of state until after his ouster from the presidency in 1845. Not even Rocafuerte, who followed political developments in Ecuador very closely, knew of the monarchical scheme.

4. Chapter 1 above.

5. Bolívar to Flores, Barranquilla, 9 November 1830, in Flores, *Correspondencia,* 284–287. Flores kept this letter in his files. The president promoted the cult of the Liberator in Ecuador by ordering spe-

cial memorial services and by placing a portrait of Bolívar in the government palace; presidential decree, 29 September 1842, *Gaceta,* 9 October 1842.

6. On Flores' sensitivity to this issue, see his letters to Santander of 25 October 1836 and 21 January 1840, in Cortázar, *Correspondencia,* VI: 22 and 39. For newspaper coverage, see *La Balanza,* 11 January 1840, and 15 February, 13, 20 June, and 25 July 1840; and *Gaceta,* 2 October 1842, and 1 January and 1 October 1843. See also Robalino Dávila, *Rocafuerte,* 165. Rocafuerte, who at first refused to believe the charge against Flores, later exploited the issue to discredit his adversary; *A la nación,* nos. 8, 9, 10, *Colección,* XIV: 130–131, 132, 151, and 234. Andrade, *Historia,* VII: 254–255.

7. Osvaldo Hurtado, *Political Power in Ecuador* (Albuquerque, 1977), 128–148.

8. For an interesting treatment of the subject of legitimacy in Latin America, see Francisco José Moreno, *Legitimacy and Stability in Latin America: A Study of Chilean Political Culture* (New York and London, 1969), esp. 91–115.

9. Robalino Dávila, *Nacimiento,* 202. The inscription gave rise to cynical jokes that denigrated both the coinage and the government, which illustrated the seriousness of the problem of legitimacy in the new nation.

10. Flores, address to Ecuadorians, 20 April 1835, Salazar, "Introducción," *Actas* (1835), ccviii–ccviv; and Flores to Santander, Guayaquil, 13 October 1835, in Cortázar, *Correspondencia,* V: 476.

11. Flores, "Manifiesto" (1842), *Gaceta,* 30 October 1842; and Flores, address to the national convention, 15 January 1843, *Gaceta,* 15 January 1843.

12. See chapter 3 above; García del Río, "Autobiografía," in his *Meditaciones,* v–xx; Burr, *Reason,* 36. And see documents published in the *Gaceta,* 22 August 1841 (relating to García del Río's mission to Peru); and Stanhope Prevost (U.S. chargé in Peru) to James Buchanan (U.S. secretary of state), Lima, 1 February 1847, in Manning, *Correspondence,* X: 550–551 (which reveals that García del Río was very well informed on Flores' monarchical plans but had turned against the Ecuadorian leader and was informing Peru of Flores' intrigues in Europe).

13. "Prospecto de un nuevo periódico: La Concordia," *Gaceta,* 10 December 1843. On the directorship of the government press, see the *Gaceta,* 21 April 1844. While Irisarri served as the editor of the *Gaceta,* this newspaper became duller than usual, for it printed very little

news. Most government documents published in its pages were of little importance.

14. Collier, *Ideas,* 238. See also 142–146, 159–160, 191, and 251–252 of the same work for more on Irisarri's changing political views. On his difficulties in Central America with the liberals and Francisco Morazán, see Irisarri's own brief account in *La Balanza,* 30 May 1840, which reprinted an article from *El Amigo del pueblo* (Lima?); and a letter from Irisarri to Flores, Guayaquil, 15 March 1843, in AJC, "Cartas a Flores," IV: f. 879.

15. "Cartas sobre las revoluciones, carta tercera," *La Balanza,* 18 April 1840. Earlier Irisarri had expressed deep pessimism regarding the political conditions of Ecuador and Spanish America in *La Verdad desnuda;* see early issues of this periodical, including the "Prospecto," in the first number of 1 June 1839, and an article entitled "A los progresistas de América," 16 August 1839.

16. "Cartas sobre las revoluciones, carta cuarta," *La Balanza,* 27 June 1839.

17. *La Balanza,* 11 July 1840, which reprinted an article from a New York newspaper whose title was given as *El correo de los Estados Unidos,* which must have been the French-language newspaper *Courrière des Etats-Unis* (New York, 1828–1837). The name of the author of the article was not provided, but statements in the article indicate that he must have been French. In succeeding months Irisarri kept up his criticism of political conditions in Ecuador and Spanish America. He denounced the Congress of 1841 for its wrangling and declared that such congresses are the "germ of tyranny and oppression." He raised questions of the suitability of republican institutions and condemned what he regarded as the unfortunate imitation of the United States; see *La Balanza,* 30 January and 15 May 1841. Since Irisarri was publishing his paper in Quito at this time he probably had much personal contact with Flores and was in good position to influence the president's thinking.

18. Irisarri to Flores, Guayaquil, 12 July and 6 September 1843, in AJC, "Cartas a Flores," IV: ff. 939–942 and 969–971. On Irisarri's continuing labors to prepare public opinion for monarchy, see *La Concordia,* 1 January 1844.

19. Rocafuerte's letters to Flores from 1839 to 1842, in Rodríguez O., *Estudios,* 305–345.

20. Santa Cruz to Flores, aboard the Frigate Lamarang, Gulf of Guayaquil, 9 March 1839; Guayaquil, 2 April 1839; Quito, 29 September and 21 October 1840, in AJC, "Cartas a Flores," I: ff. 131–153. It

is ironic to note that Santa Cruz had attempted to prevent Flores' election to a second term in the presidency, and Flores knew it; Santa Cruz to Rocafuerte, La Paz, 2 July 1838; and id. to García del Río, La Paz, 2 July 1838, in AJC, "Cartas a Flores," I: ff. 107–108, 111–112.

21. Santa Cruz to Flores, Guayaquil, 9 June 1841, with enclosed letter from J. J. de Mora to Santa Cruz, London, 18 November 1840, in AJC, "Cartas a Flores," I: ff. 193–203.

22. Orbegoso, "Resenā política," AJC, "Cartas a Flores," II: ff. 669–674.

23. Halperín-Donghi, *Aftermath*, 115–118; chap. 2 above; and Flores, address to the national convention of 1843, *Gaceta*, 15 January 1843.

24. *La Balanza*, 15 May 1841.

25. Terry, *Travels*, 61–62, 184–286.

26. Cope to Backhouse, nos. 4 and 6, Guayaquil, 1 April and 28 May 1835, in FO 25/1.

27. Hassaurek, *Four Years*, 217–218. Flores' awareness of the incongruity of the social structure and the political institutions of Ecuador was implicit in his constitutional reforms, which moved in the direction of greater aristocratic control. On this point see Rocafuerte, *A la nación*, no. 6, *Colección*, XIV: 80–88, in which the ex-president accused Flores of foisting aristocratic rule on Ecuador, of corrupting the republican system, and of moving toward monarchy. Hassaurek's dispatches are of interest here, especially no. 10, Quito, 19 December 1861, and no. 78, Quito, 2 July 1863, National Archives, Washington, D.C. (NA), Dispatches, Ecuador, Microcopy T-50/5-6.

28. Halperín-Donghi, *Aftermath*, 114–115.

29. Rocafuerte to Flores, Quito, 16 March 1836, in Rodríguez O., *Estudios*, 249–250, in which he gives unreserved approval of the draconian measures of Diego Portales; and id. to id., Quito, 13 May 1836, ibid., 260–261. Later Rocafuerte declared, " . . . la prudencia dicta que establezcamos gobiernos muy enérgicos como el de los españoles, para conservar la paz y preparar las masas al uso racional de la Libertad . . ."; id. to id., Guayaquil, 26 February 1840, ibid., 317. The influence of the Chilean example in Spanish America was considerable; see Jorge M. Mayer, *Alberdi y su tiempo* (Buenos Aires, 1963), 417.

30. On the Mexican monarchical project, see Van Aken, *Pan-Hispanism*, 42–49. The *Gaceta* carried occasional articles on the developing crisis in Mexico, as did *La Balanza*.

31. William M. Blackford (U.S. chargé in New Granada) to Daniel Webster (U.S. secretary of state), no. 3, Bogotá, 20 October 1842, in Manning, *Correspondence*, V: 591–592. Monarchism continued to have

its adherents in Colombia for some time; see Arboleda, *Historia,* II: 153–157.

32. Blackford to Webster, no. 3, Bogotá, 20 October 1842, in Manning, *Correspondence,* V: 591–592; and Potestad to first secretary of state, no. 27, Quito, 1 February 1843, in AMAE (Madrid), Ecuador, Correspondencia, Legajo 1458. General Santa Anna had expressed pessimism about liberty and republican institutions earlier (in 1834) and had declared himself in favor of benevolent despotism as a means of bringing order to Mexico. His conversion to the notion of monocratic rule followed the same lines as those of Rocafuerte and Flores. See Callcott, *Santa Anna,* 108–109, and 113, citing Clarence R. Wharton, *El Presidente: A Sketch of the Life of General Santa Anna* (Houston, 1924), 64.

33. James Semple (U.S. chargé in New Granada) to Webster, no. 43, Bogotá, 27 January 1842, in Manning, *Correspondence,* V: 581–583. The Ecuadorian chargé in New Granada, Marcos Espinel, learned of the preliminary agreement according to Semple, and doubtless reported this important news to Quito.

34. Hassaurek to Seward, no. 10, Quito, 19 December 1861, in National Archives (hereinafter NA) Dispatches, Ecuador, Microcopy T-50/5.

35. *Gaceta,* 10 July 1842, reprinting an article from *L'Estafette.*

36. Halperín-Donghi notes that the midcentury reversion to conservatism was largely the result of Spanish-Americans' experience with "the discomforts of disorder and violence," rather than an intellectual response to the "counterrevolutionary authors in Europe." Halperín-Donghi, *Aftermath,* 113–114. Halperín-Donghi's generalization appears to be valid for Ecuador in the 1840s.

37. Leonice Levrault (French consul at Guayaquil) to the French minister of foreign affairs, no. 1, Guayaquil, 10 December 1841, in AMAE (Paris), Correspondance Politique, Équateur I (microcopy); Marcos, circular to governors, Quito, 29 November 1841, *Gaceta,* 5 December 1841, which stated that Flores had gone to Guayaquil on business of "vital importance to the Republic."

38. Flores to Palmerston, Guayaquil, 31 December 1841, FO 25/7, marked received 12 May 1842. This letter was carried to London by chargé Wilson. On Wilson's role in this affair, see Cope to Bidwell (private), Guayaquil, 3 November 1843, FO 25/9; and Cope to Palmerston, no. 14, Quito, 20 December 1847, FO 25/14.

39. Flores to Palmerston, Guayaquil, 31 December 1841, FO 25/7.

40. On the importance of the Galápagos as bait for the British, see: General Leonard Stagg (son-in-law of Flores) to Thomas D. Williams,

M.D. (extract), Quito, 20 August 1843; id. to id., Quito, 6 December 1843; and Williams to Aberdeen, Belgrave Square, 10 April 1844, FO 25/10. Stagg was a British naval officer who joined Bolívar's forces, later met Flores, and rose to military eminence in Ecuador. Flores' proposal was similar to the New Granadan preliminary agreement reported by Semple in January 1842 (see n. 33, this chap.).

41. Cope to Palmerston, no. 14, 20 December 1847, FO 25/14.

42. The British government subsequently declined involvement in a monarchical project in Mexico, where the economic stakes were much higher; Van Aken, *Pan-Hispanism,* 47–48. See also the British diplomatic correspondence for the years 1841 to 1845, FO 25/7–11— esp. Dr. Thomas Williams to Aberdeen, Belgrave Square, 10 April 1844, and I. MacGregor (of the board of trade) to Lord Canning, Whitehall, 28 November 1844, in FO 25/10.

43. *Gaceta,* 14 August 1842; and *El Peruano,* 1 October 1842.

44. *Gaceta,* 14 August 1842. The same issue printed the formal greetings brought by Potestad from Antonio González (Spanish first secretary of state) to Francisco Marcos, Madrid, 4 December 1841.

45. Potestad to Spanish first secretary of state, confidential dispatch no. 3 (in cipher), Quito, 16 August 1842, in AMAE (Madrid), Ecuador, Correspondencia, Legajo 1458. I have not been able to decipher every word of this dispatch, but the sense of the communication is clear.

46. Potestad to first secretary of state, no. 7 (in cipher), Quito, 9 September 1842, in AMAE (Madrid), Ecuador, Correspondencia, Legajo 1458.

47. Ibid.

48. The national convention of 1843 approved a presidential term of eight years, not ten; see the Constitution of 1843, article 57, *Constituciones,* 169.

49. Potestad to first secretary of state, no. 7, 9 September 1842, in AMAE (Madrid), Ecuador, Correspondencia, Legajo 1458.

50. Ibid. England and France, of course, had not offered to support his project. In fact, the French correspondence of this period does not show that the consul-general even knew of Flores' plans. Flores' suggestion of protecting the Philippines was a clever tactic, but ironic in the light of his earlier proposals to Bolívar of an expedition to liberate those Spanish-held islands. Flores admitted to Potestad his involvement in an earlier project to liberate the Philippines.

51. Antonio González, Instructions to Potestad, Madrid, 4 December 1841, in AMAE (Madrid), Ecuador, Correspondencia, Legajo 1458.

52. Potestad to first secretary of state, no. 7, 9 September 1842, in AMAE (Madrid), Ecuador, Correspondencia, Legajo 1458. Concerning Potestad's inexperience, see González to Marcos, Madrid, 4 December 1841, delivered to Marcos by Potestad on arrival in Quito, in *Gaceta*, 14 August 1842. The letter reveals that Potestad had had no previous foreign assignments.

53. Potestad to first secretary of state, nos. 17, 18, 26, and 28, Quito, 30 October 1842, and 16 January and 1 February 1843, in AMAE (Madrid), Ecuador, Correspondencia, Legajo 1458.

54. Potestad to first secretary of state, nos. 7 and 26, 9 September 1842 and 16 January 1843, in ibid.

55. Potestad to first secretary of state, nos. 7, 9, and 27, Quito, 9, 10 September 1842 and 1 February 1843; and Potestad to Hipólito de Hoyos (Oficial Mayor de la Primera Secretaría de Estado), Madrid, 1 February 1843, in ibid.

56. Unsigned document, no date, found between Juan José Flores' letter to the regent of Spain, 18 August 1843, and Montúfar's dispatch no. 56, 1 April 1844, in AMAE (Madrid), Política, Ecuador, Legajo 2348. The document appears to be a decoded dispatch or a decoded enclosure forwarded by Potestad on behalf of Flores. Since the contents of this document agree entirely with the ideas of Flores as reported by Potestad, it must be a formal proposal made by Flores to the Spanish government. Chances are that the proposal was forwarded between February and August 1843. Flores' letter to the regent indicated that "varias indicaciones" were being forwarded by Potestad. The last option included the use of the shipyard at Guayaquil by Spanish warships, for the protection of the Philippines.

57. Potestad to first secretary of state, no. 28 (in cipher), 1 February 1843, in AMAE (Madrid), Ecuador, Correspondencia, Legajo 1458.

58. Potestad reported in his dispatch no. 18, 30 October 1842, that Flores showed him a document approved by several Peruvians calling upon the Ecuadorian president to assume the leadership of a great project. In all probability Potestad referred to the Reseña Política presented to Flores by Luis Orbegoso, which was Santa Cruz's plan for restoring the confederation.

59. The idea of Tahuantinsuyu continued to fascinate people in Ecuador at this time; see Rocafuerte's reference to it in his address to congress, 15 January 1839, *Actas* (1839), I: lvi.

60. The story of Flores' unsuccessful efforts to interest the British in the Galápagos is a long one, and documentation abounds in the files of the Foreign Office from 1842 to 1845. Among the many

documents, see: Gen. Leonard Stagg to Thomas Williams, M.D., Quito, 3 May 1843, and id. to id., Quito, 6 December 1843, in FO 25/ 10; Herbert (whole name not legible) to Canning, Admiralty, 6 August 1844, in FO 25/10; Williams to Aberdeen, Belgrave Square, 23 September 1844, in FO 25/10; James Murray, Memorandum—Galapagos Islands, 9 December 1844, in FO 25/10, which gives a summary of the whole affair.

61. Some of the French diplomatic correspondence on this matter seems to be missing from the files, but the broad outline of Flores' efforts to interest the French is clear.

62. Levrault to minister of foreign affairs, nos. 11 and 12, 8 December and 13 December 1843, in AMAE (Paris), Correspondance Politique, Équateur, Vol. I.

63. Stagg to William Gordon, Quito, 28 May 1844, and Stagg to Dr. Williams, Quito, 10 November 1844, in FO 25/10. The star of the Legion of Honor was conferred upon Flores by Louis Philippe.

64. James Howard Harris, Earl of Malmesbury, *Memoirs of an Ex-Minister: An Autobiography*, 2 vols. (London, 1884), Vol. I, 157–160. Louis Napoleon claimed that the Ecuadorian agents wanted him to assume the "presidency," but this must have been a cover for monarchy.

65. Spain was eager to regain lost prestige in the New World. The Spanish seizure of the Chincha islands in 1864 provoked a very strong anti-Spanish reaction on the Pacific coast of the sort that leaders in Madrid must have feared in connection with the Flores project; Van Aken, *Pan-Hispanism*, 52–53, 111–114.

66. The Spanish diplomatic correspondence does not indicate the nature of the deliberations in Madrid and the reservations that may have delayed Spanish acceptance of Flores' proposals. However, there is an interesting, unsigned and undated document that lists: "Fuerzas Marítimas de las Repúblicas que tienen puertos en el Pacífico," including, of course, the Chilean naval units. This document is next to Flores' letter to the regent of Spain, of 18 August 1843, in AMAE (Madrid), Política, Ecuador, Legajo 2384.

67. The dispatch from the first secretary of state to Juan Pío Montúfar (acting Spanish chargé in Quito) of 11 April 1843 is not in the file in the AMAE. However, Montúfar's dispatch no. 46, Quito, 1 April 1844, AMAE (Madrid), Política, Ecuador, Legajo 2384, summarizes much of the content of the missing communication. Most of this dispatch is in cipher.

68. Montúfar to first secretary of state, no. 50, Quito, 27 December 1843, in AMAE (Madrid), Correspondencia, Ecuador, Legajo 1458.

Potestad left Guayaquil for Spain on 4 December 1843. By inference, it may be assumed that either he received instructions in November to return or he decided to do so on his own. At any rate, Flores knew that Potestad would make strong representations in favor of the project.

69. Montúfar to first secretary of state, no. 56, Quito, 1 April 1844, in AMAE (Madrid), Política, Ecuador, Legajo 2384. Why it took almost a year for the minister's dispatch of 11 April 1843 to reach Quito is unknown. Montúfar makes no mention of an unusually lengthy delay.

9. THE "CHARTER OF SLAVERY," 1843–1845

1. Flores, decree of 21 October 1842, *Gaceta,* 30 October 1842; Ceballos, *Resumen,* V: 399–401; Restrepo, *Diario,* III: 325.

2. Ceballos, *Resumen,* V: 400. The councilors were acquitted of the charge; see the letter from Roberto de Ascásubi (member of the municipal council) to the governor of Pichincha, Quito, 20 October 1842, and minutes of the council for the same date, in *El Nacional,* 15 June 1847. On muffled opposition, see Tamariz to Flores, Cuenca, 14 December and 21 December 1842, in AJC, Archivo, IV: unnumbered folios.

3. Rocafuerte, *A la nación,* no. 4, *Colección,* XIV: 51–52; Rocafuerte to Flores, Guayaquil, 5 October 1842, in Rodríguez O., *Estudios,* 354–355; and Flores, "Manifiesto del Poder Ejecutivo . . .," 22 October 1842, in *Gaceta,* 30 October 1842. The Supreme Court recommended a constituent convention in order to solve the constitutional problem; "Voto de la Corte Suprema," *Gaceta,* 30 October 1842. The Court pointed out that, if the Congress could not meet, it would be impossible to elect a new president at the expiration of the incumbent's term in January 1843. The Council of Government issued a similar opinion, *Gaceta,* 30 October 1842. On the more conservative constitutions in nearby nations, see: Alcides Arguedas, *Historia de Bolivia: Los caudillos letrados, la Confederación peru–boliviana, Ingavi; o la consolidación de la nacionalidad, 1828–1848* (Barcelona, 1928), 319–320; Leon Helguera, "The First Mosquera Administration in New Granada, 1845–1849," Ph. D. dissertation, University of North Carolina, 1958, 49–72.

4. Flores, decree establishing elections rules, 21 October 1842, *Gaceta,* 30 October 1842. Ceballos, *Resumen,* V: 402, calls the rules "retrograde" and claims that they set Ecuador back "forty years on the road to public rights."

5. Deputies were required to own property worth 8000 pesos or enjoy an income of at least 1000 pesos per year. This provision was

identical to the property requirements for senators under the Constitution of Ambato (1835).

6. Potestad to first secretary of state, no. 7, Quito, 9 September 1842, in AMAE (Madrid), Ecuador, Correspondencia, Legajo 1458.

7. Rocafuerte, *A la nación,* no. 2, *Colección,* XIV: 30–34; Ceballos, *Resumen,* V: 402–403; *Gaceta,* 27 November and 11 December 1842. Rocafuerte claimed that twenty-one of the thirty-six deputies were completely loyal to Flores. See also Cope to Aberdeen, no. 18, 28 October 1843, FO 25/9. Some of the private correspondence received by Flores from his political agents revealed that the elections were being managed; letters from Tamariz of 14 and 21 December 1842, and the notable letter from General A. de la Guerra, Cuenca, 26 October 1842, in AJC, Archivo, IV: unnumbered.

8. A complete list of all deputies, *principales* and *suplentes,* appeared in the *Gaceta,* 11 December 1842.

9. Potestad to first secretary of state, no. 7, Quito, 9 September 1842, in AMAE (Madrid), Ecuador, Correspondencia, Legajo 1458.

10. Tobar Donoso, *Iglesia,* 468–495; Constitution of 1843, *Constituciones,* 153–183, especially articles 3, 17, 25, 52, and 60. The national convention was more anticlerical than Flores was, but the president received the blame for the convention's actions nonetheless. An indication of Flores' somewhat moderate position is shown in Valdivieso's opposition to the more extreme proposals of Rocafuerte and his associates. Valdivieso worked closely with Flores, while Rocafuerte did not; Tobar Donoso, *Iglesia,* 468–474.

11. *Gaceta,* 18 December 1842 and 22 January 1843; and Rocafuerte to Flores, Guayaquil, 18 January 1843, in Rodríguez O., *Estudios,* 358–359.

12. Flores, message to the national convention, 15 January 1843, *Gaceta,* 15 January 1843.

13. Ibid.; and Madariaga, *Bolívar,* 519–527.

14. Flores, message, 15 January 1843.

15. Ibid.

16. See the letters from Gual to Flores from 21 September 1842 to 22 August 1843, in AJC, "Cartas a Flores," X: 613–678.

17. Potestad to first secretary of state, no. 7, Quito, 9 September 1842, in AMAE (Madrid), Ecuador, Correspondencia, Legajo 1458; Gual to Flores, Bogotá, 23 November and 7 December 1842, in AJC, "Cartas a Flores," X: 613–623; Un Ecuatoriano (pseud.), *La libertad refugiada* (Piura, 1843); *Gaceta,* 26 February 1843; and Robalino Dávila, *Rocafuerte,* 184.

18. Potestad to first secretary of state, no. 26, Quito, 16 January 1843, in AMAE (Madrid), Correspondencia, Ecuador, Legajo 1458.

19. Article 2 of the Constitution of 1843, *Constituciones,* 153. This antimonarchical article was a rewording of a similar statement in the Constitution of 1835, ibid., 126. The inclusion of the antimonarchical clause in the draft constitution of 1843 indicates that very few delegates, if any, were apprised of Flores' monarchical plan.

20. "A la nación," *Gaceta,* 30 April 1843. This article, of anonymous authorship, must have been written by Flores, for it contains information that only Flores possessed. Rocafuerte maintained that Flores offered him the post of vice-president, and he refused it; see Rocafuerte, *A la nación,* no. 1, *Colección,* XIV: 13–18.

21. Rocafuerte, *A la nación,* nos. 3 and 4, *Colección,* IV: 40–41, 53–57, 67–68; and Flores or anonymous, "A la nación." On the Church, see Robalino Dávila, *Rocafuerte,* 186–187; and Donoso, *Iglesia,* 467–470.

22. For Rocafuerte's accusations, see his *A la nación,* no. 6, *Colección,* XIV: 83–86, 87–88, 92–96.

23. Constitution of 1843, *Constituciones,* 155–157; Robalino Dávila, *Rocafuerte,* 192. The requirement of 3000 pesos in property appears to have been more aristocratic, but the election of senators was direct rather than indirect.

24. Constitution of 1843, Títulos VII–XI, *Constituciones,* 156–168.

25. Ibid., 171.

26. Ibid., Título XII, 168–171.

27. Ibid., 159, 173–174.

28. Ibid., articles 61, 62, and 63, 171–172.

29. Ibid., Título XVII, 177–180.

30. Rocafuerte, *A la nación,* no. 4, *Colección,* XIV; 54–55. For a different version of the altercation with General Guerra, see Rocafuerte, *Colección,* XIV: vii, n. 1.

31. Rocafuerte, "Protesta" of 25 March 1843, published by the Imprenta de la Viuda de Vivero por J. F. Puga, and reprinted in the *Gaceta* of 30 April 1843. The convention refused to publish the speech in its minutes, and the *Gaceta* delayed publication for more than a month, until the government was ready to print a reply to the harsh charges of Rocafuerte.

32. Ibid.

33. A la nación, no. 4, *Colección,* XIV: 55–56.

34. On Rocafuerte's efforts to revolutionize Guayaquil and his voluntary departure to Peru, see Levrault to French minister of foreign

affairs, nos. 7, 8, and 10, Guayaquil, 26 April, 4 May, and 21 May 1843, in AMAE (Paris), Équateur, Correspondance Politique, Vol. I.

35. *Genízaro* is ordinarily translated as "janizary" or "janissary," but in Mexico, where Rocafuerte had lived, it also meant "half-breed." Racial slurs abounded in Rocafuerte's denunciations of Flores and others.

36. For the term "carta de esclavitud," see *A la nación,* no. 3, *Colección,* XIV: 43. Rocafuerte appears to have invented the term.

37. Flores, "A la nación."

38. Rocafuerte, *A la nación,* no. 6, *Colección,* XIV: 83–88 and 127.

39. *Gaceta,* 16 April 1843.

40. Ibid.; and Constitution of 1843, articles 6 and 36, *Constituciones,* 154, 161.

41. A. Farfán to Flores, Cuenca, 26 April 1843, in AJC, Archivo Flores, Vol. I; Tobar Donoso, *Iglesia,* 468–478; *Gaceta,* 16 April and 14 May 1843. The government was deeply concerned about Solano's criticism of the constitution in his newspaper *La Luz; Gaceta,* 14 May 1843.

42. Flores, decree of 15 May 1843, *Gaceta,* 21 May 1843; correspondence between the bishop of Quito and Ministro-General Hipólito Soulín, 10 to 12 June 1843, in *Gaceta,* 12 July 1843; and Tobar Donoso, *Iglesia,* 483–488. In Guayaquil many leading citizens as well as priests refused to swear allegiance; Cope to British foreign secretary, no. 18, Guayaquil, 28 October 1843, FO 25/9.

43. Ceballos, *Resumen,* V: 412–413; Tobar Donoso, *Iglesia,* 502–503; Flores, decree of 23 June 1843, *Gaceta,* 9 July 1843. Malo would later turn against Flores; see Benigno Malo's *Flores juzgado por su ministro de gobierno y relaciones exteriores* (Lima, 18—).

44. Tobar Donoso, *Iglesia,* 506–518; Wilfrido Loor, *Los Jesuitas en el Ecuador* (Quito, 1959), 38; Malo (minister of government) to the president of the Permanent Commission of the Senate, Quito, 18 September 1843, in *Gaceta,* 24 September 1843.

45. *Gaceta,* 28, May, 2 July, and 1, 8, 15 October 1843; Ceballos, *Resumen,* V: 416–417. The new press law was mildly restrictive, but it made provision for jury trials of persons accused of violating this law. Indians were exempted from military service.

46. Law of 19 June 1843, *Gaceta,* 3 September 1843; Flores to Col. Richard Wright (Ecuadorian consul-general in England), Quito, 12 October 1843, FO 25/9.

47. Payment of government salaries fell eight to ten months in arrears in Loja, and the government had to close the Colegio de Niñas in Quito; *Gaceta,* 7 January and 4 May 1844; and Cope to Aberdeen, no. 10, Guayaquil, 26 February 1844, FO 25/10.

48. See chap. 3 above.

49. Flores, address to the national convention, 15 January 1843.

50. Ibid.

51. Robalino Dávila, *Rocafuerte,* 178–179, 249–250, 257; Lei de impuestos, 5 June 1843, *Gaceta,* 20 August 1843; and decree of 5 June 1843 (the new tariff law), *Gaceta,* 2 July 1843.

52. Lei de impuestos, 5 June 1843.

53. Flores, decree of 24 June 1843, *Gaceta,* 20 August 1843.

54. "Tumultos populares," *Gaceta extraordinaria,* 2 September 1843; Levrault to minister of foreign affairs, no. 3, Quito, 4 September 1843, in AMAE (Paris), Correspondance Politique, Équateur, Vol. I; and Robalino Dávila, *Rocafuerte,* 257–259.

55. Best contemporary accounts of the riots and rebellions are two articles that appeared in the *Gaceta:* "Tumultos populares," 2 September 1843, and "Fin de los tumultos populares," 24 September 1843. See also: documents published in the *Gaceta,* 2, 3, and 24 September 1843; Restrepo, *Diario,* III: 356–357, 390; and Ceballos, *Resumen,* V: 419–427.

56. Levrault to minister of foreign affairs, no. 3, 4 September 1843, in AMAE (Paris), Correspondance Politique, Équateur, Vol. I; documents in the *Gaceta extraordinaria,* 2 September 1843; *Gaceta,* 24 September 1843; and Flores, decree of 23 August 1843 (suspending the general contribution), in *Gaceta,* 3 September 1843.

57. Levrault to minister of foreign affairs, nos. 20 and 27, 23 and 29 October 1843, in AMAE (Paris), Correspondance Politique, Équateur, Vol. I; and Ceballos, *Resumen,* V: 427–430.

58. "Tumultos populares," *Gaceta extraordinaria,* 2 September 1843; and Levrault to minister of foreign affairs, no. 3, Quito, 4 September 1843, in AMAE (Paris), Correspondance Politique, Équateur, Vol. I.

59. Levrault to minister of foreign affairs, no. 5, Quito, 6 October 1843, in AMAE (Paris), Correspondance politique, Équateur, Vol. I. Levrault's dispatches are especially interesting because he was partial to the Flores regime and gained much of his information from Ecuadorian authorities, yet he also kept abreast of current comments and popular opinion in Quito.

60. Levrault to minister of foreign affairs, no. 4, Quito, 20 September 1843, in AMAE (Paris), Correspondance Politique, Équateur, Vol. I.

61. Id. to id., no. 5, Quito, 6 October 1843, in ibid. For more on opposition to the Flores administration, see Moncayo, *Ecuador,* 167–169 and 171–172.

62. Cope to Aberdeen, no. 18, Guayaquil, 28 October 1843, FO 25/9.

63. Ibid.

64. *La Balanza,* 6 June 1840.

65. For the complete text of the law, see the *Gaceta,* 2 July 1843.

66. Ceballos, *Resumen,* V: 431; Cope to Aberdeen, no. 18, Guayaquil, 28 October 1843, in FO 25/9; "Segunda representación al Supremo Poder Ejecutivo," enclosure with Cope's dispatch no. 18; Levrault to minister of foreign affairs, no. 7, Quito, 29 October 1843, in AMAE (Paris), Correspondance Politique, Équateur, Vol. I; and "Ecuador," *El Peruano* (Lima), 20 December 1843.

67. Consejo de Gobierno, Actas, 23 October 1843, *Gaceta,* 11 February 1844; and *Gaceta extraordinaria,* 13 November 1843.

68. Levrault to minister of foreign affairs, nos. 22, 23, and 10, 5, 18 November and 7 December 1843, in AMAE (Paris), Correspondance Politique, Équateur, Vol. I; "Ecuador," *El Peruano,* 20 December 1843; and Flores to the president of the Permanent Commission of the Senate, Quito, 22 December 1843, in *Gaceta,* 24 December 1843.

69. Levrault to minister of foreign affairs, no. 14, Quito, 19 January 1844, in AMAE (Paris), Correspondance Politique, Équateur, Vol. I.

70. León Iturburu (acting French consul?) to minister of foreign affairs, no. 1, Guayaquil, 29 February 1844, in AMAE (Paris), Correspondance Politique Équateur, Vol. I; *Gaceta,* 17 March 1844 (concerning official complaints about the publication in New Granada of material written by Rocafuerte); and *Gaceta,* 28 July 1844 (concerning charges of graft against Flores).

71. Iturburu to minister of foreign affairs, no. 1, 29 February 1844, in AMAE (Paris), Correspondance Politique, Équateur, Vol. I; *Gaceta,* 24 December 1843; and Restrepo, *Diario,* III, 401–402.

72. Levrault to minister of foreign affairs, no. 16, Quito, 4 February 1844, in AMAE (Paris), Correspondance Politique, Équateur, Vol. I.

73. Montúfar to first secretary of state, no. 53, Quito, 25 December 1843, in AMAE (Madrid), Correspondencia, Ecuador, Legajo 1458; Cope to Aberdeen, no. 21, Guayaquil, 3 November 1843, in FO 25/9; and *Gaceta,* 12 and 19 March 1843. On Vivanco's monarchist views, see Vargas Ugarte, *Historia,* VIII: 285–286.

74. Basadre, *Historia,* Vol. I, 423–427; Crespo Rodas, *Santa Cruz,* 330–338 (but there is no mention of Santa Cruz's involvement with Flores in this account); Burr, *Reason,* 68–69; *El Peruano,* 20, 30 Sep-

tember and 16, 27 October 1843, and 6, 31 January and 10 February 1844 (fairly complete coverage of this topic, including some diplomatic correspondence); Montúfar to first minister of state, no. 53, 25 December 1843, in AMAE (Madrid), Ecuador, Correspondencia, Legajo 1458; Pickett to Abel P. Upshur (U.S. secretary of state), no. 90, Lima, 24 February 1844, in Manning, *Correspondence,* X: 528–529; Cope to Aberdeen, no. 21, Guayaquil, 3 November 1843, in FO 25/9; and Restrepo, *Diario,* III: 365–378.

75. Flores made several unsuccessful attempts to persuade the Chileans to release their captive; Crespo Rodas, *Santa Cruz,* 332–333.

76. First secretary of state to Montúfar, Madrid, 1 December 1844, in AMAE (Madrid), Ecuador, Correspondencia, Legajo 1458.

77. As late as the 1860s Spain encountered great hostility in Spanish America. On this, see: Van Aken, *Pan-Hispanism,* 107–114; and William Columbus Davis, *The Last Conquistadores: The Spanish Intervention in Peru and Chile, 1863–1866* (Athens, Ga., 1950).

78. Spanish American opposition to Flores' projected expedition of 1846 provided a strong indication of the vigorous hostility that was likely in 1845. On this point, see the next chapter.

79. "Prospecto de un nuevo periódico: La Concordia," *Gaceta,* 21 April 1844; and Donoso, *Irisarri,* 236–239.

80. For a denunciation of Irisarri by Guayaquil rebels, see point number twelve in their "Pronunciamiento popular de Guayaquil," 7 March 1845, Martínez-Delgado, *Traiciones,* I: 189–190. On Irisarri's unpopularity in Ecuador, see Donoso, *Irisarri,* 239.

81. "Orden público," *Gaceta,* 2 February 1845.

82. *Gaceta,* 27 April 1845. For Rocafuerte's denunciations of Roca as a contrabandist and inveterate enemy of Flores, see Rocafuerte's letters to Flores for the period 8 May 1839 to 26 August 1840, in Rodríguez O., *Estudios,* 307–341.

83. *Gaceta,* 27 April 1845.

84. Ceballos, *Resumen,* V: 437–471; Robalino Dávila, *Rocafuerte,* 265–272; *Gaceta,* 9 March, 27 April, and 4, 18 May 1845; and Restrepo, *Diario,* III: 412–413, 417–419. On Rocafuerte's continuing presidential aspirations, see Delazon Smith (U.S. special agent) to John C. Calhoun (U.S. secretary of state), Quito, 10 August 1845, in Manning, *Correspondence,* VI: 251.

85. The fighting resulted in at least eight hundred casualties, not including those who died of disease. The total number of troops engaged probably did not exceed three or four thousand. General Otamendi was gravely wounded and later was executed by the victorious rebel forces. Yellow fever killed large numbers of highland

troops. See Richard Wright to John Bidwell, Southampton, 6 September 1845, in FO 25/11.

86. The term "Treaties of La Virginia" came from the name of the hacienda on which the agreements were negotiated. *Convenios* of 17 and 18 June 1845, Martínez-Delgado, *Traiciones a la independencia hispanoamericana*, 2 vols. (Bogotá, 1974–1975), I: 205–207, also reprinted in *Libertad y orden* (Quito), 20 July 1845; Moncayo, *Ecuador*, 185–188; Cope to Aberdeen, no. 16, Quito, 8 July 1845, FO 25/11; and Montúfar to first secretary of state, no. 116, Quito, 14 July 1845, in AMAE (Madrid), Ecuador, Correspondencia, Legajo 1458. Ceballos, *Resumen*, V: 471–472, refers to the convenios as *tratados*, as did the national convention of Cuenca in 1845.

87. Restrepo, *Diario*, III: 436 (entry of 15 September 1845); Cope to Aberdeen, no. 26, Guayaquil, 25 November 1845, in FO 25/11; and id. to id., no. 13, Cuenca, 16 February 1846, FO 25/12.

88. Luis Robalino Dávila, *La reacción anti-floreana* (Puebla, 1967), 40; and Cope to Aberdeen, no. 26, Guayaquil, 25 November 1845, in FO 25/12.

89. Report of the Comisión de Seguridad Pública, 28 October 1845, *El Seis de marzo* (Guayaquil), 7 November 1845—enclosed with Cope's dispatch no. 26, 25 November 1845, in FO 25/12; Pedro José Cevallos Salvador, *El Doctor Pedro Moncayo y su folleto titulado "El Ecuador de 1825 a 1875 . . ."* (Quito, 1887), 33–34; and Robalino Dávila, *Reacción*, 16–25, and 30–42.

90. Montúfar to first secretary of state, no. 117, Quito, 14 July 1845, in AMAE (Madrid), Ecuador, Correspondencia, Legajo 1458. Flores' letter is not extant, but is referred to by Montúfar.

10. THE SPANISH PROJECT, 1845–1847

1. Montúfar to first secretary of state, no. 116, Quito, 14 July 1845, in AMAE, Ecuador, Correspondencia, Legajo 1458.

2. Cope to Aberdeen, no. 16, Quito, 8 July 1845, in FO 25/11.

3. Delazon Smith (U.S. special agent) to John C. Calhoun (secretary of state), Quito, 10 August 1845, in Manning, *Correspondence*, VI: 253 and 255.

4. Ibid.; Cope to Aberdeen, no. 26, Guayaquil, 25 November 1845, in FO 25/11; Andrade, *Historia*, VII: 2722–2723; Robalino Dávila, *Reacción*, 14–15.

5. Constitution of 1845, *Constituciones*, 185–219; Cope to Aberdeen, no. 13, Cuenca, 16 February 1846, in FO 25/12 (provides an

interesting commentary on the constitution); and Robalino Dávila, *Reacción*, 54–55.

6. *Constituciones*, 201.

7. Robalino Dávila, *Reacción*, 175–204; Le Gouhir y Rodas, *Historia*, I: 437–460; and Moncayo, *Ecuador*, 188–193, 198–199, and 203–214.

8. Le Gouhir y Rodas, *Historia*, I: 411–413; and Robalino Dávila, *Reacción*, 50, 56–60.

9. Article 63, Constitution of 1845, *Constituciones*, 201; Cope to Aberdeen, no. 26, Guayaquil, 25 November 1845, and no. 13, Cuenca, 16 February 1846, in FO 25/11–12.

10. In a desperate move to save his government, Flores sent General Leonard Stagg to Lima with "thirty thousand dollars [pesos], besides a large quantity of Jewellery [sic], diamonds, etc., etc.," according to an American diplomat, to attempt to purchase a ship or ships, with which to blockade Guayaquil. Though Stagg was captured by the rebels and relieved of his money, probably not all of the cash was returned to the treasury. See Delazon Smith to Calhoun, Quito, 10 August 1845, in Manning, *Correspondence*, VI: 252; Cope to Aberdeen, no. 26, Guayaquil, 25 November 1845, and no. 5, Cuenca, 3 January 1846, in FO 25/11–12; and extract of a letter from General Stagg to Dr. Williams, enclosed with letter from Williams to Aberdeen, Belgrave Square, 8 August 1845, in FO 25/11.

11. Restrepo, *Diario*, III: 436; and Cope to Aberdeen, no. 26, Guayaquil, 25 November 1845, FO 25/11, which deals with the adverse effects of the persecution of floreanos. On government finance and the economy see also: decree of 3 February 1846, *El Nacional*, 11 May 1846 (on suspension of salaries of floreano officers); Manuel Bustamante (minister of finance), circular to governors, Quito, 9 and 15 March 1847, in *El Nacional*, 12 and 19 March 1847 (on a forced loan); *El Nacional*, 23 February, 12 March, and 30 July 1847, and 6 February 1848; Vicente Ramón Roca (president), message to Congress, 15 September 1847, in *El Nacional*, 24 September 1847; and decree of 30 November 1847 (ordering advanced collection of tribute), in *El Nacional*, 7 January 1848.

12. Diplomatic correspondence in *El Nacional*, 23 March, 27 April, and 8 June 1846; Andrade, *Historia*, VII: 2728–2730; Robalino Dávila, *Reacción*, 42–47; and Arboleda, *Historia contemporánea*, II: 220–223.

13. Juan José Flores, *El General Flores á los ecuatorianos* (Bayona, 1847), 9–12 (hereinafter cited as Flores, *Ecuatorianos*); Jacinto Jijón y

Caamaño, *La expedición floreana de 1846* (Quito, 1943), 3–5; and Richard Wright to John Bidwell, on board the steamer *Trent,* Southampton, 6 September 1845, in FO 24/11. Wright presents a glowing account of Flores and his policies as president of Ecuador. His purpose was to give Flores entrée in government circles. A few months later Wright published a brief biographical essay on Flores intended to give the expatriate a good reputation in England; see his *Memoir of His Excellency General Flores, Late President of Ecuador* . . . (n.p., 1845).

14. Flores, *Eucatorianos,* 9–12.

15. Flores, *Ecuatorianos,* 9–11; Jijón y Caamaño, *Expedición,* 5–6; Ralph W. Haskins, "Juan José Flores and the Proposed Expedition against Ecuador, 1845–1847," *HAHR* 27 (August 1947): 469–470; Moncayo, *Ecuador,* 193–194; and Diego Barros Arana, *Un decenio de la historia de Chile, 1841–1851,* 2 vols. (Santiago, 1905–1906), I: 182–193.

16. Flores, *Ecuatorianos,* 10–12; Jijón y Caamaño, *Expedición,* 6.

17. Van Aken, *Pan-Hispanism,* 1–49; Jaime Delgado, *España y Méjico en el siglo XIX,* 3 vols. (Madrid, 1950–1953), vol. II; and Colonel Senén de Buenaga y Gazmury, "Documentos reservados sobre la expedición al Ecuador," an unpublished manuscript by Flores' second-in-command, in the private library of Sergio Fernández Larraín of Santiago, Chile (hereinafter cited as Buenaga, "Documentos").

18. "Convención sobre Santa Cruz," *El Peruano,* 31 January 1846; Monguió, *Mora,* 309–310; and Crespo Rodas, *Cóndor,* 334–337.

19. Santa Cruz, probably out of fear of the possible confiscation of his properties in Bolivia, maintained a low profile in the Flores project, but Luis Monguió has demonstrated that Santa Cruz did indeed work with Flores, chiefly through his agent Mora; see Monguió, *Mora,* 310–313; and *El Heraldo* (Madrid), 28 August 1846.

20. Monguió, *Mora,* 310–313; and Flores to Lord Palmerston, Madrid, 6 September 1846, in Martínez-Delgado, *Traiciones,* I: 350–351.

21. This long-standing question can be laid to rest on the basis of information in: Buenaga, "Documentos"; "Dictamen de la Comisión Parliamentaria de las Cortes Españolas, de 1854, sobre los actos de donā María Cristina," cited in Destruge, *Expedición,* 52–53; and the revelations of General Baldomero Espartero, Duque de la Victoria and president of the Spanish Council of Ministers in 1841, published by the *Gaceta oficial* of New Granada and cited in Robalino Dávila, *Reacción,* 145–147. For partisan denials of monarchist intent see: Flores, *Ecuatorianos,* 14–16; Antonio Flores Jijón, *El asesinato del Gran Mariscal de Ayacucho y el discurso de monseñor González Suárez* (Paris, 1900); and Jijón y Caamaño, *Expedición,* 12–17. For an interesting discussion of the monarchist issue in 1847, see Restrepo, *Diario,* III: 490, 495–496.

22. Buenaga, "Documentos." See also: Restrepo, *Diario,* III: 483–511; Moncayo, *Ecuador,* 193–196; Carlos Veyret (Ecuadorian consul-general in Paris) to Manuel Gómez de la Torre (minister of foreign relations), Paris, 14 December 1846, in *El Nacional,* 8 February 1847; Francisco Michelena y Rojas (Ecuadorian diplomatic agent in London) to unnamed minister (Gómez de la Torre?), London, 15 November 1846, in *El Nacional,* 29 January 1847; and Haskins, "Flores," 472–473.

23. One report said that Flores ought to reunite all of Gran Colombia under a single prince; letter of a Mr. Rose (not otherwise identified) to Lord Palmerston, Paris, 8 October 1846, in FO 97/156.

24. *El Tiempo* (Madrid), 1, 2, and 3 July 1846, reprinted in Angel Francisco Brice (ed.), *La proyectada expedición de Flores al Ecuador: polémica periodística y parlamentaria (1846–1847)* (Maracaibo, 1964), 57–73.

25. *El Tiempo,* 13–19 August 1846; and Brice, *Proyectada,* 81–122.

26. Buenaga, "Documentos"; corroborated in great part by the deposition of Lt. Saturnino M. de Bustamante (an officer in the expedition), made in London, 3 May 1847, in *El Nacional,* 4 May 1847. This letter asserts that thirty million pesos were committed by Spain to the expedition, while Buenaga says that Flores had a budget of only 1,178,579 reales.

27. Buenaga, "Documentos"; Bustamante, deposition, *El Nacional,* 4 May 1847. The best secondary account of Flores' preparations in Spain and the British Isles is that of Haskins, "Flores," 473–478.

28. M. M. Mosquera (New Granadan chargé in London) to Lord Palmerston, Hakes Hotel (London), 16 October 1846, in *El Nacional,* 18 January 1847.

29. Monguió, *Mora,* 311–313 (based on correspondence in the Foreign Office).

30. Colonel Wright to secretary of the Board of Ordnance, 68 Haymarket (London), 8 September 1846, in FO 97/156; and G. Butler to H. U. Addington, Office of Ordnance, 23 September 1846, FO 97/156. Wright's letter referred to Flores as "the President of Ecuador." Written on the cover of Butler's letter are the following words: "Shall this be done? No. Genl. Flores is not President and these guns are wanted for a hostile Expedition agst the existing Govt of that State. Octr. 5/46."

31. W. Barington Pemberton, *Lord Palmerston* (London, 1954), 126–157; Goldwin Smith, *A History of England* (New York, 1957), 605–609, 613–615.

32. Captain J. J. Anslow to Rear Admiral George Seymour, H.M.S.

Daphne off Chatham Island of the Galápagos, 11 March 1845, and id. to id., H.M.S. *Daphne,* off Valparaíso (Chile), 19 April 1845 (draft), FO 25/11; Canning to General Stagg, Foreign Office, 6 May 1845 (draft), in FO 25/11; Williams to Aberdeen, 14 St. James Square (London), 10 December 1845, in FO 25/11 (cites letter from Stagg dated 10 October 1845 on the Galápagos question); Cope to Palmerston, nos. 3 and 14, Quito, 3 December 1846 and 20 December 1847, in FO 97/156 and 25/14.

33. On Palmerston's pretended ignorance of the Flores expedition, see M. M. Mosquera to Lord Palmerston, Hakes Hotel (London), 16 October 1846, in *El Nacional,* 14 January 1847. See also: Buenaga, "Documentos."

34. Buenaga, "Documentos"; and Bustamante, deposition, *El Nacional,* 4 May 1847.

35. Buenaga, "Documentos."

36. Ibid.

37. Ibid. Buenaga reported that some newspapers offered their support and others promised neutrality in the matter if the government would pay them for a certain number of subscriptions.

38. For a good discussion of the role of the press in destroying the Flores expedition, see Pedro Grases, "Historia bibliográfica del tema," in Brice, *Expedición,* 45–53.

39. *El Tiempo,* 13–19 August 1846 (reproduced in Brice, *Expedición,* 81–122).

40. *El Eco del comercio* (Madrid), 19 August 1846 (reproduced in Brice, *Expedición,* 141–142).

41. Ibid.

42. *El Heraldo,* 25 August, 3 September, and 13 October 1846; and Monguió, *Mora,* 313–319, on Mora's role and *El Heraldo.*

43. *Diario de las Cortes* (Diputados), 26 September 1846.

44. Ibid. (Senado), 28 September 1846.

45. Ibid. (Diputados), 26 September 1846, and ibid. (Senado), 28 September 1846.

46. Ibid. (Senado), 19 January 1847, and ibid. (Diputados), 6, 18 February and 3 March 1847. The formal announcement of the dissolution of the Flores project appeared in a royal decree of 6 February 1846, *Colección legislativa de España (continuación de la colección de decretos,* XL: 191–192.

47. Montúfar to first secretary of state, no. 143, Quito, 10 March 1846, in AMAE (Madrid), Ecuador, Correspondencia, Legajo 1458 (incorrectly identifies the new consul-general as "José de la Riva"); *El Heraldo,* 16 July 1846. De las Rivas was a Spaniard and held the posi-

tion of director of the Banco de Fomento in Madrid. Ecuadorian agents were also appointed in London and Paris.

48. Destruge, *Expedición*, 8–11.

49. Remarks of General Serrano and of Florencio García Goyena, *Diario de las Cortes* (Senado), 28 September 1846 and 19 January 1847.

50. As early as 15 February 1846, well before receipt in Quito of news of the Flores project, the Ecuadorian foreign minister had protested to the foreign secretary about Colonel Wright's activities in the British Isles; see Gómez de la Torre to Palmerston, Quito, 17 December 1846, in *El Nacional*, 18 January 1847, which summarizes the earlier note of 25 February 1846 and registers a new complaint. For other protests see: Manuel Moreno (Argentine minister in London) to Palmerston, London, 5 October 1846, in *El Nacional*, 2 April 1847; M. M. Mosquera (New Granadan chargé) to Palmerston, Hakes Hotel, 16 October 1846, in *El Nacional*, 14 January 1847; Francisco Michelena y Rojas to Gómez de la Torre, London, 15 November 1846, in *El Nacional*, 29 January 1847; Gómez de la Torre to Palmerston, Quito, 30 November 1846, in *El Nacional*, 26 January 1847; William Parish Robertson (former consul of Peru in London) to Lord Clarendon, London, 31 January 1846, in FO 25/29; and Burr, *Reason*, 75–76.

51. Burr, *Reason*, 76; and letter from merchants and companies in London doing business with South America to William Parish Robertson, London, 26 March 1847, in *El Nacional*, 15 June 1847. The signers of this letter included representatives of the Baring brothers, Reid, Irving and Co., Finlay Hodgson and Co., N. M. Rothschild and Co., and Anthony Gibbs and Co.

52. "Boletín. Embargo de la espedición del jeneral Flores," dateline Bogotá, 18 January 1847, in *El Nacional*, 19 February 1847, news items taken from English newspapers; Carlos Veyret to the minister of foreign relations (Gómez de la Torre), Paris, 14 December 1846, in *El Nacional*, 8 February 1846; Juan Manuel Iturregui (Peruvian minister in London), 2 March 1847; and Robalino Dávila, *Reacción*, 130–131.

53. Robalino Dávila, *Reacción*, 111–118.

54. Buenaga, "Documentos"; and Destruge, *Expedición*, 23–25.

55. Bustamante, deposition, *El Nacional*, 4 May 1847.

56. De las Rivas to Ecuadorian minister of foreign relations (Gómez de la Torre), Madrid, 2 December 1846, in *El Nacional*, 9 March 1847; anonymous letter, Santander, 17 January 1847, in *El Nacional*, 4 May 1847; and Buenaga, "Documentos."

57. Anonymous letter, Santander, 17 January 1847, in *El Nacional*, 4 May 1847.

58. Ibid.

59. Anonymous letter to Ayala, San Sebastián, 4 August 1846, in Robalino Dávila, *Reaccion,* 77.

60. Cope to Palmerston, no. 3, Quito, 3 December 1846, in FO 97/156; Montúfar to first secretary of state, nos. 158 and 163, Quito, 20 July and 16 September 1846, in AMAE (Madrid), Ecuador, Correspondencia, Legajo 1584; Cevallos Salvador, *Moncayo,* 53–57 (on revolts of 1846); Destruge, *Prensa,* II: 86–87; and editorial in *El Nacional,* 30 July 1847, admitting the government's weakness in the years 1845–1846.

61. Montúfar to first secretary of state, nos. 158 and 163, 20 July and 16 September 1846, in AMAE (Madrid), Ecuador, Correspondencia, Legajo 1458. Little is known of this scheme, but Montúfar's report seems to be accurate. Rocafuerte hankered for the presidency and detested Roca. The plan was reminiscent of the move against President Rocafuerte in 1836–1837, treated earlier.

62. Montúfar to first secretary of state, no. 169, Quito, 4 November 1846, in AMAE (Madrid), Ecuador, Correspondencia, Legajo 1458; Robalino Dávila, *Reacción,* 81–82 (on Rocafuerte's diplomatic appointment); and Andrade, *Historia,* VII: 2746–2747.

63. *El Nacional,* 6 April and 11 May 1846; and Robalino Dávila, *Reacción,* 68.

64. Vicente Ramón Roca (president), message to Congress, 15 September 1847, in *El Nacional,* 24 September 1847; Seth Sweetser (U.S. consul at Guayaquil) to Buchanan, Guayaquil, 15 November 1846, NA, Consular Dispatches, Guayaquil, Vol. I; Angel Calderón de la Barca (Spanish envoy extraordinary and plenipotentiary) to first secretary of state, no. 272, Washington, 20 March 1847, in AMAE (Madrid), Ecuador, Política, Legajo 2384 (on Ecuadorian efforts to secure the aid of the U.S. Pacific Squadron); and most issues of *El Nacional* for the months of November and December 1846, and January and February 1847, as well as 12 March 1847. The forced loan was fixed at fifty thousand pesos per month, but actually raised only forty-six thousand pesos during the two months that it lasted.

65. *El Nacional,* 2 April and 28 September 1847; and Colonel Nicolás Vernaza to Mercedes Jijón de Flores, Quito, 23 March 1848, and Jijón de Flores to chief of police (Vernaza), Quito, 2 (?) March 1848, on file in the Flores Library of the Universidad Católica, Quito.

66. *El Clamor de Atahualpa* (Quito), first appeared on 19 November 1846; and *El Vengador* (Quito) appeared on 24 November 1846, published by García Moreno. The government newspaper *El Seis de marzo* also published news and editorials about the expected invasion.

67. Montúfar to first secretary of state, nos. 168, 172, and 177,

Quito 4, 10 November and 7 December 1846, in AMAE (Madrid), Ecuador, Correspondencia, Legajo 1458, and Política, Legajo 2384; and Robalino Dávila, *Reacción,* 85–87.

68. Montúfar to first secretary of state, Havana, 10 March 1847, in AMAE (Madrid), Ecuador, Política, Legajo 2384; *El Nacional,* 14 and 18 January 1847; Spanish diplomatic correspondence in Martínez-Delgado, *Traiciones,* I: 278–296, 315–328; and Roca, message to Congress, 15 September 1847, in *El Nacional,* 24 September 1847.

69. Robalino Dávila, *Reacción,* 83–86 and 122–128. Gómez de la Torre replaced Dr. Fernández Salvador in late November 1846, shortly after the latter asked for a leave of absence of four months for unspecified reasons (perhaps because he had had close ties to Flores in the past and did not feel comfortable in the role imposed upon him as foreign minister during the crisis).

70. Carlos Creus (Spanish chargé in Uruguay) to first secretary of state, nos. 155 and 205, Montevideo, 12 November 1846 and 22 March 1847, in AMAE (Madrid), Ecuador, Política, Legajo 2384; *El Constitucional* (Montevideo), 15 March 1847; Henry Savage (U.S. chargé in Guatemala) to Buchanan, no. 18, Guatemala City, 27 March 1847, in Manning, *Correspondence,* III: 246–247; Salvador Bermúdez de Castro (Spanish minister in Mexico) to Spanish first secretary of state, no. 480, Mexico City, 28 April 1847, in AMAE (Madrid), Ecuador, Política, Legajo 2384; and *El Iris español* (Mexico City), 27 January and 13 February 1847. Creus' reports from Montevideo said that a large Spanish population in Uruguay and the presence of Spanish warships in the Río de la Plata induced the Uruguayan government to adopt a very circumspect attitude toward Spain and the Flores expedition. On Venezuela's reaction, see: Pedro de las Casas (Venezuelan minister of foreign relations) to Ecuadorian minister of foreign relations), Caracas, 10 February 1847, in *El Nacional,* 7 May 1847; and Buenaga, "Documentos." According to Buenaga, the Venezuelan agent in Madrid favored Flores.

71. Saturnino de Sousa e Oliveira (Brazilian minister of foreign relations) to Ecuadorian minister of foreign relations (Gómez de la Torre), Rio de Janeiro, 27 October 1847, in *El Nacional,* 14 March 1848; and Haskins, "Flores," 484–485.

72. Sweetser to Buchanan, Guayaquil, 15 and 18 November 1846, NA, Consular Dispatches, Guayaquil, Vol. I (the second dispatch cites President Polk's reassertion of the Monroe Doctrine in December 1845); Buchanan to Stanhope Prevost (U.S. consul in Lima), Washington, 24 March 1847, in Manning, *Correspondence,* X: 238–239; and Vanbrugh Livingston (U.S. chargé in Ecuador) to Gómez de la Torre,

Quito, 22 August 1848, in Manning, *Correspondence,* VI: 261–262. The rather blasé response of the United States is somewhat mystifying. Perhaps Secretary of State Buchanan was taken in by Calderón de la Barca's denials of Spanish complicity.

73. Haskins, "Flores," 481–484; Robalino Dávila, *Reacción,* 123–128; and Restrepo, *Diario,* III: 483–494.

74. Haskins, "Flores," 481–487; Robalino Dávila, *Reacción* 144–45 and 150–162; John Randolph Clay (U.S. chargé in Peru) to Buchanan, Lima, 12 January 1848; Manning, *Correspondence,* X: 561–563; and Peru, Ministerio de Relaciones Exteriores, *Congresos americanos de Lima,* 2 vols. (Lima, 1938).

75. Domingo Delgadillo (Bolivian foreign minister) to Peruvian foreign minister, Cochabamba, 7 December 1846, in *El Nacional,* 29 January 1847; José Ramón Sucre (Bolivian consul at Guayaquil) to Ecuadorian foreign minister, Guayaquil, 6 December 1846, in *El Nacional,* 29 January 1847; and other diplomatic correspondence published in *El Nacional,* 29 January and 4 May 1847.

76. Rocafuerte to Chilean foreign minister (Manuel Camilo Vial), Lima, 15 December 1846, and Vial to Rocafuerte, Santiago, 25 January 1847, in *El Nacional,* no. 73, 21 (?) March 1847 (page with date omitted in the microfilm copy of Saint Louis University); Vial to Chilean consul at Arica, Santiago, 27 January 1847, in AMRE (Chile), Indice de Oficios Dirijidos de los Ajentes de Chile a Gobiernos Extranjeros, 1847–1851; Burr, *Reason,* 76; and Robalino Dávila, *Reacción,* 124–126.

77. Diplomatic correspondence and other documents reproduced in *El Nacional,* 14 and 18 January 1847; Robalino Dávila, *Reacción,* 112–113, 116–17; Arboleda, *Historia contemporánea,* II: 278–281; Becker, *Independencia,* 540.

78. Diplomatic correspondence and other documents reproduced in *El Nacional,* 29 January, 12 and 19 February, and 2 March 1847; *El Eco del comercio,* 20 January and 7 February 1847; *El Heraldo,* 19 January 1847; Prevost to Buchanan, no. 15, Lima, 10 December 1846, in Manning, *Correspondence,* X: 547–550; and *El Peruano,* 11, 14, and 16 November 1846, and subsequent dates.

79. Robalino Dávila, *Reacción,* 158–161; Basadre, *Historia,* II: 770–771. Flores obtained temporary asylum in New Granada and later organized a filibustering expedition in Peru.

80. *El Nacional,* 29 February 1847, reproduced a brief summary of the Congress' accomplishments.

81. On the joint action to close ports to Spanish shipping, see the editorial in *El Nacional,* 20 April 1847. The Spanish government's

deep concern over the reaction of Spanish American nations to the Flores expedition was demonstrated by the fact that the Ministry of Foreign Affairs gathered together all reports on its impact in the New World and had a report written for internal use. This interesting summary, dated 13 and 19 February 1847, is in AMAE (Madrid), Ecuador, Política, Legajo 2384.

82. Hispanophobia remained strong in Ecuador for many years; Stanhope Prevost (secretary of U.S. legation in Ecuador) to Seward, no. 10, Guayaquil, 26 April 1866, NA, Microcopy T-50/7.

11. KING OF THE NIGHT 1847–1855

1. Flores, *Ecuatorianos* (Bayona, 1847), 10–25; "Apuntes sobre Flores en los 24 días que lleva de residencia en Panamá," *El Nacional*, 12 May 1848; and extract of a letter from Flores to "un amigo en Lima," Puná, 25 May 1852, enclosed with a dispatch of John Randolph Clay to Webster, 8 June 1852, NA, Despatches, Peru, Microcopy T-52/9.

2. On filibusters, see William O. Scroggs, *Filibusters and Financiers: The Story of William Walker and his Associates* (New York, 1916, reprinted in 1963); Robert G. Caldwell, *The López Expeditions to Cuba, 1848–1851* (Princeton, 1915); and Charles H. Brown, *Agents of Manifest Destiny: The Lives and Times of the Filibusters* (Chapel Hill, N.C., 1980).

3. The British later released two of the vessels under a large bond to prevent their use in any filibuster; Manuel Camilo Vial (Chilean minister of foreign relations) to Gómez de la Torre, Santiago, 27 September 1847, in *El Nacional*, 22 October 1847.

4. Roca, address to Congress, 15 September 1847, *El Nacional*, 24 September 1847; and diplomatic correspondence published in *El Nacional*, 15 and 22 October, 30 November, 31 December 1847.

5. Flores to Buchanan, Washington, 29 September 1847, in Manning, *Correspondence*, VI: 260.

6. The Ecuadorian government claimed that Flores tried to organize an expedition in the United States at this time, but there is no evidence to confirm the claim; *El Nacional*, 24 December 1847.

7. Documents published in *El National*, 17 March 1848; Mendeville to French minister of foreign affairs, no. 167, Quito, 11 February 1848, in AMAE (France), Correspondance Politique, Équateur, Vol. I-bis; Cevallos Salvador, *Moncayo*, 53–57.

8. Cope to Palmerston, nos. 3, 5, and 7, Quito, 10 February, 8 April, and 10 May 1848, in FO 25/16. Other diplomatic agents

painted a similar picture of the disruption and disorder in Ecuador, though the political reporting of the U.S. chargé, 1848–1851, was of poor quality; Manning, *Correspondence*, VI: 260–301.

9. Minutes of the Chamber of Representatives, 18 October 1847, in *El Nacional*, 28 December 1847; and Manuel Bustamante (minister of the treasury), "Esposición que el Ministro de Hacienda presenta a las Cámaras Legislativas . . .," 14 September 1848, in *El Nacional*, 1 December 1848.

10. Roca, address to Congress, 15 September 1848, *El Nacional*, 22 September 1848; Gómez de la Torre, "Esposición," 23 September 1848, *El Nacional*, 17 November 1848; and decree of 9 October 1848, *El Nacional*, 13 October 1848.

11. Gómez de la Torre, "Esposición," 23 September 1848 (an excellent comprehensive view of general conditions in Ecuador in 1848); and Manuel Bustamante, *Esposición* (1848).

12. José Julián Ponze (Ecuadorian consul-general in Caracas) to Gómez de la Torre, Caracas, 8 December 1847 and 5 April 1848, in *El Nacional*, 15 February and 9 June 1848; *El Nacional*, 15 February 1848; Restrepo, *Diario*, III: 537, 552–553; and Cope to Palmerston, nos. 3 and 5, Quito, 10 February and 8 April 1848, in FO 25/16.

13. Ponze to Gómez de la Torre, Caracas, 5 April 1848, in *El Nacional*, 9 June 1848.

14. Flores, *Ecuatorianos*, 12–25; Ponze to Gómez de la Torre, Caracas, 8 December 1847, in *El Nacional*, 15 February 1848; *El Nacional*, 12 May 1848; and Flores' letters to Ecuadorians published in *El Nacional*, 10 March 1848.

15. Herman Menvale (of the Colonial Office) to Lord Eddisbury, Downing Street, 18 July 1848, in FO 25/16.

16. Flores, *Réplica del jeneral Flores al libelo del jeneral Mosquera . . .* (Costa Rica, [1848?]), 5–6.

17. Roca, written response to Congress, 11 November 1848, in *El Nacional*, 24 November 1848.

18. Lorenzo Montúfar y Rivera Maestre, *Reseña histórica de Centro-América*, 7 vols. (Guatemala, 1878), V: 524, VI: 56, 65, 102, 114–116, and 118.

19. Mary Wilhelmine Williams, *Anglo-American Isthmian Diplomacy, 1815–1915* (Washington, 1916), 26–56.

20. "Private observations of General Flores to Col. Wright with respect to Mr. Molina's mission," no date, but probably 7 October 1848 (which is the date of another communication from Flores to Wright), in FO 21/2. "Private observations" is obviously an English

translation of Flores' original to Wright. See also: "Translation of a paper written by General Flores and headed 'my indications delivered to Col. Wright for the information of Lord Palmerston,' " Costa Rica, 7 October 1848, in FO 21/1; and Flores to Palmerston, San José 15 December 1849, in FO 21/2.

21. Felipe Molina (Costa Rican chargé in England), London, 23 December 1848, and 5, 12 January, 17 February, 5, 23 April, 2, 3 May, and 18 July 1849, in FO 21/1; Flores to Wright, San José, 10 January and 9 February 1849, in FO 25/18; President Castro to Wright, San José, 16 February 1849, in FO 25/18; and Wright to Palmerston, Conservative Club, 12 January 1849, in FO 97/88.

22. Chatfield (British consul-general in Central America) to Palmerston, San José, 8 March 1850, in FO 15/64; and Chatfield's other correspondence of 1849 and early 1850.

23. Williams, *Anglo-American,* 67–109; Palmerston to Chatfield, no. 9, Foreign Office, 8 March 1850 (draft), in FO 97/88; id. to Molina, Foreign Office, 23 March 1850 (draft), in FO 21/33; and Molina to Palmerston, London, 23 March 1850 (cites Palmerston's oral rejection of a protectorate), in FO 21/3.

24. Palmerston to Cope, no. 1, Foreign Office, 25 January 1850 (draft), in FO 25/20; id. to Chatfield, no. 30, Foreign Office 26 June 1850 (draft), in FO 15/63; and id. to id., no. 41, Foreign Office 9 June 1851 (draft), in FO 15/69.

25. Robalino Dávila, *Reacción,* 194–216; Benigno Malo (minister of foreign relations) to Cope, Quito, 24 January 1850, enclosed with Cope's dispatch no. 1, 1 February 1850, in FO 25/50; Cope to Palmerston, nos. 5, 7, 11, Quito, 7 March, 10 April, and 10 May 1850, in FO 25/20; and Van Alen to Clayton, no. 29. Quito, 5 March 1850, NA Despatches, Ecuador, Microcopy T-50/1.

26. Cope to Palmerston, no. 21, Quito, 10 July 1850, in FO 25/20; and similar views by French consul Mendeville, dispatch no. 5, Quito, 9 June 1850, in AMAE (France), Correspondance Politique, Équateur, Vol. I.

27. Van Alen to Clayton, nos. 31 and 32, 9 May and 1 June 1850, NA, Despatches, Ecuador, Microcopy T-50/1, and other early dispatches of Van Alen in the same file.

28. Mendeville to minister of foreign affairs, no. 5, Quito, 9 June 1850, in AMAE, Correspondance Politique, Équateur; Van Alen to Clayton, nos. 32 and 33, Guayaquil, 1 June and 10 July 1850, NA, Despatches, Ecuador, Microcopy T-50/1. The Spanish chargé also kept his government in the dark about his activities aimed at bringing Flores back; Fidencio Bourman to Spanish first secretary of state, nos.

5, 8, and 36, Quito, 2, 8 March and 3 September 1850, in AMAE (Spain), Ecuador, Correspondencia, Legajo 1458.

29. Chatfield to Palmerston, no. 24, San José, 8 March 1850, and reply, no. 30, Foreign Office, 26 June 1850 (draft), in FO 15/63–64; and id. to id., no. 38, Guatemala, 25 March 1851, in FO 15/70. Flores' involvement in political controversy is seen in: Flores, *Contestación del Jeneral Flores a la Gaceta del Gobierno de San Salvador* (San José, 1850).

30. *El Nacional,* 11 July 1851; William Pitt Adams (British chargé in Peru) to Palmerston, no. 34, Lima, 9 July 1851, FO 61/129; and John Randolph Clay (U.S. chargé in Peru) to Webster, no. 73, Lima, 9 July 1851, in Manning, *Correspondence,* X: 575–577.

31. Clay to Webster, no. 97, Lima, 8 April 1852, in Manning, *Correspondence,* X: 584–585.

32. Diplomatic correspondence published in *El Nacional,* 24 June and 11 July 1851; Cushing to Webster, unnumbered and nos. 5 and 7, Guayaquil and Quito, 12 May, 5 August, and 6 September 1851, NA, Despatches, Ecuador, Microcopy T-50/1; Cope to Palmerston, nos. 13, 14, 16, and 18, Quito, 6 July, 24 August, 5 September, and 6 October 1851, in FO 25/22; and Le Gouhir y Rodas, *Historia,* I: 465–466.

33. José Rufino Echenique, *Memorias para la historia del Perú (1808–1878),* 2 vols. (Lima, 1952), I: 171–173 (Echenique denied having invited Flores to Peru in order to use him, but Flores openly admitted support from Echenique); article quoting Flores on Peruvian support, *La Democracia,* 18 May 1855; Adams to Palmerston, nos. 52 and 8, 9 November 1851 and 8 January 1852, in FO 61/130 and 133; and Basadre, *Historia,* I: 910–913, 969–970. On the red scare in New Granada, see Robert L. Gilmore, "Nueva Granada's Socialist Mirage," *HAHR* 36(May 1956):190–210.

34. Adams to Palmerston, nos. 37 and 58, Lima, 8 August and 9 December 1851, in FO 61/130; Clay to Webster, no. 73, Lima, 9 July 1851, in Manning, *Correspondence,* X: 575–577; and Juan A. Gutiérrez (Chilean consul at Guayaquil) to Varas, Guayaquil, 28 September 1851, in AMRE, Ajentes de Chile en Perú, 1845–1856, Guayaquil. Flores had to borrow money before leaving Costa Rica.

35. Adams to Palmerston, no. 9 (confidential), Lima, 8 January 1852, in FO 61/133. See also B. J. de Toro (Chilean chargé in Peru) to Varas, no. 119, Lima, 25 November 1851, in AMRE, Ajentes de Chile en Perú, 1849–1856; Adams to Palmerston, no. 58, Lima, 9 December 1851, in FO 61/130; and Bourman to first secretary of state no. 109 (encoded), Quito, 5 November 1851, in AMAE (Spain), Correspondencia, Ecuador, Legajo 1458.

36. Bourman to first secretary of state, no. 109, Quito, 5 November 1851, in AMAE (Spain), Ecuador, Correspondencia, Legajo 1458.

37. Adams to Palmerston, nos. 9 and 14, Lima, 8 January and 9 February 1852, in FO 61/133; Adams to Earl Granville, nos. 24 and 26, Lima, 9 and 23 March 1852, in FO 61/133; Clay to Webster, nos. 93, 95, and 96, Lima, 7, 9, and 23 February 1852, in Manning, *Correspondence*, X: 580–584; Cushing to Webster, no. 18, Guayaquil, 1 May 1852, in Manning, *Correspondence*, VI: 281; and Brown, *Agents*, 166–167.

38. José Villamil, (Ecuadorian minister of foreign affairs) to Cushing, Guayaquil, 26 February and 6 April 1852, in Manning, *Correspondence*, VI: 269–270 and 275–278.

39. Cushing to Villamil, Guayaquil, 28 February 1852 and 12 April 1852, in Manning, *Correspondence*, VI: 271 and 278.

40. Cushing to Captain Thomas A. Dornin, Guayaquil, 8 June 1852, enclosed with Cushing's dispatch no. 20, Guayaquil, 1 July 1852, NA, Despatches, Ecuador, Microcopy T-50/2.

41. De Toro to Varas, no. 137, Lima, 9 April 1852, in AMRE, Ajentes de Chile en Perú, 1849–1856; Montholon to minister of foreign affairs, no. 18, Guayaquil, 10 April 1852, in AMAE (France), Correspondance Politique, Équateur, Vol. I; and Philo White (U.S. minister resident in Ecuador) to Lewis Cass (U.S. secretary of state), no. 130, Quito, 21 October 1857, NA, Despatches, Ecuador, Microcopy T-50/4.

42. *El Seis de marzo*, 11 May 1852; and translation of a letter from Flores to "a friend in Lima," Puná, 25 May 1852, enclosed with Clay to Webster, no. 102, Lima, 8 June 1852, in Manning, *Correspondence*, X: 586–589.

43. Cope to Palmerston, nos. 2 and 3, Quito, 20 January and 3 March 1852, FO 25/25.

44. Montholon to French minister of foreign affairs, Guayaquil, 12 March 1852, in AMAE (France), Correspondance Politique, Équateur, Vol. I.

45. Cushing to Webster, no. 16, Guayaquil, 27 March 1852, NA, Despatches, Ecuador, Microcopy T-50/2.

46. Villamil to Cushing, Guayaquil, 7 June 1852, and Cushing to Webster, no. 20, Guayaquil, 1 July 1852, in Manning, *Correspondence*, VI: 284–286; Gutiérrez to Varas, no. 28, Guayaquil, 1 June 1852, in AMRE, Ajentes de Chile en el Perú, 1849–1856, Guayaquil; and Destruge, *Prensa*, I: 103–104.

47. Cushing to Webster, no. 20, Guayaquil, 1 July 1852, in Man-

ning, *Correspondence,* VI: 286–287; and Cope to Malmesbury, nos. 11 and 12, Quito, 30 June and 25 August 1852, in FO 25/25.

48. Cushing to Webster, nos. 20 and 21, Guayaquil, 1 July and 1 August 1852, in Manning, *Correspondence,* VI: 286–291; Villamil to Webster, Guayaquil, 31 August 1852, in ibid., 291–294; Cope to Malmesbury, no. 12, Quito, 25 August 1852, in FO 25/25; *El Seis de marzo,* 18 July 1852, and following issues to 5 October 1852; and a letter from Captain Alex Bell to an unnamed person, Panama, 2 August 1852, *Alta Californian* (San Francisco), 25 August 1852. Bell, one of Flores' California recruits, said that Flores' army "was not worth a damn, and most of his officers were not worth a———."

49. Clay to Webster, no. 105, Lima, 7 August 1852, and Clay to Edward Everett (U.S. secretary of state), no. 120 (or 121?), Lima, 12 December 1852, in Manning, *Correspondence,* X: 657–660; Adams to British secretary of foreign affairs, nos. 31, 35, 39, 43, and 49, Lima, 11 May, 10, 26 June, 11 July, and 11 August 1852, in FO 61/133; and Basadre, *Historia,* II: 971–974 and 984–986.

50. Cushing to Webster, nos. 21, 23, 27, 32, 35, and 36, Guayaquil, 1 August and 1 September 1852, and 6 January, 2 March, and 1 and 11 May 1853; and Villamil to Webster, Guayaquil, 31 August 1852, in Manning, *Correspondence,* VI: 291–305. And see Cope to Lord John Russell (British secretary of foreign affairs), no. 7, Guayaquil, 1 March 1853, in FO 25/26.

51. *La Democracia,* 9 August 1853. Cushing to Marcy, no. 39, Guayaquil, 11 August 1853; and Marcy to Villamil (Ecuadorian chargé in the U.S.), Washington, 2 November and 5 December 1853, and 31 January 1854, in Manning, *Correspondence,* VI: 231–232, 307–308, and other correspondence in ibid., 316–322. *San Francisco Commercial Advertiser,* 29 October 1853; and *Alta Californian,* 1 October 1853, citing the *Panama Herald* and *El Panameño.*

52. Diplomatic correspondence in *El Peruano,* 4 March 1854; and Varas to Chilean chargé in Peru, nos. 51 and 53, Santiago, 13 and 30 March 1854, in AMRE, "Ajentes de Chile en Estranjero, Correspondencia," 1852–1855.

53. *New York Herald,* 20 March 1855, quoted in Spanish translation in *La Democracia,* 2 May 1855, and in a broadside published in Ecuador on 27 April 1855, enclosed with White's dispatch no. 54, 16 May 1855, in NA, Despatches, Microcopy T-50/3; Ruth Ketring Nuermberger, *The Clays of Alabama: A Planter–Lawyer–Politician Family* (Lexington, Ky., 1958), 124; and White to Marcy, nos. 54 and 55, Quito, 16 and 23 May 1855, in Manning, *Correspondence,* VI: 356–360.

54. Philo White (U.S. minister resident in Ecuador) to William L.

Marcy (secretary of state), nos. 54 and 55, Quito, 16 and 23 May 1855, in Manning, *Correspondence*, VI: 356–360; and Marcy to White, no. 23, Washington, 11 July 1855, in ibid., 235–236; and other correspondence in ibid., 364–366.

55. White to Marcy, no. 54 (confidential), Quito, 16 May 1855, in Manning, *Correspondence*, VI: 356–359.

56. Cope to Lord Russell, no. 7, Guayaquil, 1 March 1853, in FO 25/25–26.

57. Copies of the convention are enclosed with White's dispatch no. 40, Quito, 20 December 1854, in NA Despatches, Ecuador, Microcopy T–50/3. See also White to Marcy, no. 25, Quito, 19 July 1854, in ibid.; Marcy to White, no. 14, Washington, 14 August 1854, in Manning, *Correspondence*, VI: 232–234; Cope to Clarendon, no. 22, Quito, 20 June 1855, in FO 25/29; Robalino Dávila, *Reacción*, 284, 347–348; Alexander James Duffield, *Peru in the Guano Age* (London, 1877); and E. Taylor Parks and J. Fred Rippy, "The Galápagos Islands, a Neglected Phase of American Strategy Diplomacy," *The Pacific Historical Review*, 9 (March 1940): 37–45.

58. Cope (now British chargé in Ecuador) to Clarendon, nos. 18 and 22, Quito, 8 and 20 June 1855, in FO 25/29; Clarendon to Cope, no. 16, Foreign Office, 13 October 1855, in FO 25/28; White to Marcy, nos. 39 and 40, Quito, 24 November and 20 December 1854, in Manning, *Correspondence*, VI: 339–342, 360–363; Gutiérrez to Varas, no. 42, Guayaquil, 10 December 1854, in AMRE, "Ajentes de Chile en el Perú," 1845–1856, Guayaquil; Burr, *Reason*, 84–85.

59. Fernando Casós, *Para la historia de la revolución de 1854* (Cuzco, 1854), cited in Basadre, *Historia*, I: 331, II: 969.

12. THE EXILE'S RETURN, 1855–1864

1. *La Democracia*, 1 April 1855; Clay to Marcy, no. 253, Lima 10 April 1855, in Manning, *Correspondence*, X: 756–759; and Stephen Henry Sulivan (British chargé in Peru) to Lord Clarendon (British foreign secretary), nos. 31 and 38, Lima, 11 and 26 March 1855, in FO 61/154.

2. White to Marcy, no. 50, Quito, 3 April 1855, in NA, Despatches, Ecuador, vol. 3, Microcopy T-50/3; proclamation of President Urbina, 3 April 1855, in *La Democracia*, 11 April 1855; and Sulivan to Clarendon, nos. 38, 41, 49, 55, 81, 90, and 111, Lima, 26 and 27 March, 11, 26 April, 25 June, 11, 25 July, and 11 September 1855, in FO 61/154–155.

3. Clay to Marcy, nos. 253 and 257, Lima, 10 April and 25 May

1855, in Manning, *Correspondence*, X: 756–761; and Antonio Varas (Chilean foreign minister) to Chilean minister in Peru, nos. 20 and 22, 30 May and 14 June 1855, in AMRE (Chile), "Copiador de los Oficios a Ajentes Diplomáticos . . ." (1855–1856), Vol. VI.

4. For background to the boundary controversy, see the extensive correspondence between Philo White and William L. Marcy, 18 January 1853 to 22 August 1854, in Manning, *Correspondence*, VI: 226–235, 317–335; and White to Marcy, unnumbered, Quito, 19 April 1854, NA, Despatches, Ecuador, vol. 3, Microcopy T–50/3. Clay to Everett, nos. 129, 130, 134, 144, and 182, Lima, 8, 11 February, 9, 11 March, 25 April, and 21 July 1853, and Clay to Marcy, no. 277, Lima, 25 September 1855, in Manning, *Correspondence*, X: 666–689 and 761–762. And see *El Peruano*, 29 September, 6 October, and 12 December 1855.

5. "El protectorado yankee y el eco de los Andes," *Voz del pueblo* (Lima), 29 March 1855—clipping enclosed with Clay's dispatch no. 253, Lima, 10 April 1855, NA, Despatches, Peru, Microcopy T-52/11; White to Marcy, nos. 54 and 55, Quito, 16 and 23 May 1855, NA, Despatches, Ecuador, Microcopy T-50/3; and Manning, *Correspondence*, VI: 359–360; and *El Comercio* (Lima), no. 4713, reprinted in *La Democracia*, 18 May 1855.

6. Clay to Marcy, no. 253, Lima, 10 April 1855, in Manning, *Correspondence*, X: 756–757.

7. Clay to Marcy, no. 257, Lima, 25 May 1855, in Manning, *Correspondence*, X: 759–760; Varas to Chilean minister in Lima, no. 22, Lima, 14 June 1855, in AMRE (Chile), "Copiador de Oficios a Ajentes Diplomáticos . . ." (1855–1856), Vol. VI.

8. White to Marcy, no. 55, Quito, 23 May 1855, and Marcy to White, no. 23, Washington, 11 July 1855, in Manning, *Correspondence*, VI: 235–236, 359–360; and Lord Clarendon to Cope, draft no. 13, Foreign Office, 24 August 1857, in FO 25/31.

9. White to Marcy, no. 55, Quito, 11 July 1855, in Manning, *Correspondence*, VI: 235–236.

10. White to Cass, no. 121, Quito, 24 July 1857, NA, Despatches, Ecuador, Microcopy T-50/4.

11. Ibid.

12. White to Cass, no. 125, Quito, 23 September 1857, and no. 138, Quito, 10 June 1848, NA, Despatches, Ecuador, Microcopy T-50/4–5; El Seis de marzo, 12 January 1858; Clarendon to Cope, no. 13, Foreign Office, 24 August 1857, in FO 25/31; and Robalino Dávila, *Reacción*, 364–379. The government's claims of innocence may have been exaggerated, because there were various reports of confiscations

of Flores' properties after the Spanish expedition. The truth in this matter is very hard to ascertain. Information independent of the Ecuadorian government may be found scattered through the British diplomatic correspondence of the years 1847 to 1849. See also the government newspaper *El Nacional,* 7 December 1847, which published records of the Senate for 21 October 1847. It is clear that the government's seizures of Flores' estates caused him large financial losses and may have forced him to sell and to default on mortgages.

13. White to Cass, nos. 125, 138, and 140, Quito, 23 September 1857, and 10 January and 2 February 1858, NA, Despatches, Ecuador, Microcopy T-50/4–5; correspondence in Manning, *Correspondence,* VI: 406–423; and Robalino Dávila, *Reacción,* 394–406.

14. Cope to Lord Malmesbury, no. 26, Quito, 22 September 1858, in FO 25/32.

15. Robalino Dávila, *Reacción,* 407.

16. Cope to Malmesbury, no. 26, Quito, 22 September 1858, in FO 25/32; and Charles R. Buckalew (U.S. chargé in Ecuador) to Cass, no. 4, Quito, 24 November 1858, NA, Despatches, Ecuador, Microcopy T-50/5.

17. Cope to Malmesbury, no. 26, Quito, 22 September 1858, in FO 25/32.

18. Robalino Dávila, *Reacción,* 355–361, 379–393; White to Cass, nos. 138 and 144, Quito, 10 January and 17 April 1858, NA, Despatches, Ecuador, Microcopy T-50/5; and Cope to Malmesbury, no. 26, Quito, 22 September 1858, in FO 25/32.

19. Buckalew to Cass, no. 4, Quito, 24 November 1858, NA, Despatches, Ecuador, Microcopy T-50/5; Cope to Malmesbury, no. 28, Quito, 20 October 1858, in FO 25/32; Moncayo, *Ecuador,* 234–235; and Robalino Dávila, *Reacción,* 414–415.

20. Buckalew to Cass, no. 4 and an unnumbered dispatch, Quito, 24 November 1858 and 22 March 1859, NA, Despatches, Ecuador, Microcopy T-50/5; Cope to Malmesbury, no. 29. Quito, 23 November 1858, in FO 25/32; Moncayo, *Ecuador,* 235–238; and Robalino Dávila, *Reacción,* 414–415.

21. Robalino Dávila, *Reacción,* 419–434.

22. Moncayo, *Ecuador,* 240–253; and Robalino Dávila, *Reacción,* 434–442.

23. Clay to Cass, no. 579, Lima, 27 April 1860, in Manning, *Correspondence,* X: 835–836; Buckalew to Cass, no. 18, Quito, 22 May 1860, NA, Despatches, Ecuador, Microcopy T-50/5; Laso, *Biografía,* 39–40; Robalino Dávila, *García Moreno,* 219–225; and Wilfrido Loor, *La victoria de Guayaquil* (Quito, 1960), 286–291. The Reconciliation of the two

leaders may have been fostered by the marriage of García Moreno's brother to Flores' daughter Virginia in 1857.

24. Laso, *Biografía*, 39–40; Robalino Dávila, *García Moreno*, 225–229; Buckalew to Cass, no. 23, Quito, 1 October 1860, NA, Despatches, Ecuador, T-50/5; Francis Mocatta (British acting consul-general at Guayaquil) to Lord Russell (British foreign secretary), nos. 23 and 24, Guayaquil, 14 and 29 September 1860, in FO 25/35.

25. *Boletín*, Quito, 28 September 1860—enclosed with Buckalew's dispatch no. 23, Quito, 1 October 1860, NA, Despatches, Ecuador, T-50/5.

26. Laso, *Biografía*, 40–42; Friedrich Hassaurek (U.S. minister to Ecuador) to William H. Seward (U.S. secretary of state), nos. 4, 6, 10, and 12, Quito, 28 August, 29 September, and 19 December 1861, and 12 January 1862, NA, Despatches, Ecuador, Microcopy T-50/5; and Benigno Malo, *Escritos*, 238 and 441–442. On Flores' advocacy of monarchy, see Hassaurek's dispatch no. 10 cited above and George Fagan (British chargé in Ecuador) to Lord Russell, no. 10 (confidential), Quito, 20 December 1861, in FO 25/37.

27. Robalino Dávila, *García Moreno*, 202–208; Hassaurek to Seward, no. 4, Quito, 28 August 1861, and enclosures, NA, Despatches, Ecuador, Microcopy T-50/5; Fagan to Russell, no. 5, Quito, 18 October 1861, and enclosures, in FO 25/37; George F. Howe, "García Moreno's Dream of a European Protectorate," *Contribuciones para el estudio de la historia de América: Homenaje al Dr. Emilio Ravignani* (Buenos Aires, 1941), 125–143.

28. Hassaurek to Seward, no. 6, Quito, 29 September 1861, NA, Despatches, Ecuador, Microcopy T-50/5, quoting in translation from Flores' article in no. 187 of the *Club de Guayas* (Guayaquil).

29. Undated letter of Flores to Palmerston (probably January 1861), in FO 25/39; Wodehouse to Fagan, Foreign Office, 30 March 1861, in FO 25/36; F. Corraia (?) to Lord Russell, Paris, 18 April 1861, in FO 25/39; and Hassaurek to Seward, no. 13, Quito, 1 August 1861, NA, Despatches, Ecuador, Microcopy T-50/5.

30. Wright to Russell, Conservative Club, 15 August 1861, in FO 25/39. Wright's letter is printed, not in manuscript. Flores corresponded with Juan Bautista Alberdi on the subject of monarchy; see Mayer, *Alberdi*, 650.

31. Hassaurek to Seward, no. 95, Quito, 20 October 1863, NA, Despatches, Ecuador, Microcopy T-50/5.

32. Hassaurek to Seward, nos. 10, 12, 18, 62, 69, 78, 95, and 131, Quito, 19 December 1861, 6 January, 11, 18 March, 20 April, 2 July,

and 20 October 1862, and 1 July 1864, NA, Despatches, Ecuador, Microcopy T-50/5–6.

33. Robalino Dávila, *García Moreno,* 214–218; and Howe, "García Moreno's Efforts," 257–262.

34. Laso, *Biografía,* 43; Hassaurek to Seward, nos. 47 and 54, Quito, 26 November 1862 and 10 January 1863, NA, Despatches, Ecuador, Microcopy T-50/6; and Fagan to Russell, no. 2, Quito, 10 January 1863, in FO 25/42.

35. Laso, *Biografía,* 42; and Hassaurek to Seward, no. 54, Quito, 10 January 1863, NA, Despatches, Ecuador, Microcopy T-50/6.

36. Hassaurek to Seward, nos. 59, 67, and 73, Quito, 18 February, 17 April, and 9 May 1863, NA, Despatches, Ecuador, Microcopy T-50/6; Fagan to Russell, no. 8 or 9 (dispatch number not visible on film), Quito, 18 April 1863—and Mocatta to Russell, no. 20, Guayaquil, 27 July 1863, in FO 25/42; and Benigno Malo, *Escritos,* 238.

37. Hassaurek to Seward, nos. 47 and 49, Guayaquil, 26 November 1862, and Quito, 10 January 1863, NA, Despatches, Ecuador, Microcopy T-50/6; and Fagan to Russell, no. 2, 10 January 1863, in FO 25/42.

38. Hassaurek to Seward, no. 90, Quito, 9 September 1863, NA, Despatches, Ecuador, Microcopy T-50/6.

39. Mocatta to Russell, no. 20, Guayaquil, 27 July 1863, in FO 25/42.

40. Robalino Dávila, *García Moreno,* 513–517; Hassaurek to Seward, nos. 45 and 121, Quito, 12 November 1862 and 4 April 1864, NA, Despatches, Ecuador, Microcopy T-50/6–7; Fagan to Russell, no. 21, Quito, 8 August 1862, in FO 25/40; and Laso, *Biografía,* 43–49.

41. Hassaurek to Seward, no. 45, Quito, 12 November 1862, NA, Despatches, Ecuador, Microcopy T-50/6.

42. Mocatta to Q. A. M. Méjer, Guayaquil, 20 May 1863, enclosed with Mocatta's dispatch to Russell dated 14 May 1864, in FO 25/44.

43. Fagan to Russell, nos. 21 and 22. Quito, 8 and 20 August 1862, in FO 25/40; Hassaurek to Seward, no. 38, Quito, 20 September 1862, NA, Despatches, Ecuador, Microcopy T-50/6; and Robalino Dávila, *García Moreno,* 456–458.

44. Mocatta to Russell, no. 32, Guayaquil, 17 September 1863, in FO, 25/42; Hassaurek to Seward, nos. 85 and 88, Quito, 19 August and 9 September 1863, NA, Despatches, Ecuador, Microcopy T-50/6; and Robalino Dávila, *García Moreno,* 462–467.

45. Hassaurek to Seward, no. 94, Quito, 20 October 1863, NA, Despatches, Ecuador, Microcopy T-50/6; Mocatta to Russell, no. 32,

Guayaquil, 17 September 1863, in FO 25/42; Robalino Dávila, *García Moreno*, 467–478; and Laso, *Biografía*, 43–44.

46. Fagan to Russell, nos. 2 and 8 (or 9, number not visible on the microfilm), Quito, 10 January and 18 April 1863, in FO 25/42; Hassaurek to Seward, nos. 54 and 59, Quito, 10 January and 18 February 1863, NA, Despatches, Ecuador, Microcopy T-50/6; Robalino Dávila, *García Moreno*, 250–260; and Loor, *Los Jesuitas*, 214–215.

47. Fagan to Russell, no. 2, Quito, 10 January 1863, in FO 25/42.

48. Laso, *Biografía*, 43; Robalino Dávila, *García Moreno*, 478; Mocatta to Russell, no. 36, Guayaquil, 17 October 1863, NA, Despatches, Ecuador, Microcopy T-50/6.

49. *El Nacional*, 17 October 1863; Hassaurek to Seward, no. 94, Quito, 20 October 1863, NA, Despatches, Ecuador, Microcopy T-50/6; Mocatta to Russell, no. 36, Guayaquil, 17 October 1863, in FO 25/42; and Robalino Dávila, *García Moreno*, 478–481.

50. Documents in *El Nacional*, 28 November 1863; Hassaurek to Seward, no. 102, Quito, 17 December 1863, NA, Despatches, Ecuador, Microcopy T-50/6; and Robalino Dávila, *García Moreno*, 480–482.

51. Hassaurek to Seward, nos. 103 and 105, Quito, 17 December 1863 and 8 January 1864, NA, Despatches, Ecuador, Microcopy T-50/6–7; *El Nacional*, 2 January 1864, which published the treaty of Pinsaquí of 30 December 1863; and Robalino Dávila, *García Moreno*, 490–494.

52. Hassaurek to Seward, nos. 115 and 121, Quito, 20 February and 4 April 1864, NA, Despatches, Ecuador, Microcopy T-50/7.

53. Hassaurek to Seward, no. 131, Quito, 1 July 1864, NA, Despatches, Ecuador, Microcopy T-50/7.

54. Hassaurek to Seward, no. 144, Guayaquil, 25 August 1864, NA, Despatches, Ecuador, Microcopy T-50/7; Mocatta to Russell, no. 32, Guayaquil, 14 September 1864, in FO 25/44. Mocatta reported that Peru may have supported Urbina out of the belief that García Moreno and General Flores were supporting Spain in her conflict with Peru which had resulted in a Spanish occupation of Peru's Chincha Islands.

55. Hassaurek to Seward, no. 144, Guayaquil, 25 August 1864, NA, Despatches, Ecuador, Microcopy T-50/7; Stanhope Prevost (secretary of the U.S. legation in Ecuador) to Seward, nos. 8, 9, and 11, Guayaquil, 11, 28 September and 13 October 1864, NA, Consular Despatches, Guayaquil, Microcopy T-209/3; Laso, *Biografía*, 49–50; and Destruge, *Prensa*, II: 147–148.

56. Robalino Dávila, *García Moreno*, 285; Destruge, *Prensa*, II: 147;

García Moreno, message to Congress, 10 August 1865, in *El Nacional,* 20 September 1865.

57. Robalino Dávila, *Reacción,* 175–305 and 476–490.

58. Robalino Dávila, *Garciá Moreno,* 274–280, 392–394, 399–401, and 628–630; Hassaurek, *Four Years,* 223–230; and Hassaurek to Seward, nos. 121 and 125, Quito, 4 and 23 April 1864, NA, Despatches, Ecuador, Microcopy T-50/7.

59. García Moreno was not the chief executive from 1865 to 1869, but he dominated the government during much of this time and seized power once more in 1869 when his handpicked president showed too much independence.

Select Bibliography

RESEARCH AIDS

Freile-Granizo, Juan. *Guía del Archivo Nacional de Historia.* Guayaquil: Archivo Histórico Nacional, 1973.

Griffin, Charles C., and Warren, J. Benedict, eds. *Latin America: A Guide to the Historical Literature.* Austin and London: University of Texas Press, 1971.

Rolando, Carlos A. *Crónica del periodismo en el Ecuador.* Guayaquil: Tip. de la Sociedad Filantrópica, 1947.

Sánchez, Carlos Enrique. *La imprenta en el Ecuador.* Quito: Talleres Gráficos Nacionales, 1935.

Tepaske, John J., et al., eds. *Research Guide to Andean History: Bolivia, Chile, Ecuador, and Peru.* Durham, N.C.: Duke University Press, 1981.

SOURCE MATERIALS

Archival Collections

CHILE

Archivo Nacional (Santiago); Ministerio de Relaciones Exteriores (AMRE)

Private Library of Sergio Fernández Larraín (Santiago)

ECUADOR

Archivo Juan José Flores, Pontificia Universidad Católica del Ecuador (Quito)

Archivo del Ministerio de Finanzas (Quito)

Archivo Nacional de Historia (Quito) (ANH)

Archivo del Poder Legislativo (Quito) (APL)

Biblioteca Jijón y Caamaño (Quito) (AJC)

FRANCE

Archives du Ministère des Affaires Étrangères (Paris) (AMAE)

GREAT BRITAIN

Public Records Office (London); Foreign Office Papers (PRO/FO)

SPAIN

Archivo del Ministerio de Asuntos Exteriores (Madrid) (AMAE)

UNITED STATES

The National Archives (Washington, D.C.) (NA)

Printed Sources

Academia Colombiana de Historia, Bogotá. *Archivo Santander*. 3 vols. Bogotá: Aguila Negra Editorial, 1914–1922.

Archivo Juan José Flores. *Correspondencia del Libertador con el General Juan José Flores, 1825–1830*. Edited by Jorge Villalba F., S. J. Quito: Banco Central del Ecuador, 1977.

Biografía del General Flores o sea Mora contra Mora. Lima: n.p., 1846.

Biografía del Jeneral Flores tomada de El Correo Peruano.... Lima: Imprenta del Correo Peruano, 1846.

Blanco, José Félix, and Azpurúa, Ramón, comps. *Documentos para la historia de la vida pública del Libertador de Colombia, Perú y Bolivia*. 14 vols. Caracas: Impr. de "La Opinión nacional," 1875–1878.

Bolívar, Simón. *Cartas del Libertador*. Edited by Vicente Lecuna. 12 vols. Caracas: Lit. y Tip. del Comercio, 1929–1959. (Vol. 11 published in New York by The Colonial Press.)

Colombia. *Rejistro oficial de los decretos i órdenes circulares del poder ejecutivo*. Cualla: n.p., 1828–. (Title varies.)

Cortázar, Roberto, comp. *Cartas y mensajes del General Francisco de Paula Santander*. 10 vols. Bogotá: n.p., 1953–1956.

———, comp. *Correspondencia dirigida al General Francisco de Paula Santander*. 14 vols. Bogotá: Academia Nacional de Historia, 1964–1970.

Ecuador, Congreso, *Actas del Congreso de ...* (followed by years 1830–1839). 9 vols. Quito: Impr. del Gobierno, 1888–1893. (Title varies.)

Flores, Juan José. *Contestación del Jeneral Flores a la Gaceta del Gobierno de San Salvador*. San Salvador: Imprenta de la República, [1850?]. (Written on 24 October 1850 in San José de Costa Rica.)

———. *Discurso pronunciado por el ilustre prócer de la independencia, gen-*

eral *Juan José Flores, con motivo de la inauguración, en Lima, de la estatua del Libertador el 9 de diciembre de 1859.* Caracas: Impr. de "La Opinión national," 1883.

———. *El general Flores á los ecuatorianos.* Bayonne: Impr. Foré et Lasserre, 1847.

———. *Réplica del jeneral Flores al libelo del jeneral Mosquera, intitulado: Respondese con hechos y documentos a la protesta del jeneral Flores.* Costa Rica: Imprenta de la república, [1848?]. (Written on 5 December 1848.)

Flores, o el panejirista de sí mismo. [Lima?]: Imprenta del Comercio, n.d. (probably 1846).

García del Río, Juan. *Meditaciones colombianas,* 2d ed. Bogotá: Impr. Nacional, 1945.

García Moreno, Gabriel. *Cartas.* Edited by Wilfrido Loor. 4 vols. Quito: La Prensa Católica, 1953–1955.

Great Britain. Foreign Office. *British and Foreign State Papers.* Vol. 1–, 1812/1814–. London: J. Ridgway and Sons, 1841–.

Humphreys, Robert Arthur, ed. *British Consular Reports on the Trade and Politics of Latin America, 1824–1826.* London: Offices of The Royal Historical Society 1940.

Irisarri, Antonio José de. *Escritos polémicos.* Edited by Ricardo Donoso. Santiago: Imprenta universitaria, 1934.

Malo, Benigno. *Escritos y discursos.* Quito: Editorial Ecuatoriana, 1940.

———. *Flores juzgado por su ministro de gobierno y relaciones exteriores.* Lima: Imprenta del "Comercio," 18– (sic).

Manning, William Ray, ed. *Diplomatic Correspondence of the United States: Inter-American Affairs, 1831–1860.* 12 vols. Washington, D.C.: Carnegie Endowment for International Peace, 1932–1939.

Martínez-Delgado, Luis, ed. *Traiciones a la independencia hispanoamericana.* 2 vols. Bogotá: Editorial Kelly, 1974–1975.

Mosquera, Tomás Cipriano. *Archivo epistolar del General Mosquera.* Edited by Joseph Leon Helguera and Robert H. Davis. 3 vols. Bogotá: Editorial Kelly, 1966–1972.

Noboa, Aurelio, comp. *Colección de tratados, convenciones, capitulaciones, armisticios y otras actos diplomáticos y políticos celebrados desde la independencia hasta nuestros días.* Guayaquil: Imprenta de A. Noboa, 1901–1902.

O'Leary, Daniel F., comp. *Correspondencia de extranjeros notables con el Libertador.* 2 vols. Madrid: Editorial-América, 1920.

O'Leary, Simón B., ed. *Memorias del General O'Leary.* 32 vols. Caracas: Impr. de la "Gaceta Oficial," 1879–1888.

Olmedo, José Joaquín de. *Epistolario*. Puebla: J. M. Cajica, Jr., 1960.
Peru. Ministerio de Relaciones Exteriores. *Congresos americanos de Lima*. 2 vols. Lima: n.p., 1938.
Peru de Lacroix, Louis. *Diario de Bucaramanga: Estudio crítico*. Edited by Nicolás E. Navarro. Caracas: Tipografía Americana, 1935.
Portales, Diego José Víctor. *Epistolario de don Diego Portales, 1821–1837*. Edited by Guillermo Feliú Cruz. 3 vols. Santiago: Dirección General de Prisiones, Imp., 1936–1937.
Primer rejistro auténtico nacional de la República del Ecuador. Quito: Imprenta del Gobierno, 1830–1841. (Title varies.)
Restrepo, José Manuel. *Diario político y militar: Memorias sobre los sucesos importantes de la época para servir a la historia de la Revolución de Colombia y de la Nueva Granada, desde 1819 para adelante*. 4 vols. Bogotá: Impr. Nacional, 1954.
Rocafuerte, Vicente. *Colección Rocafuerte*. 16 vols. Edited by Neptalí Zúñiga. Quito: Impr. del Ministerio Tesoro, etc., 1947.
Rodríguez O., Jaime E., ed. *Estudios sobre Vicente Rocafuerte*. Guayaquil: Publicaciones del Archivo Histórico del Guayas, 1975.
Sucre, Antonio José de. *Cartas de Sucre al Libertador (1820–1830)*. Compiled by Daniel F. O'Leary. 2 vols. Madrid: Editorial América, 1919.
Terry, Adrian Russell. *Travels in the Equatorial Regions of South America, in 1832*. Hartford, Conn.: Cooke & Co., 1834.

Newspapers

La Balanza (Guayaquil).
El Colombiano del Guayas (Guayaquil).
La Concordia (Quito).
La Democracia (Quito).
El Eco del Azuay (Cuenca).
El Ecuatoriano del Guayas (Guayaquil).
Gaceta del Gobierno del Ecuador (Quito and Guayaquil). Title varies; changed to *El 21 de junio, El Seis de marzo,* and *El Nacional*.
El Nacional (Quito and Cuenca). Official newspaper.
El Peruano, diario oficial (Lima).
El Quiteño libre (Quito).
El Republicano (Quito).
El Seis de marzo (Guayaquil and Quito). Official newspaper.
El Vengador (Quito).
La Verdad desnuda (Guayaquil).

SECONDARY WORKS

Books

Academia Colombiana de Historia. *Historia extensa de Colombia*. Edited by Luis Martínez-Delgado. 18 vols. in 28. Bogotá: Ediciones Lerner, 1964–1983. Four more volumes projected.

Aguirre Abad, Francisco X. *Bosquejo histórico de la república del Ecuador*. Guayaquil: Corporación de Estudios y Publicaciones, 1975.

Alberdi, Juan Bautista. *Life and Industrial Labors of William Wheelwright in South America*. Boston: A. Williams & Co., 1887.

———. *La monarquía como mejor forma de gobierno en Sud–America*. Buenos Aires: A. Peña Lillo, 1970.

Andrade, Roberto. *Historia del Ecuador*. 7 vols. [Guayaquil?]: Reed & Reed, [1934–1937?].

Arboleda, Gustavo. *Historia contemporánea de Colombia*. 6 vols. Bogotá: Arboleda & Valencia, 1918–1935.

Arguedas, Alcides. *Historia de Bolivia: Los caudillos letrados, la Confederación peru–boliviana, Ingavi; o la consolidación de la nacionalidad, 1828–1848*. Barcelona: Sobs. de López y c.ª, impresos, 1928.

Arnade, Charles W. *The Emergence of the Republic of Bolivia*. Gainesville: University of Florida Press, 1957; reprint ed., New York: Russell & Russell, 1970

Bailyn, Bernard. *The Ideological Origins of the American Revolution*. Cambridge, Mass.: Belknap Press of Harvard University Press, 1967.

Basadre, Jorge. *Chile, Perú y Bolivia independientes*. Barcelona and Buenos Aires: Salvat, 1948.

———. *Historia de la República del Perú*. 5th ed., rev. and enl. 10 vols. Lima: Editorial peruamérica, 1963–1964.

Blanksten, George I. *Ecuador: Constitutions and Caudillos*. Berkeley and Los Angeles: University of California Press, 1951.

Brown, Charles H. *Agents of Manifest Destiny: The Lives and Times of the Filibusters*. Chapel Hill, N.C.: University of North Carolina Press, 1980.

Bushnell, David. *The Santander Regime in Gran Colombia*. Newark, Del.: University of Delaware Press, 1954; reprint ed., Westport, Conn.: Greenwood Press, 1970.

Callcott, Wilfrid Hardy. *Santa Anna: The Story of an Enigma Who Once Was Mexico*. Norman: University of Oklahoma Press, 1936.

Carbo, Luis Alberto. *Historia monetaria y cambiaria del Ecuador: Desde la época colonial*. Quito: n.p., 1953.

Casós, Fernando. *Para la historia del Perú: Revolución de 1854.* Cuzco: Imprenta Republicana por J. Refino Oblitas, 1854.

Ceballos, Pedro Fermín. *Resumen de la historia del Ecuador desde su origen hasta 1845.* 5 vols. in 3. Lima: Imprenta del Estado, 1870.

Cevallos García, Gabriel. *Historia del Ecuador.* 2d. ed., enl. Cuenca: Editorial "Don Bosco," 1967.

Cid Fernández, Enrique del. *Origen, trama y desarrollo del movimiento que proclamó vitalicia la presidencia del General Rafael Carrera.* Guatemala: Publicaciones del Servicio de Relaciones Públicas, Cultura y Acción Cívica del Ejército, 1966.

Costales Samaniego, Alfredo, and Peñaherra de Costales, Piedad. *Historia social del Ecuador.* 3 vols. Quito: n.p., 1964.

Crespo Rodas, Alfonso. *Santa Cruz, El cóndor indio.* Mexico City: Fondo de Cultura Económica, 1944.

Dávalos y Lissón, Pedro. *Historia republicana del Perú.* 10 vols. Lima: Librería e Imprenta Gil, 1933–1938.

Davis, Roger P. "Ecuador under Gran Colombia, 1820–1830: Regionalism, Localism, and Legitimacy in the Emergence of an Andean Republic." Ph.D. dissertation, University of Arizona, 1983.

Destruge, Camilo. *Album biográfico ecuatoriano.* 5 vols. Guayaquil: Tip. "El Vigilante," 1903–1905.

———. *Ecuador. La expedición Flores. Proyecto de monarquía americana. 1846–47: Relación histórica por un viejo liberal.* Guayaquil: Impr. de el Tiempo, 1906.

———. *Historia de la prensa de Guayaquil.* Memorias de la Academia Nacional de Historia. 2 vols. Quito: Tipografía y Encuadernación Salesianas, 1924–1925.

Donoso, Ricardo. *Antonio José de Irisarri: Escritor y diplomático.* Santiago: Prensa de la Universidad de Chile, 1934; 2d. ed., 1966.

Echenique, José Rufino. *Memorias para la historia del Perú (1808–1878).* 2 vols. Lima: Editorial Huascaran, 1952.

Estrada Ycaza, Julio. *El puerto de Guayaquil.* 3 vols. to date. Guayaquil: Archivo Histórico del Guayas, 1972–.

Gálvez, Manuel. *Vida de don Gabriel García Moreno.* 2d ed. Buenos Aires: Editorial Difusión, S.A., 1942.

García Salazar, Arturo. *Resumen de historia diplomática del Perú, 1820–1884.* Lima: Talleres Gráficos Sanmartí y cía, 1928.

González Suárez, Federico. *Historia eclesiástica del Ecuador desde los tiempos de la conquista hasta nuestros días.* Vol. I–. Quito: Imp. del Clero, por I. Miranda, 1881. (No more vols. published.)

———. *Historia general de la República del Ecuador.* 9 vols. Quito: Imprenta del Clero, 1890–1903.

Halperín-Donghi, Tulio. *The Aftermath of Revolution in Latin America.* New York and London: Harper Torchbooks, 1973.

Hamerly, Michael T. *Historia social y económica de la antigua Provincia de Guayaquil, 1763–1842.* Guayaquil: Archivo Histórico del Guayas, 1975.

Hassaurek, Friedrich. *Four Years among Spanish-Americans.* New York: Hurd and Houghton, 1868.

Helguera, Joseph Leon. "The First Mosquera Administration in New Granada, 1845–1849." Ph.D. dissertation, University of North Carolina, 1958.

Holinski, Alexandre. *L'Équateur, Scènes de la Vie Sud-Américaine.* Paris: Amyot, 1861.

Huerta, Pedro José. *Rocafuerte y la fiebre amarilla de 1842. La ciudad triste y desolada.* Guayaquil: Imprenta de la Universidad, 1947.

Jaramillo Alvarado, Pío. *El indio ecuatoriano.* 4th ed. Quito: Edit. Casa de la Cultura Ecuatoriana, 1954.

Larrea Holguín, Juan Ignacio. *La iglesia y el estado en el Ecuador: La personalidad de la iglesia en el modus vivendi entre la Santa Sede y el Ecuador.* Sevilla: Escuela de Estudios Hispanoamericanos, 1954.

Laso, Elías. *Biografía del General Juan José Flores.* Quito: n.p., 1924.

Le Gouhir y Rodas, José. *Historia de la república del Ecuador.* 2d ed. 3 vols. Quito: Editorial Ecuatoriana, 1935.

Lecuna, Vicente. *Crónica razonada de las guerras de Bolívar.* 3 vols. New York: Colonial Press, 1950.

Loor, Wilfrido. *Los Jesuitas en el Ecuador: Su ingreso y expulsión, 1850–1852.* Quito: La Prensa Católica, 1959.

Madariaga, Salvador. *Bolívar.* New York: Pellegrini & Cudhy, 1952.

Martínez-Delgado, Luis, *Berruecos: Asesinato del gran mariscal de Ayacucho.* Medellín: Editorial Bedout, 1973.

Martz, John D. *Ecuador: Conflicting Political Culture and the Quest for Progress.* Boston: Allyn and Bacon, 1972.

Masur, Gerhard. *Simon Bolivar.* Rev. ed. Albuquerque: University of New Mexico Press, 1969.

Mecum, Kent B. *El idealismo práctico de Vicente Rocafuerte (un verdadero americano independiente y libre).* Puebla: Editorial Cajica, S.A., 1975.

Mitre, Bartolomé. *Historia de San Martín y de la emancipación americana.* 2d ed. 4 vols. Buenos Aires: F. Lajouane, 1890.

Moncayo, Pedro. *El Ecuador de 1825 a 1875: Sus hombres, sus instituciones y sus leyes.* Santiago: R. Jover, 1885.

Montúfar y Rivera Maestre, Lorenzo. *Reseña histórica de Centro-America.* 7 vols. Guatemala: Tip. de "El Progreso," 1878–1887.

Pareja y Diez Canseco, Alfredo. *Historia del Ecuador.* 4 vols. Quito: Casa de la Cultura Ecuatoriana, 1954.

Parra-Pérez, Caracciolo. *La monarquía en Gran Colombia.* Madrid: Ediciones Cultura Hispánica, 1957.

Pérez Concha, Jorge. *Ensayo histórico-crítico de las relaciones diplomáticas del Ecuador con los estados limítrofes.* 3 vols. Quito and Guayaquil: Editorial Casa de la Cultura, 1958–1965.

Pfeiffer, Ida. *A Lady's Second Journey Round the World: From London to the Cape of Good Hope, Borneo, Java, Sumatra, Celebes, Ceram, the Moluccas, etc., California, Panama, Peru, Ecuador, and the United States.* 2 vols. London: Longman, Brown, Green, and Longmans, 1855.

Piccirilli, Ricardo. *Rivadavia y la diplomacia: Episodios de una empresa monárquica frustrada, 1818–1820.* Buenos Aires: Edit. Guillermo Kraft ltda., 1945.

Pike, Fredrick B. *The United States and the Andean Republics: Peru, Bolivia, and Ecuador.* Cambridge, Mass., and London: Harvard University Press, 1977.

Reyes, Oscar Efrén. *Breve historia general del Ecuador.* 4th ed., enl. 2 vols. Quito: Editorial "Fray Jodoco Ricke," 1950.

Robalino Dávila, Luis. *Orígenes del Ecuador de hoy* (a general title given to a work of seven volumes published between 1948 and 1970, but each volume bears its own title, and volume members are not always included; see following specific titles under Robalino Dávila).

———. *García Moreno.* Quito: Talleres Gráficos Nacionales, 1949.

———. *Nacimiento y primeros años de la República.* Puebla: Editorial José M. Cajica, Jr., S.A., 1967.

———. *La reacción anti-floreana.* Puebla: Editorial José M. Cajica, Jr., S.A., 1967.

———. *Rocafuerte.* Quito: Talleres Gráficos Nacionales, 1964.

Rodríguez, Linda Alexander. *The Search for Public Policy: Regional Politics and Government Finances in Ecuador, 1830–1940.* Berkeley, Los Angeles, London: University of California Press, 1985.

Rodríguez, Mario. *A Palmerstonian Diplomat in Central America: Frederick Chatfield, Esq.* Tucson: University of Arizona Press, 1964.

Rodríguez. O., Jaime. *The Emergence of Spanish America: Vicente Rocafuerte and Spanish Americanism, 1808–1832.* Berkeley, Los Angeles, London: University of California Press, 1975.

Sanders, Frank J. "Proposals for Monarchy in Mexico, 1823–1860." Ph.D. dissertation, University of Arizona, 1967.

Scroggs, William O. *Filibusters and Financiers: The Story of William*

Walker and His Associates. New York: Macmillan, 1916; reprint ed., New York: Russell & Russell, 1969.

Tobar Donoso, Julio. *La iglesia ecuatoriana en el siglo XIX*. Quito: Editorial Ecuatoriana, 1934.

Van Aken, Mark J. *Pan-Hispanism: Its Origin and Development to 1866*. Berkeley and Los Angeles: University of California Press, 1959.

Vargas, José María. *Historia de la iglesia en el Ecuador durante el patronato español*. Quito: Editorial Santo Domingo, 1962.

Vargas Ugarte, Rubén. *Historia general del Perú*. 2d ed., rev. 10 vols. Lima: Editor Carlo Milla Batres, 1971.

Villanueva, Carlos A. *La monarquía en América*. 4 vols. Paris: P. Ollendorff, 1912–1913.

Villavicencio, Manuel. *Geografía de la república del Ecuador*. New York: Impr. de R. Craighead, 1858.

Williams, Mary Wilhelmine. *Anglo-American Isthmian Diplomacy, 1815–1915*. Washington, D.C.: The American Historical Association, 1916.

Wolf, Teodoro. *Geografía y geología del Ecuador*. Leipzig: Tipografía de F. A. Brockhaus, 1892.

Scholarly Articles.

Bushnell, David. "The Development of the Press in Great Colombia." *The Hispanic American Historical Review* 30 (November 1950): 432–452.

———. "The Last Dictatorship: Betrayal or Consummation?" *The Hispanic American Historical Review* 63 (February 1983): 65–105.

Haskins, Ralph W. "Juan José Flores and the Proposed Expedition against Ecuador, 1845–1847." *The Hispanic American Historical Review* 27 (August 1947): 467–495.

Howe, Frederick George. "García Moreno's Efforts to Unite Ecuador and France." *The Hispanic American Historical Review* 17 (May 1936): 257–262.

Kendall, Lane Carter. "Andrés Santa Cruz and the Peru–Bolivian Confederation." *The Hispanic American Historical Review* 16 (February 1936): 29–48.

Lockey, Joseph B. "A Neglected Aspect of Isthmian Diplomacy." *American Historical Review* 41 (January 1936): 295–305.

McGann, Thomas F. "The Assassination of Sucre and Its Significance in Colombian History, 1828–1848." *The Hispanic American Historical Review* 30 (August 1950): 269–289.

Morse, Richard. "The Heritage of Latin America." In *The Founding of New Societies*, ed. Louis Hartz, (New York, 1964), 123–177.

Parks, E. Taylor, and Rippy, J. Fred. "The Galápagos Islands: A Neglected Phase of American Strategy Diplomacy." *The Pacific Historical Review* 9 (March 1940): 37–45.

Robertson, William Spence. "García Moreno's Dream of a European Protectorate." In *Contribuciones para el estudio de la historia de América: Homenaje al Dr. Emilio Ravignani* (Buenos Aires, 1941), 125–143.

Van Aken, Mark J. "The Lingering Death of Indian Tribute in Ecuador." *The Hispanic American Historical Review* 61 (August 1981): 429–459.

Index

Designer:	U.C. Press Staff
Compositor:	Huron Valley Graphics, Inc.
Text:	11/13 Baskerville
Display:	Baskerville
Printer:	Braun-Brumfield, Inc.
Binder:	Braun-Brumfield, Inc.